Involuntary Resettlement Sourcebook

Planning and Implementation in Development Projects

Involuntary Resettlement Sourcebook

Planning and Implementation in Development Projects

THE WORLD BANK

ISBN 0-8213-5576-7

Library of Congress Cataloging-in-Publication Data

Involuntary resettlement: planning and implementation in development projects.
     p. cm.
  Includes bibliographical references and index.
  ISBN 0-8213-5576-7
  1. Economic development projects—Developing countries. 2. Land Settlement—Developing countries. 3. Forced migration—Developing countries. 4. Migration, Internal—Developing countries. I. World Bank.

HC59.72.E44I467 2003
325—dc22

2003065763

Contents

Foreword . . . . **xvii**

Acknowledgments . . . . **xxi**

Introduction . . . . **xxiii**

Abbreviations . . . . **xxxiii**

Section 1: Policy Issues in Involuntary Resettlement **1**

1. Scope of OP 4.12 . . . . **3**

Scope of OP 4.12 3
    Land Acquisition and Restriction of Access to
    Conservation Areas 4
    Coverage of the Terms "Resettlement" and "Displaced Persons" . . 5
    The Policy Objective of Minimizing Land Acquisition
    and Resettlement 5
When OP 4.12 Becomes Effective and When
It Remains in Force 8
    Initial Applicability 8
    Project Closing 9
Linkages between Bank and Other Donor or National Projects 10
When OP 4.12 Does Not Apply 15
    Structural Adjustment Loans 15
    Natural Disasters, War, or Civil Strife 16
    Indirect Economic Impacts 18
    Adverse Environmental and Other Socioeconomic Impacts 19
    National or Regional Resource Management Programs 20
    Open-Market Purchase of Project Land 20
    Voluntary Resettlement 21
Notes 25

2. Resettlement Instruments and Disclosure **27**

Resettlement Plan 27
Policy Framework 27
Process Framework 29
    Preparation and Implementation of Specific Components
    of the Project 30
    Selection of Criteria for Determining Eligibility for Assistance . . 30
    Identification of Measures to Improve or Restore Livelihoods
    and Living Standards 31
    Resolution of Potential Conflicts or Grievances 31
    Administrative and Legal Procedures 32
    Monitoring Arrangements 32
Disclosure 33

3. Eligibility Criteria and Units of Entitlement **35**

Eligibility Criteria: Land Tenure and Severity of Impact 35
    Land Tenure 36
    Severity of Impact 38
Open Access and Other Property 42
    Open Access or Common Property 42
    Residences 43
    Businesses 43
    Temporary Permits 45
Temporary Involuntary Acquisition 45
Appropriate Unit of Entitlement 47

4. Compensation and Income Restoration **51**

Calculation and Application of Replacement Cost 52
    General Principles 52
    Replacement Cost for Land 54
    Replacement Cost for Houses and Other Structures 57
    Replacement Cost for Other Assets 60
Income Restoration Alternatives: Land, Cash, and Jobs 61
    General Principles for Replacing Income-Generating Assets 62
    Land-Based Options 64
    Cash Compensation and Rehabilitation 66
    Employment as Rehabilitation 69
Note 70

5. Vulnerable Populations 71

The Poor 72
Women 75
Indigenous Peoples 78
Those Less Able to Care for Themselves 81
    Children 81
    The Elderly 83
    The Disabled 84
Other Groups Not Protected by National Land
Compensation Law 85
    People without Title or Use Rights 85
    Host Communities 87
    Community Members Remaining in the Original Area
    after Resettlement 90
Note 91

Section 2: Technical Aspects of Involuntary
             Resettlement 93

6. Resettlement Planning and Processing
   Requirements 95

Processing Requirements at Each Stage
of the Project Cycle 97
    Preidentification 97
    Project Identification 102
    Project Quality Enhancement Review 105
    Project Preparation 107
Preappraisal 110
    Project Decision Meeting 111
    Project Appraisal 114
    Negotiations 115
    Effectiveness 116
    Supervision 116
    Irregular Processing: Late Identification of the Need
    for Resettlement 119
Annex: Resettlement Site Selection,
Movement of Displaced Persons, and
Organization of Community Life 120

Phase 1: Criteria for Site Selection 120
Phase 2: Feasibility Studies 121
Phase 3: Detailed Designs and Land Purchase 121
Phase 4: Final Designs and Construction 122
Movement of DPs 122
Organization of Community Life and Support Services 122

7. Consultation and Participation 123

What OP 4.12 Says 123
Consultation and Participation Defined 124
The Importance of Participation 125
Issues in Consultation and Participation 126
Consultation and Participation in the Project Cycle 128
Project Identification 129
Project Preparation 130
Project Preappraisal 138
Project Appraisal 138
Project Implementation 140
Project Completion 142
The Role of the Bank in Supporting Participation 142
Note 143
Annex: Consultation and Participation Matrix 144

8. Income Improvement 153

What OP 4.12 Says 153
Definition of Income Restoration in Operational Terms 155
Issues in Income Restoration 157
Risk Analysis 162
Design of Income Restoration Strategies 164
Stage 1: Analyzing Existing Sources of Income 165
Stage 2: Surveying and Analyzing Current
Economic Conditions 166
Stage 3: Identifying New Opportunities 167
Income Restoration through Land Replacement 169
Strategic Use of Project Opportunities 171
Other Income Restoration Strategies 176
Requirements for Reporting and Review of Income
Restoration Plans 176
Monitoring and Supervision of Income
Restoration Measures 177

Annex: Microfinance as a Tool for Income Restoration 181

    Microfinance as an Income Restoration Strategy 182

    Collateral 183

    Creditworthiness 183

    Character 183

    Promotion of Favorable Practices among

    Financial Institutions 184

9. Costs, Budgeting, and Financing 185

What OP 4.12 Says 185

Identifying and Reporting Resettlement Costs 186

    Compensation 186

    Community Infrastructure and Services Costs 187

    Relocation Costs 187

    Resettlement Site Preparation Costs 188

    Income Restoration and Improvement Costs 188

    Administrative Costs 189

Estimating Resettlement Costs 189

    Planning Costs 191

    Compensation Costs 192

    Community Infrastructure Costs 192

    Relocation and Resettlement Site Preparation Costs 193

    Income Restoration or Improvement Costs 194

    Administrative Costs 195

Financial Flows, Arrangements, and Contingencies 196

    Key Issues 196

    Financial Arrangements for a Resettlement Policy Framework . . 198

    Financial Arrangements for Income Restoration 200

Bank Disbursement for Resettlement 200

Notes 203

10. Surveys, Monitoring, and Supervision 205

What OP 4.12 Says 205

Identification: Land Acquisition Assessment 208

Census of DPs and Inventory of Assets 209

    Data Collection Formats 211

    Staffing 211

    Field Operations 212

    Data and Records 212

RP Preparation: Socioeconomic Analysis 213
Implementation: Monitoring 215
    Internal Monitoring 219
    External Monitoring 219
Bank Supervision of Resettlement Operations 221
    Supervision 222
    Early Review of Resettlement Implementation 225

11. Organizations for Planning and Implementation . . 229

What OP 4.12 Says 229
Organizational Responsibility for Resettlement Preparation and
Planning 230
    Land Acquisition Assessment 231
    Census and Socioeconomic Surveys 233
    Eligibility Criteria and Resettlement Entitlements 234
    Consultations 234
    Feasibility Study of Resettlement Sites 235
    Feasibility Study of Income Improvement Measures
    and Formation of DP Committees 235
Implementation 237
    Project Launch Workshop 238
    Organizational Units 239
    Organizational Models for Resettlement Implementation 248
    Checklist for Organizations Involved in Resettlement
    Implementation 250
    Coordination with Local Governments 251
Monitoring and Evaluation 252
    Internal Monitoring 252
    External Monitoring 253
Training and Capacity Building 253
Notes 255

12. Implementing Resettlement Plans 257

Getting Ready for Implementation 257
Initiating Implementation 258
    Payment of Compensation 259
    Relocation 259
    Linkage of Resettlement Progress and Pace of
    Project Construction 260

Reconstruction and Relocation to New Housing 260
Civic Infrastructure 262
Income Improvement Strategies 263
Monitoring and Evaluation 264
Grievance Redress 264
Adaptation When Things Do Not Go According to Plan 264
Circumstances Likely to Require Planning Changes 266
Documentation of Planning Changes 268

Section 3: Involuntary Resettlement in Selected Sectors

Section 3: Involuntary Resettlement in Selected Sectors **269**

13. Resettlement in Urban Areas

13. Resettlement in Urban Areas **271**

The Context of Urban Resettlement 271
Importance of Initial Planning 272
Minimizing Displacement 272
Preventing Fraudulent Claims of Eligibility for Compensation . . 274
Encouraging Public Participation and Responsiveness 274
Considering Gender Issues 276
Coordination of Administrative and Financial Responsibilities 277
Administrative Coordination 277
Financial Planning and Coordination 279
Limits of Bank Financing in Urban Projects 280
Resettlement of Urban Squatters 280
Entitlements for People without Security of Tenure 280
Adverse Impacts on Mobile Enterprises 283
Residential Relocation in Urban Projects 284
Replacement Cost for Urban Land 284
Replacement Housing in Urban Areas 285
Location Issues in Urban Resettlement 287
Urban Improvement: Opportunities
for Resettlement as Development 289
Improvement of Housing Standards 289
Slum Improvement Programs 290
Land Consolidation Programs 291
Economic Rehabilitation in Urban Projects 292
Distance of Relocation 293
Obstacles to Income Restoration at the Relocation Site 295

Community and Public Infrastructure in Urban Projects 295
    Restoring or Replacing Public Infrastructure 296
    Creating Public Spaces 296
Urban Linear Projects 297

14. Resettlement in Linear Projects 299

The Context of Linear Resettlement 299
Linear Projects and Their Corridors of Impact 300
    Roads and Highways 300
    Gas and Oil Pipelines 302
    Water and Sanitation Systems 303
    Irrigation Systems 304
    Transmission Lines 304
    Railways 305
Participation and Minimization of Resettlement 306
Impacts on Vulnerable Populations 309
    Informal Economic Enterprises 309
    Residents without Secure Title 310
    Indigenous People 311
Project Phasing, Censuses, and Studies 312
Administrative Coordination 316
Monitoring 318
Summary of Key Elements 319

15. Dams and Resettlement: Building Good Practice 321

The Context of Dam Construction 321
Organizational Capacity and Commitment 323
    Assessment of Institutional Capacity for Resettlement
    Planning and Implementation 323
    Capacity Building in All Relevant Agencies 324
    Involvement of Local Institutions Likely to Be Engaged
    in Operation and Maintenance 325
Resettlement Planning 325
    A Panel of Experts for Preparing and Implementing
    the Resettlement Program 325
    Systems for Preparing, Reviewing, and Approving
    Resettlement Plans 326
    Framework for Compliance with Agreements 326

Minimization of Displacement 327
    Selection of Dams for Construction 327
    Use of Dam Design to Reduce Displacement
    and Resettlement Impacts 328
    Use of Barriers to Minimize Displacement
    and Resettlement Impacts 328
Assessment of Resettlement Impacts 329
    Early, Detailed Surveys of Who Is Affected,
    How, and When 329
    Upstream and Downstream Impacts 330
    Temporary, Partial, and Other Impacts 330
    Consequences of Inadequate Surveys of Impacts
    and Affected People 331
    Impacts of the Long Gestation Period for Dam Construction ... 333
Consultation and Participation 334
    Mechanisms for Consulting Affected People throughout
    Planning and Implementation 334
    Provision of Information to Affected People 335
    Consequences of Inadequate Involvement
    of Affected People 337
    Consultation with the Host Communities 338
    Systems for Grievance Redress 338
Rehabilitation Strategies 339
    Resettlement as Development 339
    Feasibility of Sharing Project Benefits with DPs 340
    Affected People as Shareholders in the Dam Project 341
    Land-Based Resettlement Strategies 341
    Non-Land-Based Resettlement Strategies 344
    Technical, Legal, Financial, and Economic Feasibility
    of Strategies and Options 345
    Feasible Resettlement Alternatives
    and Mitigation of All Impacts 347
    Detailed Feasibility Assessment of Resettlement Sites 348
Financial Arrangements 349
    Resettlement Entitlements and Activities 349
    Compensation for Affected Assets 349
    Nonmonetary Costs of Resettlement 350
    Internalized Resettlement Costs 350
    Project Revenues Used to Finance Resettlement Costs 352
Assessment of Risks to the Resettlement Program 353

Institutional Arrangements 354
    Adequate Arrangements During the Resettlement
    Transition Period 354
    Strong Institutional Design to Deliver What
    the Project Has Promised 355
Linkage of Dam Construction to the Implementation
of Resettlement 356
Monitoring and Supervision 357
    Clear Benchmarks and Indicators for Monitoring
    Implementation 357
    Resettlement Supervision beyond the Resettlement Program . . . 358
Notes 359

16. Resettlement in Natural Resources Management and Biodiversity Projects 361

Policy Applicability 361
Policy Objectives 363
Policy Instruments 363
Elements of a Resettlement Process Framework 365
Plan of Action 368
    Bank Procedures for the Resettlement Process
    Framework and Plan of Action 369

Appendix 1: World Bank Involuntary Resettlement Policy, OP/BP 4.12 371

Involuntary Resettlement OP 4.12 371
    Policy Objectives 371
    Impacts Covered 372
    Required Measures 372
    Eligibility for Benefits 375
    Resettlement Planning, Implementation, and Monitoring 376
    Resettlement Instruments 377
    Assistance to the Borrower 379
Notes 380
OP 4.12—Annex A 384
    Resettlement Plan 384
    Abbreviated Resettlement Plan 389
    Resettlement Policy Framework 389
    Process Framework 390
Notes 391

Involuntary Resettlement BP 4.12 393
    Appraisal 394
    Supervision 396
    Country Assistance Strategy 397
  Notes 397

Appendix 2: Checklist for Census Information 399

Appendix 3: Census Forms 400

Appendix 4: Terms of Reference for a Socioeconomic Study 404

Introduction 404
Objectives of the Study 405
The Study 405
Scope of the Study 406
Methodology of the Study 407

Appendix 5: Matrix of Resettlement Impacts 408

Appendix 6: Resettlement Entitlement Matrix China Yangtze Basin Flood Control Project 410

Appendix 7: Resettlement Budget 412

Appendix 8: Resettlement Timetable 413

Appendix 9: Resettlement Supervision Guidelines . . . 414

Glossary 417

List of Boxes

Box 3.1   Suggested Compensation Guidelines for Temporary
             Acquisition of Assets 46
Box 4.1   When Replacement Land Is Unacceptable to DPs 65
Box 4.2   Cash Compensation Does Not Ensure Asset Replacement . . . 67
Box 6.1   Assessing the Need for Consultant Services 104
Box 6.2   Meeting the Special Needs of New Borrowers 106
Box 6.3   Estimating the Time Required for Resettlement Preparation . 109
Box 7.1   Disclosure Requirements for Bank Resettlement Documents . 143

Box 8.1   Impoverishment Risks and Reconstruction: A Framework for
            Resettlement Analysis and Planning 163
Box 8.2   Microfinance and Market Failure 182
Box 10.1   Censuses, Surveys, and Computer Technology 213
Box 13.1   Vertical Resettlement: A Tool for Urban Renewal 288
Box 13.2   Housing Affordability and Willingness to Pay 290
Box 14.1   Consultation and Minimizing Displacement in Guatemala . . 309
Box 14.2   Inconsistent Treatment of Squatters and Encroachers 311
Box 15.1   Criteria for Assessing Adequacy of Institutional
            Commitment and Capacity 324
Box 15.2   Typical Adverse Social Impacts of Reservoirs 331
Box 15.3   Laws for Hydropower Revenue Sharing with Affected
            Communities 352

List of Figures

Figure 2.1 Decision Tree: Resettlement Instruments 28
Figure 8.1 Income Restoration Objective in Regions of
            Economic Growth 156
Figure 8.2 Income Restoration Objective in Regions
            of Economic Contraction 157

List of Tables

Table 3.1   Severity of Impact of Land Taking and Recommended
            Entitlement Options 40
Table 7.1   Participation and the Project Cycle 130
Table 8.1   Comparing Compensation and Income Restoration 158
Table 10.1 The Project Cycle and Information Requirements 208
Table 10.2 Land Acquisition Assessment 209
Table 10.3 Elements of a Census 210
Table 10.4 Topics of a Week-Long Training Program 212
Table 10.5 Elements of a Socioeconomic Analysis 215
Table 10.6 Elements of a Monitoring System 216
Table 10.7 Process Model for Tracking Project Performance 217
Table 10.8 Suggested Generic Indicators of Resettlement Performance . 218
Table 11.1 Preparation Activities and Agencies Responsible 232
Table 16.1 Choice of Resettlement Instruments 364

Foreword

Economic development relies on construction of new physical infrastructure to cater to the increasing needs of growing populations. Infrastructure development, in turn, often requires acquisition of land and other assets that are privately owned. Such acquisition can adversely affect the socioeconomic well-being of the people whose assets are acquired, as well as the communities they live in. Impacts include physical relocation, disruption of livelihoods, and potential breakdown of communities.

Resettlement can have serious repercussions that cannot be exclusively measured in economic terms. Breakdown of established community relationships, social disarticulation among people who find themselves in a different sociocultural environment after resettlement, and the psychological trauma of moving into an alien environment can be severe if efforts to design and implement resettlement programs are not sensitive to the needs and preferences of communities.

Well-designed and well-implemented resettlement can, however, turn involuntary resettlement into a development opportunity. The challenge is to not treat resettlement as an imposed externality but to see it as an integral component of the development process and to devote the same level of effort and resources to resettlement preparation and implementation as to the rest of the project. Treating resettlers as project beneficiaries can transform their lives in ways that are hard to conceive of if they are viewed as "project-affected people" who somehow have to be assisted so that the main project can proceed. For example, in the Mumbai Urban Transport Project in India, slum dwellers living along the railroad tracks were helped to become owners of apartments in urban housing cooperatives, which are often beyond the reach of the middle-class residents of Mumbai, a city with some of the highest real estate prices in the world. In a Bank-assisted irrigation project in Bahia, Brazil, people from whom land was acquired were given priority in the allocation of irrigated land, thus becoming the first project beneficiaries.

Implementing resettlement as a development program not only helps the people who are adversely affected but also promotes easier, less-troubled implementation of development projects. Projects that do not address resettlement issues adequately are often subject to delays because of opposition from displaced persons (DPs). Bank experience shows that the additional economic gains from expeditious implementation of projects with generous resettlement provisions for DPs can far outweigh the incremental costs of providing adequate resettlement assistance. Good resettlement, therefore, also makes good economic sense.

Displacement necessitating involuntary resettlement of populations can be caused by a variety of triggers, including natural disasters, such as earthquakes, hurricanes, and floods; political events, such as wars and internal conflicts; and development projects. The World Bank's operational policy on involuntary resettlement addresses only issues related to development-induced displacement. Development projects, more than any of the other triggers for displacement, offer the means and mechanisms to help DPs improve their standards of living. Development-induced displacement provides a unique opportunity for the project team to systematically plan and implement the resettlement program on the basis of consultations with the DPs, along with making adequate provisions for funding, implementation arrangements, monitoring, and redress of grievances. Failure to capitalize on the tremendous potential of development-induced displacement to improve the lives of resettlers would impose a high opportunity cost on the development process.

Realizing the development impact of well-implemented resettlement programs, some countries, states, and private sector companies consciously design development-oriented programs that follow standards higher than the minimum needed to restore people's standards of living. The argument for providing such resettlement assistance is that the incremental effort helps achieve overall development of the displaced community and that this overall development results in savings because the resettled community does not need to be targeted for different development programs. It could be years before the development process "touches" a resettled community again, so it makes good sense to address most of the community's development needs as part of the resettlement program.

We need to view resettlement as a sector issue and not an externality, given the pervasive need for land acquisition, physical relocation, and economic rehabilitation in infrastructure projects. For example, resettlement is as integral to road building as the engineering design of roads, so both should be given the same amount of attention by transport sector staff. Resettlement is not simply an issue to be dealt with in implementing a roads project—it is a part of the project. The implementation of resettlement will substantially improve when Bank and borrower staff working in various sectors start treating resettlement as a core sector issue.

The challenge of resettlement is no longer restricted to large infrastructure projects with substantial resettlement impacts; many projects require minor land acquisition or relocate people only a few hundred meters. A linear project cuts through many administrative jurisdictions, posing a unique institutional challenge to resettlement practitioners. An increasing number of projects do not involve any land acquisition or physical relocation, but they impose restrictions on people's access to legally designated parks and protected areas. Diverse approaches are needed to address the impacts of such restrictions on the livelihoods of affected people. Resettlement practitioners have duly responded to the challenge of emerging forms of resettlement by developing a variety of approaches and methodologies applicable to different situations. This book offers a wide range of approaches. The authors also realized that it would be almost impossible to anticipate all types of resettlement situations and provide guidance for each one. This book, therefore, is a living document, to be periodically updated on the basis of the experience of practitioners and the findings of new research.

Involuntary resettlement is an essential and historically underappreciated aspect of development. Unsuccessful resettlement has often been the result of both a lack of sensitivity to this issue and a deficiency of operational guidance on the "how to" of resettlement design and implementation. Today, many governments are convinced of the need to adopt a "resettlement-with-development" approach and provide affected people with benefits from the projects that displace them. Although attitudes toward resettlement have undergone a sea change for the better over the past decade, this book aims to fill the current gap in available guidance on resettlement. It is hoped that global practice will benefit from lessons learned by the World Bank and that this book will help meet the need for capacity building, not only in projects where the Bank is involved, but also in non-Bank projects and in national policies and institutions more generally. By helping people plan and implement better resettlement programs, this book will make a difference in the lives of people displaced by development projects around the world.

Ian Johnson
Vice President
Environmentally and Socially
Sustainable Development

Acknowledgments

The preparation of this book was coordinated by a team consisting of Maninder Gill (team leader), Dan Gibson, Lars Lund, Warren Van Wicklin, and Gordon Appleby. The present version of the book draws substantially on an earlier draft prepared in 1996–97 for the two Asia regions (South Asia and East Asia and Pacific) by a team led by Ellen Schaengold and consisting of Dan Gibson, Lars Lund, and Maninder Gill. Other contributors who helped write or substantially review a specific chapter of this book were Lou Scura ("Resettlement in Natural Resources Management and Biodiversity Projects"), Reidar Kvam ("Resettlement in Linear Projects"), Tosun Aricanli ("Surveys, Monitoring, and Supervision"), Pramod Agrawal and Maria Clara Mejia ("Resettlement in Urban Areas"), Mary Judd ("Consultation and Participation"), and Chaohua Zhang ("Costs, Budgeting, and Financing"). Significant contributions in the form of comments, suggestions, and case examples were made by Pramod Agrawal, Tosun Aricanli, Dan Aronson, John Briscoe, Michael Cernea, Charles Di Leva, Carlos Escudero, Ashraf Ghani, Dan Gross, Scott Guggenheim, Steen Jorgensen, Mary Judd, Reidar Kvam, Stephen Lintner, Alessandro Palmieri, I.U.B. Reddy, Salman Salman, Lee Travers, Warren Waters, and Chaohua Zhang. Warren Van Wicklin selected and organized the appendices. Leili Makki helped identify useful appendices, both for the paper version of the book and for the accompanying CD-ROM. Gerardo Cruz helped standardize the format of the appendices.

The contributions of the above are gratefully acknowledged.

Introduction

In December 2001, the World Bank officially adopted its revised Operational Policy on involuntary resettlement (OP 4.12). The policy is part of an integrated suite of 10 social and environmental safeguard policies. Unlike the format of previous policy coverage, the format of OP 4.12 distinguishes between policy principles, standards, and requirements (OP 4.12) and the Bank's own procedures (BP 4.12). Several other safeguard policies also distinguish between mandatory policy provisions and recommendations for good practice; the latter are offered in a separate good-practice section. The resettlement policy has no good-practice section; instead, it refers readers to this sourcebook for guidance on good practice.

The chapters that follow provide resettlement practitioners (whether from the Bank, other donor agencies, borrower agencies, civil society organizations, the private sector, consultants, or others) with guidance on the implementation of policy principles, the procedural requirements for projects, the technical aspects of resettlement planning, and the actual implementation of resettlement. This guidance is intended to increase the likelihood that Bank-financed projects will achieve the objectives of OP 4.12:

- To avoid or minimize adverse impacts and to conceive and execute resettlement activities as sustainable development programs
- To give displaced persons opportunities to participate in the design and implementation of resettlement programs
- To assist displaced persons in their efforts to improve their livelihoods and standards of living, or at least to restore these to pre-project levels.

This sourcebook draws its lessons mainly from the Bank's project experience. In many respects, these lessons are encouraging: they indicate that most egregious forms of impoverishment and harm inflicted in the past can now be avoided through thorough planning and diligent implementation. Many of the people subjected to land acquisition or other adverse impacts have emerged as beneficiaries, with higher incomes or living standards than before the projects. Nonetheless, much remains to be learned. Involuntary resettlement is a complicated subject. To achieve resettlement objectives remains an inherently risky proposition (otherwise there would be no reason to avoid or minimize the adverse impacts of involuntary resettlement). And new projects bring to the fore—with surprising frequency—new resettlement issues or challenges.

This introductory note briefly explains the purposes of the book, highlights some of the key recurring lessons from project experience that informed it, and offers some simple guidance on using the book itself.

Why a Sourcebook on Involuntary Resettlement?

In all countries, providing public facilities or public infrastructure sometimes requires acquisition of private land or even relocation of people. To ensure that public facilities or infrastructure is provided at reasonable cost and is sited appropriately, all governments sometimes invoke legal powers—that is, eminent domain—to expropriate land or other fixed assets. In virtually all countries of the world, governments are legally required to pay "just" or "fair" compensation for expropriated private property.

If governments in all borrowing countries already are legally required to justly compensate those whose property is taken, why does the World Bank need its own involuntary-resettlement policy? And why is the Bank now publishing an involuntary-resettlement sourcebook?

The Bank adopted its first involuntary-resettlement policy in 1980, after it recognized the painful shortcomings in development practice that in some cases led to the impoverishment of thousands of people. Most obvious among these shortcomings, perhaps, was the failure of some governments to pay fair compensation for expropriated assets as their own laws required. But for many reasons impoverishment also occurred in projects in which compensation was duly paid. In an effort to ensure that Bank-supported projects do not contribute to impoverishment through land acquisition and resettlement, the Bank initiated a policy differing in three significant aspects from most borrower legislation.

First, Bank policy is directed at improving (or at least restoring) incomes and living standards, rather than merely compensating people for their expropriated assets. This improvement of incomes and living standards broadens the objective of the policy to include the restoration of income streams and retraining of people unable to continue their old income-generating activities after displacement. The broader focus on living standards brings a wide array of factors into resettlement discourse, including social and cultural relationships, public health, and community services. The resettlement process in Bank-assisted projects is no longer the mere mitigation of externalities but an integral part of the development project itself. This new view of the process poses practical and legal challenges to borrowers.

Second, the emphasis on incomes and living standards, in contrast to the conventional emphasis on expropriated property, expands the range and number of people recognized as adversely affected. Recognition of this broader range of adverse impacts leads to a greater appreciation of the issues to be considered in resettlement. However, this recognition has also contributed to confusion in the use of terminology, as the aggregate number of people statistically categorized as "resettled" or "displaced" fails to reflect the variety and severity of resettlement impacts. Whereas the conventional approach is to compensate only people with property rights, as defined by domestic law, the Bank policy extends assistance to others who are affected but did not own property—renters, sharecroppers, and wage-earners, for example—and those who lacked legally recognized property rights for the land or assets they occupied or used. This policy explicitly recognizes people whose welfare may otherwise be overlooked, but in so doing it also brings complex and contentious issues into project planning.

Finally, the Bank policy underscores the importance of explicit and distinct resettlement planning. Compensation for expropriated assets requires little more than the identification of eligible persons, the establishment of compensation rates, and a one-time payment process. Improvement (or restoration) of incomes and living standards, by contrast, may require attention to many potentially relevant variables and the synchronized or coordinated action of many agencies over an extended period. This approach poses numerous issues of responsibility. A compensation-only approach transfers all risk management to the affected persons after payment of the compensation. A focus on incomes and living standards, by contrast, requires careful delineation of responsibilities and elaborate risk management.

Since 1980 resettlement planning and practice have improved significantly. The Bank, along with other development agencies and borrower governments, is now more attentive to the lessons of resettlement experience. Most development agencies and many borrowing-government agencies have adopted resettlement policies, often founded on similar principles and standards. Today, the major costs that development projects impose on individuals and communities through expropriation of land or other assets are far more likely to be identified, and plans are more likely to be formulated to avoid or mitigate these costs.

Although much has been learned about involuntary resettlement, planning and practice often yield unsatisfactory results as a result of any of several factors:

- Project planners (including Bank staff) do not recognize all adverse impacts, or they recognize them only at a late stage, when mitigating them is far more difficult.
- Plans may focus only on narrow mitigation, overlooking resettlement-created opportunities to improve local incomes or living standards.
- Plans and options may be developed without meaningful consultation with displaced persons, which can make the plans difficult to implement.

- Project agencies may lack the technical, organizational, or financial capacity to implement resettlement plans.
- Project agencies may lack the legal authority or political commitment to implement the plans.
- Plans do not elicit the behavioral responses from project-affected people that are necessary for successful resettlement.
- Resettlement plans become inappropriate, ineffective, or obsolete because of changing conditions in the project area.
- New projects—and new kinds of projects—produce unanticipated problems requiring innovation in resettlement methods and strategies.

A major portion of this book is aimed at resolving or minimizing such issues in resettlement planning. Although there continues to be room for improvement in resettlement planning for standard infrastructure projects, the book also focuses on new policy considerations and resettlement-planning instruments created in response to a changing project portfolio. Special planning is needed, for example, when people are adversely affected, not by land acquisition, but by restrictions on resource use in conservation areas. Special arrangements also may be needed to accommodate small-scale land acquisition (or voluntary contributions of land) in community-based lending activities.

With the adoption of OP 4.12 and its attendant shift in policy format, this book also serves a useful purpose in elaborating on, or further clarifying, distinctions between mandatory policy provisions and good-practice recommendations and between borrower obligations and Bank obligations. Consensus on such distinctions is expected to help borrowers and the Bank improve the efficiency of project processing. The Bank's task team leaders, for example, have sometimes complained that lack of clarity on resettlement-policy principles and procedures forces them to give too much time and attention to resettlement. They also sometimes find it difficult to differentiate, for borrower counterparts, what precisely the Bank requires of them and what the Bank is asking them to consider. Some team leaders have indicated that they prefer to avoid projects involving involuntary resettlement, even if these projects are otherwise of great developmental potential. To the extent that this book succeeds in providing useful guidance on implementing policy, projects will benefit from more efficient and manageable processing.

Still another major strategic purpose of this book is to increase the emphasis on the project implementation phase. As a guide to practice, the book promotes improved resettlement on the ground by helping to distill lessons from implementation experience and by providing guidance on monitoring and supervision and on how to best respond to problems identified in implementation.

Lessons from Experience

The following are some recurring lessons derived from Bank projects. These lessons are treated in greater detail in the various chapters on specific issues.

- *Systematic resettlement planning is important*—Although this statement may now seem banal, it bears remembering that resettlement planning is fairly new. The risks of impoverishment that involuntary resettlement may pose to affected people are by now well known. But systematic planning involves far more than the identification of potentially adverse impacts. Unsatisfactory outcomes also result from failure to coordinate the actions of different agencies and to establish clear lines of responsibility and contingency arrangements.
- *An early start is often the key to effective planning*—Effective resettlement planning can be time-intensive. In many projects, several months may be needed to gather the required information to establish a range of potentially adverse impacts, estimate the extent of impacts and the number of people affected, and devise alternative approaches to mitigate such impacts. The most effective approach is to have a balanced project design. If too many elements of project design are considered fixed, the range of alternatives available for avoiding, minimizing, or mitigating adverse impacts may be drastically reduced. However, opportunities to minimize the transition period for affected people or to minimize the costs of the resettlement to the borrowing government might also be sacrificed if appropriate planning steps are not taken at early stages. As well, failure to identify issues of policy interpretation at early stages of preparation makes it more difficult to find appropriate and mutually acceptable solutions and frequently contributes to delays in project processing.
- *Effective plans should be crafted to fit the particular project context*—Earlier formulations of resettlement policy, as well as much of the resettlement literature (external commentary and Bank evaluations and reviews), focused on large-scale resettlement in reservoir projects. Because of the potentially severe impacts on individuals and communities, reservoir resettlement remains a subject of great concern (and the topic of an entire chapter of this book). With time, however, application of the policy has spread to a wider array of investment projects, with widely varying impacts. This broader application may present new obstacles in planning; for example, linear projects that stretch across multiple administrative jurisdictions may run into coordination problems. New investment modalities may also create difficulties in policy interpretation, as when community-based lending activities propose voluntary contribution of

private land in return for community benefits. In many standard infra-structure projects, the extent of land acquisition and the severity of adverse impacts are fairly minor. In such cases, resettlement planning should be more narrowly tailored to fit the practical need. Experience has demonstrated that applying a planning template designed for large-scale reservoir resettlement to projects with small-scale or fairly insignificant impacts can be more than merely ineffective; in some cases, communities lose access to public investment because planners (including Bank proj-ect team members) expect the resettlement planning process to be too cumbersome or too expensive.

- *Effective plans should elicit positive responses from the affected population*— Many aspects of project design require technical or professional expert-ise. A lesson clearly emerging from resettlement experience, however, is that successful resettlement—and sometimes the success of the project itself—may hinge on the responses that the affected people make to the changes imposed on them. Effective resettlement planning recognizes the need to inform affected populations about project impacts and reset-tlement opportunities, to encourage the affected populations to partici-pate in formulating and choosing resettlement options, and to engage the affected people as active participants in the resettlement process. As emphasized in chapter 7, giving affected populations opportunities to participate in the process reduces the likelihood of resistance to, and delay of, the resettlement and increases the likelihood that the affected people will adapt to their changed circumstances.
- *Resettlement plans should be conceived as development opportunities*—In most projects, a narrow emphasis on compensation for lost assets or mitigation of adverse impacts leads planners to overlook significant development opportunities. Especially when projects generate large-scale or severe impacts, the extent of disruption to community services or infrastructure may create an opportunity for community improvement. Restoring inad-equate or obsolete urban infrastructure, for example, is virtually pointless when resettlement creates an opportunity to improve or modernize infra-structure to meet current or future needs. Similarly, with careful and participatory planning, opportunities can be identified for the affected people to derive project-related benefits or to capitalize on opportunities to improve their incomes or productivity.
- *Resettlement plans should not be conceived as blueprints*—Although plan-ning may be a necessary condition for effective resettlement, it is usually not sufficient. Even the most thorough and detailed resettlement plans may require adjustment to fit the changing circumstances of the actual implementation, particularly projects involving complex resettlement,

those unfolding over several years, and those situated in rapidly changing environments. Rigid adherence to plans prepared before implementation may be ineffective or even counterproductive as unanticipated changes occur in the project environment or planning assumptions or estimates prove erroneous. To achieve positive practical results on the ground, as Bank experience clearly demonstrates, resettlement monitoring and supervision are critical. Both are needed for assessing the extent to which plans are being implemented effectively and for signaling when the plan itself is out of step with changing circumstances.

- *Early resettlement supervision should identify any need to make changes*—Even the best-designed resettlement programs are likely to face some problems during implementation and may need to be fine-tuned. Close monitoring and supervision of the resettlement program should be carried out early so that the necessary changes in resettlement design can be made.

- *Close monitoring of resettlement should continue until the likelihood of achieving resettlement objectives is established*—Qualified experts should regularly monitor and supervise the resettlement. Most problems in resettlement planning and implementation can be solved if they are quickly and adequately identified. If routine resettlement problems are not identified or solved as soon as they arise, they can become difficult to resolve.

- *Outstanding resettlement issues should be documented at project completion and discussed between the Bank and the borrower*—As the main contractual obligation of the borrower is to implement the agreed resettlement instrument, Bank-assisted projects can be considered complete after the resettlement plan has been implemented. However, resettlement outcomes generally take longer to achieve. Therefore, the prospects of achieving desirable resettlement outcomes and the issues likely to affect these outcomes should be well documented at the completion of the project and should be discussed between the Bank and the borrower. If resettlement plans have been implemented but resettlement objectives are not likely to be fully achieved, the Bank and the borrower should discuss possible follow-up measures. The Bank should also determine whether supervision of the resettlement component beyond project completion is necessary.

How to Use This Volume

This book is divided into four sections:

- *Policy issues in involuntary resettlement*—Because projects involving land acquisition and resettlement take place under a seemingly infinite variety of circumstances, questions often arise about how to apply certain concepts or procedures under unique or unanticipated conditions. Similarly, over the past 20 years, the terminology and definitions have shifted to incorporate broader patterns of experience. This section (chapters 1–5) conveys the current consensual definitions of terms and their application in resettlement policy. The guidance provided in this section is not itself official policy, and consensus views on application may continue to evolve. Nonetheless, this section should be useful to task teams or others involved in resettlement operations who are making informed judgments in a wide variety of circumstances.

- *Technical aspects of involuntary resettlement*—Chapters 6–12 present the Bank's procedural requirements, good-practice guidance, and lessons from project experiences with various technical aspects of resettlement planning and implementation.

- *Involuntary resettlement in selected sectors*—Chapters 13–16 examine unique or especially significant planning and implementation problems in particular categories, specifically urban resettlement projects, linear infrastructure projects, dams and reservoir projects, and sustainable natural resource management promotion projects.

- *Appendices and glossary of terms*—The appendices provide samples of various planning documents, as well as supplementary sources of information on various aspects of resettlement policy, planning, and implementation. Already evident to all resettlement practitioners is chronic and widespread confusion about the use of terms and concepts. In some cases, existing patterns of word usage are likely to continue to impede clear communication of ideas. For example, the use of "displaced persons" in OP 4.12, as a reference to all adversely affected people, may cause many readers to grossly overestimate the severity of actual resettlement impacts and the number of people subjected to them. The glossary seeks to provide some clarity about the meaning of such difficult resettlement terms as "displaced persons" and "replacement cost."

This book is structured as a reference work. For convenience of presentation and reading, each chapter is designed to serve more or less as a stand-alone guide to a selected aspect of resettlement planning or practice. Of course, any actual resettlement process involves complex relationships among various aspects of planning and practice. Dividing this complex whole into a set of stand-alone chapters leads unavoidably to some redundancy.

While avoiding redundancy is desirable, the greater challenge for a book like this one is to provide all the available practical guidance on a topic in a reasonably accessible format. Each chapter is intended to cover its topic as succinctly as possible. However, this book includes three other features to enable the reader to obtain additional information:

- *Case references,* which briefly highlight relevant lessons from the Bank's project experience, including project identification details for help in finding additional information on a given project;
- *Cross references,* which link treatment of the same subject or closely related subjects in different chapters, sections, or appendices; and
- *The index,* which helps the reader search for specific subjects, as well as relationships among them.

Learning from experience is a recurring theme in this book. Of course, such learning implies that standards of good resettlement most likely will continue to evolve as today's practice produces tomorrow's lessons. Although most of its guidance is likely to be pertinent for years to come, this book, as a published volume, cannot stay abreast of all future developments. Therefore, the reader is encouraged to explore the following more timely sources of information and guidance:

- *Electronic updates*—The sourcebook is available on the World Bank's Web ite, http://www.worldbank.org/, and may be updated periodically. In addition, information updates will be provided to highlight significant changes in resettlement planning or project processing and significant developments in good practice.
- *Direct assistance*—For people seeking more specific guidance on resettlement issues, assistance is available through the World Bank Safeguards Help Desk (safeguards@worldbank.org).

For issues of policy interpretation, the policy itself will continue to be the fundamental reference. Appendix 1 contains the entire text of the policy. The various chapters of this book contain excerpts from OP 4.12 that are relevant to their subject areas. The resettlement committee, constituted under the provisions of the policy, will provide guidance on application in a particular context.

Abbreviations

BP   Bank Procedure
CDD   community-driven development
Cr   Credit
DP   displaced person
GNP   gross national product
ICR   Implementation Completion Report
IPDP   indigenous peoples development plan
IRR   impoverishment risks and reconstruction
ISDS   Integrated Safeguards Data Sheet
LEG   Legal Department
Ln   Loan
NHAI   National Highways Authority of India
NGO   nongovernmental organization
OD   Operational Directive
OP   Operational Policy
PAD   Project Appraisal Document
PIC   public information center
PSR   Project Supervision Report
QER   quality enhancement review
RP   resettlement plan
SAL   Structural Adjustment Loan
TF   Trust Fund
ZESCO   Zambia Electricity Supply Corporation

Policy Issues in Involuntary Resettlement

Scope of OP 4.12

The World Bank first adopted its policy on involuntary resettlement, in 1980, as an Operational Manual Statement. The policy was revised, in 1990, as Operational Directive (OD) 4.30. The primary focus of the Operational Manual Statement and subsequently of the OD was on resettlement associated with large dams. When OD 4.30 was converted to Operational Policy (OP) 4.12, in 2002, the policy incorporated the experience with resettlement over a wide range of sectors across all regions of the Bank.

Bank policy on involuntary resettlement covers only the direct economic and social impacts of the expropriation of land or the restriction of access to natural resources and does not cover all of the social issues and impacts of an investment, whether or not it involves resettlement. These additional issues are appropriately identified through other instruments, including environmental assessments and social assessments.[1]

This chapter examines basic issues of the applicability of OP 4.12: the project activities that trigger OP 4.12, the times when the OP comes into force, the linkages between project components, and the domains where the policy applies (see Appendix 1, "OP/BP 4.12, Involuntary Resettlement," for the entire text of the Bank's policy and procedures on involuntary resettlement).

Scope of OP 4.12

Paragraph 3 of OP 4.12 describes the coverage of the policy: "direct economic and social impacts that both result from Bank-assisted investment projects, and are caused by

(a) the involuntary taking of land resulting in
   (i)   relocation or loss of shelter;
   (ii) loss of assets or access to assets; or
   (iii) loss of income sources or means of livelihood, whether or not the affected persons must move to another location; or
(b) the involuntary restriction of access to legally designated parks and protected areas resulting in adverse impacts on the livelihoods of the displaced persons."

1

> OP 4.12 (endnote 1) specifies that both loans and projects are subject to the OP: " 'Loans' includes credits, guarantees, Project Preparation Facility (PPF) advances and grants; and 'projects' includes projects under (a) adaptable program lending; (b) learning and innovation loans; (c) PPFs and Institutional Development Funds ... if they include investment activities; (d) grants under the Global Environmental Facility and Montreal Protocol, for which the Bank is the implementing/executing agency; and (e) grants or loans provided by other donors that are administered by the Bank. The term 'project' does not include programs under adjustment operations."

Land Acquisition and Restriction of Access to Conservation Areas

Involuntary land acquisition is always an OP 4.12 issue.[2]

When, in a Bank-financed project, land is acquired through the application of state powers, such as eminent domain, the acquisition is involuntary, and OP 4.12 applies. "Involuntary" connotes the lack of informed consent and power of choice on the part of the people directly affected by the acquisition.

Involuntary taking of land includes situations in which the state acquires new lands for development or exerts ownership of land to which it has title but which is nonetheless occupied or used by others. The OP applies regardless of the number of people affected; whether or not they will benefit from the acquisition; and whether or not they are fully satisfied with the provisions for compensation, relocation, or rehabilitation, as relevant.

OP 4.12 covers only the direct impacts of land acquisition and restrictions of access to legally designated parks and protected areas. "Direct impact" means any consequence immediately related to the taking of a parcel of land or to restrictions in the use of legally designated parks or protected areas. People directly affected by land acquisition may lose their home, farmland, property, business, or other means of livelihood. In other words, they lose their ownership, occupancy, or use rights, because of land acquisition or restriction of access. The key factor is that the state has taken some or all of the land that people owned, used, or occupied; or, in legally designated parks and protected areas, the state has limited people's use rights.[3]

Restriction of traditional access to resources in legally designated parks and protected areas is also an OP 4.12 issue.

OP 4.12 applies when the state restricts access to resources "in legally designated parks and protected areas." Conservation schemes (for example, wildlife reserves, national parks, classified forests) may not acquire land through eminent domain. But the declaration of nature reserves, the upgrading of forest areas to the status of parks, or the enforcement of earlier directives limits access to resources in the protected area and directly affects livelihoods and incomes. These conservation projects fall within the purview of OP 4.12 because the new restrictions on resource use affect the livelihood and well-being of the people who were using the newly restricted area.

In these instances, the Bank has instituted a process framework to promote a participatory approach to conservation activities in legally designated parks and protected areas. Encouraging community participation in the design and enforcement of conservation activities helps identify acceptable alternatives to unsustainable patterns of resource use and promotes community support for such alternatives. If sustainability requires that local residents stop or reduce their activities, these residents must be confident that they can find alternative sources of food or livelihoods.

Coverage of the Terms "Resettlement" and "Displaced Persons"

"Resettlement," in Bank terminology, covers all direct economic and social losses resulting from land taking and restriction of access, together with the consequent compensatory and remedial measures. Resettlement is not restricted to its usual meaning—physical relocation. Resettlement can, depending on the case, include (a) acquisition of land and physical structures on the land, including businesses; (b) physical relocation; and (c) economic rehabilitation of displaced persons (DPs), to improve (or at least restore) incomes and living standards.

Finally, "displaced persons" are defined as "persons who are affected in any of the ways described in para. 3 of this OP" (OP 4.12, endnote 3). The word thus connotes all those people who lose land or the right to use land (para. 3a) or who lose "access to legally designated parks and protected areas resulting in adverse impacts on the livelihoods" (para. 3b). The term "displaced persons" is synonymous with "project-affected persons" and is not limited to those subjected to physical displacement.

The Policy Objective of Minimizing Land Acquisition and Resettlement

OP 4.12 states that "involuntary resettlement should be avoided where feasible, or minimized, exploring all viable alternative project designs" (para. 2a). This fundamental policy objective reflects the recognition that resettlement can be severely harmful to people and their communities. Moreover, the planning and implementation of mitigation measures can be both complex and costly, and

1

even so the measures provide no guarantees of complete success. A project design that reduces the number of people potentially affected and minimizes the severity of potential impacts also helps reduce the resettlement costs, responsibilities, and liabilities of the project.

The simplest way to minimize resettlement is to design projects that minimize land acquisition and the number of people affected by loss of land, by physical relocation, or by disruption of income-generating activities. All things being equal, facilities and transportation corridors, for example, are obviously better sited in or through areas with little or no population, to minimize the number of people affected. Of course, a host of economic, technical, and other factors must also be considered, so land acquisition and resettlement are often impossible to avoid altogether.

Bank experience shows that two points deserve attention in striking a balance between accommodating project initiatives and avoiding harm to those potentially affected. First, the severity of the impacts of resettlement can vary tremendously. Some projects (rehabilitation of existing roads, for example) may affect only a few people and in only minor ways. Others (reservoir construction is the usual example) may uproot whole communities, forcing them to reestablish lives in unfamiliar surroundings that are less favorable than those they left behind. Because the most severe impacts are also the most difficult and costly to mitigate, minimizing or avoiding the potentially most severe impacts is often more important than focusing simply on minimizing the aggregate number of people affected or amount of land acquired.

The second (and related) point is that minimizing or eliminating land acquisition may not always minimize or eliminate adverse impacts. People should not be allowed to continue using or occupying land or structures, for example, if their doing so poses a hazard to themselves or others. Similarly, acquiring only part of a land parcel or structure would be inappropriate if the remainder is of no practical use.

With careful attention, however, project design can significantly reduce the number of people affected, the severity of potential impacts, and the costs and burdens for the project itself.

> **Project example:** In Brazil, the Water Quality and Pollution Control Project (São Paulo–Guarapiranga component: Ln 3503, Ln 3504, Ln 3505) originally intended to move slum dwellers out of a watershed and into more distant apartment complexes. However, because of the expense of acquiring land near the city and the difficulties of relocating thousands of poor people, the program was revised. Some slum dwellers were moved to apartments already built nearby, but most remained in the slum area. The slum area was provided with sewers, drains, roads, and other infrastructure, to protect the water supply for the city.

1

Project example: In China, the Shanghai Sewerage Project (Ln 2794, Cr 1779) made an extraordinary effort during the design and implementation stages to minimize potentially adverse impacts of the project. By optimizing alignment and changing construction methods, the project dramatically reduced the amount of land to be acquired, from 2,814 mu to 470 mu (15 mu = 1 hectare); the number of households to relocate, from 1,092 to 946; and the number of affected enterprises, from 209 to 144. These reductions almost halved the resettlement budget, from 1.018 billion yuan to 552 million yuan (in 2003, 8.2872 Chinese yuan renminbi [CNY] = US$1.00).

Project example: Also in China, the Hunan Power Development Project (Ln 4350) increased the height of transmission towers, where topography allowed, so that nearby residences would have more than the required 6.5-meter clearance and therefore legally would not have to be relocated.

Project example: In Kenya, the Tana River Conservation Project (TF 28601) first proposed that people be removed from a legally designated park area. Further studies suggested that an endangered monkey species lived in a symbiotic relationship with the people in the area. The project planners decided to allow the people to remain but created incentives to promote out-migration.

Project example: In Uganda, the Bujagali Power Project (Cr B0030) diverted high-voltage transmission lines around a large residential area in the capital city, Kampala. The reorientation of the transmission lines resulted in a longer and more costly route but eliminated much of the need for resettlement. The overall cost–benefit of the initiative was not significantly affected.

Project example: In Zambia, the Power Rehabilitation Project (Cr 3042) follows the Zambia Electricity Supply Corporation's (ZESCO's) policy of negotiating with landowners and users, rather than resorting to involuntary acquisition through the *Land Acquisition Act*. The corporate policy also requires that its engineers design three alternative routes for each transmission line, to help avoid the lands of landowners and occupiers who refuse to accept the line across their land. In addition, once the line is designed, ZESCO's Environmental and Social Affairs Unit surveys the route to determine the number of properties and structures to be affected. On the basis of these surveys, planning engineers fine-tune the final alignment of the transmission lines, to reduce the number of residences and buildings affected.

1

When OP 4.12 Becomes Effective and When It Remains in Force

Sometimes the temporal boundaries of projects are unclear. Sometimes land acquisition takes place before a project is formally identified, but the acquisition is closely linked to a Bank-financed project. Sometimes the resettlement remains incomplete at project closure. The following section addresses several questions raised by these situations.

Initial Applicability

OP 4.12 applies whenever land is taken involuntarily for a Bank-financed project.

OP 4.12 applies whenever, in a Bank-financed project, land is acquired involuntarily or access is restricted in legally designated parks or protected areas. If resettlement *for the project* begins before initial discussions with the Bank and the acquisition of the area is directly linked to the Bank project, then the substantive aspects of OP 4.12 apply retroactively. In other words, if an area is being cleared *in anticipation of, or preparation for, a project*, OP 4.12 would apply.

If, however, earlier resettlement is not directly linked to the project (even though it may facilitate the project), the OP would not apply. For example, a national land regularization or titling program might evict squatters and encroachers, following due process as prescribed by law. If subsequently and independently that area is required for a project, OP 4.12 does not apply. In other words, if the people were resettled with due process for reasons unrelated to the Bank-financed initiative, they are not covered under OP 4.12.[4] (See also "People without Title or Use Rights," in chapter 5.)

If necessary, task team leaders can seek guidance from the resettlement committee to determine whether a previous displacement is attributable to a project and, if so, to establish retroactive eligibility and entitlement criteria. Whatever the legal determination, Bank experience shows that to resolve previous issues of inequitable or insufficient rehabilitation is good practice and can help avoid resistance by DPs to the project.

> *Project example:* In Vietnam, a government decree led to the clearing out of people living within highway rights-of-way in areas designated for Bank-funded improvements under the Highway Rehabilitation Project (Cr 2549). The Bank, insisting that previous project discussions had established the applicability of OD 4.30, halted preparation of the

project until the DPs were identified and covered under the resettle-ment plan (RP).

Project Closing

> Bank policy requires full provision of all resettlement measures before a project closes: "A project is not considered complete—and Bank supervision continues—until the resettlement measures set out in the relevant resettlement instrument have been implemented" (BP 4.12, para. 16).
>
> Moreover, it is the borrower's responsibility to document that the resettlement instrument has been fully implemented: "Upon completion of the project, the bor-rower undertakes an assessment to determine whether the objectives of the resettle-ment instrument have been achieved" (OP 4.12, para. 24).

The borrower assesses achievement in the restoration of incomes and living standards before project closing.

A project cannot be deemed officially completed until the RP is fully implemented.

Outstanding resettlement issues can be pursued during the loan repayment period.

> OP 4.12 (para. 23) specifies that the borrower has the obligation "to carry out the resettlement instrument and to keep the Bank informed of implementation progress" and that this obligation is "provided for in the legal agreements for the project." Further, "before project completion, an assessment will be made by the borrower, to determine whether the main objectives of the resettlement instrument have been real-ized." BP 4.12 (para. 16) provides that the Bank will verify the accomplishments, specifically that "upon completion of the project, the Implementation Completion Report . . . evaluates the achievement of the objectives of the resettlement instrument and lessons for future operations and summarizes the findings of the borrower's assess-ment." OP 4.12 states further that "if the assessment reveals that these objectives may not be realized, the borrower should propose follow-up measures that may serve as the basis for continued Bank supervision" (para. 24).

Even if all agreed compensation and other assistance have been provided, complexities inherent in resettlement may lead to failure in achieving the objectives. Therefore, before the scheduled project closing, the Bank task team first verifies that all agreed forms of assistance in the RP have been provided. The borrower is obligated to obtain an evaluation of incomes and living standards based on baseline data and on monitoring and supervision results. If all agreed forms of assistance have been provided but evaluation results show that incomes or living standards have not been restored—or are not likely to be restored—for a significant proportion of the affected population, the Bank should initiate discussions with the borrower regarding possible follow-up actions. Continued Bank supervision may be necessary.

> *Project example:* In India, the Upper Krishna Irrigation Project (Ln 3050, Cr 2010) closed on June 30, 1997, and an Implementation Completion Report (ICR) was issued on June 29, 1998. The ICR documented that 20 of the 37 legal covenants were incompletely fulfilled and that 3 had not been complied with. The 20 partially fulfilled covenants related largely to the resettlement and rehabilitation of project-affected people and to the participation of farmers in irrigation management (for example, formation of water-user committees). According to the ICR, the project was far from complete as envisaged, so Bank management still had a responsibility to follow the progress of outstanding activities. Because the Bank and the Government of Karnataka were still bound by the provisions of the project agreement, they both agreed that the Bank would continue to supervise these activities until completed. As of October 2003, four post-completion missions have taken place: April 1999, January 2000, November 2000, and February 2002.

Linkages between Bank and Other Donor or National Projects

Resettlement caused by non-Bank–financed activities critical to the design or performance of Bank projects requires due diligence by the Bank.

If a non-Bank–financed activity that causes resettlement is critical to the design or performance of the Bank project, the Bank would carry out due diligence concerning resettlement resulting from such activity by obtaining information on the procedures to identify and address adverse impacts, the applicable standards, the outcomes that are expected, and any significant issues. Bank management and the Board would be fully advised on resettlement issues associated with such non-Bank–financed activity. A key factor in determining whether the OP applies is the sequencing of activities. Activities causing resettlement are usually contemporaneous with the Bank investment. To address the fact that these activities are not a part of the World Bank project, the Bank applies a due diligence approach.

> In terms of the policy, OP 4.12 applies "to other activities resulting in involuntary resettlement, that in the judgment of the Bank, are (a) directly and significantly related to the Bank-assisted project, (b) necessary to achieve its objectives as set forth in the project documents; and (c) carried out, or planned to be carried out, contemporaneously with the project" (para. 4).

In many cases, the Bank finances physical works that are part of broader, integrated infrastructure systems. Systems such as roadways may be constructed incrementally, sometimes over several decades. In some cases, the period of construction is much more contemporaneous, as part of an integrated development scheme. For various reasons, borrowers may rely on two or more external financing agencies, as well as domestic resources, to fund various parts of the construction. Sometimes, Bank-financed activities are essential to the functioning of non-Bank–financed activities. In such cases, the integrally linked components would require due diligence by the Bank, regardless of financing source.

Judgment may be needed in assessing the significance of such linkages. In some networks (roads, railways, or transmission grids, for example), all segments within the system are broadly linked to some extent, but the functioning of the overall system may not be critically affected by construction in one segment. Constructing or improving that single segment may be economically feasible and desirable on its own merits, without regard to effects elsewhere in the system. In such cases, OP 4.12 does not apply. However, if the construction or improvement of connection points (e.g., intersections) is occurring at about the same time as a Bank-financed road construction project, judgment is needed to determine to what extent the policy is applicable.

By contrast, a Bank-financed power plant could certainly not deliver electricity or generate economic benefits without transmission lines. Similarly, a Bank-financed wastewater treatment plant could not function without a sewerage system. If such facilities are to be built contemporaneously with the Bank-supported project, any land acquisition and resettlement needed for them would be reviewed using the Bank's due diligence approach.

To determine whether Bank-financed activities and non-Bank–financed activities are contemporaneous, the task team leaders may first have to determine the sequencing of events. In some cases, significant parts of the infrastructure may have been constructed many years before the Bank's investment. In such cases, it would make no practical sense to attempt to review investments undertaken in the distant past. Due diligence is required, however, when the Bank is financing part of an integrated development scheme. When other facilities essential to the functioning of the Bank-financed works are to be constructed at the same time as, or shortly after, the Bank-financed work, it is good practice to incorporate the resettlement arrangements for the non-Bank–financed activities into the RP. If the other facilities are newly constructed or are under construction at the same time as the Bank project is under preparation, it is recommended that these arrangements be reviewed for general consistency with Bank policy objectives and standards. If such reviews show that resettlement in these activities falls significantly short of Bank policy standards, good practice would be to discuss with the borrower some retroactive measures to mitigate the impacts of these shortcomings. The following are examples of the application of this guidance:

Project example: In Burkina Faso, the Ouagadougou Water Supply Project (Cr 3476) financed construction of a water line to the city. The line would draw water from a new dam financed by other donors. Because the only purpose of the main was to provide water to the capital city, the Bank carried out due diligence concerning resettlement resulting from the project.

Project example: In China, the Tuoketuo Thermal Power Project (Ln 4172) required construction of transmission lines that would not be part of the Bank project. Because the transmission lines were essential to the Bank project, however, the Bank required submission of a resettlement framework for the transmission lines that was consistent with Bank standards.

Project example: Also in China, illegal structures within the right-of-way were removed along a few of the streets in the Shijiazhuang Urban Transport Project (Ln 4600), then under preparation. The Bank determined that its resettlement policy would not apply to removal of these structures because they were removed as part of a broader, nationally sanctioned enforcement and beautification campaign.

Project example: Also in China, the Bank-financed Wanjiazhai Water Transfer Project (Ln 4179) would divert water from the Wanjiazhai Reservoir, which had been financed locally. Because the water main was a critical component of the reservoir, the Bank held that resettlement standards applicable to the reservoir need to be reviewed by the Bank.

Project example: In Côte d'Ivoire, the Azito Thermal Power Project near Abidjan (Cr B0010) required, but did not finance, a dedicated gas pipeline from the fractionating plant, as well as transmission lines to the main power grid. The pipeline was built and operated with separate funding from a private firm. Another firm built the transmission lines under contract to the government, which owns them. Because both the gas supplies and the transmission lines were critical to the Bank-funded project, due diligence review of the land acquisition and resettlement for all components of the power plant was carried out by the Bank.

Project example: In India, the Bank-financed Hyderabad Water and Sanitation Project (Cr 2115) depended on access to water stored behind a dam nearing completion but financed without Bank assistance. Because the Bank project was directly linked to dam construction, the project included infrastructure improvements and rehabilitation assistance to supplement compensation provided to DPs affected by dam and reservoir construction.

Project example: Also in India, displacement in a non-Bank–financed dam project was expected to encourage encroachment into wildlife protection reserves to be supported by the Bank-financed Eco-development Project (Cr 2916). Though encroachment might impair effectiveness of the reserves, the dam itself was not linked directly to the Bank-supported project. To discourage encroachment, the Bank obtained assurances that adequate measures would be taken to restore the incomes of those displaced by the dam project.

Project example: In the Republic of Korea, one component of the Pusan Urban Transport Management Project (Ln 3828) financed the purchase of 280 railroad cars for the Pusan Urban Transit System. Because the cars would serve no other purpose than transit on a rail line under construction but not financed by the Bank, the Bank conducted a due diligence review of resettlement associated with rail-line construction.

Project example: In Mali, Mauritania, and Senegal, the Regional Hydropower Development Project (Cr 2970, Cr 2971, Cr 2972), which financed transmission lines from the Manantali Dam to demand centers in the member countries, did not review resettlement in the reservoir area because dam construction and reservoir filling had taken place more than 10 years earlier.

Promotion of domestic resettlement policy adoption may eliminate or reduce project linkage issues or problems.

In projects involving cofinancing with other multilateral or bilateral agencies, Bank policy is to ensure that, at a minimum, Bank policies are met by the borrower for all components, regardless of other sources of funds. As OP 4.12 states, the "policy applies to all components of the project that result in involuntary resettlement, regardless of the source of financing" (para. 4).

(continued)

(continued from p. 13)

This insistence on minimum standards for the entire project accords with OP 14.20 on cofinancing, which states that Bank funding is intended "to supplement investment from other sources" (para. 1) and, in part, to "help establish common policies or investment priorities among financing sources at the project and sector level" (para. 2). Of course, the borrower or other financiers may require higher standards.

Divergent policies and standards can complicate project implementation. Therefore, reconciliation of the borrowers' and donors' approaches to resettlement issues is highly recommended whenever distinct subprojects are funded by different donors under the same program. OP 4.12 (para. 32) provides for Bank support for development of resettlement policies in borrower countries, as good practice is to encourage development of policies consistent with Bank policy objectives and standards. To the extent that Bank and borrower policies are consistent, temporal- and spatial-linkage issues are less likely to arise and are easier to resolve when they do arise.

Project example: In Colombia, Bogota city officials accepted the need to implement OD 4.30 in the Bank-financed portion of a ring road when they negotiated the project in the early 1990s. The officials later came to recognize the usefulness of these procedures, and today they have adopted these principles for urban resettlement operations in the city.

Project example: In India, the National Thermal Power Corporation (Ln 3632) adopted the principles of OD 4.30 for a Bank-financed project in the early 1990s. Today, the corporation not only has a policy on resettlement for all of its projects, but also has a cadre of dedicated social units to implement the unified policy in the field.

Project example: In Rwanda, the National Highway Project (project number not known) reserved Bank financing for stretches of rural highway that required no resettlement. The project used other donor funding for peri-urban stretches that would likely require resettlement. In accordance with OP 14.20, the Bank insisted that OD 4.30 be applied to the entire highway, as individual segments of road merely constituted parts of an integral investment.

Project example: In Vietnam, the Bank's Highway Rehabilitation Project (Cr. 2549) financed one stretch of highway, while another donor financed an immediately adjacent stretch. Because the government was applying widely divergent standards in adjacent areas, DPs in the non-Bank–financed area complained that they should be treated equitably, in accordance with Bank resettlement standards.

1

When OP 4.12 Does Not Apply

OP 4.12 clarifies the situations in which the policy does not apply. The essential criteria for the application of the policy are (a) the resettlement being involuntary; (b) the project being location specific; and (c) the taking of land or restriction of access being for a Bank-financed investment. The policy does not apply when these criteria are not met.

Structural Adjustment Loans

OP 4.12 (endnote 1) specifically exempts adjustment operations, such as Structural Adjustment Loans (SALs), from the specifications of the OP: "The term 'project' does not include programs under adjustment operations." Adjustment operations provide general budgetary transfers to support economic policy reform and are therefore not location-specific investments. SALs typically do have socioeconomic impacts, such as those resulting from a restructured economy. (See also "Indirect Economic Impacts," below.) But because these consequences are not the direct result of land acquisition, the Bank's policy does not apply.

Sectoral Adjustment Loans are a type of adjustment operation, as they may provide general budgetary support in a sector. These loans may, however, list specific investments, and they are also subject to OP 4.01's environmental-assessment instrument, which cross-references OP 4.12. Thus, where construction of new infrastructure at an existing facility or construction of a new facility entails land acquisition, OP 4.12 may apply on the basis of this reference in OP 4.01. Further, the proactive provisions of the Bank's policy on involuntary resettlement would help support policy and institution building in the concerned sector.

People with income losses attributable to policy or program lending are not entitled to rehabilitation assistance under OP 4.12.

Policy or program lending (for example, structural adjustment programs) can lead to economic hardships by, among other things, eliminating subsidies or closing state enterprises. Such programs do not entail land acquisition for physical infrastructure linked directly to the Bank-supported program. Therefore, loss of jobs or incomes resulting from such programs is beyond the scope of OP 4.12. Such matters can usually be considered under social analyses related to the project. The following are examples of this guidance:

> *Project example:* In India, the Coal Sector Environmental and Social Mitigation Project (Cr 2862) was designed to mitigate the adverse effects of a Bank-supported sectoral reform program. The project included

1

compensation and rehabilitation provisions for people displaced by mining subcomponents; an indigenous peoples' development plan for affected tribal peoples; and some remedial measures developed to address inadequate resettlement from an earlier mine development. Some jobs were also lost due to economic restructuring associated with the project. However, since the loss of jobs resulted not from land acquisition but from economic restructuring—including workforce reductions and closing of unsustainable mines—the Bank project did not include entitlements under OP 4.12 for miners expected to lose their jobs.

Project example: In Poland, Romania, the Russian Federation, and Ukraine, projects to restructure the coal sector had significant social consequences. The program in each country closed many mines and downsized those remaining in operation. The impact of these layoffs was significant at every level—personal, familial, communal, regional, and national. In each of these instances, the project instituted major programs for severance payments and economic rehabilitation as part of good project design. But it did so without recourse to the Bank's policy on resettlement, because none of these initiatives required involuntary acquisition of land.

Natural Disasters, War, or Civil Strife

OP 4.12 (endnote 6) states that "this policy . . . does not cover refugees from natural disasters, war, or civil strife (see OP/BP 8.50, Emergency Recovery Assistance)."

Resettlement after a natural disaster or war that may require physical relocation and economic rehabilitation is generally exempt from OP 4.12 and therefore does not need to follow the standards prescribed in it. The OP would apply, however, to any land acquisition undertaken by the state to relocate the environmental or war refugees. Also, if the people affected by disasters or war are resettled for a second time, after a few years, from their temporary locations, such subsequent resettlement would be subject to OP 4.12.

Project example: In the Azerbaijan Republic Pilot Reconstruction Project (Cr 3109), when refugees from Armenia who had been resettled in temporary locations for 12 years were resettled to permanent sites, the second relocation to permanent sites was covered by OP 4.12.

Natural disasters create emergency situations that require speedy processing. OP 4.12 (endnote 23) recognizes that "an exception to this requirement [of having a draft resettlement instrument as a condition of appraisal; see para. 22] may be made in highly unusual circumstances (such as emergency recovery operations) with the approval of Bank Management." In these situations, "decisions that would have been made at the design stage in regular investment projects may have to be made after approval of an ERL [Emergency Recovery Loan] (OP 8.50, endnote 5). Specifically for resettlement operations, "the Management's approval stipulates a timetable and budget for developing the resettlement plan" (OP 4.12, endnote 24) This stipulation accords with the requirement in OP 8.50 (Annex A, para. 4) that the Memorandum and Recommendation of the President . . . append a technical annex that details the "requirements for rehabilitation, reconstruction, or new construction."

In natural disaster or civil strife, OP 4.12 would apply if the state used its powers of eminent domain to acquire areas for the relocation of citizens in places other than their original residences and places of business. Similarly, OP 4.12 would apply if, in a Bank-financed project, abandoned land that reverted to the state for reallocation were encumbered by pre-existing use claims.

In Emergency Relief Projects (ERP), designed to mitigate adverse impacts of a disaster or civil strife on affected people, detailed resettlement planning can be carried out during the project implementation stage.

Project example: In China, the Taihu Basin Flood Control Project (Cr 2463) was designed after the 1991 flood. The RP was prepared on the basis of an incomplete census and inventory, as the project components were at various stages of technical design at that time. Nonetheless, during implementation detailed census and inventory surveys were conducted on the basis of preliminary technical designs for each component of the project. As a result, the project experienced substantial changes in its estimated impacts: although land acquisition increased, project authorities strove to minimize the number of people affected, the number of homes demolished, and the amount of land leased temporarily.

Project example: In Ecuador, the El Nino Emergency Project (Ln 4259) was designed to rehabilitate roads and bridges washed out in floods and to provide new housing for poor families, which had been living in environmentally unsafe areas in 10 provincial towns. The RPs were developed in consultation with the families, after project approval, and were implemented within two years of the project start.

Project example: In Turkey, the Marmosa Earthquake Recovery Project (Ln 4517) was designed, and quickly approved, to provide new housing for families with homes destroyed in the disaster. Early in implementation,

1

project authorities discovered that three sites designated for new apartment blocks were actually privately owned farmlands with a few structures. As a consequence, an RP that accorded with OD 4.30 was developed to guide the acquisition of these plots and the implementation of measures to compensate and rehabilitate their owners.

Project example: In Azerbaijan, the Pilot Reconstruction Project (Cr 3109) resettled some 5,000 returnees in an area that had been abandoned during the war and legally alienated from its original owners. Because pastoralists who remained in the area had customary use rights, OD 4.30 applied to the herders' situation, but not to that of the landowners who did not return to the area.

Project example: In Sri Lanka, the Northeast Irrigated Agriculture Project (Cr 3301) is rehabilitating irrigation systems in a war-torn area. OP 4.12 does not apply in the southern part of the project area, because people can return to their former homes if they wish. They can do so because the southern part remained under titular government control during the conflict. OP 4.12 does apply in the northern part, however, where the de facto government forcibly expelled Muslims and resettled other populations on the lands, an act not recognized by the official government.

Indirect Economic Impacts

> OP 4.12 explicitly covers "direct economic and social impacts" caused by Bank-assisted investment projects (para. 3). By implication, the policy does not apply to impacts indirectly related to land acquisition. OP 4.12 states that in these instances, "Where there are adverse indirect social or economic impacts, it is good practice for the borrower to undertake a social assessment and implement measures to minimize and mitigate adverse economic and social impacts, particularly upon poor and vulnerable groups" (endnote 5). (See also "Land Acquisition and Restriction of Access to Conservation Areas," above.)

Income losses not directly attributable to land taking are not covered by OP 4.12.

Projects can indirectly affect incomes with or without expropriation of land, physical relocation of people, or restrictions on use. Often, development components (road building, electricity generation) can deleteriously affect incomes by altering competitive environments, traffic or consumption patterns, or other income-related factors. In the case of commercial enterprises, for example, OP 4.12 requires compensation and various forms of relocation assistance, but the policy cannot address long-term impacts on customer loyalty, differences in local tastes, or other forms of intangible cost. Such indirect effects are not covered by OP 4.12, but they may be identified through social assessment and mitigated by attentive project design or other special measures. (See also "Calculation and Application of Replacement Cost," in chapter 4.)

Adverse Environmental and Other Socioeconomic Impacts

Environmental, social, and economic impacts that do not result from land taking may be identified and addressed through environmental assessments and other project reports and instruments" (OP 4.12, endnote 5).

Environmental externalities are beyond the scope of OP 4.12.

Projects often create environmental externalities not directly caused by, or related to, land acquisition. In principle, negative environmental externalities that are not caused by land acquisition and do not, themselves, lead to forced relocation are to be addressed by OP 4.01. In those instances, the environmental assessment (or environmental management plan) can include measures for compensation and other assistance, and the standards of OP 4.12 can be used to assist in the definition of those measures.

If the externalities create conditions that pose a serious risk to health or safety, good practice is to include formal land acquisition in project specifications. People forced to relocate by environmental hazards directly related to project-induced changes in land use are covered by the environmental management plan. This plan may have provisions similar to those in OP 4.12.

> *Project example:* In Bangladesh, the Jamuna Bridge Multipurpose Project (Cr 2569) provided resettlement benefits for people affected by riverbank and channel-island erosion in the vicinity of the project. At issue was determining erosion attributable to the project in a generally erosion-prone environment. Accordingly, spatial- and temporal-proximity criteria (distance from construction areas and timing of erosion) were used to establish entitlement.

> *Project example:* In China, the Shanghai Sewerage Project (Ln 2794, Cr 1779) used tunneling to minimize displacement. Vibrations from the tunneling, however, damaged houses. The project paid repair costs, and authorities agreed to resettle people whose houses were damaged beyond repair.

1

Project example: In India, effluent odors and coal dust severely affected 84 households following implementation of the Tamil Nadu Newsprint Project (Ln 2050). The affected households were resettled under the follow-on Renewable Resources Development Project (Ln 3544).

Project example: In Thailand, persistent health and safety complaints arising from blasting during the Pak Mun dam construction led the officials of the Third Power System Development Project (Ln 3423) to offer both temporary and permanent resettlement options to DPs living near blast zones.

National or Regional Resource Management Programs

National programs to regularize resources are not covered under OP 4.12, because these programs neither require land nor restrict access to legally designated parks or protected areas. This exemption holds, for example, when the program imposes restrictions on the use of natural resources, such as limitations on pumping from aquifers. As OP 4.12 (endnote 8) states, "This policy does not apply to regulations of natural resources on a national or regional level to promote their sustainability, such as watershed management, groundwater management, fisheries management, etc. The policy also does not apply to disputes between private parties in land titling projects, although it is good practice for the borrower to undertake a social assessment and implement measures to minimize and mitigate adverse social impacts, especially those affecting poor and vulnerable groups."

Open-Market Purchase of Project Land

OP 4.12 does not apply if land is acquired through voluntary sale at market price. That the sale is voluntary is important to document, however, because such sales can sometimes be coerced. Also, the land in question is to be free of rival claims or encumbrances. If resident agricultural laborers or others with customary claims to the land are involved, OP 4.12 would apply, and the claimants would be provided with alternative opportunities to earn their livelihood.

Project example: In Malawi, the upcoming land-reform program (Project 075247) will provide funds to local communities to purchase bankrupt tobacco farms on the open market. If the farms have resident agricultural laborers, the project will take a census of the workers, determine their employment preferences, and present a menu of rehabilitation options.

Project example: In South Africa, the government intends to enlarge an existing national park by buying scores of large but highly marginal farms. These sales are to be voluntary. Most of the farms have resident farm workers, many with long tenure and various privileges (for housing, crop land, grazing rights, and so on). These assets and rights are being delineated according to the Bank's resettlement policy. Mechanisms are being designed to restore incomes and living standards; these mechanisms will include employment opportunities within the enlarged park or in the growing tourism industry that will result from enlarging the park.

Project example: In Tanzania, the Boundary Hills Lodge Project (Project 9579), funded under the International Finance Corporation's Africa Project Development Facility, developed a private park and lodge, just outside the Tanangire Game Reserve, on 2,000 hectares of land. This land was sold by the Masai to the developers for a part interest in the investment. The International Finance Corporation hired consultants to verify the free sale of the lands, and subsequent studies have documented that the development is paying royalties to the community, as originally agreed.

Voluntary Resettlement

"Voluntary resettlement" refers to any resettlement not attributable to eminent domain or other forms of land acquisition backed by powers of the state. The operative principles in voluntary resettlement are *informed consent* and *power of choice*. "Informed consent" means that the people involved are fully knowledgeable about the project and its implications and consequences and freely agree to participate in the project. "Power of choice" means that the people involved have the option to agree or disagree with the land acquisition, without adverse consequences imposed formally or informally by the state. By definition, power of choice—and thus voluntary resettlement—is only possible if project location is not fixed. The route of a rural road, for example, could be changed if a landowner objected. The area of a reservoir behind a local dam, by contrast, is immutable. The former instance would allow for voluntary resettlement; the latter would not. To have only informed consent is insufficient without the power of choice.

Voluntary Migration Projects

In Bank experience, some projects involve voluntary resettlement, such as government programs that provide options for resettling people from one area to another. The area of out-migration is exempt from OP 4.12 if the state does not acquire any land from the resettlers or the émigrés have the option to keep their holdings or sell their land on the open market. The voluntary move should nonetheless be documented, including the full disclosure of conditions in the receiving area and the risks migrants may face there. If the state acquires the area for in-migration through use of its powers of eminent domain, however, OP 4.12 applies to the host or receiving area.

> **Project example:** In China, the Bank-supported Gansu Hexi Corridor Project (Ln 4028, CR 2870) is sponsoring the migration of 200,000 people volunteering to move into areas newly developed for agricultural production. OP 4.12 did not apply to the migrants, but it would apply to any people in a "host community" adversely affected by land acquisition for project development. In this case, the OD applied only to about 600 people affected by reservoir construction in the population-receiving area.

> **Project example:** In the Russian Federation, the Northern Restructuring Project (Ln 4611) offers people in the arctic regions the opportunity to return to their areas of origin or to move to larger communities in that region. Migration is voluntary, so OP 4.12 does not apply in the area of out-migration. Further, migrants receive housing vouchers to buy new homes in their areas of origin or to buy available alternative housing of equal quality in the arctic region. So OP 4.12 does not apply to the areas of in-migration either.

Voluntary Land Donations for Community Projects

In some projects, communities may agree to voluntarily provide land in exchange for desired community benefits. The OP does not apply if people or communities make *voluntary* land donations in exchange for benefits or services related to the project. Land donations can be voluntary only if the infrastructure is not location specific. That is, a school or clinic can be sited in a different location if the landowner objects. But in case of location-specific infrastructure, such as a dam or reservoir, voluntary donation is precluded, since objectors can be coerced into acceptance. Thus, if the location of the proposed infrastructure cannot be changed, OP 4.12 would generally apply.

Further, arrangements for voluntary resettlement are expected to involve no physical displacement or significant adverse impacts on incomes (or they are expected to include community-devised mitigatory mechanisms acceptable to those affected). OP 4.12 defines "minor impacts" as loss of less than 10 percent of an individual's holdings (endnote 25).

Because determining informed consent can be difficult, the following criteria are suggested as guidelines:

1. The infrastructure must not be site specific.
2. The impacts must be minor, that is, involve no more than 10 percent of the area of any holding and require no physical relocation.
3. The land required to meet technical project criteria must be identified by the affected community, not by line agencies or project authorities (nonetheless, technical authorities can help ensure that the land is appropriate for project purposes and that the project will produce no health or environmental safety hazards).
4. The land in question must be free of squatters, encroachers, or other claims or encumbrances.
5. Verification (for example, notarized or witnessed statements) of the voluntary nature of land donations must be obtained from *each* person donating land.
6. If any loss of income or physical displacement is envisaged, verification of voluntary acceptance of community-devised mitigatory measures must be obtained from those expected to be adversely affected.
7. If community services are to be provided under the project, land title must be vested in the community, or appropriate guarantees of public access to services must be given by the private titleholder.
8. Grievance mechanisms must be available.

Project example: In China, in the Sichuan Agricultural Development Project (Cr 2411), infrastructure and facilities were proposed by the villages and planned as part of the project. The project financed the purchase of building materials, such as cement, sand, and stones. The farmers contributed the land for tertiary canals, but all donations were less than 10 percent of each holding.

Project example: In India, the Bombay Sewage Disposal Project (Cr 2763) provided improved sanitation in a slum community, without involuntary resettlement. The slum dwellers themselves made project site decisions and provided replacement housing materials or other benefits for those agreeing to move. Those relocating were to remain within 100 meters of their previous dwellings.

Project example: In Indonesia, the Village Infrastructure Project (Ln 3888) allocated funds to villages specifying their own development priorities. The Bank accepted the practice of villagers' voluntarily contributing minor strips of land. Replacement lands or alternative

1

rehabilitation packages were to be offered to anyone losing more than 10 percent of their holdings.

Voluntary Restriction of Access to Resources: Community-Based Natural Resource Projects

Community-based natural resource projects on communal lands are a specific case of projects in which communities donate land in expectation of other benefits. OP 4.12 specifies that the OP "does not apply to restrictions of access to natural resources under community-based projects, i.e. where the community using the resources decides to restrict access to these resources, provided that an assessment satisfactory to the Bank establishes that the community decision-making process is adequate, and that it provides for identification of appropriate measures to mitigate adverse impacts, if any, on the vulnerable members of the community" (endnote 6).

OP 4.12 is premised on the involuntary nature of land acquisition under the powers of eminent domain. Decisions by local communities to voluntarily restrict access to resources or their use and, where necessary, to institute measures to mitigate adverse impacts on community members must allow informed consent and the power of choice. The community has the prerogative to husband its resources in this manner if the whole community participates in the decisionmaking and if weak or vulnerable segments of the population are protected. The Bank verifies that the decisionmaking process is truly community-based—if it isn't truly so OP 4.12 could apply. The determination hangs on the nature of voluntary agreement, which must be premised on truly community-based decisionmaking.

Restrictions on resource use require scrutiny.

The Bank is required to review the decisionmaking process, as well as the framework for protecting vulnerable groups. The decisionmaking process must be inclusive; that is, women, the landless, and seasonal and other users must be represented as well. Similarly, the action plan needs to take full account of the particular issues and needs specific to these groups. The plan must document the ways these concerns are integrated into the overall program. Recording not only who attends meetings convened with each group, but also the positions expressed by each participant, is helpful in this regard. The following is an example of how a community got involved in planning access to seven new wildlife reserves:

Project example: In India, the Eco-development Project (Cr 2916) seeks to strengthen the effectiveness of seven wildlife reserves. As part of the project, migration into the reserves is restricted. People within the reserves who indicate a willingness to move to adjacent areas are given incentives to move there. People wishing to remain within the reserves have been assured that they will not be involuntarily resettled during the life of the loan. Project objectives and designs did not require expulsion of all people, and the existing desire of some residents for relocation assistance eliminated the need to apply OD 4.30.

Notes

1. Practitioners concerned about other social issues and impacts should refer to the guidelines for social analysis available from the Social Development family website.
2. The instances where land acquisition does not trigger OP 4.12 are detailed in the section "Where OP 4.12 Does Not Apply."
3. Indirect impacts may be covered under other Bank instruments. Land acquisition may affect other people indirectly; that is, their properties and assets are not expropriated, but they suffer adverse effects from other people's losses. Communities downstream from a dam or reservoir provide a common example: downstream communities lose no land to the project, but they may be severely affected by the change in water flow. Such indirect impacts are not covered under OP 4.12 because they are not the result of involuntary taking of land used by the affected people, but of other consequences of the project. Other instruments, such as OP 4.01's environmental assessment instrument, cover such impacts. Project design should take indirect impacts into consideration, however, regardless of whether other safeguard measures apply.
4. The principle here is analogous to that used in resettlement operations for dealing with people who do not have legal rights or claims. The Bank accepts the date of the baseline survey as the cutoff date for eligibility: those in the area before the census begins are eligible for compensation and assistance, as relevant, and those who arrive after the cutoff date are not. (Squatters and encroachers are entitled to "resettlement assistance in lieu of compensation for the land they occupy . . . if they occupy the project area prior to" the date of the beginning of the census or prior to the date the project area was delineated, whichever date is earlier [OP 4.12, para. 16]).

Chapter 2

Resettlement Instruments and Disclosure

When operational policy (OP) 4.12 applies, the task team must determine which instrument is appropriate for the project under development. One of three main instruments will be required by appraisal: a resettlement plan (RP) (or an abbreviated RP), a policy framework, or a process framework. This chapter discusses in some detail only the process framework, which, formally, is a new instrument introduced with OP 4.12; later chapters take up the development of a resettlement policy and an RP.

Resettlement Plan

All projects that entail resettlement require an RP. "The scope and level of detail of the resettlement plan vary with the magnitude and complexity of resettlement" (OP 4.12, Annex A, para. 2). A full RP is required at appraisal whenever land acquisition in a project affects more than 200 people, takes more than 10 percent of any holding, and involves physical relocation of population (OP 4.12, para. 25; Figure 2.1). An abbreviated RP is acceptable if fewer than 200 people are displaced. Even if more than 200 people are affected, if all land acquisition is minor (10 percent or less of all holdings is taken) and no physical relocation is involved, an abbreviated RP is acceptable. If fewer than 200 people are displaced but some physical relocation is involved, the abbreviated RP is expanded to include a rehabilitation program (OP 4.12, Annex A, endnote 6).

OP 4.12, para. 6, and Annex A, paras. 2–21, provide the outline and recommended content for an RP.

Policy Framework

A policy framework needs to be prepared if the extent and location of resettlement cannot be known at appraisal because the project has multiple components, as typically happens in sectoral investments, projects with financial intermediaries, and other projects with multiple subprojects. The policy framework establishes resettlement objectives and principles, organizational arrangements, and funding mechanisms for any resettlement operation that may be

2

Figure 2.1 Decision Tree: Resettlement Instruments

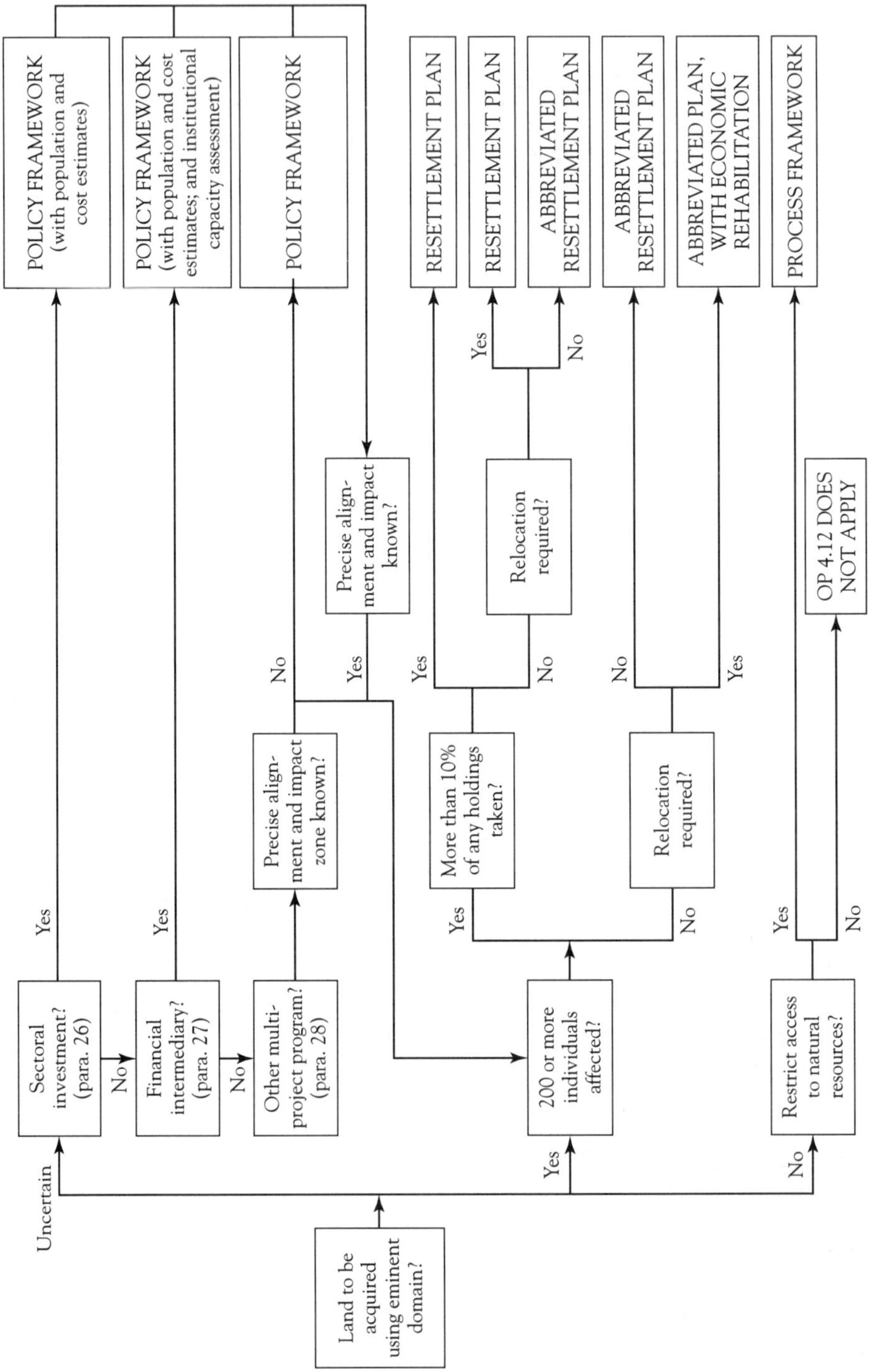

necessary during project implementation. The framework also estimates the probable number of affected persons and resettlements, and especially for financial intermediary projects, assesses the institutional capability to design, implement, and oversee resettlement operations. When during project implementation the extent of resettlement in any subproject becomes known, an RP (or an abbreviated RP, depending on the scale and severity of impacts) is prepared before the investment is approved for funding (OP 4.12, paras. 29–30) (see Appendix 27, "Resettlement Policy Framework," on the CD-Rom accompanying this book for sample resettlement policy frameworks from several Bank projects).

OP 4.12, paras. 26–28, and Annex A, paras. 23–25, provide the outline and recommended content for a policy framework.

Process Framework

Finally, conservation projects that restrict access to legally designated parks or protected areas without acquiring the land outright require a process framework (OP 4.12, para. 7). The purpose of the framework is to describe the process by which potentially affected communities will participate in planning. In these projects, the participation of the affected population in designing the restrictions, as well as in proposing the mitigation measures, is critical for success (see CD Appendix 28, "Resettlement Process Framework," for a sample resettlement process framework from a Bank project).

The process framework describes how any action plan will be developed with the local population. Once developed, the action plan, which may be part of a natural resources management plan, is submitted to the Bank for approval.

"In projects involving involuntary restriction of access to legally designated parks and protected areas, the nature of restrictions, as well as the type of measures necessary to mitigate adverse impacts, is determined with the participation of the displaced persons during the design and implementation of the project. In such cases, the borrower prepares a process framework acceptable to the Bank, describing the participatory process by which

- specific components of the project will be prepared and implemented;
- the criteria for eligibility of displaced persons will be determined;
- measures to assist the displaced persons in their efforts to improve their livelihoods, or at least to restore them, in real terms, while maintaining the sustainability of the park or protected area, will be identified; and
- potential conflicts involving displaced persons will be resolved.

The process framework also includes a description of the arrangements for implementing and monitoring the process" (OP 4.12, para. 7).

(continued)

2

> *(continued from p. 29)*
>
> The process framework establishes how the "affected communities [will] partici-pate in the design of project components, [in the] determination of measures necessary to achieve resettlement policy objectives, and [in the] implementation and monitoring of relevant project activities" (OP 4.12, Annex A, para. 26).
>
> "For a project involving restriction of access . . . the borrower provides the Bank with a draft process framework that conforms to the relevant provisions of this policy as a condition of appraisal. In addition, during project implementation and before to [*sic*] enforcing of the restriction, the borrower prepares a plan of action, acceptable to the Bank, describing the specific measures to be undertaken to assist the displaced per-sons and the arrangements for their implementation. The plan of action could take the form of a natural resources management plan prepared for the project" (OP 4.12, para. 31).

Key elements of a process framework are identified in OP 4.12 (paras. 7, 31). These are described below.

Preparation and Implementation of Specific Components of the Project

The framework describes the components or activities that may involve new or more stringent restrictions on the use of natural resources. The key aspect of this section is to describe how potentially affected communities are to participate in deciding the scope of the restrictions and the mitigative measures proposed, including the methods of participation and decisionmaking (for example, open meetings, selection of leaders or councils).

Selection of Criteria for Determining Eligibility for Assistance

The framework describes how potentially affected groups or communities will be involved in identifying, and assessing the significance of, adverse impacts of the restrictions. The framework also describes how the local population will be involved in establishing the criteria for determining who is eligible for any nec-essary mitigation assistance. While the process framework approach requires that the local population participate in decisionmaking relating to eligibility criteria, another important aspect is to ensure the support of government agen-cies involved in the program.

The framework must identify groups who may be particularly vulnerable to hardship as a result of new or strengthened restrictions on access to natural resources. Two additional issues warrant careful consideration in specific cases.

First, the framework should consider the interests of nonresidents who also use the resources in question. Second, the framework may need to explain how the project is going to address the claims of people engaging in some form of illicit or unsustainable resource use (for example, poaching of protected wildlife or opportunistic encroaching into areas already subject to customary resource management).

Identification of Measures to Improve or Restore Livelihoods and Living Standards

The framework describes how groups or communities will be involved in identifying (a) the most equitable basis for sharing access to resources under restricted use, (b) alternative resources available for use, and (c) other opportunities to offset losses. This section describes the participatory method by which adversely affected community members will make collective decisions about the options available to them as eligible individuals or households. The framework also describes enforcement provisions and clearly delineates responsibilities of the community and government agencies to ensure that use restrictions are observed.

In general, affected communities will likely use one or more of four strategies in devising alternatives:

- Devising reliable and equitable ways of sustainably sharing the resource at issue. (Attention to equitable property rights or more efficient practices may significantly reduce pressure on forest products, for example.)
- Obtaining access to alternative resources or functional substitutes. (Obtaining access to electricity or biomass energy may eliminate overuse of timber for firewood, for example.)
- Obtaining public or private employment (or financial subsidies) to provide local residents with alternative livelihoods or the means to purchase resource substitutes.
- Providing access to resources outside of the park or protected area. Of course, a framework promoting this strategy must also consider impacts on people and the sustainability of the resources in these alternative areas.

Resolution of Potential Conflicts or Grievances

The framework describes processes for addressing disputes among affected groups or communities. A key aspect of these processes will be the role of government in both mediation and the enforcement of agreements. The framework also describes processes for addressing grievances raised by affected individuals

2

or households that are dissatisfied with eligibility criteria, the design of mitigation measures, or patterns of actual implementation. The framework should describe how responsibilities will be distributed among government agencies and the communities themselves in the event that unanticipated problems or impacts arise or mitigation measures cannot be implemented successfully.

In addition, a process framework includes at least two elements that may not necessarily be directly related to community participation.

Administrative and Legal Procedures

The framework reviews the legal basis for acceptance and enforcement of measures and terms included in the framework or policy. As necessary, the framework delineates the responsibilities of various government entities involved in the project or in delivery of services within the affected area. It establishes the minimum period for agreements with affected communities to remain in effect. It also establishes measures to protect the affected communities' interests if these agreements are superseded or rendered ineffective by any other government actions.

Monitoring Arrangements

The framework establishes arrangements for monitoring progress during project implementation. A general principle is that these arrangements include opportunities for the affected population to participate in monitoring activities. The framework describes the scope and methods for monitoring, taking into account both the extent and significance of adverse impacts and the effectiveness of measures intended to improve (or at least restore) livelihoods and living standards.

For a process framework approach to be acceptable, the Bank must be convinced that the people affected will have a voice in the decisionmaking process. OP 4.12 emphasizes that affected communities should participate in determining both the nature of restrictions on resource use and the measures needed to mitigate the adverse impacts of these restrictions. Such a high degree of community involvement is essential whenever local cooperation and collaboration are critical for the success of an initiative. And like any framework for participatory processes (see chapter 7), the process framework must address issues about the quality of the process, such as leadership, representation, equity, and treatment of individuals vulnerable to specific hardships.

In projects that involve both land taking and restriction of access, an RP and a process framework will have to be prepared. Task teams with specific questions can refer their queries to their regional resettlement specialist, the resettlement specialist for the Environmentally and Socially Sustainable

Development Unit—Environment Department, or, if necessary, the Resettlement Committee.

Disclosure

The Bank insists on both integral participation of displaced persons (DPs) and public disclosure of RPs. "Displaced persons should be meaningfully consulted and should have opportunities to participate in planning and implementing resettlement programs" (OP 4.12, para. 2[b]). "The borrower informs potentially displaced persons at an early stage about the resettlement aspects of the project and takes their views into account in project design" (OP 4.12, para. 19). Furthermore, "as a condition of appraisal of projects involving resettlement, the borrower provides the Bank with the relevant draft resettlement instrument which conforms to this policy, and makes it available at a place accessible to displaced persons and local NGOs [nongovernmental organizations], in a form, manner, and language that are understandable to them. Once the Bank accepts this instrument as providing an adequate basis for project appraisal, the Bank makes it available to the public through its InfoShop. After the Bank has approved the final resettlement instrument, the Bank and the borrower disclose it again in the same manner" (OP 4.12, para 22).

Bank Procedure (BP) 4.12 reiterates these instructions: "Once the borrower officially transmits the draft resettlement instrument to the Bank, Bank staff—including the Regional resettlement specialists and the lawyer—review it, determine whether it provides an adequate basis for project appraisal, and advise the Regional sector management accordingly. Once approval for appraisal has been granted by the Country Director, the TT [task team] sends the draft resettlement instrument to the Bank's InfoShop. The TT also prepares and sends the English language executive summary of the draft resettlement instrument to the Corporate Secretariat, under cover of a transmittal memorandum confirming that the executive summary and the draft resettlement instrument are subject to change during appraisal" (BP 4.12, para. 9).

For projects that entail the involuntary restriction of access to legally designated parks and protected areas, "the TT assesses the plan of action to determine the feasibility of the measures to assist the displaced persons to improve (or at least restore in real terms to pre-project or pre-displacement levels, whichever is higher) their livelihoods with due regard to the sustainability of the natural resource, and accordingly informs the Regional Management, the Regional social development unit, and LEG [Legal Department]. The TL [team leader] makes the plan of action available to the public through the InfoShop" (BP 4.12, para. 15).

The DPs are informed about the possibility of resettlement and are consulted in a meaningful way throughout the process. To this end, the borrower may work directly with the DPs and their local groups, contract an intermediary agency to assist in the work, or both. Whatever the organizational arrangement, the borrower is obligated to hear the views of the DPs and to integrate these

2

views fully into the resettlement instrument and its implementation (see chapter 7 for further details).

Formal public disclosure entails distribution of the appropriate instruments, both in the project area and through the Bank's InfoShop: the borrower is responsible for dissemination of the documents in the project area in a form and language understandable to the local populations, and the Bank undertakes distribution through the InfoShop.

Chapter 3

Eligibility Criteria and Units of Entitlement

Operational Policy (OP) 4.12 uses land ownership and severity of impact as guides to determine eligibility for resettlement entitlements. Land ownership includes title, customary, and traditional rights, as well as formal and informal contractual rights. The severity of impact may range from minor to severe. Minor impacts occur when, as defined in OP 4.12, endnote 25, "less than 10% of their productive assets are lost," with no physical relocation. Severe impact is when more than 10 percent of land (or resources) is taken, physical relocation occurs from one's residence or place of business, or people suffer significant loss of livelihood and income. The type of ownership or claim, in combination with the severity of impact, determines the relevant resettlement entitlements, which are generally defined in proportion to the impact on displaced persons (DPs) (see also Appendix 5 and CD Appendix 11, "Matrix of Resettlement Impacts," for several examples from Bank projects).

Eligibility Criteria: Land Tenure and Severity of Impact

OP 4.12 recognizes the adverse impact that land acquisition and involuntary resettlement can have on local populations (para. 1): "Bank experience indicates that involuntary resettlement under development projects, if unmitigated, often gives rise to severe economic, social, and environmental risks: production systems are dismantled; people face impoverishment when their productive assets or income sources are lost; people are relocated to environments where their productive skills may be less applicable and the competition for resources greater; community institutions and social networks are weakened; kin groups are dispersed; and cultural identity, traditional authority, and the potential for mutual help are diminished or lost."

OP 4.12 defines categories of eligibility in terms of land tenure (para. 15): "Displaced persons may be classified in one of the following three groups:

(a) those who have formal legal rights to land (including customary and traditional rights recognized under the laws of the country);

(continued)

(*continued from p. 35*)

    (b) those who do not have formal legal rights to land at the time the census begins but have a claim to such land or assets; provided that such claims are recognized under the laws of the country or become recognized through a process identified in the resettlement plan . . . ; and

    (c) those who have no recognizable legal right or claim to the land they are occupying."

OP 4.12 also specifies the general measures required for specific impacts: "prompt and effective compensation at full replacement cost for losses of assets attributable directly to the project" (para 6[a]); "assistance (such as moving allowances during relocation;" and "residential housing, or housing sites, as required" "if impacts include physical relocation" (para. 6[b]); and "support after displacement, for a transition period," and "development assistance in addition to compensation measures" if incomes have been affected (para. 6[c]).

Responsibility for establishing eligibility criteria rests with the borrower.

"The borrower also develops a procedure, satisfactory to the Bank, for establishing the criteria by which displaced persons will be deemed eligible for compensation and other resettlement assistance" (para. 14).

Land Tenure

Bank policy clearly distinguishes legal tenure from occupancy without legal title, which is often termed encroachment or squatting. Legal tenure covers both ownership through legal title (or lease) or occupation or use based on customary and traditional rights that are or can be legally recognized.

Land tenure—registered title, as well as customary and traditional rights—constitutes the initial eligibility criterion.

Land tenure takes a variety of forms. In the simplest case, an individual or collectivity possesses freehold title to the area: that is, the area is registered in the name of the individual, corporation, or collectivity. In other cases, parties may hold land through leasehold and therefore have legal rights. This type of landholding is particularly common in urban areas, where the state holds title but leases land to individuals on a long-term basis (for example, 99 years).

Under OP 4.12, customary or traditional rights that are recognized or are recognizable under the laws of the country have the same force as formal legal title. As the OP says, displaced persons include "those who have formal legal rights to land (including customary and traditional rights recognized [or recognizable] under the laws of the country)" (para 15[a]).

Even in straightforward situations such as freehold tenure, land ownership can be complicated. Land records may be incomplete, out of date, lost, or destroyed. Even seemingly duly registered parcels of land may be subject to dispute for any number of reasons. Owners may have informally subdivided the plot. Registered owners may be surrogates for landlords with large landholdings. Inheritance on death of the owner may not have been recorded.

In other instances, formal title might not exist, even though people have recognized, customary and traditional rights to use the area. In Africa, for example, village clans may exercise control over surrounding areas, which village elders allot to farmers for slash-and-burn agriculture. Similarly, in the South Pacific, land is held communally and cannot be alienated without a consensus of the community.

Customary title also occurs in many special circumstances. In some countries, colonial powers gazetted areas as forest or nature reserves, even though indigenous populations had resided there for generations. These populations usually remained in the newly demarcated area and continued their customary use of local resources. Even where groups that occupied the area before gazetting still have recognized claims in law, the administrative actions to formally transfer title have sometimes not been completed. This situation can cause difficulties because, today, better communications, heavier population densities, and changing sensitivities about natural resource management have combined to restrict local resource exploitation on land that people regard as effectively theirs.

A different situation arises in cities, where merchants and vendors ply their trades in places that in principle belong to the state. The state may have tolerated the encroachment and may even have imposed taxes and other fees on the occupants, thus effectively establishing the occupants' informal or customary rights to that land.

Elsewhere, groups may have seasonal rights to use the land. Transhumant pastoralists, for example, may have traditional rights to graze their animals on fields after the harvest. Itinerant fishers may have seasonal rights to work in specific riverine or coastal areas. Field hands may have the traditional right to glean from the fields after harvest.

Given the complexity of land-tenure situations, the census and asset inventory should record not only each plot to be acquired but also the owner or occupier, the type of tenure, and the documentation for title or the claim to occupancy.

Land acquisition may qualify nonlandowners for assistance.

Land acquisition affects anyone who owns, resides in, or works in the area taken by the state. Although only the legal or customary owner is compensated for the loss of the land, other people may be directly affected because of loss of occupancy or of other assets and may qualify for alternative forms of assistance.

3

Three major categories of nonowners are renters, businesses, and workers and employees. Renters occupying residences to be acquired are eligible for relocation assistance because they have to move. Relocation assistance typically covers assistance in locating replacement housing, as well as in packing and moving; financial payment for the cost of the move and possibly for refitting the new residence; and follow-up services for the individuals in their new locations.

Businesses are similarly eligible for relocation and other assistance, regardless of whether they own the property or building. Businesses using rented properties are given assistance in finding a new location, compensation at replacement value for any immovable assets, compensation for the loss of income during transition, assistance with the physical transfer, and follow-up services. Workers and employees, meanwhile, may be eligible for wages during the transition.

In addition, several categories of informal occupiers, often termed squatters and encroachers, may be eligible for specific assistance (see "People without Title or Use Rights," in chapter 5).

Severity of Impact

Resettlement entitlements are generally commensurate with the severity of impact.

The effect on economic viability determines severity of impact.

Severity of impact on landholdings varies with the extent of the DPs' holdings. But landholdings vary by size, use, and productive capacity, so viability determines severity of actual impact. But no proportional formula can be relied on to consistently meet the compensation and rehabilitation requirements of OP 4.12.

As a general rule, if a project-affected family loses less than 10 percent of a holding, the impact is minor, because the remaining area is likely to remain economically viable. This rule might not hold if the holdings are very small, in which case even a minor acquisition might render the entire plot unviable. Similarly, as a general rule, if a project-affected family loses less than 20 percent of its productive assets and the remainder is economically viable, the family may receive cash compensation. Again, if the holding is small and the remaining area is not economically viable, the family is compensated both for the lost asset and for the remaining unproductive asset.

Furthermore, land may be only one source of income. Families may earn money from any number of activities, such as collecting secondary forest products, marketing produce, producing artisanal goods, migrating for seasonal labor, and receiving remittances. Determination of the severity of impact takes into account not only landholdings but also all the income sources available to the DPs. This approach recognizes that families with holdings of the same size and losing the same amount of land might have different incomes and standards of living and hence suffer different probable impacts.

Resettlement planning involves two instruments that help in assessing severity of impact. Land surveys are used to determine the proportion of land acquired from each household and thus the probable severity of the impact of the project on landholding. Socioeconomic surveys are used to assess other income sources and thus the severity of the impact on total family income.

The nature of the land tenure system, particularly collective land tenure, can mitigate the severity of impact.

Unlike individual land tenure, in which the impact of land acquisition falls on the individual or household, collective land tenure can mitigate the severity of impact by distributing the loss among all community members. In rural China, for example, farmers own land collectively, and the farmer group (the production team under the commune system) is the unit of land ownership. When the state acquires land within a village, the remaining area is reallocated to all the community members. (If the average landholding in the village falls below a regional average, the authorities will invoke other mechanisms, such as migration permits and industrial employment, to ensure that all remaining farmers have plots of at least the average holding size.) Such collective sharing of the loss of land reduces the loss any one family must bear and means that the severity of impact needs to be measured at the level of the collectivity.

Collective tenure may not guarantee communal sharing of land loss if plots are locally identified as individual holdings. This situation arises, for example, in Vietnam and parts of southern China, where land is legally held collectively, but in some localities, specific plots are considered effectively the property of individuals. In such instances, the impact of land acquisition will be collective in theory but individual in practice, and entitlements would need to be designed individually (see CD Appendix 4, "Guidelines for Land Acquisition Assessment," for guidance in conducting a land acquisition assessment that will help determine the resettlement implications and impacts of land acquisition).

Total income (landholdings and income diversification) affects severity of impact.

As mentioned, assessment of the severity of impact is based on a DP's total income. Both the amount of land held and the proportion of income that agriculture contributes to family earnings are factors. To more accurately assess the actual impact of land acquisition, a good practice is to have the asset inventory cover both the total lands held by a family (rather than just the amount of land to be acquired) and the nonagricultural income available to the family. The impact of land acquisition is likely to be less severe for DPs who derive only a small proportion of their income from land-based activities (see CD Appendix 10, "Household Income Stream Analysis," for the variety of income streams that need to be considered in designing income restoration strategies).

In situations in which farmers depend entirely on farming for their income (rural situations), the loss of one tenth or more of their holdings is considered severe, according to OP 4.12, and "preference should be given to land-based resettlement strategies" because the DPs' livelihoods are land-based (para. 11).

Households commonly have both farm and nonfarm sources of income, especially in densely populated rural and in peri-urban areas. In such areas, the extent of land loss alone is insufficient for estimating the impacts of land acquisition. Estimating the total family income in these cases also requires analysis of household employment patterns and income structures. Furthermore, in areas with diversified income streams, giving a range of options to DPs allows them to protect (or enhance) their incomes, as they deem appropriate. Either a land-replacement option or cash compensation and rehabilitation assistance may be appropriate in these instances (Table 3.1). OP 4.12 accepts cash compensation "where (a) livelihoods are land-based but the land taken for the project is a small fraction of the affected asset and the residual is economically viable; (b) active markets for land, housing, and labor exist, displaced persons use such markets, and there is sufficient supply of land and housing; or (c) livelihoods are not land-based" (para. 12).

Cash compensation is generally sufficient for DPs losing less than 20 percent of their landholding.

Generally, DPs losing access to less than 20 percent of their landholding can be paid cash compensation at replacement cost for the portion of land lost to them.

Table 3.1 Severity of Impact of Land Taking and Recommended Entitlement Options

	Amount of holdings acquired	Option of replacement land for that taken	OR	Prorated cash compensation	Rehabilitation package	PLUS	Option to sell residual land
Residual holdings economically viable	Less than 20%			×			
	More than 20%	×		×	×		
	More than 80%	×		×	×		×
Residual holdings no longer economically viable	Percentage irrelevant	×		×	×		×

Of course, design or land-consolidation considerations may lead governments to offer more than this minimum entitlement.

DPs losing more than 20 percent of their total agricultural land are entitled to a land-replacement option.

DPs losing more than 20 percent of their total agricultural land are generally considered severely affected. Those whose livelihoods are land-based and who are losing more than 20 percent of their total productive agricultural land are to be given an option allowing them to acquire comparable replacement land. They may, at their option, choose cash compensation and economic rehabilitation, instead of land replacement. Those severely affected whose income is not land-based may receive only cash compensation and rehabilitation assistance to allow them to restore or improve their incomes.

Residual landholdings that do not remain viable after land acquisition may be acquired, at the option of the DPs.

> "If the residual of the asset being taken is not economically viable, compensation and other resettlement assistance are provided as if the entire asset had been taken" (OP 4.12, endnote 12).

A good practice is to give those people losing 80 percent or more of their total agricultural land an option allowing them to relinquish the remainder at replacement cost, acquire replacement land equivalent in size or productive value to their entire holdings, or choose among other rehabilitation measures, as appropriate. However, in cases in which acquisition of less than 80 percent of the landholding renders the remainder of the landholding no longer viable, Bank policy recommends that the entire plot be acquired.

Landless laborers can be offered reemployment options.

Landless laborers have no reasonable chance of reemployment if landowners involuntarily cede their property and move away. A good practice in these instances is to establish arrangements for the laborers' economic rehabilitation. (The same approach is followed for open-market purchase of project land; see "When OP 4.12 Does Not Apply," in chapter 1).

> *Project example:* In Malawi, the upcoming land-reform program (Project 075247) will provide funds to local communities for purchasing bankrupt tobacco farms on the open market. If the farms have resident agricultural laborers, the project will census the workers, determine their employment preferences, and present a menu of rehabilitation options.

3

Open Access and Other Property

Open Access or Common Property

Bank projects frequently affect people whose rights to land or other resources are not legally recognized. Such projects are especially likely to be carried out in regions where the regularization of formal property remains incomplete. Some households depend on open access to resources in unregulated areas. Some communities have long-standing or ancestral customary rights to collectively regulate common property, or individuals or families may assert customary property ownership. As OP 4.12 recognizes, the most devastating effects of displacement may be borne by individuals or groups who depend on open access to resources, whose customary rights are not legally recognized, or whose resource use differs from dominant patterns.

Project example: In the Republic of Korea, the Ports Development and Environmental Improvement Project (Loan [Ln] 3793) gave licensed ocean fishers directly affected by land reclamation and port construction the equivalent of eight years' earnings. Indirectly affected fishers were to receive compensation amounting to 30 percent of earnings for 2.5 years.

Project example: In Pakistan, as a result of a mid-term review of resettlement implementation, roughly 200 grazing households displaced by reservoir construction in the Left Bank Drainage Outfall Project (Credit [Cr] 1532) were granted continued use of the reservoir drawdown for grazing (in addition to standard DP entitlements). Roughly 20 households without access to grazing areas received agricultural land acceptable to them. The resettlement package also included income-generation programs, including a milk-collection center.

Project example: In India, the indigenous peoples' development plan for tribal peoples affected by the Orissa Water Resources Consolidation Project (Cr 2801) provided a mix of entitlements, including access to forest resources. The plan provided regularized title to land with up to a 30-degree slope and common-use rights on land or in forests in steeper areas.

Resettlement plans include a survey of existing uses of all land directly affected by the project.

Resettlement plans (RPs) detail the use and tenure of all affected plots in the project area. To ensure that resettlement does not cause secondary displacement, task teams ascertain at appraisal that the existing use of land to be acquired, including proposed resettlement sites, has been investigated. This verification extends to public lands allocated for the project, because these lands may be used privately. A good practice is to hold public consultations to find out whether anyone has pre-existing private claims to public lands not in active use. Such nominal public ownership cannot serve as a bar to compensation (or rehabilitation) for those with customary claims to resources.

Replacements for common property are also communally owned.

When affected lands are communally owned, ownership of replacement lands remains vested in the community (see also "Appropriate Unit of Entitlement," below). Because relocation can disrupt modes of production and social relationships within communities and households, a good practice is to review the arrangements for redistribution established by the community.

Residences

For partially affected residential land, necessity of relocation is often used to determine severity of impact.

Rural

If partial land acquisition leaves insufficient area for existing residential structures and family farming activities, the impact is considered severe. Accordingly, the affected household, at its option, is entitled to alternative land of the same size or of a size that permits relocation of the affected structures and resumption of small-scale farming activities, such as fish ponds, chicken coops, or vegetable plots. Compensation at replacement cost is also required for relocation or reconstruction of structures or facilities. If land acquisition does not directly affect residential structures, cash compensation at replacement cost for the portion of land acquired (and any assets on it) is sufficient, provided an area acceptable and appropriate for farming activities remains.

Urban

In urban areas, yard areas required for a project may be acquired for cash, through a process of negotiation with the owner. If parts of the residence must be demolished, a good practice is to acquire the entire structure, unless the owner wishes to keep the structure and doing so does not create a threat to public safety.

Businesses

For enterprises, the necessity to relocate is often used to determine severity of impact.

If industrial or commercial activity cannot be continued following partial acquisition of land, the affected enterprise is entitled to the cost of reestablishing its

3

activities elsewhere. This means the enterprise is provided alternative land of the same size or of a size that permits relocation of the affected enterprise. In addition, the affected enterprise is entitled to compensation at replacement cost for structures, compensation for lost net income during the period of transition, and compensation for the costs of the transfer and reinstallation of the plant and machinery. If an enterprise can be relocated within the existing holding, compensation at replacement cost for the affected portion of the land must be paid, along with any transfer or reconstruction costs for affected structures, plants, or machinery.

Project example: In China, the Shanghai Sewerage Project (Ln 3987) compensated all 144 enterprises for their physical losses and reimbursed collective and private enterprises for salary expenses.

Project example: Also in China, the Shandong Environment Project (Ln 4237) relocated three enterprises and one shop affected by its program; paid the workers' salaries during the transition; and waived, for two years after relocation, the contract fee levied on enterprises.

Usefulness determines severity of impact for partially affected structures.

For fully affected structures, full compensation at replacement cost (including any costs of relocation) is required. If a partially affected structure can continue its existing use, or if reconstructing only the affected portion of the structure can restore existing use, compensation at replacement cost is required for the affected portion of the structure. If a partially affected structure can no longer serve its normal functions, compensation at replacement cost (including provision of a comparable building site), or compensation for all costs of complete restoration, is required.

For wage employees, duration of joblessness determines severity of impact.

If wage employees are to lose their incomes temporarily because of dislocation or disruption directly related to the Bank project but are likely to eventually be reemployed, they may be given a transition allowance equivalent to lost wages for the duration of their unemployment. If employees do not have a reasonable opportunity for reemployment (at equal or higher wages), a good practice is to provide them with alternative jobs or to take other rehabilitation measures to allow them to restore their incomes. Workers not assured of alternative employment are normally given the equivalent of at least three years' wages.

Project example: In the Republic of Korea, the Pusan Port Project (Ln 2726) disrupted employment of both waiters in portside restaurants and landless laborers. The waiters were given a transitional allowance, because they could find reemployment in restaurants elsewhere in the city. However, the landless laborers at the port were given assistance to qualify for and find other employment.

Temporary Permits

People with valid temporary permits or use rights are eligible for compensation or other assistance.

People with valid permits or licenses for temporary use or occupancy of land or structures are eligible for compensation or equivalent forms of assistance. This compensation or assistance should be prorated for the remaining period of validity. These people should also be compensated for loss of crops or for other damages incurred. People whose temporary-use rights have already expired or who have been allowed temporary use in areas acknowledged to be reserved for the project are not generally eligible for compensation. However, a good practice is to provide such people with relocation or transition assistance.

Temporary Involuntary Acquisition

Infrastructure projects frequently require temporary use of private lands or structures for access, material storage, borrow pits, work sites, or other purposes. In many cases, temporary access can be obtained voluntarily through renting or leasing. In some cases, borrowers may find they need to exercise legal or regulatory authority. Because temporary loss of lands or structures can adversely affect incomes or standards of living, task teams must ensure that involuntary temporary acquisition is minimized and that project plans provide compensation for any involuntary temporary acquisition (Box 3.1).

People temporarily affected are to be considered DPs.

The primary emphasis of OP 4.12 is on mitigating adverse impacts, including temporary ones (for example, impacts of the relocation process). Those people involuntarily bearing costs of temporary acquisition directly attributable to Bank projects are to be considered DPs. The RPs therefore address the issues of temporary acquisition.

Mechanisms to regulate prolonged temporary acquisition are provided.

Because of contingencies during project implementation, the length of time required for temporary use of land or structures cannot be reliably determined at appraisal. But open-ended or prolonged temporary displacement lessens the

3

Box 3.1 Suggested Compensation Guidelines for Temporary Acquisition of Assets

For land

Good practice recommends that DPs receive (a) compensation equivalent to the net average income that would have been obtained from the land during the period of temporary acquisition; and (b) restoration of the land to its original productive use or full compensation for the cost of restoration. Another good practice is to explicitly delineate in contractors' agreements the responsibility for restoring the land to its former productive use.

> *Project example:* In China, plans for the Second National Highways Project (Ln 4124) included temporary acquisition of agricultural land for four years. Compensation for loss of access and cultivation was calculated as five times the average annual value of agricultural production.

For structures

Good practice recommends that DPs receive compensation based on the remaining extent of access or use. If temporary land acquisition produces only minor inconveniences (for example, periodic disruption of access), compensation to restore the structure to its original condition and an inconvenience allowance can be paid. If structures themselves are temporarily acquired, or if use of the structures is precluded, alternative comparable accommodations, a rental allowance for equivalent temporary housing, or payment for constructing temporary housing of a reasonable standard can be provided. Compensation should also be paid for any moving or restoration expenses.

For businesses

Temporary loss of access to facilities, suppliers, or customers can diminish business income significantly. A good practice is to pay compensation equivalent to the estimated net loss to the owner of the business. Because estimating may be unavoidable when planners are determining losses (or incomes), compensation amounts are usually negotiated with business owners. If an affected business cannot continue in its current location, another good practice is to provide new premises or a rental allowance for new premises (including the cost of relocating business personnel and equipment to and from these new premises).

> *Project example:* In China, replacement accommodations for businesses temporarily affected by the Second Shanghai Sewerage Project (Ln 3987) were to be provided at least six months before displacement. Compensation was also to be provided for relocation expenses, lost wages, and net losses.

For wages

Good practice recommends paying allowances, equivalent to regular wages, to workers temporarily losing employment.

> *Project example:* In China, the Shandong Environment Project (Ln 4237) paid the workers' salaries in affected shops during the transition.

ability of DPs to restore their livelihoods and plan for the future. A good practice is to agree with the borrower on arrangements for, and duration of, temporary acquisition. Beyond that duration, additional allowances can be provided for the landowners and occupiers, in part as incentive for official agencies to speed up the process. Temporary compensation already paid is not to be deducted from the compensation at full replacement cost if the project agency ultimately decides to acquire the property.

> *Project example:* In China, the Taihu Basin Project (Ln 3560; Cr 2463) required 44,736 mu of land for dumping soil (15 mu = 1 hectare). A 1.5-year lease was originally planned. But the heavy, clayey soil took several years to dry out. Therefore, the Taihu Basin Authority and local governments extended the land-rental period and allocated funds to speed up the restoration of the soil dumps.

Appropriate Unit of Entitlement

OP 4.12 recognizes individual, family or household, and community losses. "Upon identification of the need for involuntary resettlement in a project, the borrower carries out a census to identify the persons who will be affected by the project" (para. 14). "Alternative or similar resources are provided to compensate for the loss of access to community resources (such as fishing areas, grazing areas, fuel, or fodder)" (para. 13[b]).

The "unit of entitlement" is the individual, the family or household, or the community that is eligible to receive compensation or rehabilitation benefits. Determining the appropriate unit of entitlement, especially if the resettlement process disrupts current household relationships, is necessary to ensure that entitlements target those adversely affected and to clarify the responsibilities of agencies managing compensation and rehabilitation (see also Appendix 6 and CD Appendix 13, "Entitlement Matrix," for several entitlement frameworks from Bank projects).

As a rule, the unit of loss determines the unit of entitlement.

As a general rule, those losing assets are compensated for their losses. If an individual loses a small business or access to income-generating resources, the individual is entitled to compensation or rehabilitation. If more than one person owns or customarily uses expropriated resources, then they are entitled to share in compensation. For example, if a household of eight loses a house and 2 hectares of land held in the name of one person, the members of the household are collectively entitled to at least a house and 2 hectares of land of comparable value or to another form of compensation or rehabilitation acceptable to them.

When the unit of entitlement is collective, resettlement arrangements need to take into account the interests of all affected individuals.

In countries such as China, where rural land is collectively owned and compensation is typically paid to the collective as the unit of entitlement, the use of collective compensation varies from case to case, but typically it is used to benefit the whole collective. Resettlement planning should identify the individuals within the collective who are actually affected by land loss and ensure that adequate arrangements are provided for their economic recovery (through collective land redistribution or other means).

The Bank accepts the borrower's census definition of "household."

When the household is the appropriate unit of entitlement, the definition of "household" as used in the borrower's censuses can be used in RPs. If the borrower's practice is to categorically exclude certain groups, such as female-headed households, a good practice is to agree with the borrower on a general principle of compensation for the effective owner or user (see also "Gender Issues," in chapter 5).

Household entitlements are typically payable to the head of the household.

In practice, title to replacement land, structures, and any other household assets is generally vested in the head of the household. In principle, the household as a group should jointly decide on an equitable distribution of entitlements. Social assessment may be needed to determine the equitability of existing household practices and the potential effects of resettlement on the distribution of opportunities and rights within the household. The following are common examples of such effects:

- The shift from customary use to legal property title vested in the head of household may undermine the position of women. Social assessment may be necessary to determine whether joint title should be encouraged or required, especially if gender discrimination in income regeneration or estate transfer might result.
- The shift from rural agriculture to wage employment for the head of household may undermine the productive opportunities and potential of other adults within the household. Social assessment may be necessary to determine whether these other adults have skills that would be applicable in the resettlement area or whether alternative entitlements, such as training, education, small-business grants, or other opportunities, can be encouraged or required.

- Prolonged moving delays from the time of project identification to actual implementation can also distort normal household patterns (for example, lack of investment, land divestiture, or inheritance). Updating the census surveys is useful in identifying children who have reached adulthood in the interim, as well as families within households who may have lost productive opportunities because of the project, but well before displacement.

Adult offspring in the household are not eligible for separate entitlements.

As a general principle, Bank policy does not make adult offspring residing within the household individually eligible for the complete household entitlement. If, in the example above, the household of eight includes two adults still residing with their natal family, giving each of them entitlement to a house and 2 hectares of land would go far beyond compensation for losses. Of course, nothing in OP 4.12 precludes the borrower from providing land to adult sons or daughters if the borrower wants to go beyond minimum standards.

> *Project example:* In India, the policy of the Upper Krishna (Phase II) Irrigation Project (Ln 3050; Cr 2010) was to entitle each of two sons over 18 years of age (adult brothers living separately) and unmarried daughters over 35 years of age to a house plot and a construction grant for replacement housing.

Adult offspring are entitled to compensation for lost assets they own.

Adult offspring (sons and daughters alike) residing within a household are entitled to compensation for loss of any productive assets in their name, assuming the losses are directly attributable to the project.

Adult offspring are eligible for rehabilitation assistance for loss of employment income.

Adult sons and daughters residing within the household are entitled to rehabilitation assistance for any direct loss of employment income. If household entitlement packages are sufficient to restore household labor arrangements (for example, an agricultural household receives replacement agricultural lands), adult offspring living within the household are not automatically eligible for alternative rehabilitation assistance. A good practice is to extend such eligibility, if direct replacement of household assets is not feasible or sources of household income are expected to change as a result of resettlement.

Chapter 4

Compensation and Income Restoration

4

Operational Policy (OP) 4.12 distinguishes between compensation for expropriated assets and rehabilitation measures to help improve, or at least restore, incomes or standards of living.[1] To compensate displaced persons (DPs) for expropriated assets, the OP requires actual replacement of expropriated assets, when land-based households so desire, or compensation at replacement cost and alternative rehabilitation measures acceptable to the DPs. This chapter first provides guidance for applying the principle of replacement cost; it, then, examines experience with rehabilitation measures.

According to OP 4.12, the resettlement plan (RP) provides "prompt and effective compensation at full replacement cost for losses of assets attributable directly to the project" (para. 6).

For households with land-based livelihoods that lose a significant portion of their holdings, Bank policy gives preference to land-based strategies. "These strategies may include resettlement on public land, or on private land acquired or purchased for resettlement. Whenever replacement land is offered, resettlers are provided with land for which a combination of productive potential, locational advantages, and other factors is at least equivalent to the advantages of the land taken" (para. 11).

Payment of cash compensation may be appropriate "where (a) livelihoods are land-based but the land taken for the project is a small fraction of the affected asset and the residual is economically viable; (b) active markets for land, housing, and labor exist, displaced persons use such markets, and there is sufficient supply of land and housing; or (c) livelihoods are not land-based. Cash compensation levels should be sufficient to replace the lost land and other assets at full replacement cost in local markets" (para. 12).

"'Replacement cost' is the method of valuation of assets that helps determine the amount sufficient to replace lost assets and cover transaction costs. In applying this method of valuation, depreciation of structures and assets should not be taken into account. . . . For losses that cannot easily be valued or compensated for in monetary terms (e.g., access to public services, customers, and suppliers; or to fishing, grazing, or forest areas), attempts are made to establish access to equivalent and culturally acceptable resources and earning opportunities. Where domestic law does not meet the standard of compensation at full replacement cost, compensation under domestic law is supplemented by additional measures necessary to meet the replacement cost standard" (endnote 11).

51

Calculation and Application of Replacement Cost

Asset valuation procedures in many borrowing countries do not result in payment of replacement cost of affected assets. Under these procedures, valuation of structures usually takes depreciation into account, and valuation of land is often based on land registers that do not always reflect market price. It is, therefore, important to agree on asset valuation procedures to help DPs replace affected assets with equivalent alternative ones.

General Principles

4

One source of operational confusion is the distinction between compensation at replacement cost and compensation at market cost. Where markets provide reliable information about prices and availability of comparable assets or acceptable substitutes, market cost plus transaction costs (for example, all preparation and transfer fees) is equivalent to replacement cost.

Bank policy uses the principle of replacement cost to ensure that DPs secure assets equivalent to those lost. In many countries, legal compensation criteria are based on a registered "market value" that underestimates actual market value, so landowners are unable to replace their assets. Elsewhere, private property markets are thin or do not exist, and compensation is set administratively, which may also result in undervaluation. The situation is even more complex where legal compensatory practices discount local resource valuations, recognize customary claims but compensate them at a discounted value, or, in some instances, fail to recognize customary claims to land at all. Bank experience has shown that in the long run, insufficient valuation of assets often ends up costing more, in terms of project delays and benefits foregone, than sufficient valuation and compensation would.

The use of replacement cost as the compensation standard usually complements borrower legislation and is meant, in part, to streamline project implementation. Where legal stipulations result in undervaluation of assets, the mandated values can be supplemented by additional payments agreed to with the borrower. Although the borrower usually has no disagreement in principle, the manner in which supplementary compensation is determined is often the subject of close negotiation in practice (see CD Appendix 12, "Matrix of Compensation Unit Prices," for several lists of compensation rates for various impacts from Bank projects).

Replacement cost addresses tangible assets only.

Replacement cost addresses compensation for tangible assets, primarily land, houses, other structures, trees, crops, access to water, and improvements on the land (see CD Appendix 7, "Asset Inventory," for examples of assets for which several Bank projects provided compensation). Because valuation cannot be established for intangibles—sentimental attachments; proximity to neighbors or relatives; spiritual sites; aesthetic qualities, such as the view—compensation at replacement cost refers to compensation for tangible assets only. Intangible factors can have economic value (for example, customer goodwill), however, and intangible attachments can be important to DPs. As a matter of good practice, such concerns are addressed through attentive project design or negotiation (see also "Indirect Economic Impacts," in chapter 1).

Replacement cost includes all administrative fees.

Any administrative charges, title fees, or other legal transaction costs must be paid by the project or waived. OP 4.12 (Annex A, endnote 1) notes that "the cost of any registration and transfer taxes," whether for land in rural or urban areas or for houses or other structures, is included in the calculation of replacement cost.

The reason for including administrative fees as part of replacement cost is simple. The DPs have not elected voluntarily to sell their property. As this property is being acquired by the state, the DPs cannot be expected to pay the state taxes or fees for land sales or purchases.

Replacement cost includes a provision for inflation if payments are delayed.

Compensation can fall below replacement cost because of delays in actual payment of compensation. In many countries, the national law on land acquisition requires an interest payment if compensation is not paid within a specified period. Where such provisions are not legally mandated, project-specific provision must be made for interest to accrue to offset inflation (or other price contingencies) if payment of compensation is significantly delayed.

Potential project benefits are not counted toward replacement cost.

Potential project benefits, such as access to irrigation or job-training programs, are properly part of rehabilitation, not compensation. However, borrowers may want to count such benefits against the compensation they are obliged to pay. Such benefits are not counted toward replacement cost, because they do not replace lost assets. "The value of benefits to be derived from the project [is not to be] deducted from the valuation of an affected asset" (OP 4.12, Annex A, endnote 1.) The benefits may be accepted as an income improvement measure, if chosen as an alternative by DPs who are informed of their options. But even in this instance, well-informed choice is critical because such benefits may never be realized or may be realized only after lengthy delays.

Supplemental mechanisms can be counted toward compensation.

The most direct way to achieve the compensation objective of OP 4.12 is to formally calculate compensation on a replacement-cost basis. If legal codes or

4

institutional practices in borrower countries present obstacles to direct compensation at replacement cost, supplementary payments can be used to ensure the overall adequacy of compensation. Relocation, construction, subsistence, transition, or rehabilitation allowances and grants in excess of actual transition costs can be counted as contributing to replacement cost. Only the additional amount in each measure can be counted informally as part of the supplement, however, because the original allotment for each measure represents a necessary payment for some aspect of the resettlement operation.

Disclosure and grievance mechanisms are required.

Markets that furnish reliable information about the supply of alternatives and costs provide transparent institutional mechanisms for negotiating the value of land, housing, and other structures. Even in these situations, however, disputes over valuation are common. Accordingly, OP 4.12 requires that the RP include "affordable and accessible procedures for third-party settlement of disputes arising from resettlement; such grievance mechanisms should take into account the availability of judicial recourse and community and traditional dispute settlement mechanisms" (Annex A, para. 17).

Replacement Cost for Land

If land is not directly replaced, compensation is to be based on market value, productive potential, or equivalent residential quality.

OP 4.12 specifies either direct replacement of land or provision of full replacement cost, along with rehabilitation measures, in order to restore livelihoods. In principle, the replacement cost of agricultural land "is the pre-project or pre-displacement, whichever is higher, market value of land of equal productive potential or use located in the vicinity of the affected land, plus the cost of preparing the land to levels similar to those of the affected land, plus the cost of any registration and transfer taxes" (Annex A, endnote 1). Where land is not provided by the project, the cost of identifying acceptable replacement land is included in the budget estimate.

"For land in urban areas, it is the pre-displacement market value of land of equal size and use, with similar or improved public infrastructure facilities and services and located in the vicinity of the affected land, plus the cost of any registration and transfer taxes" (Annex A, endnote 1).

Where markets are active, replacement cost of affected land, in either rural or urban areas, is based on fair market value (plus transaction costs and, in rural areas, any preparation costs). Alternatively, where markets are weak, replacement cost is calculated from the productive potential of agricultural or commercial land of equivalent size. Formulations are likely to vary, depending on land systems and market conditions in the borrower country.

Replacement Cost in Countries with Active Land Markets

Determining replacement cost of affected land can be fairly easy where active land markets exist. Projects can engage private and independent real estate agencies, banks, or mortgage firms to determine market prices or evaluate the adequacy of administratively set compensation. Alternatively, committees that include DPs or representatives of nongovernmental organizations can be formed to establish land valuation and help DPs identify and purchase replacement land.

> *Project example:* In Bangladesh, in the Jamuna Bridge Multipurpose Project (Credit [Cr] 2569), provision of administratively set compensation and an automatic 50 percent solatium (or premium) was replaced with land-purchase committees guaranteeing supplemental compensation sufficient to purchase replacement lands from a willing seller, identified by the DP. As long as the replacement land was within the maximum allowable cost, the DP could choose between more land of lower quality or less land of higher quality.

> *Project example:* In India, land committees have been established for several projects to identify or purchase replacement land from willing sellers. In the Orissa Water Resources Consolidation Project (Cr 2801), legal compensation was to be supplemented by rehabilitation assistance grants to purchase replacement land or other productive assets. The projects also promised reimbursement for, or exemption from, all transfer fees or taxes.

Replacement Cost in Countries with Mixed Land Markets and Property Systems

In some borrower countries, or regions within them, formal property titling remains incomplete, leaving a complex mélange of competing legal and customary claims. In areas lacking unitary property systems, resource valuations may vary substantially and some property claims are likely to go unrecognized. (In Indonesia, for example, some land is still untitled, even in downtown Jakarta, and titled land is valued 10–60 percent higher than untitled land.) Hence, establishing replacement cost requires much greater attention to the type of title and use rights held by affected persons. For projects acquiring land in such areas, good practice is to encourage vigorous disclosure of information and the use of negotiation or arbitration procedures and independent grievance mechanisms.

> *Project example:* In the Philippines, RPs for the Leyte-Luzon Geothermal Project (Loan [Ln] 3746) called for the National Power

Corporation to negotiate land acquisition with the DPs. Because an agreement could not be reached, an independent appraisal committee was established to address the compensation disputes. The committee consisted of a real estate expert and representatives from the local land bank and the Philippines National Bank.

Project example: Also in the Philippines, DPs in the Transmission Grid Reinforcement Project (Ln 3996) could choose between compensation as evaluated by an independent appraiser or replacement land provided by the project.

Project example: In Indonesia, RPs for the Second Sulawesi Urban Development Project (Ln 4105) give DPs with insecure tenure (and those now in rental housing) tenurial rights in developed house plots, which cannot be sold for at least 10 years.

Replacement Cost in Countries without Land Markets

In China, the Russian Federation, and Vietnam, land remains collectively or publicly owned and cannot be alienated, although these countries are experimenting with mechanisms to increase individual or household tenure. In countries like these, the value of land is calculated as equal to the productive value of the land (usually, the value of the crops grown) times a multiplier representing land value in various places (typically set by the distance from major consumer centers).

Project example: In China, compensation for expropriated rural land is based on the average annual value of agricultural production over the preceding three years. Normally an amount of 6–10 times that value is paid as land compensation, and an additional 4–6 times that original value is paid as a resettlement subsidy, depending on the extent of land acquisition and its impact on average landholdings. In recognition that many factors can make land in some areas extraordinarily valuable, the law allows land compensation and resettlement subsidy combined to reach 30 times the average agricultural output value. The law also provides a procedure for obtaining even higher rates of compensation. This provision is often used in peri-urban areas, where land values are not a function of agricultural output.

Project example: In Vietnam, an emerging market permits buying and selling of land-use rights at highly fluctuating prices. Compensation rates payable in cash to project-affected households were introduced by national decree (87-CP) in 1994. This decree sets lower and upper limits on prices for various categories of land. The prices established in this decree are set administratively and may not be equal to replacement cost. Bank experience in Vietnam has so far mainly focused on replacing land for people losing more than 20 percent of their total holding, along with cash compensation for people losing less than 20 percent. More recent laws also allow for outright ownership (and alienation) of house plots of up to 200 square meters. The Irrigation Rehabilitation Project (Cr 2711) provides 60 percent of replacement cost for homesteads not privately or legally owned (plus full compensation for the house or other structures), to be used for purchase of privately owned homesteads. In all instances, compensation is to be sufficient to purchase a 200-square-meter parcel. The conversion from informal use rights to outright alienable ownership is considered as contributing to replacement cost.

Replacement Cost for Houses and Other Structures

"For houses and other structures, [replacement cost] is the market cost of the materials to build a replacement structure with an area and quality similar or better than those of the affected structure, or to repair a partially affected structure, plus the cost of transporting building materials to the construction site, plus the cost of any labor and contractors' fees, plus the cost of any registration and transfer taxes" (OP 4.12, Annex A, endnote 1).

Where markets provide adequate information about the supply and cost of comparable substitutes, any replacement structure of equivalent market value, plus any transaction and relocation costs, may be appropriate. Where such market signals are absent or inadequate, replacement cost is equivalent to the delivered cost of all building materials, labor costs for construction, and any transaction or relocation costs (the cost of the land under the structure is considered in "Replacement Cost for Land," above).

Replacement cost can be calculated using the infrastructure schedule or contractors' quotes

Replacement cost can be calculated on the basis of the following:

- *The schedule of rates obtained from the infrastructure department*—The infrastructure construction departments in all countries have a schedule of rates for preparing estimates for construction projects, which borrowers themselves use to estimate costs for construction materials and labor. When applied to calculation of replacement cost, rates current for the period of actual replacement should be used.

- *The rates quoted by contractors for similar structures in other construction projects or programs*—Where rate schedules do not exist or are out of date, recent contractor quotations for similar types of construction in the vicinity of the project can be used for calculating replacement cost. In projects offering the options of cash compensation or alternative accommodation, the cost estimates for constructing alternative accommodation could be used for calculating cash compensation payable.

Project example: In China, several projects—including Inland Waterway III (Ln 4621), Jiangxi Highway II (Ln 4608), and Inner Mongolian Highway (Ln 4663)—used unit-rate analysis for replacement cost of structures.

Project example: In Vietnam, the Mekong Delta Water Resources Development Project (Cr 3198) has a dynamic process for evaluating compensation rates. To meet the stipulations of the provincial governments, an independent monitor and the project office use market surveys and contractor interviews to periodically evaluate compensation rates.

Depreciation is not deducted in calculating replacement cost for structures.

"In determining the replacement cost, depreciation of the asset and the value of salvage materials are not taken into account" (OP 4.12, Annex A, endnote 1).

Where housing markets are active, the replacement value of a structure can be readily determined. The compensation is generally enough to buy a similar structure elsewhere. However, many countries have no residential housing markets or provide no reliable information about the appreciation or depreciation of housing. Moreover, under some compensation regulations, depreciation is used to calculate the present value of structures and improvements. If compensation at depreciated cost is paid to DPs under these conditions, the DPs are unable to replace their lost assets. In this instance, Bank policy requires replacement of assets or compensation at actual cost so that people involuntarily displaced can secure equivalent assets. Therefore, where borrowers apply depreciation in calculating compensation, other mechanisms are typically used to help provide DPs with compensation at replacement cost. In various projects, the Bank has accepted some combination of supplemental devices to bring actual compensation up to replacement cost. Such supplemental devices include moving and house reconstruction grants, transition allowances, free access to salvageable materials, and other entitlements above actual DP requirements.

Salvage materials may belong to the acquiring agency but are not deducted from replacement cost.

Salvage materials become the property of the acquiring entity. Accordingly, borrowers could, in principle, deduct from compensation the value of salvage materials sought by DPs. Because complexities arise in calculating the value of salvage materials, OP 4.12 does not allow for a deduction of the value of salvage materials from compensation. "In determining the replacement cost, . . . the value of salvage materials [is] not taken into account" (OP 4.12, Annex A, endnote 1).

> *Project example:* In China, a common practice is to allow DPs to keep and reuse any salvageable materials, and the value of these materials is not deducted from the compensation fund.

> *Project example:* In the Philippines, the Transmission Grid Reinforcement Project (Ln 3996) team made no claim to salvage materials. The RP provided DPs with a "disturbance fee" equivalent to the minimum wage for 60 days, in part to pay for the cost of gathering and transporting salvage materials. Materials left behind by the DPs became the property of the project agency.

A good practice is to improve substandard living conditions, after displacement.

OP 4.12 does not require compensation in excess of replacement cost. In the case of substandard housing or house plots or economically inviable land parcels, however, compensation at replacement cost is likely only to recreate and perpetuate poverty. Careful project design, targeted compensation, and flexibility in compensation arrangements can often improve living standards for the poor. As OP 4.12 notes, particular attention and consideration must be paid "to the needs of vulnerable groups among those displaced" (para. 8).

> *Project example:* In Colombia, the Calle 80 Urban Transport Project (Ln 4021) team assessed the economic vulnerability of DPs and provided supplemental payments to the poorest segments to improve the quality of their housing.

> *Project example:* In India, the Mumbai Urban Transport Project (Ln 4665; Cr 3662) is providing slum dwellers with new housing in apartment complexes. The new housing is in each case better than the previous residences. The project has put several common measures, such

as collective title, into effect to prevent the sale of the apartments and help collect utility and maintenance fees.

Comparable replacement sites are required for movable structures.

OP 4.12 makes no reference to movable housing or other structures. A good practice, however, is to calculate replacement cost for such structures as the cost of alternative sites, the cost of replacing improvements (such as foundations), and relocation expenses or other transaction costs (including provisions for replacing any materials ruined in transit).

> **Project example:** In India, the National Highways Authority of India's road rehabilitation projects (Ln 4559) provides a small payment to cover the costs of shifting each vendor's movable structure to a new location.

Replacement Cost for Other Assets

Public Infrastructure

Public infrastructure includes a wide array of facilities, such as roads, telephone lines, electric lines, water mains, public telephone offices, police stations, schools, and health clinics. In-kind replacement under force account, within an agreed time schedule, or full compensation to the agency replacing the service, is required. In the latter instance (cash compensation), project planners may need to ensure contractually that the service agency actually replaces the lost infrastructure.

> **Project example:** In China, the Shanghai Sewerage Project (Ln 2794; Cr 1779) paid the responsible municipal agencies the requisite amounts to replace public facilities and infrastructure. The project team ensured that the relocation areas were promptly provided with complete infrastructure.

Community-Owned Facilities

Communities may enjoy a wide range of community-owned facilities: churches, mosques, temples, or shrines; private or community-operated schools; village meeting houses; and local libraries. In-kind replacement or compensation at replacement cost is required for land and structures. In addition, for religious structures, ceremonies may be required to deconsecrate the old structure, give thanks to a deity, or consecrate the new structure. A good practice is to include these costs in the total compensation payment.

Some assets, such as graveyards, have high emotional value. Another good practice is to select an appropriate plot, acceptable to the DPs, and conduct all the necessary ceremonies.

Crops

When arrangements cannot be made to allow for harvest, the market value for lost cash crops is paid. In some countries the value of the harvest is determined by the average market value of crops for the previous three years. Whatever the multiplier, if food supplies are sold in the area enough cash compensation is paid to purchase equivalent supplies, taking into account the possibility of price increases caused by heightened demand from DPs. In areas of predominantly subsistence production, good practice recommends that in-kind compensation be made for subsistence crops.

Trees

Where markets exist, the value of a tree of a specified age and use can be used to determine compensation rates. Where markets do not exist, surrogate values must be determined. For timber trees, the value of a tree equals that of the lumber. For fruit or fodder trees, the value is equal to the cumulative value of the fruit crop for its productive life (and any timber value). If replacement trees are provided, good practice indicates that compensation be based on the value of the harvests lost until the replacement trees come into full production (typically, 7–10 years). In the case of immature trees, a less costly alternative may be to directly supply seedlings as a replacement and provide compensation for the resulting delay in reaching fruit-bearing capacity.

Other Assets

Other productive assets—such as tubewells, fishponds, poultry houses, and fences—are usually replaced in kind (or with functional equivalents), relocated, or compensated for at replacement cost.

Income Restoration Alternatives: Land, Cash, and Jobs

To restore people's income-earning opportunities after land acquisition and resettlement, OP 4.12 specifies that "displaced persons are . . . provided with development assistance in addition to compensation measures . . . , such as land preparation, credit facilities, training, or job opportunities" (para. 6[c]).

OP 4.12 maintains the preference for land-based solutions, where appropriate. "Preference should be given to land-based resettlement strategies for displaced persons whose livelihoods are land-based. These strategies may include resettlement on public land . . . , or on private land acquired or purchased for resettlement. Whenever replacement land is offered, resettlers are provided with land for which a combination

(continued)

4

(*continued from p. 61*)

of productive potential, locational advantages, and other factors is at least equivalent to the advantages of the land taken" (para. 11).

OP 4.12 also recognizes a number of circumstances in which other options may be desirable and feasible. "If land is not the preferred option of the displaced persons, the provision of land would adversely affect the sustainability of a park or protected area, or sufficient land is not available at a reasonable price, non-land-based options built around opportunities for employment or self-employment should be provided in addition to cash compensation for land and other assets lost. The lack of adequate land must be demonstrated and documented to the satisfaction of the Bank" (para. 11).

General Principles for Replacing Income-Generating Assets

The Bank established its initial resettlement policy in response to problems with large-scale resettlement in rural areas, including widely publicized episodes of displacement that reduced agricultural families to landless poverty. Although alternative forms of compensation or rehabilitation may have been provided, they often failed to help DPs acquire productive assets and restore their incomes. Recognizing that cash compensation or other benefits can impose a high risk on DPs, Bank policy emphasizes land-centered remedies for loss of land-based incomes.

In practice, three sets of issues complicate land-centered resettlement strategies. First, replacement land available to borrower agencies is scarce or of poor quality in many densely populated areas. Excessive reliance on direct land replacement in some instances has encouraged conversion of forest to agricultural land, unacknowledged secondary displacement, or granting of wastelands to replace productive agricultural lands. Second, a growing proportion of people affected by land acquisition live in nonagricultural settings or are only partially affected by land acquisition, as in linear projects. Third, in peri-urban settings or areas with general economic growth, DPs may prefer other income-generating options. This section discusses appropriate income-generating strategies for DPs. The aim of these strategies is to protect the land-based livelihoods of DPs who prefer to remain in agriculture and to enable others to pursue alternative opportunities (see CD Appendix 10, "Household Income Stream Analysis," for the variety of income streams to be considered in designing income restoration strategies).

DPs with land-based livelihoods are to receive the option of obtaining comparable replacement land.

RPs are designed to fit specific project circumstances, as well as the preferences of DPs. In rural areas, preliminary consultations with DPs are likely to show that many agriculturalists prefer replacement land. In these cases, all DPs who lose productive land are to have the option of obtaining comparable replacement land through either direct exchange or intermediary mechanisms. Two exceptions are discussed below:

- *Cash compensation is appropriate for marginal land takings*—In many linear projects, small portions (less than 10%) of land parcels are expropriated for transmission lines, drains, or roads. If the impact is likely to be marginal and replacement of small parcels is likely to result in fragmented holdings, cash compensation at prorated replacement cost is enough. If preliminary assessment indicates that some DPs who are losing more than 10 percent of land want this land replaced, a replacement option would be required. DPs must also have the option of having the entire parcel replaced if the area not taken is no longer economically viable. As OP 4.12 notes, "If the residual of the asset being taken is not economically viable, compensation and other resettlement assistance are provided as if the entire asset had been taken" (endnote 12). (See also "Eligibility Criteria: Land Tenure and Severity of Impact," in chapter 3.)
- *An agricultural land option is not required in peri-urban (or urban) settings*— OP 4.12 stipulates the option of land replacement for people with land-based livelihoods. In urban or peri-urban areas, where income may be derived from nonagricultural activities, DPs have no need of an agricultural land option, although direct or indirect replacement of house plots remains a requirement. In peri-urban areas with mixed land use, an option for direct or indirect replacement of land would be required if preliminary assessment of DP preferences indicated that the DPs desire it.

Good practice recommends that DPs be able to choose from other feasible options.

Bank policy does not bind people to agricultural livelihoods. The consultative process informs DPs about feasible options, including those to obtain replacement land or start non-land-based income-generating activities. Some people may not be satisfied with the quality or location of available replacement land. Some may prefer to shift to wage employment or to start a small business as markets expand. Some may prefer to diversify sources of income. Some in peri-urban areas may already derive much of their income from non-land-based activities. In these instances, good practice suggests that gauging the viability of the non-land options should take into account the risk-bearing capacities of the DPs. All options offered to the DPs should be technically, financially, and economically feasible, and the DPs should have the necessary skills and capacity to undertake them.

Project example: In China, the designers of the RPs for the Shuikou Hydroelectric Project (Ln 2775) assumed that about 30 percent of the DPs would opt for nonagricultural rehabilitation. Spurred by rapid economic expansion, however, about 65 percent chose non-land-based rehabilitation.

Land-Based Options

Direct replacement is always an acceptable option.

Land can be replaced directly or through indirect mechanisms. Direct replacement of expropriated land with land identified by the borrower is acceptable as an option to be presented to DPs. These replacement lands—typically government land, converted forest, or degraded lands—must be of equivalent productive potential (or developed to make them so) and must be acceptable to the DPs themselves. In the terms of OP 4.12, "Whenever replacement land is offered, resettlers are provided land for which a combination of productive potential, locational advantages, and other factors is at least equivalent to the advantages of the land taken" (para. 11). Attempts to move DPs to replacement lands without their approval has been a major recurring source of protests and project delays (see below).

In some circumstances, direct replacement is encouraged.

"Bank experience has shown that resettlement of indigenous peoples with traditional land-based modes of production is particularly complex and may have significant adverse impacts on their identity and cultural survival. For this reason, the Bank satisfies itself that the borrower has explored all viable alternative project designs to avoid physical displacement of these groups. When it is not feasible to avoid such displacement, preference is given to land-based resettlement strategies for these groups . . . that are compatible with their cultural preferences and are prepared in consultation with them" (OP 4.12, para. 9).

When displacement affects indigenous peoples with little exposure to markets, these peoples must be offered the option of direct land replacement. (If indigenous lands were collectively owned, replacement lands are usually vested in the collectivity; see "Appropriate Unit of Entitlement," in chapter 3, and "Indigenous Peoples," in chapter 5.) When agricultural projects bring unirrigated land under irrigation, DPs who are losing land can be given the option of obtaining irrigated land as a direct land replacement.

Project example: In India, an estimated 75 percent of DPs received irrigated land in the Orissa Water Resources Consolidation Development Project (Cr 2801). Average incomes were then expected to increase fourfold. DPs who did not receive irrigated land were to be eligible for twice as much unirrigated land or for wastelands converted into lands suitable for plantation agriculture at project expense.

Indirect replacement mechanisms are also acceptable as an option.

Intermediate mechanisms using cash compensation and supplemental assistance may be effective in helping DPs (or local representatives) identify and purchase suitable replacement land from willing sellers. Land-purchase committees composed of DPs, project officers, and technical specialists can be instrumental in identifying land and verifying its productivity (Box 4.1). Disbursement of compensation can be tied to the purchase of replacement land (or other productive assets).

Box 4.1   When Replacement Land Is Unacceptable to DPs

In some projects, DPs have refused to accept replacement land provided by project agencies. Poor land quality or inconvenient location is a common reason for refusal. This situation tends to arise when projects fail to establish technical feasibility studies, site inspections by DPs, or oversight committees. The DPs' refusal of land can have serious consequences: it can lead to public protests and costly delays for the modification of RPs; it can also lead to cost overruns in implementation. A good practice is to have projects not only help DPs participate in identifying land, but also provide alternative land options, as well as non-land-based options. Such preparation helps avoid land refusal.

Project example: In China, one of the sites designated for agricultural use in the Xiaolangdi Resettlement Project (Cr 2605) was redesigned as an industrial settlement at the request of the DPs. In addition, an increase in cost of 36 percent over South Asia Region estimates has been observed in land compensation and construction of houses and infrastructure at redesigned resettlement sites.

Project example: In India, a resettlement area was provided 125 kilometers away from the Upper Indravati Hydroelectric Project (Ln 2278) site. The DPs rejected the proposed site because it provided little access to natural resources and off-farm employment and because they did not want to move that far from their home villages and relatives. Project authorities subsequently established a joint account to enable the DPs to purchase replacement lands they identified closer to their original homes.

Project example: In Indonesia, RPs for the Kedung Ombo Multipurpose Project (Ln 2543) estimated that 90 percent of the DPs would join the transmigration program. During implementation, however, more than 80 percent did not want to join. Local resistance contributed to delays in construction, to court challenges, and to international controversy and eventually led to makeshift measures to resettle the DPs closer to the site. Bank evaluations attribute much of the resistance to a lack of consultations with DPs during the planning process.

Project example: In Thailand, Third Power System Development Project (Ln 3423) planners selected a Pak Mun Dam resettlement site, but they failed to adequately consult the DPs. Although the implementing agency had already developed demonstration farm plots, a fish pond, a poultry farm, and a dairy farm at the site, and installation of electricity and water supply was in progress, no displaced families took up residence. The agency added an option to enable the DPs to resettle in their own villages, and the proposed site was abandoned.

Project example: In Bangladesh, the Jamuna Bridge Multipurpose Project (Cr 2569) tied compensation to the purchase of replacement land identified by the DP. The level of compensation was increased by the project team to complete the purchase of the replacement land, subject to a maximum allowable replacement value.

Project example: In India, RPs for the Upper Krishna II (Ln 3050; Cr 2010) and Sardar Sarovar (Ln 2497; Cr 1552) projects included the creation of local land committees to identify, evaluate, and purchase land for DPs.

Project example: Also in India, RPs for the Orissa Water Resources Consolidation Project (Cr 2801) and the Upper Indravati Project (Ln 2278) created joint accounts for depositing compensation. The release of compensation required the approval of both DPs and designated authorities and was tied to the DP's identification or purchase of replacement land from a willing seller.

Cash Compensation and Rehabilitation

Under certain conditions, cash is an acceptable option for compensation.

DPs sometimes prefer cash compensation, because it may provide them with a wider range of opportunities for income restoration or improvement. Cash compensation may be enough to start, extend, or diversify a private business, especially in areas with rapid economic growth. In some cases, cash compensation following displacement may help the DPs retire or migrate, or it may give them educational or training opportunities otherwise beyond their reach.

Cash compensation may require careful preparation. The consultative process should not only enable DPs to identify the range of opportunities they may wish to pursue, but also inform them of the potential risks of such activities. Whenever DPs have such options, a good practice is to have the program include independent monitoring to identify, early on, options that are working best and those that require additional support (Box 4.2). To enable DPs to make productive use of cash compensation, it should be paid in its entirety and in a timely manner. Partial or delayed cash payments to do not allow productive investment sufficient to restore incomes.

Mechanisms for converting cash into productive investments or replacement assets enable DPs to restore their livelihoods.

DPs may have strong views about the activities they would like to pursue after resettlement, but they may have less clear ideas about what exactly is required

Box 4.2   Cash Compensation Does Not Ensure Asset Replacement

In theory, cash compensation valued at replacement cost allows DPs to restore incomes and living standards. In practice, several obstacles have impeded conversion of cash into replacement assets (or alternative income-restoration measures). Most obviously, the amount of compensation may be insufficient. The timing of compensation (either too early or too late) can also reduce the likelihood of income's being restored. Cash may not be convertible into productive assets if markets or opportunities are thin. Or local practices may encourage the use of compensation to pay debts or for social reciprocities, rather than for purchasing replacement assets.

The Operations Evaluation Department reported several such inadequacies within a single project, the Karnataka Irrigation Project (Cr 788):

- *Undercompensation*—Despite provision of an additional 15 percent solatium, compensation for land based on registered land values reportedly averaged about 44 percent of actual replacement cost. Widespread court appeals led to an average 37 percent enhancement in compensation. But with legal fees, final compensation still amounted to only 54 percent of replacement cost. Compensation for housing was also inadequate, but DPs had little or no reported recourse to the courts.
- *Delayed compensation*—Compensation amounts were determined at the time of preliminary notification of intent to acquire lands, whereas actual payment of compensation often lagged by several years, with the adequacy of compensation further eroded by inflation. Payment of compensation in installments (gaps ranged from 2 to 15 years) further aggravated this problem.
- *Use of compensation*—Because some installments were received in advance of actual dislocation, compensation was often used for house improvements, consumption, ceremonial expenses, repayment of loans, or other activities.
- *Results*—The cost of similar replacement housing exceeded compensation for housing in 76 percent of survey cases and was three times the amount of compensation in about half of the cases. In 42 percent of the cases, the cost of replacement housing exceeded compensation for land and house combined.

Only 25 percent of survey households in fully affected villages reported using compensation for purchase of replacement land. In partially affected villages, the proportion fell to 8 percent.

Source: Operation Evaluation Department, "Early Experience with Involuntary Resettlement: Impact Evaluation on India Karnataka Irrigation Project," World Bank, Washington, DC, 1993.

to succeed. Project rehabilitation teams therefore typically undertake technical and economic feasibility studies and put in place a number of extension, training, and small-business loan programs to support the DPs, particularly in the risky, early years of an endeavor. The project itself may provide these services, or existing agencies may be contracted to provide this assistance. A good practice is to assess the delivery and use of cash compensation, through regular monitoring, throughout the recovery period.

Annuities, dividends, or shares may be high-risk forms of compensation.

Some DPs may prefer annuities that contribute regularly to the income stream while leaving time available for other productive or personal endeavors. One innovative approach used in power projects is to impose a small surcharge on power sales and put this surcharge in a local development fund. When annuities are presented as forms of compensation, task teams need to determine that DPs have other options and have been informed of the risks (for example, income volatility of dividends or declining equity value of shares). Supplementary measures will be required if annuities alone are unlikely to restore incomes.

> *Project example:* In China, the Liaoning Environment Project (Ln 3781) deposited some of its land compensation funds in the bank and distributed the annual interest to the elderly, students, and laborers, in prorated shares.

> *Project example:* In India, RPs for the Coal Sector Environment and Social Mitigation Project (Cr 2862) included optional annuities or lump-sum grants for DPs with small landholdings, for DPs not provided with employment options, or for DPs not seeking land-for-land options.

> *Project example:* In Lesotho, land sales are illegal, so the project authority of the Highland Water Project (Ln 4339) determined a use value for the land and was to establish an annuity fund to generate interest income equivalent to the amount each farmer would have harvested annually. However, the project authority could not obtain from the government the total sum in one year to establish the annuity fund, so the authority now makes annual payments to the farmers in compensation.

Provision of pensions requires careful review.

In principle, early-retirement pensions are acceptable as options for DPs. Task teams need to review mandatory pension programs to ensure that capable people are given opportunities to remain productive. A good practice is to have the borrower guarantee pension programs (if these are substituted for income restoration measures). Good practice is to ensure that the programs are equitable (with regard to gender or ethnic identity) and financially adequate (for example, compensation for assets and pension together might restore previous incomes and living standards).

> *Project example:* In China, RPs sometimes include pensions for workers. In the Shanghai Second Sewerage Project (Ln 3987), for example, pensions were provided for all male workers aged more than 55 years and all females workers aged more than 45 years. But the implementing agency

and local authorities assured the DPs supplementary jobs or other rehabilitation measures, as necessary.

Employment as Rehabilitation

Provision of employment is an acceptable option to present to DPs.

Employment (public or private) can be an effective way of restoring and improving incomes, in effect creating assets in the form of skills and human capital. Promising jobs without providing other options, however, is not good practice. Similarly, providing employment training without access to employment cannot be construed as adequate rehabilitation.

> *Project example:* In China, the Shanghai Second Sewerage Project (Ln 3987) provided some DPs with specialized training at technical schools, municipal vocational training centers, or training centers at large enterprises. The training was linked to jobs already promised to the DPs.

> *Project example:* In China, the Second Red Soils Area Development Project (Cr 2563) provided one permanent job per household in construction or in the agroprocessing enterprise causing their displacement.

A good practice is to guarantee employment for a minimum of three years.

The employment must last long enough for the DPs to acquire the skills needed to reestablish their living standards. A good practice is for RPs to include provisions for at least three, and preferably five, years of employment for those DPs choosing employment options.

> *Project example:* In China, RPs for the Xiaolangdi Resettlement Project (Cr 2605) encouraged nonagricultural employment for some displaced farmers. To ensure sufficient employment to acquire skills, the project provided five-year job guarantees.

Temporary jobs are not acceptable as rehabilitation measures.

Permanent income restoration and creation of human capital are the goals when the project provides employment as a rehabilitation measure. Accordingly, employment provided in lieu of compensation cannot be temporary (for example, construction of project works or service roads). Temporary jobs are, nonetheless, appropriate as supplemental sources of household income.

Note

1. OP 4.12 (para. 6) discusses three sets of required measures: (a) "prompt and effective compensation at full replacement cost for losses of assets"; (b) in the instance of physical relocation, "measures to ensure that the displaced persons are provided assistance" during the move, as well as provided with housing or house sites; and (c) where necessary, "measures to ensure that displaced persons are offered support after displacement . . . and provided with development assistance in addition to compensation measures."

4

Vulnerable Populations

Involuntary resettlement affects poor and vulnerable segments of populations more severely than those that are better off. Bank project experience shows that the poor, women, children, the handicapped, the elderly, and indigenous populations are often susceptible to hardship and may be less able than other groups to reconstruct their lives after resettlement. However, the extent, nature, and severity of their vulnerabilities may vary significantly. Good practice therefore calls for careful screening in project design and attentive resettlement to help vulnerable groups improve or at least reestablish their lives and livelihoods. This chapter examines Bank policy and practice for various vulnerable groups: the poor, women, and indigenous peoples; those less able to care for themselves (children, the elderly, and the disabled); and other groups not protected by national land compensation law (those without land or use rights; host communities; and community members remaining in the original area after resettlement) (see also CD Appendix 14, "Assistance to Vulnerable People," for an example of one Bank project's approach to assisting vulnerable people).

Operational Policy (OP) 4.12 specifies the development objectives of resettlement operations and emphasizes the need to assist vulnerable groups in achieving those objectives.

"Involuntary resettlement may cause severe long-term hardship, impoverishment, and environmental damage unless appropriate measures are carefully planned and carried out. For these reasons, the overall objectives of the Bank's policy on involuntary resettlement are the following:

(a) Involuntary resettlement should be avoided where feasible, or minimized, exploring all viable alternative project designs.

(b) Where it is not feasible to avoid resettlement, resettlement activities should be conceived and executed as sustainable development programs, providing sufficient investment resources to enable the persons displaced by the project to share in project benefits. . . .

(c) Displaced persons should be assisted in their efforts to improve their livelihoods and standards of living or at least to restore them, in real terms, to pre-displacement levels or to levels prevailing prior to the beginning of project implementation, whichever is higher" (para. 2).

(continued)

> *(continued from p. 71)*
>
> "To achieve the objectives of this policy, particular attention is paid to the needs of vulnerable groups among those displaced, especially those below the poverty line, the landless, the elderly, women and children, indigenous peoples, ethnic minorities, or other displaced persons who may not be protected through national land compensation legislation" (para. 8).
>
> Participatory approaches provide one means of integrating the needs of vulnerable groups into project design and implementation. Measures ensure that displaced persons (DPs) are "(i) informed about their options and rights pertaining to resettlement" and "(ii) consulted on, offered choices among, and provided with technically and economically feasible resettlement alternatives" (para. 6).

5

The Poor

> "Sustainable poverty reduction is the Bank's overarching objective. Since the complete range of programs and policies affect the well-being of the poor, there are many complementarities between poverty reduction and other operational priorities. . . . The burden of poverty falls disproportionately on women; so it is essential to increase their income-earning opportunities, their food security, and their access to social services. Maintaining the environment is critical if gains in poverty reduction are to be sustained and if future increases in poverty are to be avoided. If poverty reduction is to be sustainable, institution-building and investing in local capacity to assess poverty and to analyze, design, implement, and finance programs and projects are essential" (Operational Directive [OD] 4.15 [Poverty Reduction], para. 6).

In concert with overall Bank policy, OP 4.12 seeks to ensure that resettlement improves the lives of the poor and does not reduce more people to poverty. This goal is achieved by requiring compensation at replacement cost and by providing measures for income restoration and improvement. The policy also recognizes that many people were in poverty before displacement. In these instances, resettlement can offer opportunities to improve living standards, rather than merely re-creating poverty in new surroundings, especially for people who suffer substantial impacts. Because such actions constitute economic improvements, they contribute to the economic justification for projects and may make them eligible for additional Bank financing.

This section discusses opportunities to make resettlement an integral part of the development process and engage in nonmandatory but proactive efforts on behalf of the very poor. Specifically, rehabilitation entitlements can provide the poor with assistance to secure landholdings or residential housing of some suitable standard, regardless of their circumstances before displacement.

Disaggregation into socially meaningful groups identifies specific segments of the population below the national poverty line.

The Bank accepts the national definition of poverty when identifying DPs who warrant special attention in resettlement operations. However, resettlement affects specific groups of the poor in different ways. For this reason, good practice recommends that the generic definition of "poor" be disaggregated into socially meaningful categories, such as the elderly, women-headed households, and the disabled.

Every resettlement operation requires a baseline count of the people to be affected, along with, among other things, an inventory of their fixed property and an estimate of their annual income. This information provides an objective, quantitative measure of the extent of poverty, and the socioeconomic surveys ensure that all vulnerable people are included under the project and disaggregated into specific vulnerable groups.

> **Project example:** In Colombia, the Calle 80 Urban Transport Project (Loan 4081) team in Bogotá categorized the vulnerability of DPs as high, medium, and low. Those with high vulnerability included the elderly, women-headed households, widows, people entirely dependent on the property to be acquired, and special cases, such as the disabled and people whose incomes were insufficient for them to reestablish their situation after resettlement. These groups were targeted for specific assistance, according to their needs.

Good practice is to have the project design include the poorest of the poor.

To reach the poorest of the poor affected by involuntary resettlement is difficult. They are sometimes ineligible for compensation, because they own no land or other fixed assets (for example, pavement dwellers). Furthermore, they may not qualify for income restoration, because they may have no identifiable income source.

To assist the poorest of the poor affected by resettlement operations, project plans and designs may need to go beyond the requirements of OP 4.12. Within the project framework, a good practice is to have the socioeconomic surveys identify the source of income of the poor and their access to common resources, which are often vitally important to their survival. Good practice also recommends reaching out to the poorest of the poor in the consultative process, as they may not always participate in public forums. Good resettlement planning also provides supplemental measures, such as giving the poorest DPs priority for opportunities generated by the project, particularly project-related employment, or assistance through special funds or services.

5

Taking land from the very poor may deepen their poverty.

OP 4.12 has defined a 10 percent loss of any parcel as the threshold below which the loss of land is generally considered minor. For those people already in poverty, however, or for those with substandard landholdings, loss of even a small percentage of holdings may render the rest of their land unviable. In these cases, where monetary compensation alone is likely to re-create poverty, additional benefits may be extended to such DPs, even if the project is acquiring less than 10 percent of their landholding.

Other rehabilitation measures can contribute to economic viability.

In the case of very poor households, good practice suggests that non-land-based rehabilitation measures go beyond the goal of income restoration, which, in these circumstances, would simply be re-creating poverty. Rather, Bank goals and good practice suggest that households be provided specific opportunities to reach economic viability.

Another good practice is to explore prospects for providing agricultural tenants and landless laborers with employment in the project. Preferential hiring during the construction phase is a common practice, as is awarding jobs or contracts once the enterprise is on-line. In the more successful endeavors, the project agency will have provided support services specifically for the poor, to give them a clear understanding of their work obligations and help alleviate difficulties (such as children's illnesses) that can impede their performance.

Good practice recommends that replacement housing and plots meet or exceed existing local standards.

In many projects, especially in urban areas, a section of the affected population may reside in structures that are far from meeting local health or safety standards. The objective of a resettlement program for such groups cannot be restricted to restoration of substandard housing, if for no other reason than that the alternative housing and house plots provided by the project would likely have to meet local standards. Many of the poor want to improve their housing, and many would have at least some means of doing so if bureaucratic obstacles, such as mortgage requirements, were relaxed. Good practice suggests that arrangements be made to provide housing that meets acceptable local standards. Such an arrangement would be credit facilities with group responsibility for repayment. If project terms call for construction of replacement housing, another good practice is to include adequate drainage and sanitation.

Project example: In Brazil, municipal authorities in the Nova Jaguaribara Project (not a Bank project) found an innovative way to

5

provide new houses for landless people. The municipality drew up a list of tasks for which additional help was needed, for example, street cleaning, gardening, and kindergarten and primary school support. Landless families without the financial resources to pay for the new plots were offered the opportunity of doing community work for the municipality for four hours a day, over a five-year period. In return, the families received title to their new plot. The work obligations were kept flexible. One or more members of the family could work at any time, according to their ability and availability. Any member of the family could fulfil the obligation on any day, and the four hours could be contributed at any time during the day.

Project example: In China, some projects are explicitly designed to improve housing standards following displacement. In the Shanghai Sewerage Project (Loan [Ln] 2794; Credit [Cr] 1779), most DPs expressed satisfaction with provisions that, on average, increased their rents but provided nearly double the housing space and included indoor kitchens and sanitation facilities. Plans for the Second Shanghai Sewerage Project (Ln 3987) allowed DPs to choose between government apartments supplied on a rental basis or private apartments available at one-third of construction costs. Furthermore, in the early stages of the Xiaolangdi Resettlement Project (Cr 2605), DPs received more space in replacement housing, often leaving behind dank, poorly lit cave dwellings for brick structures with modern conveniences.

Project example: In India, compensation at replacement cost for the housing of Scheduled Caste and Scheduled Tribe DPs in the Hyderabad Water Supply and Sanitation Project (Cr 2115) would likely be enough to supply only substandard housing. Therefore, the project provided these DPs with free housing, built to state housing norms.

Women

Women constitute a vulnerable group because they may be excluded from participation and because they are often exposed to greater risk of impoverishment. "The Bank aims to reduce gender disparities and enhance women's participation in the economic development of their countries by integrating gender considerations in its country assistance program" (OD 4.20 [Gender Dimensions of Development], para. 1). Women have an important role in household management and in economically productive activities, especially by making nonwage contributions to household subsistence. The socioeconomic studies conducted during project preparation must detail these activities and contributions.

The resettlement process incorporates opportunities for women's participation.

Participation is fundamentally important in resettlement operations, because people are directly affected and must, in some cases, reestablish their lives. As people's interests and concerns can be very different, resettlement operations strive to include all segments of the population.

Good resettlement programming ensures that meaningful consultations with women are included. In many settings, good practice suggests that female project representatives conduct these consultations. Separate venues for participation, such as focus group discussions that involve only women, can also be made available, as consultations of this nature give women a forum to voice their issues and concerns. Another good practice is to pretest the baseline survey with women to ensure that it covers issues of concern to them, such as the design of replacement housing, access to educational and health-care services, availability of fuel and water, and income-generating activities. Yet another good practice is to issue information on resettlement entitlements and choices to every adult member of the household, not just to the head of the household.

Baseline surveys document economic contributions of women to household income and living standards.

Women contribute financially to the household economy, through both formal and informal economic activities. Formal income derives from wage labor, artisanal production, marketing of produce, and other activities outside the home. Informal contributions to household subsistence include subsistence agriculture and collection of fuel and water, not to mention cooking, cleaning, and childcare. All of these activities are to be included in the baseline survey for calculating household incomes.

> **Project example:** In India, the Upper Krishna Irrigation Project (Ln 3050; Cr 2010) originally failed to take gender considerations into account. A survey conducted late in the project (1997) to assess the impacts on women found that most women had fewer chances to work, their incomes from farming and livestock had decreased, they had less personal disposable income, and thus they had less voice in family decisions. As a consequence, two thirds of the women surveyed believed their lives had become worse as a result of displacement, and more than three quarters of the women said they were less happy than in their old village.

*Access to basic resources must be provided in the areas where
households are to be relocated.*

Fuel and water collection are major household chores that in many countries
fall to women and girls. Resettlement site planning can help ensure that access
to these basic subsistence resources and the use of them are improved, or at least
restored.

Resettlement provides an opportunity to introduce new stove technologies.
The redesign of local stoves can benefit greatly from the input of women. The
new technologies have several benefits. When successful, they can reduce the
time spent in collecting fuel. Well-designed stoves can also reduce the pollution in kitchens, which otherwise causes respiratory disease among women and
children.

Women can also participate in making decisions about water sources in
many resettlement operations. The siting of wells and water taps within the
community is a social, as well as a technical, decision. Consulting users about
their preferences helps ensure that everyone will have equal access to water and
that the users are willing and able to maintain the facility.

Seemingly simple measures, such as the redesign of cooking stoves or siting of water points, can have major consequences. When fuel or water
resources become scarce because of land acquisition or relocation of populations, the women—and especially the girls—often find they have to spend
significantly more time collecting these basic materials. As a result, girls
more often drop out of school to help out at home. Providing improved
fuel and water sources helps avoid such adverse, secondary consequences of
resettlement.

*Baseline surveys include a section on health, for monitoring people's
physical well-being, especially women's and children's health status.*

Bank policy recognizes the importance of considering health issues during and
after resettlement. "Provision of health care services, particularly for pregnant
women, infants, the disabled and the elderly, may be important during and after
relocation to prevent increase in morbidity and mortality due to malnutrition,
the psychological stress of being uprooted, and the increased risk of disease"
(OP 4.12, Annex A, endnote 2).

Because resettlement can be stressful for people and can have adverse consequences on nutrition, health, and even mortality rates, baseline surveys in
Bank practice now include a section on the health status of DPs, for monitoring
the physical repercussions of resettlement. In addition, resettlement operations
usually construct infrastructure to address problems such as child malnutrition
and waterborne disease.

Female adults may be the appropriate unit of entitlement in male-headed households.

Households headed by women are entitled to the same resettlement benefits as those headed by men. In some cases, however, women-headed households are no longer independent, as they reside within larger extended families. Widowed women, for example, may live with their fathers or fathers-in-law. Similarly, households headed by a divorced woman may be part of her extended natal family. Such cases need to be carefully enumerated, because they may be entitled to compensation and rehabilitation assistance as independent households.

Where assets (for example, small enterprises or encroached land) are owned or controlled by a female spouse, she is the individual entitled to compensation or rehabilitation. Joint registration of household assets in the names of both husband and wife may be considered if gender discrimination in income generation or estate transfer might otherwise result (see also "Appropriate Unit of Entitlement," in chapter 3).

> *Project example:* In Côte d'Ivoire, the Rural Land Management and Community Infrastructure Development Project (Cr N022) dealt with issues of access, control, and management of land rights. Under customary principles of tenure, land could not be alienated by sale. Consequently, the country had no local institutional framework for transmitting land through market mechanisms. Because the certification of use rights had to take the form of titling, and access rights to land and other productive resources were usually recorded in the name of the male head of the household, some major stakeholders could lose their access rights. The project study found that women, youth, and pastoralists might fall through the cracks of the land-titling system, as their rights were usually not legally recognized.

Indigenous Peoples[1]

> OP 4.12 makes particular mention of the issues that may arise for indigenous peoples. "Bank experience has shown that resettlement of indigenous peoples with traditional land-based modes of production is particularly complex and may have significant adverse impacts on their identity and cultural survival. For this reason, the Bank satisfies itself that the borrower has explored all viable alternative project designs to avoid physical displacement of these groups. When it is not feasible to avoid such displacement, preference is given to land-based resettlement strategies for these groups . . . that are compatible with their cultural preferences and are prepared in consultation with them" (para. 9).
>
> *(continued)*

(continued from p. 78)

The development of resettlement measures reiterates these points: "In addition to being technically and economically feasible, the resettlement packages should be compatible with the cultural preferences of the displaced persons, and prepared in consultation with them" (OP 4.12, Annex A, para. 11).

Indigenous peoples are often vulnerable to hardship following displacement. They are usually vulnerable because legal codes and government practices may not recognize their claim to resources, they may lack avenues for representation in the project, or their sociocultural institutions may disintegrate after displacement.

Two general issues complicate the resettlement of indigenous peoples. One involves the recognition of customary communal rights to resources (see "Open Access and Other Property," in chapter 3). Second, the valuation of losses and the design of rehabilitation measures require careful qualitative study, as some characteristics of indigenous living standards (for example, subsistence production, labor reciprocity, and importance of minor forest products) are difficult to quantify.

Although income restoration is the main objective of OP 4.12, preserving standards of living may be just as important to indigenous groups. To achieve both objectives, culturally appropriate mechanisms for consultation and participation, including procedures for addressing grievances, need to be designed.

Customary land claims of indigenous peoples are to be identified and, if possible, regularized.

In areas used by indigenous peoples, land-acquisition assessments ascertain whether public lands and privately titled lands to be affected by the project are clear of customary claims. If potentially affected indigenous peoples do not have legal ownership or use rights for the land or resources on which they customarily rely, the Bank discusses prospects for regularization of such claims with the borrower.

Indigenous peoples with nonregularizable land claims require special forms of assistance.

OP 4.12 establishes that affected people with nonregularizable land claims need not be formally compensated, but they are nonetheless eligible for "other assistance, as necessary, to achieve the objectives set out in this policy" (para. 16). For indigenous peoples with primarily land-based livelihoods, it is important that such assistance include the option of replacement land.

5

Direct replacement of land is preferred if displacement affects indigenous peoples.

If acquisition of lands held communally by indigenous peoples is unavoidable, direct replacement of land is the preferred option, with title vested in the community as a whole. OP 4.12 establishes the general policy that "preference should be given to land-based resettlement strategies for displaced persons whose livelihoods are land-based" (para.11). The policy also specifically emphasizes this preference when dealing with indigenous peoples: "When it is not feasible to avoid such displacement, preference is given to land-based resettlement strategies for these groups . . . that are compatible with their cultural preferences and are prepared in consultation with them" (para. 9).

Social assessment is crucial in projects likely to affect indigenous peoples.

Social assessment, with an emphasis on appropriately designed mechanisms for communication and participation, is important for projects likely to require resettlement of indigenous peoples (see chapter 7). If social assessment shows that the customary rights of indigenous peoples are not recognized by the borrower or that special socioeconomic provisions may be necessary for resettlement, the Bank can provide assistance to the borrower in addressing such issues. If consultations with indigenous peoples indicate widespread opposition to the project or significant problems that will be inordinately difficult to mitigate, the Bank can ask the borrower to consider making appropriate changes in the project. Similarly, as part of its own project assessment and appraisal, the Bank determines the capacity and commitment of the borrower agency to do what is necessary to protect the interests of indigenous peoples. If analysis shows that the interests of the indigenous peoples are not likely to be protected, the Bank may find it necessary to reconsider its collaboration in the investment.

The cultural preferences of affected indigenous peoples determine acceptable resettlement measures.

Where indigenous peoples make a unique use of resources, they may assign a unique value to them. For this reason, whenever feasible, the resettlement plan (RP) incorporates measures to replace assets, or at least to provide alternative access to desired resources. When neither of these options is feasible, alternative measures that are "compatible with the cultural preferences" of those affected are to be devised (OP 4.12, Annex A, para. 11). The indigenous peoples are consulted to identify acceptable substitute assets or resources or alternative income-generating activities.

Relevant resettlement planning instruments and indigenous peoples development plans are distinct documents, but they can be prepared in tandem.

OD 4.20 calls for an indigenous peoples development plan (IPDP) for projects affecting indigenous groups. In projects involving involuntary resettlement of indigenous groups, the IPDP and the RP can be prepared in tandem to ensure that the IPDP fully reflects the mitigation measures included in the RP. Similar coordination is needed for projects that affect indigenous peoples and also require a resettlement policy or process framework.

> *Project example:* In India, the Coal India Environmental and Social Mitigation Project (Cr 2862) involved coordination of RPs and IPDPs for 25 of Coal India's 495 mines. The RPs covered all those people whose land or other assets would be acquired for the mining operations, and the IPDPs covered all the inhabitants of the villages and hamlets located in the vicinity of the mines. The two plans complemented each other: the RPs basically gave entitlements to individuals and households for compensation and economic rehabilitation, and the IPDPs gave entitlements to the communities for their facilities and local capacity building. The plans were not intended to be mutually exclusive; some people were covered under both plans.

Those Less Able to Care for Themselves

Good resettlement planning and implementation recognize that some segments of the displaced population—children, the elderly, and the disabled—may be unable to express their interests and concerns effectively. A good practice is to design resettlement operations to incorporate the concerns of these often voiceless groups. This section takes up this issue.

When large-scale displacement threatens to disrupt communities, RPs include measures to mitigate adverse impacts on vulnerable groups, such as children, the elderly, and those with physical or mental disabilities. Socioeconomic surveys should identify the very young segments of the population (for example, children less than 6 years old) or the elderly (for example, adults more than 65 years old). Especially in projects disrupting entire communities, surveys can also identify people with physical or mental disabilities and the services available to them.

Children

Bank policy pays "particular attention . . . to the impact of sector policies [and other work] on poor women and children, food security, . . . and the links

81

5

between environmental issues and poverty" (OD 4.15 [Poverty Reduction], para. 13).

Children typically lack the legal, political, and economic capacity to protect their own standards of living. In resettlement, school-aged children may lose physical or economic access to education, despite the prominent role that education plays in development and Bank lending. Unless special arrangements are made to help children continue schooling in the transition phase of resettlement, some of them may find it difficult to resume education once permanent schools are constructed and staffed at resettlement sites. Disruption of household access to resources can also expose children to nutritional deficiencies. And in many rural areas, where children contribute significantly to household income or subsistence, poor households may especially rely on the economic activities of children and be severely affected if such losses are not recognized and mitigated. Resettlement operations, therefore, need to ensure children's nutritional needs are met, along with their access to education. In addition, if children contribute economically to family welfare, resettlement operations must include measures to eliminate child labor to the fullest extent possible.

Education and health standards are to be surveyed.

A good practice is to have baseline socioeconomic surveys document existing community education and health facilities and services before displacement. Such surveys should identify any significant problems likely to occur in child development during resettlement. Ideally, the education section covers both quantitative information, such as attendance rates by grade and gender, and qualitative information, such as parents' attitudes about their children's schooling and domestic chores and obligations. Similarly, information covered in the section on health should be quantitative, such as average distance to clinics, the average use of their services, and the range of services provided; and qualitative, such as people's perceptions of the availability and quality of health services.

RPs for projects with large-scale displacement should describe health and education safeguards or improvements.

Large-scale displacement can be stressful for people and have immediate consequences for their health and their children's schooling. As the Bank's development experience confirms, improved healthcare and education generally come with social integration and economic growth. In projects involving large-scale displacement, the RP should include provisions for improving, or at least restoring, health and educational facilities and standards.

Education and health indicators for children are to be monitored in projects with large-scale displacement.

A good practice is to have resettlement monitoring include the impacts of resettlement on school enrollment, children's nutritional levels, and healthcare services. When the monitoring identifies a decline in educational attainment or health services, the borrower can implement measures previously agreed on with the Bank.

Productive activities of children are to be counted in calculating household entitlements.

That children are an important source of household income in many areas is a fact of life. Children's wage incomes and subsistence production are to be counted in calculating household entitlements. (However, children, as legal wards, are not entitled to separate compensation.) As good practice suggests, households dependent on child labor can benefit from alternative income-earning opportunities for adults while the children's access to educational opportunities is improved. The incidence of child labor should thus be reduced. Returning children to a situation of child labor is contrary to development policy.

The Elderly

Resettlement experience worldwide shows that the elderly often fail to adapt following displacement. They may have a lifelong "place attachment," lack the economic opportunity or physical capacity to obtain new sources of income, and lose traditional leadership roles or social standing as a result of community dispersion or social change. The elderly (like young children) are disproportionately vulnerable to disease and even death in resettlement operations, so project planners and implementers need to be aware of their needs.

Special care must be taken to prevent premature and involuntary retirement.

To discourage alienation or dependency of the elderly, a good practice is for task teams to ensure that non-recognition of losses or inadequate entitlement criteria do not result in premature and involuntary retirement of productive adults.

RPs and implementation arrangements should include arrangements for the elderly.

The effects of displacement on the elderly will depend on a host of demographic, social, and cultural conditions. Social assessment may be necessary to gauge the

5

5

probable impacts of displacement on such individuals, as well as the capacity of existing public health services and social institutions to address those impacts. Social assessment may also be necessary to suggest any necessary special remedies or arrangements. During implementation, monitoring arrangements and grievance procedures especially attentive to the concerns of the elderly or of handicapped people can help project managers identify these issues and implement remedial measures.

> *Project example:* In China, the Guangzhou City Center Transport Project (Ln 4329) provided, for more than a year, transportation to enable the elderly and other DPs to see their doctors in the area of former residence.

> *Project example:* Also in China, many urban projects use lotteries to allocate high-rise apartment housing to DPs. Because older people may have difficulty with stairs, many projects reserve the ground floors of buildings for the elderly, although apartments are still allotted by lottery to people in this group.

> *Project example:* In many rural projects in which resettlers use their own labor and compensation to build replacement housing, special arrangements have been made to assist elderly people with the construction of new housing.

The Disabled

The health section of baseline surveys should include an enumeration of physical and mental disabilities.

A good practice is to have RPs and implementation activities include the necessary arrangements for the disabled, particularly in large-scale resettlement operations.

People with physical or mental disabilities, depending on their situation, may require special assistance to understand the need to relinquish property, orient themselves to new areas, construct housing, reach their medical providers, and meet a whole suite of other specific needs.

A good practice is to have the resettlement operation enumerate the number and types of disabilities in the displaced population and make arrangements to provide the assistance needed by these individuals or their families.

Other Groups Not Protected by National Land Compensation Law

People without Title or Use Rights

Many Bank projects displace people lacking legal title to land or structures. These people are often described as squatters in urban or rural areas or as encroachers in agricultural or forest areas, although the two terms are more or less similar. Unlike people asserting long-standing or ancestral customary claims to property, squatters and encroachers typically claim use rights or even ownership after fairly recent occupation of unused or unprotected land.

Seeking to enforce legal property systems, borrowers may refuse to extend eligibility for entitlements to people without legal title or other forms of official recognition. OP 4.12, however, explicitly states that those without legal title to affected land may be compensated for their structures and may qualify for other resettlement and rehabilitation assistance. Squatters and encroachers in occupation of land *before* project initiation are likely to have invested in structures or land improvements that are eligible for compensation. Bank policy seeks redress for all people directly and adversely affected by land acquisition or changes in land use required for its projects. But both the borrower and the Bank have a legitimate interest in preventing fraudulent claims from squatters or encroachers arriving in the project area *after* project initiation, specifically to obtain resettlement benefits.

A good practice is to have RPs distinguish between the poor and other occupiers without title or claim to land.

Bank policy aims to assist the poor and vulnerable in resettlement operations to avoid re-creating or worsening the extent of their poverty. A good practice is therefore to have RPs distinguish between poor occupiers who have no other property and others who will not be significantly affected by the investment.

> *Project example:* In India, the Andhra Pradesh Highways Project (Ln 4192) distinguished between predominantly poor squatters residing in highway rights-of-way and agricultural encroachers supplementing their own substantial land holdings with use of highway rights-of-way. Plans entitled residential squatters to rehabilitation assistance. Agricultural encroachers who owned land equivalent to minimum economic holding outside the right of way, however, were to receive no assistance for losing the use of the rights-of-way and were to be warned not to replant following the harvest of existing crops.

5

DPs without legal title or claims receive compensation equivalent to replacement cost for structures and other nonland assets.

Squatters and encroachers may have a personal investment in structures or agricultural crops. Under OP 4.12, they are entitled to compensation at replacement cost (or an equivalent amount of rehabilitation assistance) for these lost assets.

> *Project example:* In India, special rehabilitation plans were drafted after planners discovered that more than 3,000 households were to be displaced by flood- and disease-prone storm drains in the Tamil Nadu Urban Development Project (Ln 4478). The government agreed to provide standard rehabilitation packages, including free house plots or subsidized flats, plus grants sufficient to cover loan repayments or rent for 13–25 months.

DPs lacking legal title to land can be offered resettlement assistance in lieu of compensation for land.

To help obtain assistance for those with de facto use or occupation rights, the Bank accepts provision of assistance as a substitute for compensation if such packages help achieve the objectives of the Bank's resettlement policy. Resettlement assistance can consist of land, cash, jobs, or other forms of assistance acceptable to the borrower.

Landlords in public safety zones are not entitled to compensation or rehabilitation.

The rationale for requiring rehabilitation of squatters living in public safety zones is to protect or improve the living standards of poor and vulnerable groups. Bank policy does not require protection of illegal rents accruing to squatter landlords from structures built in public safety zones.

Unlicensed street vendors and pavement dwellers are not considered directly affected.

Unlicensed street vendors (such as mobile enterprises lacking structures or other fixed improvements to land) lose no land or assets through displacement and hence are not covered by OP 4.12. Vendors with official site licenses, however, have recognized rights and must be provided with an alternative site and compensation for any transition expenses. Good practice recommends provision of a transition allowance to unlicensed vendors.

> *Project example:* In Indonesia, the Jabotabek Urban Development Project (Ln 2932) displaced many vendors who were operating kiosks along roads selected for widening. Roughly 1,600 vendors were given alternative sites in a newly developed market area.

Cutoff dates and land-use surveys are essential for protection against fraudulent claims.

> As OP 4.12 states, "Normally, this cut-off date is the date the census begins. The cut-off date could also be the date the project area was delineated, prior to the census, provided that there has been an effective public dissemination of information on the area delineated, and systematic and continuous dissemination subsequent to the delineation to prevent further population influx" (endnote 21).

To prevent false claims for compensation or rehabilitation appearing after disclosure of project plans, a good practice is for the Bank and the borrower to agree on an explicit eligibility cutoff date. If no acceptable cutoff dates have been established by the time the Bank becomes involved in the project, a census and socioeconomic survey can determine the number of DPs and the extent of impact on their structures and other assets. Another good practice is to examine public lands allocated for the project for evidence of private use.

Project example: In Bangladesh, the Jamuna Bridge Multipurpose Project (Cr 2569) encountered the types of problems that arise when safeguards against fraudulent claims are inadequate. In the absence of a full census or socioeconomic survey, an estimated 10,000 structures rapidly appeared in an area designated for expropriation. Aerial mapping and other methods were used to distinguish between legitimate and fraudulent claims.

Host Communities

> OP 4.12 specifically considers the position of host communities receiving displaced populations and promotes the host communities' participation in the resettlement operation.
>
> The OP states (para. 13) that "(a) displaced persons and their communities, and any host communities receiving them, are provided timely and relevant information, consulted on resettlement options, and offered opportunities to participate in planning, implementing, and monitoring resettlement. Appropriate and accessible grievance mechanisms are established for these groups."
>
> Furthermore, "(b) in new resettlement sites or host communities, infrastructure and public services are provided as necessary to improve, restore, or maintain accessibility and levels of service for the displaced persons and host communities. Alternative or similar resources are provided to compensate for the loss of access to community resources (such as fishing areas, grazing areas, fuel, or fodder)."
>
> *(continued)*

(continued from p. 87)

Also, "(c) Patterns of community organization appropriate to the new circumstances are based on choices made by the displaced persons. To the extent possible, the existing social and cultural institutions of resettlers and any host communities are preserved and resettlers' preferences with respect to relocating in pre-existing communities and groups are honored."

OP 4.12, Annex A (para. 16), provides further guidance on the integration of displaced populations with host communities. Specifically, "measures to mitigate the impact of resettlement on any host communities" should include

"(a) consultations with host communities and local governments;

(b) arrangements for prompt tendering of any payment due the hosts for land or other assets provided to resettlers;

(c) arrangements for addressing any conflict that may arise between resettlers and host communities; and

(d) any measures necessary to augment services (e.g., education, water, health, and production services) in host communities to make them at least comparable to services available to resettlers."

Bank policy explicitly seeks to mitigate adverse social and environmental impacts on the host communities. Sudden population growth, especially in large-scale resettlement operations, can render existing public infrastructure and services inadequate. Competition between resettlers and hosts for resources, as well as the sudden meeting of socially and culturally incompatible groups of people, can slow social integration or may even spur social conflict. The relationship between resettlers and host communities, therefore, warrants careful attention during project planning and implementation.

Consultations with host communities are essential to social integration.

The host communities have as much right to information about the project as the displaced populations. Good practice recommends that projects disseminate information among the host communities, just as they do among the displaced communities. Assessing the receptiveness of host communities and the potential for social conflict is important, especially when hosts and resettlers belong to different ethnic communities, have very different standards of living, or engage in different modes of production.

Once the feasibility and selection of host communities have been determined, public meetings and consultations with those communities can be carried out before RPs and site selections are finalized. Later, meetings of potential resettlers with members of the host communities enable all of them to assess the suitability of the proposed resettlement and identify potential issues. In short, the host communities' full participation is just as critical as that of DPs in the integration of the two groups.

Socioeconomic surveys can be used to assess the impact on host communities.

Socioeconomic surveys need to be carried out in host communities to determine potential resettlement impacts. The surveys in the host communities cover public infrastructure (such as schools, clinics, electricity, water supply) and employment conditions (for artisans, service personnel, salaried employees, independent entrepreneurs, and so on). The surveys often detail the compatibility of the ethnic composition of the host communities with that of incoming groups. The surveys may also assess the willingness of local people to accept the additional population. Finally, a good practice is to train the interviewers to answer questions from the host community about the project and its consequences.

A good practice is to set up a grievance committee in host communities.

An accepted procedure is to establish a grievance committee for displaced populations in projects with large-scale resettlement into host communities. Similar committees can be established for host communities (usually as a part of the local administration). Such committees would include representatives from the local communities and their leaders.

Another good practice is to maintain or improve public infrastructure in host communities.

Public infrastructure and services, if substantially affected by a sudden influx of resettlers scattered throughout host communities, must be maintained. They may have to be expanded to maintain, at least, pre-existing levels and quality of service. Furthermore, if existing infrastructure or services in the host communities are of a lower standard than those provided for resettlers in the immediate vicinity, the host community infrastructure warrants upgrading to the same level, to allay suspicions of preferential treatment.

Infrastructure and services can be expected to contribute significantly to the relations between old and new populations. If existing infrastructure is not upgraded to the same level as that provided for the resettlers, the host community may come to believe that it has sacrificed its own interests for those of the incoming population and not received commensurate benefits. If the resettlers are dispersed in the host communities, but infrastructure is not improved, everyone may see a deterioration in service, which will be blamed on the newcomers. Conversely, improving infrastructure provides everybody with better services and communicates the message to both the old and the new residents that the project is assisting them because they have endured such adverse impacts.

*Maintaining or, if necessary, replacing common resources
is a good practice.*

In rural areas, resettlement sites or scattered resettlements need to be planned so as not to contribute to depletion of common resources (for example, access to water, grazing lands, and forests). Where access to, or supply of, such resources is disrupted, good practice recommends some open access or equivalent be provided to meet the needs of hosts and resettlers (see also "Open Access or Common Property," in chapter 3).

Community Members Remaining in the Original Area after Resettlement

Issues with community members remaining in the original home area after resettlement may be more significant in rural areas. People in rural areas are more likely to be closely linked to their communities, and their economic dependence on each other may amplify disruptive effects.

*People not displaced by an investment but put in economically unviable
circumstances can be offered the full resettlement package.*

OP 4.12 establishes the principle that if the household assets remaining after involuntary acquisition are not viable, the project will acquire the entire asset as if the total had been required. Specifically, "if the residual of the asset being taken is not economically viable, compensation and other resettlement assistance are provided as if the entire asset had been taken" (endnote 12). OP 4.12 makes no specific allowances for people who remain in the original community and are not directly affected themselves but may be adversely affected by the displacement of others within their community. Good practice suggests, however, that to the extent that communities are no longer viable, the people remaining be offered the same resettlement options as those displaced. Otherwise, with the relocation of the DPs, those remaining in the community may find re-creating their livelihoods to the same levels as before extremely difficult. Good practice is to determine whether displacement of some members deprives communities of the "critical mass" needed to sustain economic productivity (for example, access to customers or suppliers) or community services (such as schools, healthcare, or religious activities). A social assessment is the appropriate instrument to determine these issues.

> **Project example:** In India, the Sardar Sarovar Project (Ln 2497; Cr 1552) relocated communities likely to face disruption of transport links, as well as those more directly affected, because the cost of building infrastructure to restore access (bridges, roads) was likely to be almost

10 times higher than relocation costs. The communities themselves demanded that they be relocated, rather than waiting for construction of infrastructure.

Project example: Also in India, a resettlement policy and an IPDP for the Bank-financed Orissa Water Resources Consolidation Project (Cr 2801) each contained provisions for community members left behind. The Orissa Water Resources Department's general resettlement policy allowed unaffected residents in villages more than 75 percent submerged to opt for treatment as DPs. Under an interpretation of the project IPDP, a tribal community that was split roughly in half by displacement was treated in effect as two communities, and both the resettlement site and the community left behind received infrastructure and other services.

Access routes and services severed by a project need to be restored.

Some infrastructure projects (such as expressways, waterways, and reservoirs) can isolate a portion of the community, effectively creating a community left behind. The impact on access is examined as part of the socioeconomic survey. The best solutions in such cases are those that restore access by, for example, constructing well-sited overpasses or underpasses. Where equivalent infrastructure is accessible (such as, busing to school), no action may be required. But if technical alternatives are unavailable, infrastructure (such as roads, sewer lines, or power transmission) must be replaced.

Project example: In China, consultations with people in areas to be affected by the Second Henan Provincial Highway Project (Ln 4027) led to the design of highway underpasses at regular intervals to restore access to divided lands, markets, or other facilities.

Note

1. A separate policy, OD 4.20, Indigenous Peoples, treats in detail the issues that may arise from development investments in areas where indigenous peoples reside. If a resettlement operation or restriction of access to legally designated parks or protected areas will affect indigenous groups, the task team must consult OD 4.20 for guidance, in addition to complying with the requirements of OP 4.12.

Technical Aspects of Involuntary Resettlement

Resettlement Planning and Processing Requirements

When a Bank-supported project involves involuntary resettlement, the planning and processing requirements include steps to facilitate effective design and flexible implementation of the resettlement program. The first principle of the Bank's resettlement policy is to avoid resettlement, if feasible, or to minimize it. Bank experience shows that if resettlement is unavoidable, poorly planned resettlement rarely leads to satisfactory implementation. Results are also likely to be poor if resettlement is overplanned and plans are viewed as blueprints to be followed regardless of changes in local circumstances.

To improve performance, Bank task teams should view resettlement as part of a development *process*. Formal project processing requirements should be compatible with, and responsive to, this development process. Resettlement success depends most directly on borrower capacity and commitment. In addition, Bank Procedure (BP) 4.12 emphasizes that Bank task teams need to pay careful attention to resettlement issues, from the earliest stages of project identification all the way through project implementation. At each stage of the project cycle, the task team (and other elements within the Bank) need to address substantive resettlement issues and meet the corresponding processing requirements.

This chapter focuses on these substantive planning and processing steps (many of which are considered in greater detail in subsequent chapters). It discusses indicative costs and time required for preparation, as well as the essential planning elements to be addressed before the next stage of project processing. It distinguishes between the processing requirements of resettlement plans (RPs) for specific investment loans and those of resettlement policy frameworks for sector investment loans, financial intermediation loans, and other multiphased projects. It also provides guidance on emerging areas of special concern, including new borrowers and late identification of resettlement.

Experience has shown that several drafts of resettlement planning documents sometimes must be reviewed and revised before becoming acceptable for clearance. Specifying what preparatory steps should be taken at each stage of the project cycle helps make the clearance process shorter and smoother (see CD Appendix 2, "Planning Matrix," for a list of major tasks during identification, planning, and implementation and for an example from a Bank project and Appendix 8 and CD Appendix 20, "Resettlement Timetable," for resettlement timetables from Bank projects).

How is the resettlement component of a project processed?

Processing the resettlement component requires the following:

- *Determining whether a project entails resettlement and, if so, what type of resettlement instrument is required.* Step 2 provides further details on how to agree on which resettlement instrument is required.
- *Taking the steps to prepare the resettlement component*—If Operational Policy (OP) 4.12 applies to the project, the following tasks must be completed: (a) conducting a census and socioeconomic surveys to identify impacts and the people that will be affected; (b) finalizing the resettlement entitlements for each category of impact; (c) selecting adequate resettlement sites and income-improvement activities (if necessary); (d) establishing institutional mechanisms for delivering entitlements and for undertaking other resettlement activities; (e) preparing budgets and making arrangements to ensure the timely flow of funds for resettlement; (f) coordinating implementation arrangements among relevant agencies; (g) establishing mechanisms for continued participation of displaced persons (DPs) in resettlement, as well as for redress of their grievances; and (h) making arrangements for internal and independent monitoring of resettlement activities.
- *Arranging for preparation of the resettlement planning documents*—The borrower engages qualified organizations to prepare RPs or resettlement frameworks and coordinates the activities of agencies contributing to planning documentation.
- *Reviewing and clearing the resettlement planning documents*—The borrower, any consultants, and the Bank specialists collaborate in preparing the resettlement documentation and arranging for their review and clearance.
- *Arranging for monitoring and supervision during implementation*—Plans for Bank supervision, project monitoring, and independent resettlement monitoring should specify arrangements for responding to obstacles or opportunities arising during implementation. Projects with significant resettlement require an early review during resettlement, ahead of any mid-term project review, to identify and address implementation problems when they are more manageable.

Processing Requirements at Each Stage of the Project Cycle

Preidentification

Bank Procedures (BP) 4.12 (para. 2) specifies required actions by Bank and borrower staff. "When a proposed project is likely to involve involuntary resettlement, the TT [task team] informs the borrower of the provisions of OP/BP 4.12. The TT and borrower staff

(a) assess the nature and magnitude of the likely displacement;
(b) explore all viable alternative project designs to avoid, where feasible, or minimize displacement;
(c) assess the legal framework covering resettlement and the policies of the government and implementing agencies (identifying any inconsistencies between such policies and the Bank's policy);
(d) review past borrower and likely implementing agencies' experience with similar operations;
(e) discuss with the agencies responsible for resettlement the policies and institutional, legal, and consultative arrangements for resettlement, including measures to address any inconsistencies between government or implementing agency policies and Bank policy; and
(f) discuss any technical assistance to be provided to the borrower."

The task team should discuss land acquisition and resettlement with the borrower as soon as possible following identification of potential projects or components. Late detection of resettlement issues has often led to procedural delays that could have been averted. BP 4.01 (Environmental Assessment) requires that any potential resettlement issues be identified during the initial environmental screening. Specifically, task teams should do the following:

- Provide OP 4.12 to the borrower and use it as a basis for resettlement discussions.
- Ask the borrower to provide an assessment of all lands to be used for the project (for additional details, see "land acquisition assessment," in chapter 11, and CD Appendix 4, "Guidelines for Land Acquisition Assessment").
- Inquire whether any resettlement was undertaken before discussion of Bank involvement in the project or whether any resettlement results from activities outside the Bank project that are critical to, or facilitate the design or performance of, the Bank project. If such resettlement needs to be covered under Bank policy, additional information on the

policies and procedures that were used may be required (for applicability of Bank policy in such circumstances, see "Linkages between Bank and Other Donor or National Projects," in chapter 1).

- Include a resettlement specialist (or consultant) as a regular member of the project task team if the scale or complexity of resettlement is potentially significant.
- Provide the project resettlement specialist (if one is included) with project feasibility studies. Ask the specialist to review sections dealing with resettlement or other social impacts and determine how resettlement should be addressed in the overall social assessment for the project (if one is conducted).
- Conduct at least a preliminary assessment of resettlement processing requirements for the project when interacting with the borrower at the preidentification stage (see above).

Step 1: Determine Whether a Project Triggers the Bank's Policy on Involuntary Resettlement

OP 4.12 is triggered by either of the following two conditions:

- Involuntary taking of land; or
- Involuntary restriction of access to parks or protected areas.

Once project components are known, a quick and inexpensive land acquisition assessment can be undertaken to help determine whether OP 4.12 applies to the project. The assessment provides answers to the following questions:

- *How much land area is required for the project?* If the project does not need any land, OP 4.12 is not triggered.
- *Who owns the land?* If part of the land has private owners and the project planners intend to acquire the land using eminent domain, OP 4.12 is triggered. If, however, all privately owned land is going to be sold voluntarily in the open market and the state is not going to use its right of eminent domain and if the potential DPs have the option to refuse land acquisition or purchase, OP 4.12 is not triggered.
- *If this project requires state-owned land, is this land subject to customary claim, squatters, or encroachers?* If all of the land required for the project is state-owned and is not subject to competing customary claims, grazing rights, or squatters or encroachers, OP 4.12 is not triggered. However, if the land is state-owned but is subject to competing claims, OP 4.12 is triggered.
- *How is the land, including state-owned land, currently used?* This question helps to determine the scope of resettlement issues in the case of private land and to identify possible temporary or seasonal use of state-owned land, even though the land may appear to be empty.

6

- *What is the rough estimate of resettlement impacts to result from acquisition?* This question helps the project team assess the scale of resettlement and determine the type of resettlement instrument to use (see step 2).
- *Will the project team be able to identify, before appraisal, all the land required for the project?* This question helps determine the type of resettlement instrument required for the project (see step 2). If all the land parcels required for the project cannot be identified before appraisal, a resettlement policy framework must be prepared for the project.
- *If the project is in a legally designated park or protected area, will the access of the people living inside or around the park be restricted?* If yes, OP 4.12 is triggered and a process framework is required under para. 31 of OP 4.12.

Step 2: If the Project Triggers the Bank's Resettlement Policy, Agree on the Type of Resettlement Planning Instrument Required

If the project requires resettlement, the Bank task team, the respective regional social development unit, and the Legal Department should agree on the type of resettlement planning documentation required. The choice of resettlement instrument depends on the scale and severity of resettlement, as well as the type of project. The various types of projects that require resettlement planning (some of which are discussed below) are as follows:

- Specific investment loans;
- Specific investment loans with minor resettlement impacts;
- Sector investment loans;
- Private sector financial intermediation projects;
- Other projects (including community-driven development [CDD] projects) with multiple subprojects; and
- Financial intermediation projects in which resettlement, if any, is likely to be minor.

In projects for which all the resettlement impacts are known by the time of project appraisal, the borrower must submit a resettlement plan to the Bank as a condition for project appraisal. (For further details about the RP, see OP 4.12, Annex A [Resettlement Instruments], paras. 1–21. A proposed outline of the resettlement plan is also given in the annex to this chapter.)

If the resettlement impacts are minor or the project displaces fewer than 200 people an abbreviated RP can be prepared instead of an RP. Resettlement impacts are considered minor if (a) all of the DPs lose less than 10 percent of their land, regardless of the number of DPs; (b) the remainder of their land is economically viable; and (c) they have no need for physical relocation. (For further details on abbreviated RPs, see OP 4.12, Annex A, para. 22.)

6

In projects for which the specific resettlement impacts cannot be known from a project appraisal, the borrower needs to submit a resettlement policy framework as a condition of appraisal. (For further details on the resettlement policy framework, see OP 4.12, Annex A, paras. 23–25. See CD Appendix 27, "Resettlement Policy Framework," for sample resettlement policy frameworks from several Bank projects.) Subproject- or component-specific RPs need to be submitted to the Bank for approval as a condition of its financing of the respective subproject or component.

In projects involving restrictions of access to legally designated parks or protected areas, the borrower needs to submit a process framework as a condition for appraisal. (For further details, see CD Appendix 28, "Resettlement Process Framework," for a sample resettlement process framework from a Bank project.) The process framework describes the consultative process to be used for deciding the restrictions of access and the proposed mitigation measures. Specific plans of action describing the mitigation measures agreed to by the affected communities need Bank approval before the restrictions can be imposed.

Several types of projects and the resettlement planning instruments required for each are described below.

Specific Investment Loans—For specific investment loans, where preliminary designs for all project components can be known by appraisal, submission to the Bank of a time-bound RP or abbreviated RP consistent with the Bank's operational policy on involuntary resettlement (OP/BP 4.12) is a condition for appraisal. The RP or abbreviated RP needs to be finalized by the time of negotiations, at the latest, and the borrower's obligation to carry out RP requirements should be reflected in legal documents.

Sector Investment Loans—For sector investment loans (as described in OP 4.12, para. 26), the Bank requires that the borrower submit a resettlement policy framework (for details, see OP 4.12, Annex A), as a condition for project appraisal. In addition, the RPs or abbreviated RPs for subprojects to be implemented during the first year of the project also need to be submitted, as a condition for appraisal. Bank approval of RPs or abbreviated RPs for subprojects to be undertaken during subsequent years would be a condition of financing these subprojects.

Private Sector Financial Intermediation Projects—The Bank increasingly supports private sector intermediation in infrastructure development projects. In such cases, the Bank extends a line of credit to one or more financial intermediaries for lending to private developers that are implementing subprojects. Because specific subprojects are usually not known at the time of appraisal, the Bank requires an approved resettlement policy framework as a condition for project appraisal. The resettlement policy framework should also describe the institutional arrangements for preparation, review, and approval of subproject-specific RPs. These RPs or abbreviated RPs for the subprojects need to be approved as a condition of financing of the subprojects.

Other Projects with Multiple Subprojects—Some projects, although not sector investment loans in the strict definition of the term, have one or more components or subprojects that cannot be known by appraisal. Resettlement planning requirements for such projects are generally the same as those for sector investment loans, described above. In such cases, RPs or abbreviated RPs must be submitted for components or subprojects for which preliminary designs can be prepared by appraisal. However, a resettlement policy framework would need to be prepared for the remaining subprojects or components. Bank approval of subproject RPs or abbreviated RPs is a condition of approval for financing.

Community-driven development (CDD) projects are a common type of project with multiple subprojects and usually have the following features:

- They involve several subprojects, typically in the hundreds.
- Each subproject is typically small, with the total outlay of most subprojects ranging from $5,000 to $50,000 or more (all dollar amounts are current U.S. dollars).
- Any adverse impacts of such activities are likely to be slight; the number of people affected by them, small.
- The subprojects are identified and often implemented by the communities themselves, based on some agreed-on parameters.
- The subprojects are not individually appraised beforehand by Bank staff or even by a project-implementing agency.
- Many individuals may be willing to voluntarily provide small pieces of land necessary for delivery of CDD benefits, but involuntary taking of land within participating communities may also be a possibility.

To accommodate the special characteristics of CDD projects, task teams need to alter the general approach to resettlement planning. (The general approach was devised primarily for application in large-scale projects initiated by government agencies, rather than in small projects initiated by communities.) Even the policy framework approach adopted in other forms of projects with multiple subprojects may be inappropriate for CDD projects, because the task team cannot anticipate the range of resettlement issues that might arise in various subprojects (which often span many sectors). Also, for communities implementing small subprojects, preparing an RP can be cumbersome, time-consuming, and costly and may not have adequate capacity to appraise resettlement issues in each subproject before implementing them.

The new approach reflects the fairly small and simple impacts that may accompany CDD activities, but it also meets the requirements of involuntary resettlement policy. The new approach has the following key features:

- An assessment of the likely resettlement issues is made at the time of project identification and is based on the nature of anticipated activities.

- A "positive list" or a "negative list" (delineating the range of acceptable activities in the CDD program) is used to decide whether activities with significant impacts and the need for more intensive resettlement planning should be excluded from funding.
- If program arrangements allow for voluntary contributions of land, special provisions must be included in the project operation manual, which is prepared for all CDD projects. Contributions of land must be shown to be voluntary and of insufficient magnitude to impoverish the individuals involved. Verifying that the community is voluntarily contributing land belonging to the community and not to individuals is important. If the land involved belongs to individuals, voluntary contributions need to be made by the respective individuals.
- The project operational manual describes the process communities use to identify and address resettlement issues if resettlement is anticipated. This description is accepted in lieu of a policy framework.
- Receipt of the draft operational manual, including an adequate description of resettlement issues, is a condition for appraisal. The draft manual is disclosed, both at the Bank's InfoShop and in the borrower country before project appraisal.
- The draft operational manual is finalized during appraisal, including the provisions relating to resettlement issues, and agreed on with the borrower at negotiations. The revised operational manual is also disclosed at the InfoShop and in the borrower country, so as to be accessible to communities in the project.
- Capacity-building efforts include initiatives to build the resettlement-related capacity of the project-implementing agency and communities.

Supervision of subprojects with significant resettlement issues is carried out by the project-implementing agency. Bank supervision missions review resettlement implementation and supervision arrangements and make selective site visits.

Project Identification

BP 4.12 describes how the Bank and the borrower determine which resettlement framework to use. "Based on review of relevant resettlement issues, the TT [task team] agrees with the Regional social development unit and LEG [Legal Department] on the type of resettlement instrument (resettlement plan, abbreviated resettlement plan, resettlement policy framework, or process framework) and the scope and the level of detail required. The TT conveys these decisions to the borrower and also discusses with the borrower the actions necessary to prepare the resettlement instrument, agrees on the timing for preparing the resettlement instrument, and monitors progress" (para. 3).

For projects involving substantial resettlement, the task team needs to establish an adequate framework for advanced resettlement preparation at the project identification stage itself, especially for projects involving community relocation or change in occupation of a large number of people. The following activities need to be initiated at this stage:

- If some project-related resettlement has already been completed, an agency needs to be engaged to evaluate the outcome. If it is unsatisfactory, retrofit activities may be necessary.
- The regional social development unit and regional legal unit should be consulted on resettlement issues. In projects entailing substantial resettlement, a resettlement specialist and a country lawyer should be included in the project task team (see CD Appendix 23, "Legal Framework for Resettlement and Compensation," for resettlement legal frameworks from Bank projects and CD Appendix 24, "Project Loan Agreement Section on Resettlement," for an example of how resettlement issues are incorporated into the project loan agreement for a large resettlement operation).
- All Bank resettlement requirements should be explained to the borrower. The task team leader, the borrower, the resettlement specialist, and the project lawyer should agree on the scope of resettlement, the required planning documentation, and the timing of preparation and submission of plans.
- The borrower, the task team, the regional social development unit, and the Legal Department should agree to a timetable for submission of planning documents to the Bank for review. The task team or resettlement specialist should inform the borrower about the normal response time after Bank receipt of plans.
- For projects with large-scale or complex resettlement, the task team (in collaboration with the borrower) should decide whether a free-standing resettlement (or environment and social mitigation) project should be prepared.
- The task team should assist the borrower, as necessary, in establishing organizational arrangements for resettlement preparation and planning. These arrangements could involve a central project resettlement unit, with assistance from relevant national or state agencies; local consultants; and international consultants (if needed). Qualified consultants are usually essential for conducting studies for community relocation or for designing income restoration programs (Box 6.1). Terms of reference for the consultants should be approved by the Bank's regional social development unit.
- Project identification is the most appropriate stage to discuss modifications in design to minimize resettlement. The task team should facilitate

6

Box 6.1 Assessing the Need for Consultant Services

Early in the preparation process (preferably during the identification stage), the task team and the borrower should assess the need for consultants to prepare for the resettlement. The assessment should consider the following factors:

- *The scale and complexity of resettlement impacts*—Projects with substantial resettlement and relocation of communities, such as reservoir and major urban resettlement projects and complex resettlement situations involving a number of components or requiring changes in occupations of affected people, would usually require consultants.
- *Resettlement experience of the project organization*—If the project organization has successfully implemented projects with substantial resettlement in the past, its in-house resettlement expertise may be sufficient for resettlement planning.
- *Resettlement planning experience in the country, region, or sector*—If sufficient resettlement experience is available domestically and transferable to the local project, local consultants (from an experienced organization) can be engaged. However, if resettlement experience is inadequate or not transferable to the local project, international consultants may be required.
- *Background studies or impact assessments already carried out*—Sometimes project feasibility studies already give a clear assessment of the need for resettlement preparation consultants.
- *Presence of social scientists or resettlement specialists on the engineering design consultant's team*—Adding a qualified resettlement specialist to the design consultant's team is useful after upstream identification of the need for resettlement. If timely assessment of the need for consultants can be made, the project design team can include a social scientist or resettlement planner. A multidisciplinary team with design engineers and project managers allows better coordination of resettlement planning and project design and implementation.

---

discussion between project engineers and resettlement planners to explore ways of reducing adverse impacts. Changes in project design may require some project reformulation.

- The resettlement specialist should determine whether indigenous peoples are affected by the project, and if so, ensure that the requirements of OD 4.20 are addressed (see "Indigenous Peoples," in chapter 5).
- Links between Bank-financed projects or components and non-Bank-financed projects or components, if any, should be assessed. OP 4.12 applies to resettlement impacts of projects or components that are not financed by the Bank but are essential to the design or performance of Bank-funded projects (see "Linkages between Bank and Other Donor or National Projects," in chapter 1).
- Once the scope of the project is determined, organizational and budgetary arrangements for conducting a census and socioeconomic survey

should be discussed and, if possible, finalized. This initiative allows for smooth resettlement planning at the preparation stage.

- The borrower's need for technical assistance in resettlement preparation and planning should be assessed. If necessary, the task team should seek support for this purpose through the various trust funds.

Project identification sets the stage for the quality enhancement review (QER). By this time, the scope of resettlement and the main issues to be addressed during project preparation should be identified. For various reasons, however, some resettlement impacts may not be identified until later in the project cycle. (Procedures for handling these impacts are discussed at the end of this chapter.)

Project Quality Enhancement Review

BP 4.12 specifies what resettlement information is necessary at the project concept stage: "The TT [task team] summarizes in the Integrated Safeguards Data Sheet (ISDS) accompanying the Project Concept Note (PCN) and the Project Information Document (PID) available information on the nature and magnitude of displacement and the resettlement instrument to be used, and the TT periodically updates the PID as project planning proceeds" (para. 4).

6

A description of resettlement impacts and main resettlement issues identified as part of project identification should be provided in the Integrated Safeguards Data Sheet (ISDS) prepared at the QER stage. BP 4.01 (Environmental Assessment), para. 3, requires that the task team record in the ISDS at the QER stage and the initial Project Information Document the key social and environmental issues, including any resettlement. Therefore, the environmental assessment process will also identify any resettlement issues. Usually, the regional social development unit and the Legal Department will submit written comments in advance of the QER. Unit representatives should attend the QER meeting to ensure that resettlement issues are addressed. The objective of the QER is to identify and agree on the main resettlement issues to be addressed during project preparation. At the meeting, the task team should seek the necessary guidance on addressing these issues later, during project preparation. Issues commonly raised include the following:

- Have all project activities or components that will cause resettlement been identified? Are all adverse impacts of resettlement identified? Have these impacts been minimized?

- Has agreement been reached on the type of resettlement instrument required? When is it to be submitted to the Bank and reviewed?
- What are the key challenges and issues for the resettlement process? Especially difficult are situations in which replacement land is unavailable for people displaced from land-based livelihoods; indigenous peoples must be relocated; the need to assist DPs without legal rights to the land being acquired (squatters or encroachers) is not acknowledged by the borrower; resettlement operations are large and complex; and past resettlement in the same sector or region has been inadequate.
- Does the borrower have sufficient organizational capacity for resettlement planning and implementation? If not, how can this capacity be strengthened? Evaluating this capacity is especially important when dealing with new borrowers (Box 6.2).

If an agency, state, or province is a new borrower, special provisions may be needed to ensure adequate resettlement preparation and planning. Box 6.2 gives an indicative list of the means for assisting new borrowers.

Before the QER, the task team also ensures that resettlement information is provided for the project's ISDS. This information should cover the nature and

---

Box 6.2   Meeting the Special Needs of New Borrowers

- The resettlement specialist and project lawyer should review local land acquisition and resettlement laws, regulations, procedures, and implementation experience. Gaps between Bank policy and local regulations and practice should be identified and discussed with the borrower, preferably with senior-level decisionmakers.
- The rationale behind Bank resettlement policy should be explained to the borrower in detail. A consensus on resettlement objectives and on mechanisms to reach these objectives is important.
- A resettlement training program for resettlement planners and implementation staff should be organized, where possible, to provide clear instructions and necessary clarifications.
- When consultants are engaged to prepare or plan resettlement in a new project, introducing capacity-building arrangements is important so that the borrower gains skills and knowledge in preparing resettlement to Bank standards. Absence of such capacity building would substantially dilute the long-term benefits of this exercise and would not reduce borrower dependency on consultants.
- The Bank country team should substantially involve a resettlement specialist and the country lawyer in the first few projects as a long-term investment in smooth, efficient resettlement preparation and implementation. The country team should share the expense of these measures with the task team that is preparing these projects for the Bank. The Bank should also offer assistance, including financial assistance, for review and revision of domestic laws and regulations related to land acquisition and resettlement.

magnitude of anticipated adverse impacts, any preliminary planning arrangements, and any other points that may appear particularly relevant, given the preliminary stage of project development. The task team also ensures that the ISDS is sent to the InfoShop (see CD Appendix 26, "Integrated Safeguards Data Sheet," for a sample ISDS from a Bank project). (For information on the ISDS, and guidance on filling it out, visit the Intranet website: http://essd. worldbank.org/essd/internal.nsf/wSPHD/ISDS.)

Project Preparation

BP 4.12 (paras. 5–6) outlines the assessments required during project preparation. "For projects with impacts under para. 3 (a) of OP 4.12, the TT [task team] assesses the following during project preparation:

(a) the extent to which project design alternatives and options to minimize and mitigate involuntary resettlement have been considered;
(b) progress in preparing the resettlement plan or resettlement policy framework and its adequacy with respect to OP 4.12, including the involvement of affected groups and the extent to which the views of such groups are being considered;
(c) proposed criteria for eligibility of displaced persons for compensation and other resettlement assistance;
(d) the feasibility of the proposed resettlement measures, including provisions for sites if needed; funding for all resettlement activities, including provision of counterpart funding on an annual basis; the legal framework; and implementation and monitoring arrangements; and
(e) if sufficient land is not available in projects involving displaced persons whose livelihoods are land-based and for whom a land-based resettlement strategy is the preferred option, the TT also assesses the evidence of lack of adequate land (OP 4.12, para. 11).

For projects with impacts under para. 3 (b) of OP 4.12, the TT assesses the following during project preparation:

(a) the extent to which project design alternatives and options to minimize and mitigate involuntary resettlement have been considered; and
(b) progress in preparing the process framework and its adequacy in respect to OP 4.12, including the adequacy of the proposed participatory approach; criteria for eligibility of displaced persons; funding for resettlement; the legal framework; and implementation and monitoring arrangements.

Most resettlement preparation and planning work usually occurs during project preparation. At this time, consultations with DPs, task team discussions with resettlement counterparts, background studies needed for resettlement (for example, studies related to resettlement sites and income improvement programs), site inspections of affected areas and relocation areas, and finalization

6

of resettlement entitlements and organizational arrangements normally culminate in a draft RP. Past experience has shown that several drafts need to be reviewed by the Bank's resettlement specialist and Legal Department during project preparation. This helps ensure that the draft to be formally reviewed by the regional social development unit and Legal Department, as a condition for appraisal, is in an acceptable form. The specific resettlement-related actions that need to be taken by the task team (or other Bank personnel) during project preparation are the following:

- Review the borrower's resettlement policies and procedures to identify gaps between Bank and borrower policies and procedures. The review should be carried out by the Legal Department and the regional social development unit.
- Identify ways to address the above-mentioned gaps in resettlement policies and procedures. Some common mechanisms for bridging these gaps are as follows: (a) The borrower issues a project-specific policy to comply with Bank requirements. This typically includes special provisions to (i) assist DPs that have no legal rights to the land acquired for the project or other DPs that are not eligible for assistance under local law; and (ii) provide for compensation for lost assets at replacement cost. (b) The project team obtains government waivers on provisions in local laws or regulations conflicting with the resettlement plan prepared in accordance with Bank policy. (c) When compensation at replacement cost is the issue, borrowers sometimes use additional grants or allowances to top up the compensation prescribed by law or regulation (see "Calculation and Application of Replacement Cost," in chapter 4). (d) When the eligibility of those lacking legal land title or residency permits becomes an issue, project-specific cutoff dates can be used to discourage entry into the area by people seeking to establish illegitimate claims for assistance (see "People without Title or Use Rights," in chapter 5). (e) The project can serve as a vehicle for dialogue between the Bank and borrower on developing national, regional, or sectoral resettlement policies that will be broadly consistent with Bank and other donor requirements.
- Help the borrower obtain qualified consultant services, if required, for detailed resettlement planning. Trust funds used to engage consultants for this purpose should be operated by the borrower and not by the Bank. Consultants engaged through a trust fund operated by the Bank cannot be used to prepare borrowers' documents, including RPs.
- If the resettlement program involves community relocation to new sites or identification and design of income improvement programs for DPs who have to change occupations, emphasize that the level of detail in the RP, the extent of participation of affected communities, the number

of preparatory studies for planning, and the time required to prepare the RP are substantially greater than for projects without these impacts (Box 6.3). (Details of income improvement strategies and programs, as well as the requirements for development of resettlement sites, are discussed in chapter 8.)

- Ensure that the census and socioeconomic surveys are completed. Because these activities provide the basis for preparing the RP, they should be completed as soon as possible during the project preparation stage.

Box 6.3   Estimating the Time Required for Resettlement Preparation

For normal investment projects, "resettlement preparation" describes the period of time between identification of resettlement and the completion of project appraisal. All things being equal, the time required for resettlement preparation tends to grow if resettlement involves any of the following:

- Large-scale resettlement
- The need for community relocation
- Multijurisdictional coordination
- Impacts on indigenous peoples
- Several resettlement components
- The need for income restoration programs
- Project agency inexperienced with resettlement

Steps can also be taken to reduce the preparation period, or at least to relieve project processing bottlenecks, while sustaining the quality of preparation:

- Appointing consultants or increasing the frequency of resettlement missions can shorten preparation time.
- Beginning preparation as early as possible in the project identification process can relieve processing bottlenecks during appraisal (or negotiations).

Ordinarily, the minimum time required to complete resettlement preparation for various categories of projects is as follows:

- Reservoir resettlement   1–1.5 years
- Major urban resettlement   9 months–1 year
- Rural linear resettlement   6–9 months
- Resettlement involving indigenous peoples   1–1.5 years
- Resettlement with mainly marginal impacts   4–6 months

The preparation activities requiring substantial amount of time are the following:

- Census and socioeconomic surveys   3–6 months
- Identification of the need, and feasibility studies,
  for resettlement (especially agricultural) sites 4–8 months
- Design of appropriate economic rehabilitation programs   3–6 months

Carrying out the above activities simultaneously, as much as possible, helps reduce the overall preparation time required.

6

- Ensure that the census and socioeconomic survey data are used to categorize impacts and DPs. All impacts must be reflected in this categorization, as it forms the basis for determining eligibility and for designing assistance packages. The categorization process should trigger consultation between the Bank and the borrower and between the borrower and DPs (or their representatives) on assistance options, economic rehabilitation strategies, and relocation sites. The process should culminate in a draft entitlement matrix (see Appendix 6 and CD Appendix 9, "Entitlement Matrix," for several examples of entitlement matrices from Bank projects).
- Obtain agreement on methods for valuation of lost assets and procedures for compensation or asset replacement, after categories of impact have been established.
- Ensure that DPs are consulted on relevant aspects of resettlement planning, especially selection of relocation sites and development of income improvement strategies and programs. The task team should assess the extent to which DPs' views have been considered in planning. A preliminary list of income restoration programs, based on consultations with DPs, should be prepared. Proposed programs should be assessed for technical, economic, and financial feasibility. If economic rehabilitation of many DPs is needed, experienced agencies should be contracted to conduct these studies. The capacity of DPs to implement or manage program activities should also be assessed.
- Discuss and finalize, if possible, organizational arrangements for resettlement. These arrangements include delivery of all forms of resettlement assistance, coordination of the various implementation agencies, clear delineation of financial responsibilities, and procedures for internal monitoring. If independent monitoring is required, draft terms of reference and a short list of candidate agencies should be prepared.
- Assist the borrower, if necessary, with the preparation of tentative cost estimates and budget measures, including clear indication of financial responsibility for all aspects of the resettlement program.

After completion of the above activities and before the preappraisal mission arrives in the field, a draft RP should be prepared. Review of draft plans by the regional social development unit and the Legal Department can help the preappraisal mission focus on any key outstanding issues.

Preappraisal

By the end of the preappraisal stage (if not before), resettlement policy entitlements for various categories of impacts should be finalized. Relocation sites and income restoration programs should be acceptable to DPs. Any outstanding issues identified during project preparation should be resolved during the preappraisal mission, before a draft RP (or policy framework) is to be submitted to the Bank for approval.

Specifically, the following steps should be taken during preappraisal:

- Prepare an agreed resettlement entitlement matrix, detailed layout and design of relocation sites, and operational details of income restoration programs (including an estimate of the number of DPs likely to opt for each program).
- Finalize organizational arrangements for implementation, including mechanisms for redress of grievances. Incorporate in the draft RP an organization chart of the project resettlement unit and agencies, and if necessary, a capacity building plan.
- Review external monitoring proposals, if applicable, and arrange meetings with short-listed agencies during the preappraisal mission.
- Compute detailed cost estimates based on finalization of the resettlement entitlement matrix, final selection of relocation sites, and income restoration programs.
- Include in the draft RP a description of the participatory processes that contributed to its preparation. Include a strategy for consultation with DPs during project implementation (see chapter 7).
- Encourage the borrower to prepare resettlement information (in a booklet, pamphlet, or other media) for distribution to DPs. Include in the draft RP an outline of the information to be provided, as agreed with the borrower.
- Complete the evaluation of any project resettlement undertaken before the Bank's involvement in the project. Incorporate in the draft RP any provisions for remedial actions, if necessary.
- By the end of the preappraisal mission, submit a revised draft RP (if a draft was previously submitted) to the Bank for legal and technical review.
- If any significant issues are outstanding, seek clarification or guidance from the regional safeguards coordinator, the Bankwide resettlement coordinator, or the Resettlement Committee.

Project Decision Meeting

"The borrower submits to the Bank a resettlement plan, a resettlement policy framework, or a process framework that conform[s] with the requirements of OP 4.12, as a condition of appraisal for projects involving involuntary resettlement (see OP 4.12, paras. 17–31). Appraisal may be authorized before the plan is completed in highly

(continued)

6

> *(continued from p. 111)*
>
> unusual circumstances (such as emergency recovery operations) with the approval of the Managing Director in consultation with the Resettlement Committee. In such cases, the TT [task team] agrees with the borrower on a timetable for preparing and furnishing to the Bank the relevant resettlement instrument that conforms with the requirements of OP 4.12." (BP 4.12, para. 8)
>
> "Once the borrower officially transmits the draft resettlement instrument to the Bank, Bank staff—including the regional resettlement specialists and the lawyer— review it, determine whether it provides an adequate basis for project appraisal, and advise the Regional sector management accordingly. Once approval for appraisal has been granted by the Country Director, the TT sends the draft resettlement instrument to the Bank's InfoShop. The TT also sends the English language executive summary of the draft resettlement instrument to the Corporate Secretariat, under cover of a transmittal memorandum confirming that the executive summary and the draft resettlement instrument are subject to change during appraisal" (BP 4.12, para. 9).

The draft RP should be submitted for legal and technical review at least 15 days before the project decision meeting. The regional Legal Department manager and the safeguards coordinator ensure that the draft RP is reviewed. Although clearance procedures may vary from region to region, clearance should be based on there being an adequate description of the following key planning attributes in the RP:

- Census and socioeconomic data necessary to establish baseline conditions and formulate entitlements
- Legal framework
- Entitlement policy and assistance packages covering all categories of impacts
- Budget and identification of funding sources
- Organizational arrangements for RP implementation
- Time-bound implementation schedule linked to civil works
- Selection of relocation sites, based on consultations with DPs
- Feasible income restoration programs, based on consultation with DPs
- Plans for housing, infrastructure, and social services
- Plans for environmental protection and management
- Consultation with DPs and host communities
- Accessible grievance procedures
- Monitoring plan.

In the event that the draft RP is generally acceptable but requires some additional improvement or clarification, specific deficiencies are identified. A conditional clearance is provided in this case. Then, after outstanding issues are satisfactorily completed, the appraisal process will be considered complete. However, if key planning issues have not been addressed at this stage and the RP is found not to form an adequate basis for project appraisal, project appraisal can be delayed. In many cases, the technical specialist reviewing the document provides the task team with detailed technical comments on RP deficiencies or outstanding issues. All identified deficiencies or outstanding issues should be resolved during the appraisal mission, and a revised RP must be submitted to the Bank for review. Project appraisal is considered complete only when an RP is determined to be acceptable to the Bank. (The review process described above also applies to draft resettlement policy frameworks submitted as a condition for project appraisal.)

"In the Project Appraisal Document (PAD), the TT [task team] describes the resettlement issues, proposed resettlement instrument and measures, and the borrower's commitment to, and institutional and financial capacity for, implementing the resettlement instrument. The TT also discusses in the PAD the feasibility of the proposed resettlement measures and the risks associated with resettlement implementation. In the annex to the PAD, the TT summarizes the resettlement provisions, covering, inter alia, basic information on affected populations, resettlement measures, institutional arrangements, timetable, budget, including adequate and timely provision of counterpart funds, and performance monitoring indicators. The PAD annex shows the overall cost of resettlement as a distinct part of project costs" (BP 4.12, para. 11).

Before the formal project decision meeting, the task team should summarize the status of resettlement preparation in the Project Appraisal Document (PAD). This summary should address resettlement issues (including scope and magnitude of adverse impacts), proposed resettlement measures to be undertaken, the borrower's capacity (organizational and financial) for and commitment to implementing the RP. The PAD should also assess any risks (to DPs and to the Bank) posed by the resettlement. Typically, more detailed information relating to various aspects of resettlement is provided in an annex to the PAD.

BP 4.12 defines the use of the Resettlement Committee to obtain guidance. "The TT [task team] may request a meeting with the Resettlement Committee to obtain endorsement of, or guidance on, (a) the manner in which it proposes to address resettlement issues in a project, or (b) clarifications on the application and scope of this policy. The Committee, chaired by the vice president responsible for resettlement, will include the Director, Social Development Department, a representative from LEG [Legal Department], and two representatives from Operations, one of whom is from the sector of the project being discussed. The Committee is guided by the policy and, among other sources, [this book], which will be regularly updated to reflect good practice" (para. 7).

Before the project decision meeting, the task team should seek guidance on strategies for resolving outstanding issues, if any, and for RP revision, if required. (Any resettlement-related conditionality attached to formal project negotiations should be discussed at the meeting.)

Before the project decision meeting, the task team should review the draft legal documentation to ensure that references to resettlement-related matters are accurate and that actions legally required of the borrower are adequately identified.

Before the project decision meeting, the task team should also ensure that the borrower has fulfilled its obligations to publicly disclose the RP. The task team should send the revised RP to the Bank's InfoShop and the host country PIC, update the ISDS, obtain clearance from the regional safeguards coordinator, and send the ISDS to the InfoShop as well. The draft RP should also be made available to DPs, other affected people, and local nongovernmental organizations (NGOs) through local government offices, the project office, the resettlement agency office, and other locations convenient to the DPs.

In projects involving emergency recovery operations (such as earthquakes, floods, hurricanes, or other disasters), the managing director can waive the requirement to submit resettlement plans as a condition of appraisal. In such cases, the written waiver provided by the managing director should describe the proposed alternative schedule for preparing the RP.

Project Appraisal

"During project appraisal, the TT [task team] assesses (a) the borrower's commitment to and capacity for implementing the resettlement instrument; (b) the feasibility of the proposed measures for improvement or restoration of livelihoods and standards of living; (c) availability of adequate counterpart funds for resettlement activities; (d) significant risks, including risk of impoverishment, from inadequate implementation of the resettlement instrument; (e) consistency of the proposed resettlement instrument with the Project Implementation Plan; and (f) the adequacy of arrangements for internal, and if considered appropriate by the TT, independent monitoring and evaluation of the implementation of the resettlement instrument. The TT obtains concurrence of the Regional social development unit and LEG [Legal Department] to any changes to the draft resettlement instrument during project appraisal. Appraisal is complete only when the borrower officially transmits to the Bank the final draft resettlement instrument conforming to Bank policy (OP 4.12)" (BP 4.12, para. 10).

Comments raised during RP review or the project decision meeting should be conveyed in time to allow the borrower (including planning and implementation agencies) to address outstanding issues as much as possible before the arrival of the appraisal mission. The following issues usually need to be addressed during appraisal:

- Deficiencies or outstanding issues identified during the review of the project decision package should be addressed.
- Terms of reference for independent monitoring and selection of the monitoring agency should be finalized. Internal monitoring procedures (including formats) and responsibilities should also be finalized.
- In addition to the appraisal requirements (see box above), other issues or clarifications are likely to be outstanding at the appraisal stage. These issues are addressed during the appraisal mission, in addition to the specific objectives of appraisal. All outstanding issues need to be resolved and incorporated into a revised RP, if necessary, before the appraisal can be considered complete.
- The schedule and arrangements for staffing the resettlement unit and engaging independent monitors (if applicable) should be discussed during appraisal.
- A revised RP, if necessary, should be submitted for technical and legal review. Following review, regional clearance procedures are essentially the same as those used for the initial draft.
- If applicable, the draft resettlement policy framework or the process framework should be further discussed with the borrower at appraisal and finalized by the end of the appraisal mission.

Negotiations

> "The project description in the Loan Agreement describes the resettlement component or subcomponent. The legal agreements provide for the borrower's obligation to carry out the relevant resettlement instrument and keep the Bank informed of project implementation progress. At negotiations, the borrower and the Bank agree on the resettlement plan or resettlement policy framework or process framework. Before presenting the project to the Board, the TT [task team] confirms that the responsible authority of the borrower and any implementation agency have provided final approval of the relevant resettlement instrument" (BP 4.12, para. 12).

Sometimes issues may still need to be addressed or clarified after completion of the appraisal mission. If the issues are significant, resolution may be required as a condition of negotiations. This means that revisions to the RP or policy framework must be found acceptable by the regional safeguards unit and the Legal Department before an invitation to formal project negotiations can be issued. However, minor clarifications and presentational issues can be addressed during negotiations.

At the time of negotiations or before a Board presentation, the task team must confirm that the borrower and responsible implementation agencies have provided final and official approval of the RP. Once the RP has been finalized, the task team should send the final RP to the Bank InfoShop and the host country public information center (PIC), finalize the ISDS, and send that to the Bank InfoShop as well. The final RP should be distributed to the same locations as the draft RP.

Effectiveness

Any resettlement-related conditions of effectiveness must be complied with before the project is declared effective. Such cases require clearance by the regional social development unit and the Legal Department.

Supervision

BP 4.12 defines Bank requirements for resettlement supervision. "Recognizing the importance of close and frequent supervision to good resettlement outcomes, the Regional vice president, in coordination with the relevant country director, ensures that appropriate measures are established for the effective supervision of projects with involuntary resettlement. For this purpose, the country director allocates dedicated funds to adequately supervise resettlement, taking into account the magnitude and complexity of the resettlement component or subcomponent and the need to involve the requisite social, financial, legal, and technical experts. Supervision should be carried out with due regard to the Regional Action Plan for Resettlement Supervision" (para. 13).

"Throughout project implementation the TL [team leader] supervises the implementation of the resettlement instrument ensuring that the requisite social, financial, legal, and technical experts are included in supervision missions. Supervision focuses on compliance with the legal instruments, including the Project Implementation Plan and the resettlement instrument, and the TT [task team] discusses any deviation from the agreed instruments with the borrower and reports it to Regional Management for prompt corrective action. The TT regularly reviews the internal, and where applicable, independent monitoring reports to ensure that the findings and recommendations of the monitoring exercise are being incorporated in project implementation. To facilitate a timely response to problems or opportunities that may arise with respect to resettlement, the TT reviews project resettlement planning and implementation during the early stages of project implementation. On the basis of the findings of this review, the TT engages the borrower in discussing and, if necessary, amending the relevant resettlement instrument to achieve the objectives of this policy" (para. 14).

(continued)

(continued from p. 116)

"For projects with impacts covered under para. 3(b) of OP 4.12, the TT assesses the plan of action to determine the feasibility of the measures to assist the displaced persons to improve (or at least restore in real terms to pre-project or pre-displacement levels, whichever is higher) their livelihoods with due regard to the sustainability of the natural resource, and accordingly informs the Regional Management, the Regional social development unit, and LEG [Legal Department]. The TL makes the plan of action available to the public through the InfoShop" (para. 15).

"A project is not considered complete—and Bank supervision continues—until the resettlement measures set out in the relevant resettlement instrument have been implemented. Upon completion of the project, the Implementation Completion Report (ICR) evaluates the achievement of the objectives of the resettlement instrument and lessons for future operations and summarizes the findings of the borrower's assessment referred to in OP 4.12, para. 24. If the evaluation suggests that the objectives of the resettlement instrument may not be realized, the ICR assesses the appropriateness of the resettlement measures and may propose a future course of action, including, as appropriate, continued supervision by the Bank" (para. 16).

6

BP 4.12 makes regional management and country program directors responsible for ensuring that adequate resources are committed to resettlement supervision. Regional resettlement supervision plans should be prepared to ensure that supervision resources are allocated appropriately and that the supervision team includes a skills mix appropriate for the project context.

The RP should contain a detailed plan for internal and independent monitoring, including a timetable for periodic submission of monitoring reports to the Bank. Any project monitoring indicators should be consistent with the resettlement monitoring indicators. If well prepared, these reports, supplemented with project supervision by the Bank, constitute an effective mechanism for reviewing implementation of resettlement activities (see chapter 10). Specifically, the following actions need to be taken by the task team during implementation:

- The team ensures that monitoring reports are prepared and submitted according to the schedule provided in the RP. Monitoring reports should be reviewed by a resettlement specialist, whose comments should be conveyed to the relevant implementing agency or agencies.
- Supervision activities should be based on the project's legal documents, the RP, and monitoring reports. At the end of each supervision mission, any outstanding issues should be discussed with project counterparts. A timetable for resolving issues identified during supervision should be agreed on. Repeated lack of compliance with salient agreements in the RP or supervision reports should be reported to senior management.

6

- An early review of resettlement implementation should be held to identify implementation problems or RP deficiencies, especially if the project is large scale or has complex resettlement operations and when ample time is available for adaptation or correction. If necessary, the task team and the borrower should revise or amend the RP so that policy objectives are more likely to be achieved.
- In the case of sector investment loans or other projects for which a resettlement policy framework has been prepared, the borrower prepares subproject-specific RPs. These RPs are submitted to the regional social development unit for review and approval, as a condition for Bank approval of the subproject for financing. In projects with many subprojects, the authority to approve subproject RPs may be delegated to responsible government agencies or, if applicable, to private financial intermediaries. In projects with only a few subprojects or where counterpart agencies or financial intermediaries lack capacity for RP review, the Bank retains this responsibility.
- If conditions have been applied to initiation of civil works or Bank disbursement, the task team and the Legal Department need to ensure compliance with these conditions during project supervision before lifting them.
- During resettlement supervision, the task team's periodic Project Supervision Report should include accurate information gleaned from supervision or data relating to resettlement.

The project is not considered complete unless a resettlement plan has been fully implemented.

Because the resettlement program is one of the components of the project, the project cannot be considered complete until the resettlement plan agreed to by the borrower is fully implemented.

The Bank's resettlement policy requires an assessment, at the time of project completion and after the RP has been fully implemented, of the extent to which the DPs have improved or restored their standards of living. This assessment is usually based on the results of a follow-up socioeconomic survey conducted by the borrower at the time of project completion (see CD Appendix 33, "Implementation Completion Report Section on Involuntary Resettlement," for an example of how an ICR should report on involuntary resettlement, including whether the resettlement instrument is fully implemented and if any additional actions are required or recommended).

If the assessment reveals that a majority of DPs have already improved or restored their standards of living and that the remaining DPs are likely to reach this stage in the near future, no further supervision is necessary.

If the assessment reveals that a significant proportion of DPs have not been able to improve or restore their incomes and are also unlikely to do so in the near future and that this failure is due to the design of the resettlement instrument or its implementation, the task team should discuss additional measures with the borrower to assist DPs. The task team may decide, in consultation with the borrower, to continue supervision of the resettlement program after the formal completion of the project, as necessary.

Irregular Processing: Late Identification of the Need for Resettlement

Sometimes, the need for resettlement is discovered late in the project preparation stage or even during project implementation. Late discovery is typically a result of one of three unanticipated situations:

- Addition of project components requiring resettlement;
- Redefinition of the scope of a component; or
- Impacts unforeseen during project identification

Processing requirements for resettlement under these circumstances can vary. A major consideration is whether an RP or a resettlement policy framework is already under preparation or in place. Amending an existing RP or framework will usually be less of a problem than producing such a document in midcourse. If an RP already exists or is under preparation, components such as mechanisms for participation, redress of grievances, and monitoring normally would not change, and only the institutional arrangements and budgets may need minor modifications.

If no other resettlement has been identified in the project, and no RP or framework is in place, the task team should convene a meeting with the borrower and Bank technical and legal specialists as soon as possible to determine what kind of planning documents needs to be prepared and under what timetable.

When the need for resettlement is identified during implementation, submission of an acceptable RP will be a condition of disbursement for the given component. If land acquisition and displacement have occurred before the need for resettlement is brought to the attention of the Bank, the borrower must conduct a retroactive assessment. This assessment should provide the Bank with basic information relating to the scope and magnitude of adverse impacts, the compensation paid for assets, and other forms of assistance extended to DPs. If baseline data are available, a socioeconomic survey should be conducted to determine whether incomes and living standards have at least been restored. If no baseline data are available, DPs should be consulted regarding their views on the effectiveness of resettlement measures. The task team and the borrower

6

should subsequently discuss and agree on any supplementary resettlement measures necessary to meet Bank policy requirements.

Annex: Resettlement Site Selection, Movement of Displaced Persons, and Organization of Community Life

Resettlement site selection and feasibility studies of the proposed actions and economic packages are the most important steps for successful implementation of RPs. The major objectives of these steps are to ensure that the resettlement sites have been properly selected and that the proposed income restoration activities are not only technically, economically, and financially viable, but also within the capacity of the DPs to manage.

The site selection, feasibility studies, and site development process can be divided into four phases as follows.

Phase 1: Criteria for Site Selection

Site selection must be carried out systematically. Criteria for site selection must be determined. For evaluating the potential sites against the prescribed site selection criteria, basic data sources must be assembled. These sources might include national survey authority or agency topographical maps, at a scale of 1:100,000 or 1:50,000, satellite imagery, aerial photography, and any other available maps or data.

Site selection criteria are suggested below. These criteria should be discussed with the DPs, their representatives, and local officials before being finalized. In general, potential sites should

- Be as close as possible to the affected areas (this criterion needs to be balanced with the potential of these sites for sustainable economic activities);
- Be easily accessible via existing roads or capable of becoming so via construction of inexpensive, economically feasible roads (accessibility, not remoteness, is the issue);
- Include no protected areas, classified forests, nature reserves, or environmentally sensitive lands, such as sloping terrain or shallow soils;
- Have an even and smooth topography and no mountainous areas, rolling topography, or steep slopes;
- Have soils adequate for irrigated or rainfed agriculture after minimal reclamation works (saline soils or lands susceptible to floods and water logging should be avoided unless inexpensive reclamation works can be implemented);

6

- Have good potential for surface or groundwater irrigation; and
- Have, preferably, a low population density, large holdings, and good potential for further development (areas already developed should be avoided, unless a market for land purchase is active).

Phase 2: Feasibility Studies

During the feasibility studies stage of site selection, planners should carry out detailed studies to determine the technical and economic feasibility of the proposed activities. The studies should include the resettlement component for the DPs and the land development component for the host community, over the entire study area. Cost estimates should be prepared, and sites found to be economically unviable or environmentally unsuitable should be rejected. Phase 2 should include the following components:

- A detailed demographic and land-ownership survey of the host community, by sampling;
- A topographical survey, at a scale of 1:10,000, with 1-meter contours;
- A land-cover or land-use map, at a scale of 1:10,000;
- A soil survey and soils map, at a scale of 1:10,000, to determine the capability of the soil to support rainfed and irrigation agriculture;
- An agro-meteorological survey of rainfall, temperature, sunshine hours, pan evaporation, and consumptive use of water;
- A survey of surface water and groundwater resources, taking into account actual discharges and data generated over 30 years to determine the available surface water and groundwater resources;
- A proposal of various agricultural development options for the area as a whole, that is, without any distinction between the DP and host communities;
- A study of the economic and financial viability of the proposed agricultural development options; and
- A recommendation, with cost estimates and semidetailed plans, of selected development options.

Phase 3: Detailed Designs and Land Purchase

At the design and land purchase stage of site selection, resettlement planners need to obtain (a) the DPs' final agreement on the suitability of the proposed sites and site development options; and (b) the host community's consent to allow or sell the land to be used for the relocation. During this phase, contiguous tracks of land should be purchased to rationalize the layout of the resettlement villages and agricultural plots and reduce the cost of road, irrigation, and

6

drainage infrastructure. Care should also be taken to lay out the resettlement villages along the lines of former DP villages.

Phase 4: Final Designs and Construction

The final design and construction stage is rather straightforward. The construction of provisional housing for each displaced family and the provision of basic amenities, such as water supply, access roads, and partial electrification, are prerequisites for the movement of the DPs and their families. Phase 4 comprises the following steps:

1. Final designs, cost estimates, and tender documents for the construction of the resettlement sites;
2. Bidding and award of contracts; and
3. Construction of works.

Movement of DPs

The movement of DPs and their families needs to be carefully planned. The movement should take place only when the sites are ready with basic amenities, that is, provisional housing, water supply, and good access roads. The planning of this phase requires the preparation and medical checkups of the DPs and their families to ensure that they are all fit for travel, the mobilization of buses and trucks to move the DPs and their belongings, and the assistance of social workers and NGOs as the DPs take over their new residences. Usually, some food distribution is necessary during the transport of DPs and their belongings and during the first few days after their arrival at the new site. Some cash, basic tools, seeds, and fertilizers should also be distributed to enable the DPs to start working their land from the beginning.

Organization of Community Life and Support Services

Community life will need to be organized. Local groups will need to be established for village administration and for operation and maintenance of the resettlement villages and public facilities, such as roads, water supply, power supply, and irrigation and drainage systems. These organizations also increase the effectiveness of various support services, such as agricultural extension, credit, input supply, and seed distribution. Initial training of resettlement staff, extension workers, and DP representatives should start before the actual movement of DPs so that community life can be organized soon after their arrival at the new sites.

Chapter 7

Consultation and Participation

What OP 4.12 Says

Operational policy (OP) 4.12 states, as a policy objective, that "displaced persons should be meaningfully consulted and should have opportunities to participate in planning and implementing resettlement programs" (para. 2[b]).

The OP further requires that the resettlement plan or resettlement policy framework include measures to ensure that "the displaced persons are . . . consulted on, offered choices among, and provided with technically and economically feasible resettlement alternatives" (para. 6[a]).

The OP provides the additional guidance that "displaced persons and their communities, and any host communities receiving them, are provided timely and relevant information, consulted on resettlement options, and offered opportunities to participate in planning, implementing, and monitoring resettlement. Appropriate and accessible grievance mechanisms are established for these groups" (para. 13[a]).

OP 4.12 provides a detailed outline of the elements of a participation plan: "Involvement of resettlers and host communities, including

(a) a description of the strategy for consultation with and participation of resettlers and hosts in the design and implementation of the resettlement activities;

(b) a summary of the views expressed and how these views were taken into account in preparing the resettlement plan;

(c) a review of the resettlement alternatives presented and the choices made by displaced persons regarding options available to them, including choices related to forms of compensation and resettlement assistance, to relocating as individuals[,] families[,] or as parts of preexisting communities or kinship groups, to sustaining existing patterns of group organization, and to retaining access to cultural property (e.g. places of worship, pilgrimage centers, cemeteries); and

(d) institutionalized arrangements by which displaced people can communicate their concerns to project authorities throughout planning and implementation, and measures to ensure that such vulnerable groups as indigenous people, ethnic minorities, the landless, and women are adequately represented" (Annex A, para. 15).

Similarly, for projects involving restriction of access to legally designated parks and protected areas, OP 4.12 requires a process framework. The process framework describes "the participatory process by which (a) specific components of the project will be prepared

(continued)

(*continued from p. 123*)

and implemented" (para. 7[a]). Indeed, "the nature of restrictions, as well as the type of measures necessary to mitigate adverse impacts, is determined with the participation of the displaced persons during the design and implementation of the project" (para. 7).

Consultation and Participation Defined

Participation is conventionally divided into two dimensions: information exchange and decisionmaking, each of which in turn has two component activities. Information exchange conventionally comprises dissemination and consultation. Decisionmaking comprises collaboration and direct extension of choice to affected individuals, households, or communities. Participation includes, on this view, four levels or types of activities:

- "Dissemination" refers to the one-way transfer of information, in this case, from project staff to the affected population. Providing early and accurate information to displaced persons (DPs) allays fears, dispels misconceptions, and builds trust, providing a foundation for collaboration between DPs and project authorities.
- "Consultation" refers to two-way transfer of information or joint discussion between project staff and the affected population. Systematic consultation implies a sharing of ideas. Bank experience shows that consultation often yields the best resettlement alternatives, fruitful procedures for continued participation, and independent information on actual conditions or implementation.
- "Collaboration" refers to joint decisionmaking through membership in committees, tribunals, or other formal or informal bodies. The DPs and their representatives not only are consulted but also have a voice in decisionmaking.
- "Extension of choice" refers to the transfer of decisionmaking power to the people affected (for example, providing DPs with options for their rehabilitation, among which they choose). Participation, in this sense, involves empowerment and represents a step by which DPs resume responsibility for their lives. Extension of choice may be more relevant in projects involving physical relocation or economic rehabilitation than in projects that have not greatly disrupted peoples' lives.

These dimensions often occur, and should occur, during resettlement planning and implementation in an iterative, rather than a sequential, fashion. For example, an initial dissemination of information to the potentially affected public usually begins the participatory process, because this information is necessary for informed consultations. Subsequent dissemination of resettlement plans (RPs), for example, helps to ensure that information obtained through consultations has been considered appropriately and accurately, leading to further refinement of those plans through additional consultation. By the time of project preparation, consultation and collaboration become more significant, as people can contribute to the design of the project and its implementation, especially regarding the aspects that affect them most directly. Finally, participation in decisionmaking usually occurs during the later stages of project planning and implementation.

The Importance of Participation

Participation is important because the success of resettlement depends in part on the responsiveness of the people affected. A fundamental objective of OP 4.12 is to assist DPs *in their efforts* to improve, or at least restore, their incomes and living standards. The DPs must themselves be able and willing participants if they are to return to productivity and resume responsibility for their lives. Providing appropriate mechanisms for participation is likely to benefit the project—it decreases the likelihood of delays, or even cancellations, which may occur when people are forced to participate outside the project (for example, in the media or in the courts).

> *Project example:* In India, the Upper Krishna Project (Loan [Ln] 3050; Credit [Cr] 2010) long failed to provide participatory forums for DPs. As a consequence, 96 percent of DPs had taken their cases to court by 1997. The courts generally doubled the compensation offered by the government. After 1997, participation and compensation increased, and the number of court cases decreased.

Participation plays an important role in resettlement operations for many reasons:

- Information allays fears. In the absence of information, rumor and interpretation hold sway. Such misinformation can create fears about what may happen once the project gets under way. Calibrated information programs help fill the void that gives rise to misinformation and apprehension.
- Consultation provides some of the detail that planners cannot foresee. Land acquisition and displacement often generate a wide variety of impacts, even within the same project. Consultation helps identify impacts, sources of vulnerabilities, and the people and groups likely to be affected.

125

- Similarly, because the DPs know their economic, social, and physical surroundings best, consultation is useful in formulating resettlement options that balance the DPs' needs and capabilities with the technical requirements of the options.
- Consultation helps avoid unnecessary and costly development of options that people do not want.

Project example: In Thailand, the Pak Mun Hydroelectric Project (Ln 3423) started to develop a relocation site, complete with an irrigation system and model houses. These facilities were being introduced next to a reservoir built in an earlier project, at some distance from the affected houses. But no DPs at all moved to the relocation site, as they preferred to move short distances from their previous homes.

Project example: In Guatemala, the Chixoy Hydroelectric Project (Ln 1605) built houses in closely spaced rows, neglecting to leave room for household gardens. The DPs refused to move into the houses, and the project was compelled to offer alternative housing with room for gardens.

Collaboration helps to verify empirical facts, such as the identity of the people affected or the amount of assets to be acquired, and helps to make delivery of entitlements and services transparent.

Collaboration is essential to reaching consensus on issues not subject to technical solutions. Such issues include negotiated valuation standards in the absence of markets; the acceptability of substitute sites or other assets; bases for social integration of DPs into host communities; and legitimization for the project, itself.

Participation per se can have a powerful impact on perceptions and behaviors. In the resettlement context, the participation of DPs in decisions affecting their lives helps diminish risk aversion and perceptions of acute vulnerability, thus reducing the dependency of DPs and the incidence of failure to adapt to their new surroundings.

Finally, participation engenders commitment or ownership, increasing the likelihood that resettlement programs will operate satisfactorily and sustainably once assistance from the project ends.

Issues in Consultation and Participation

Although participatory approaches contribute significantly to resettlement success, some practical issues may arise. Because approaches often need to be tailored to fit widely varying circumstances, only limited guidance can be offered regarding these issues. Nonetheless, task teams can improve the efficiency of

7

project preparation (and often project performance) if they take steps to avoid or manage issues such as the following:

- *How can participation be structured efficiently?* Participatory processes can be time- and labor-intensive, but project preparation usually has a restrictive time line. Initiating participatory processes at the earliest feasible opportunity will reduce pressure on the project preparation time line.
- *How can a meaningful participatory process be ensured?* Effective participation provides people with an opportunity to express their interests and concerns and suggest alternatives and options. Current measures of participation, however, are typically formal and minimal: they emphasize the numbers of meetings and participants, instead of the quality, content, and impact of interaction. Participation should not become just one more thing to check off on the list of things to do.
- *How can sufficiently representative participation be ensured?* Participation is frequently constrained by issues of representation. Who should legitimately represent others can be difficult to establish. The desire to represent others may heighten conflict or impede compromise. Alternatively, compromise, as part of project participation, may lead to claims of false representation or new demands from others.
- *What happens if people make poor decisions?* As OP 4.12 recognizes, participation ultimately involves decisionmaking and responsibility for decisions. But DPs may fail to participate according to plan. They may change their minds about resettlement options. They may decide on short-term rather than long-term goals. And they may choose poorly—they may favor improvement of living standards over income restoration, even though by most measures successful resettlement programs emphasize the latter.

Project example: In Brazil, in the Itaparica Resettlement and Irrigation Project (Ln 2883), Polo Sindical, the main NGO representing the affected people, insisted that land-based resettlement next to the reservoir was the only acceptable option. But the costs of preparing substandard lands for irrigated agriculture proved to be exorbitant (almost $250,000 per household [all dollar amounts are current U.S. dollars]). Incomes from irrigated plots were still insufficient and had to be supplemented with additional income assistance and with subsidies for irrigation water. However, direct dialogue with the affected people might have identified other, feasible alternatives.

- *How can the borrower support the participatory process?* Officials may be biased against participatory processes if they believe they already know

7

what is needed at the local level. In the extreme case, attempts by the Bank to promote collaborative decisionmaking can be seen as political interference by some borrowers. Conversely, the involvement of government officials in consultative processes may be perceived as intimidating by some DPs in some areas.

Participation cannot be entirely structured, thoroughly planned, or politically stage-managed. In the Bank's experience, the assumption that people cannot or would not find alternatives for obtaining information if denied formal channels for participation has often proven erroneous. Without an open and flexible process of communication, people are likely to view resettlement design as inadequate and to shift their participation to the courts or the streets. Under such circumstances, even otherwise proficient project plans may become subject to delays, overruns, or outright cancellation, all of which might have been avoided.

Consultation and Participation in the Project Cycle

The consultation and participation matrix in the annex to this chapter provides general guidelines for incorporating participation in resettlement planning and implementation.[1] The following sections provide elaboration, relating participation to the various stages of the project cycle. In practice, the stages of participation themselves often overlap, coming together at various times in project preparation and implementation. Participation is a fluid process. The specific form, sequence, and content of participatory processes vary significantly by country, project, and local environmental and social factors. Accordingly, the time and funding required for participatory resettlement processes can vary substantially (see CD Appendix 21, "Possible Participation Outputs," for examples of participation at each stage of the project cycle).

Early initiation of participation helps synchronize local contributions over the project cycle.

Participatory processes begin as early in the project cycle as is feasible. Delay in disclosure of basic information increases the likelihood that misinformation will generate uncertainty, distrust, and possibly hostility among those rumored to be affected. Therefore, a good practice is to have the initial information campaign describe and justify the project, explain why resettlement is necessary, give a preliminary assessment of its impacts, and disclose the fundamental principles on which the resettlement program will be designed, the procedures for assessing compensation, and the timetable for any displacement and relocation.

Oral or visual presentations may be necessary to inform the illiterate. Special efforts may be necessary to reach isolated groups and vulnerable populations.

7

If the project authority has little experience in conducting local dissemination campaigns, it can hire a local organization familiar with this work. In that case, a representative of the project authority should attend the meetings to provide any needed clarification of technical matters. The information dissemination campaign includes any host communities, if these have already been identified.

Deciding when to initiate participatory processes is complicated. Bank borrowers have legitimate reasons to undertake some project-related activities and agenda-setting functions before inviting public involvement. Potential projects must be identified, usually with an initial emphasis on technical criteria. Feasibility assessments can be kept confidential to some extent if disclosure is likely to provoke unrest or high levels of uncertainty early in the process. In some projects, it may be necessary to undertake steps such as site selection and census taking at a very early stage in order to prevent land speculation, in-migration, or various forms of rent seeking. In such instances, project agencies would do well to devise culturally and politically appropriate approaches to dissemination, consultation, and participation.

Participatory processes shift over the project cycle.

Ideally, resettlement planning and implementation will involve most or all of the activities identified in Table 7.1. In many cases, participation deepens over the course of the project cycle (the steps are the same as in the consultation and participation matrix in the annex).

Project Identification

Step 1: Identification of Stakeholders and Analysis

Project identification entails collection and analysis of basic information from stakeholders. In this effort, the borrower, with the task team, identifies the groups with an interest in the investment, along with their composition, concerns, and potential influence on resettlement design and outcomes. Cast broadly, stakeholders usually include the project sponsor; other government agencies involved in the project; the people to be adversely affected by the operation; those who will benefit; and others, such as civil society groups with a possible interest in the project or the implications of resettlement.

Stakeholder analysis provides an initial list of local organizations and leaders whose cooperation may be necessary or important in resettlement planning, implementation, and monitoring. This initial list also gives a preliminary idea of the support for the project and of possible obstacles. Furthermore, the preliminary analysis of probable impacts helps in assessing the viability of project design and identifying potential sources of conflict and ways to mitigate them.

Table 7.1 Participation and the Project Cycle

Project cycle	Steps
Identification	1. Identification of stakeholders and analysis
Preparation (Concept Paper)	2. Preliminary dissemination of information; consultation
	3. Gathering of information (census and socioeconomic survey)
	4. Dissemination of information (socioeconomic surveys, social assessment, preliminary RPs, options, and entitlements) and consultations with DPs, their representatives, and local NGOs; participation on decisions regarding resettlement sites and income restoration options.
Preappraisal	5. Preparation of the RP (exploration of site and income restoration options)
Appraisal	6. Finalization of the RP; dissemination of information
Implementation	7a. Participation in committees
	7b. Participation in delivery of assistance
	7c. Participation in monitoring
Completion	8. Participation in evaluation

Note: RP, resettlement plan.

Project Preparation

Step 2: Preliminary Dissemination of Information and Consultation

Once basic project information is available, the project team can begin to promote dissemination, consultation, and collaboration. The earliest document containing information related to resettlement is the Integrated Safeguards Data Sheet (ISDS). The ISDS should be made publicly available by sending it to the Bank InfoShop before the first formal review of the proposed operation is held by Bank management, generally the project concept review meeting.

Participatory approaches should fit the project's scale and nature.

In large-scale projects, whether urban or rural, the large number of displaced or affected people makes the quality of participatory processes important. Many people feel intimidated by large gatherings, meaning that the voices and demands heard there are not likely to be representative. The remedy is disaggregation, arranging for consultations on a smaller scale or supplementing general proceedings with focus group consultations.

Project example: In China, in the Shanghai Sewerage Project (Ln 2794; Cr 1779), strenuous efforts were made to disseminate information. Project offices and local governments used pamphlets, booklets, posters, films, and neighborhood and individual meetings. These media were used to inform people of a wide range of issues, such as compensation policy and rates, entitlements, and relocation schemes and schedules. The project then sponsored neighborhood meetings to inform people and allow them to air issues. These meetings were followed up with individual visits, as required. Finally, the project team published the phone numbers, locations, and working hours of both the project office and the grievance committee, giving people better access to project authorities.

Project example: Also in China, the Guangzhou City Center Transport Project (Ln 4329) strongly emphasized participation and transparency. Information on policy and entitlements was disseminated through booklets and pamphlets (more than 10,000 were printed), large and small meetings, work unit meetings, and door-to-door consultation by resettlement staff. Information on resettlement was also widely disseminated via radio, television, and newspapers. Resettlement offices were established throughout the city. Telephone hot lines were set up for anyone to call for more information or consultation.

Project example: In India, the Mumbai Urban Transport Project (Ln 4665; Cr 3662) held large public meetings to explain the goals of the project and the fact that the alignment of the arteries had yet to be finalized. Although these meetings helped allay fears of mass relocation, the large public meetings were also followed by small-group consultations. These consultations were facilitated by a local nongovernmental organization (NGO), and they provided a forum for answering specific answers.

In linear projects, treating participatory processes uniformly may be impossible. Some linear projects run across two or more geographic, cultural, or linguistic zones, requiring adjustments in participatory strategies or methods.

In rural areas, the DPs are often too dispersed to gather together and communicate among themselves. Often they are culturally or linguistically diverse, as well. One remedy is to work with smaller groups; doing so provides a greater degree of geographic, cultural, and linguistic opportunity to participate. Another method, appropriate for highway or road projects, is to convene local community meetings to discuss the route.

Project example: In India, the Third National Highways Authority of India Project (Ln 4559) team convened local meetings with villagers to discuss the proposed routing of the rehabilitated highway. These meetings involved both DPs and other residents and often provided useful local information for the highway engineers. In one village, for example, the villagers preferred to route the highway around the settlement, rather than widen the road through it. They actually walked the engineers along their proposed alignment and noted that most of the land that would be taken already belonged to the government. This meant that land acquisition costs would be no greater than those already budgeted. The project engineers accepted the suggested alignment and redrew their plans accordingly.

In projects involving restriction of access to resources in nature parks or other legally designated conservation areas, an inherently participatory process framework should be prepared. In these circumstances, the cooperation of the local people is needed to achieve sustainable resource use, as they know the area and use its resources. People must be consulted meaningfully if they are to accept limitations on their access to resources. Moreover, the local population can usually suggest feasible alternatives to illegal use and are often the most efficient enforcers of such restrictions.

Representativeness is a concern in consulting with local notables.

A good practice is to have project agencies consult, formally or informally, with leaders and representatives of the affected groups or communities. Particular attention must be paid at this stage to determining the legitimacy of the leaders and representatives as spokespeople accepted by the DPs. This initial consultation solicits early reactions to the project and to tentative resettlement arrangements. The purpose of these discussions is to reexamine the preliminary concepts and premises of project design so that local preferences are addressed, displacement will be minimized, and adverse social impacts will be reduced. Efforts to reduce the impacts must balance and consider the benefits and trade-offs of various technical, economic, and social criteria. The project authority should keep a record of the meetings, including a detailed list of recommendations and concerns, along with project action on these concerns. This information will make it easier to assess the extent of local participation.

NGOs can represent DP interests, but their acceptability to the DPs should be verified.

Affected people often trust NGOs to represent their interests. NGOs usually have more knowledge of, and experience with, the relevant legal frameworks than the DPs. NGOs also know the best ways to deal with project and government staff and can advocate for the interests and positions of DPs. Care must be taken to ensure that NGOs represent the DPs' interests, rather than their own agendas. A good practice is for the project team to meet with NGOs and DPs together, to minimize the risk that the NGOs will fail to represent the DPs' interests.

The media can be effective allies in information dissemination.

Local and familiar media can be used for dissemination and consultation. Media representatives can be invited to public meetings at village or community centers, schools, places of worship, or other places where people usually gather. The media representatives can be given the project information, printed in local languages, that has been disseminated to all groups, including those often marginalized in local deliberative processes (such as indigenous peoples, ethnic minorities, or women). In dealing with the media, the project authorities should emphasize that many aspects of resettlement planning at the project preparation stage are preliminary and may change significantly before final designs are approved and implementation begins. For projects likely to attract considerable media attention throughout the implementation process, the borrower may decide to assign a liaison officer to handle media requests for further information.

Step 3: Gathering of Information

Consultation during project preparation can take various forms. Scoping the environmental impact assessment provides one opportunity for wide participation. Subsequently, the population census of DPs and the socioeconomic survey give other opportunities for consultation.

Scoping the environmental assessment provides a useful forum for participation.

While initial stakeholder analysis identifies the various interested groups, scoping the environmental assessment is an opportunity to involve these key stakeholders early in the project design process. Government officials, technical experts, academics, and NGOs all have their own expertise and can help define terms of reference for the environmental studies. The affected people can provide information on potential impacts of alternative designs, including information on land tenure arrangements. This approach not only taps into the existing pool of national expertise, but also provides a forum for meaningful consultation on the issues that may arise during project design and implementation.

> **Project example:** In Lesotho, the Highland Water Project (Ln 4339) team invited government officials and technical staff, academic researchers, and NGO representatives to the scoping exercise for the environmental assessment. The participants formed groups according to their substantive expertise (for example, terrestrial, aquatic, or social) and identified and ranked the key issues that, in their experience, they thought might arise in the project. The substantive groups presented

7

their ranked lists of key issues at the plenary. The following day, the workshop as a whole harmonized the lists prepared by experts into a master list of key issues that integrated all sectors. The master list became the basis for the terms of reference for the environmental studies. In this way, the project not only defined the major issues, but also involved key stakeholder groups in this task.

The resettlement census and other surveys provide an opportunity to consult the directly affected people.

The establishment of entitlements and the design of RPs require a census, an asset inventory, and a socioeconomic survey, conducted in tandem or separately (see chapter 10 for details.).

The census identifies and enumerates individuals to be affected and is often combined with an inventory of fixed assets to be expropriated. The asset inventory, in turn, lists all the immobile property that will have to be acquired. It also records the use and condition of that property and may establish a preliminary valuation of the affected assets. Preparatory work done before the census (or various feasibility studies) sometimes provides an opportunity to disseminate information and to record views about the possible impact of the investment in local areas.

> *Project example:* In Senegal, the Regional Hydropower Development Project (Cr 2970, Cr 2971, Cr 2972) team convened meetings in each province traversed by the power lines. The initial meetings, chaired by the district prefects, informed all local officials, including village heads, about the nature and timing of the project and its probable local impact. Subsequently, each village head chaired local meetings to convey the same information to the populace, and field surveyors were instructed to inform landowners of the reason they were surveying in the area and of the probable area of impact of the transmission lines.

The purpose of the socioeconomic survey is broader. This survey provides the baseline information on income and socioeconomic indicators in the affected population and helps identify and develop a range of preliminary resettlement options. Socioeconomic information is gathered to determine the social dynamics likely to hinder or help the effectiveness of resettlement measures. The survey, then, solicits a much wider range of information not captured in a census or in an asset inventory. Accordingly, the survey uses a mix of both quantitative and qualitative methods to

- Record intrahousehold and community divisions of labor;
- Record information regarding sources of income or access to resources;

7

- Identify groups especially vulnerable to impoverishment or marginalization as a result of land acquisition or displacement;
- Identify social relationships and local institutions that DPs use and trust;
- Assess the acceptability of measures proposed to restore or improve incomes and living standards;
- Identify DP needs and aspirations; and
- Record basic education and health information, including access to schools and health services.

Key-informant interviews can provide important overview information.

Surveys for quantitative analysis provide only some of the necessary information. Consultation is required to identify and gain an understanding of the role of leadership, the mechanisms of informal intrahousehold and community relationships, and the social impacts of the project. Local government officials, traditional elders, or others with similar status may speak with authority on resettlement issues, and their words may shape the perceptions and influence the actions of other DPs.

Focus groups can provide vitally important local information.

Bank experience shows that formal surveys of social impacts have frequently failed to capture the productive role of women or the prevalence of common property that supports community living standards. Quantitative surveys alone do not capture attitudinal and cultural nuances. Other methods, such as focus group discussions (semistructured interviews of small groups composed by gender, age, income levels, occupations, interests, etc.), help fill this information void. A good practice is to conduct personal interviews with affected people and with experts and leaders with first-hand knowledge of local conditions. The findings of these interviews can be incorporated in the socioeconomic survey, to complement and qualitatively validate the quantitative findings.

Focus groups can be invaluable in identifying people most likely to be vulnerable to hardship and those whose voices are not likely to be heard in the project process. Focus group discussions allow people with similar life circumstances to voice their concerns among peers. In many cases, focus group participants will speak more thoughtfully and freely than they would in a larger, open meeting attended by a wider variety of DPs or officials.

Step 4: Dissemination of Information and Preparation for Participation

The census and socioeconomic survey together identify the extent of impacts and establish baseline data, providing the necessary foundation for resettlement planning.

Once collected and analyzed, information can be shared to validate results and foster public involvement.

A good practice is for the project team to disseminate the census and survey results to the DPs. This exercise in communication may require the establishment of a public information unit. To be effective, the unit would have to be accessible to the DPs. Depending on the local culture, information may best be disseminated through various media (printed, visual, or oral). In fact, a combination of media is recommended, because each approach has its own advantages and may reach a different segment of the potentially affected population. Meetings with communities is a standard method of communication; each meeting would cover a neighborhood or village. Television and radio are best suited to communicating general information. Printed materials allow for repeated reference whenever questions arise. In some areas, social workers can answer specific questions and provide more detailed information when visiting households.

Project agencies may be tempted to use census and survey information to produce a blueprint for resettlement. Therefore, a good practice is to emphasize that consultation is needed at this stage to help define feasible resettlement options and to discourage resistance to resettlement or to the broader project. Specifically, at this stage, consultation with DPs helps the project agencies formulate options for replacement land, community resettlement sites (if needed), income restoration measures, and so on. Consultation on replacement land will give the DPs an opportunity to identify desirable parcels of land on the basis of fertility, location, or other preferred attributes. The formulation of income restoration measures may require consultations with DPs, local government agencies, and NGOs to identify the range of alternative opportunities available and the skills required to take advantage of these opportunities. Identifying community resettlement sites, by contrast, requires community consultations and site visits, as well as consultation with host communities. More significantly, consulting DPs about their options may diminish their sense of dependency and risk aversion and increase their responsiveness and commitment to chosen options.

> *Project example:* In the Lao People's Democratic Republic, the IFC Sepon Gold Mine Project (Project 10626) team extensively consulted the multiethnic population in the project area to identify appropriate relocation sites for three villages of 28 households. Site selection balanced the desire of the DPs to be close to their farmland (and the main road) with the need for general safety in the area (blasting and heavy truck traffic). Consultations resulted in the inhabitants of one village settling within the boundaries of another existing village and the inhabitants of the other two villages selecting a new site. The company prepared the site, removed unexploded ordnance, built houses, and installed

7

potable water and irrigation. It also established a trust to support public health, agricultural extension, and small-enterprise development for the entire population.

Project example: In China, the Yunnan Environment Project (Ln 4055; Cr 2892) supported participatory planning for economic rehabilitation. At village meetings, the villagers participated in planning how to use compensation funds. They decided to improve their power supply system, repair the irrigation and drainage system, and build pumping stations and a village center.

This stage of consultation may be protracted, depending on geographic distances between DPs and host communities, seasonal access, cultural and social issues, and other factors. Culturally distinct and geographically remote DPs are often costly to interview because they are scattered in small groups and difficult to reach. In Bank experience, however, these DPs may be most vulnerable to impoverishment, because they are socially or politically marginalized and their relationships with each other and to their physical environment are often not well understood by project planners. Therefore, consultation with such groups is important.

7

DPs commonly make decisions on the basis of short-term considerations.

As the project evolves, consultation is likely to shift gradually into collaboration and participation. In the blueprint approach, DPs simply choose among presented options or are given no options at all. A more participatory approach incorporates the DPs' preferences into the formulation of the options, which is important in developing a functional RP. The RP can be executed much more effectively if it reflects choices made by the DPs themselves, but the DPs need to be given time to formulate their choices. The choices they make at the earliest stages of project dissemination are likely to be more risk-averse than those they might make after community consultations and the identification of alternatives. When feasible, DPs should be offered sufficient time and opportunity to consider options before making final, binding choices.

Project example: In China, the Guangzhou City Center Highway Project (Ln 4329) team developed a computerized resettlement and rehabilitation information system to enable DPs to select apartments. The DPs could select from eight resettlement sites by scrolling through a computer program (30 terminals were set up in the five project offices, all connected through a main server). As long as units were available, the DPs could change their minds as often as they wished after visiting the apartments. One DP reportedly changed his mind 20 times.

Project Preappraisal

Step 5: Preparation of the Resettlement Plan

The census and survey, supplemented with other interviews, inform the draft RP. If the resettlement process is to be *responsive* to DP concerns, however, some aspects of the resettlement and rehabilitation process must wait to be fully addressed after project appraisal or negotiations. To promote a responsive process, the RP must specify venues for consultation with affected people, not only during planning, but also during implementation. The RP therefore describes decisionmaking responsibilities and procedures for making resettlement decisions, mechanisms for participatory planning, mechanisms for making modifications during implementation, and grievance mechanisms available to DPs.

Project Appraisal

Step 6: Finalization of the Resettlement Plan and Dissemination of Information

Submission of a draft RP acceptable to the Bank is normally a condition of project appraisal. Even before the draft RP is formally submitted for Bank acceptance, however, a good practice is to share the document with various community leaders and with the local agencies responsible for implementation. The draft RP (or draft policy framework or draft process framework) should be made available in the resettlement agency office, the project office, government offices of the borrower, and other locations in the project area that can be conveniently accessed by the DPs, other affected people, and local NGOs and in a language and format that is understandable to these groups. The draft RP must also be sent to the Bank InfoShop and the Bank PIC in the project country. The ISDS should also be updated at this time and sent to the Bank InfoShop. Making the draft RP (or other resettlement instrument) public is a precondition for appraisal.

If the project requires a resettlement policy framework or process framework, rather than an RP, then the appropriate draft resettlement instrument should be made locally available and also be sent to the Bank InfoShop and the host country PIC. In these instances, it may not always be possible to disseminate a policy framework at the local level because the location of the impacts is not yet known. The draft resettlement instrument should be made available at government offices within the administrative unit where the project is known to be located.

To supplement the draft RP, the Bank should encourage the resettlement agency to produce a resettlement information booklet that summarizes the key impacts, compensation rates, entitlements, rehabilitation options, grievance procedures, and other information of greatest interest to DPs. This booklet should be proactively distributed to the DPs in their villages by the local government or the resettlement agency. (See CD Appendix 16 for an example of a resettlement information booklet from a Bank project.)

In principle, clearance of the RP by the Bank technical and legal departments binds the borrower to meet contractual obligations. The final RP, accordingly, reflects the final range of options presented to the DPs and, usually, their final choices. If final choices have not been made, the RP should indicate how and when choices are to be finalized. Although preliminary consultations can be group based, final resettlement options must be chosen by individual DPs, heads of households, or (in the case of community entitlements) affected communities. Such choices always involve elements of risk and responsibility.

Before RPs are submitted to the Bank for review and clearance, another good practice is for task teams to ascertain that DPs

- Have been presented with options consistent with OP 4.12 objectives;
- Have been adequately informed about the range of options available (the options must not have been misrepresented);
- Are aware that formal acceptance of options may be irreversible; and
- Are aware of the responsibilities they assume when accepting options.

In the case of compensation or replacement land, the DP's acceptance generally extinguishes the liability of the borrower. In the case of alternative income restoration, responsibility is likely to remain shared, and clear assignment of responsibility is likely to be more difficult. Therefore, good practice is to have the RP describe procedures for altering income restoration provisions during implementation, along with procedures to extend protective measures when failure to achieve income restoration is attributable to factors beyond the control of the DPs. Having been given a range of choices, DPs may prefer the advantages of a certain location or situation (for example, proximity to relatives or home villages, or relocation as part of an existing community) over a narrow emphasis on income restoration. The objective of OP 4.12 is improvement or at least restoration of incomes and living standards, so a good practice is to make a concerted effort to provide DPs with options that will allow them to achieve these objectives. But the OP does not guarantee indefinite income maintenance; nor does it require DPs to sacrifice preferred living standards. In a resettlement context, these obligations are part of what "choice" means.

Project example: In China, some of the people affected by construction of the Jiangya dam and reservoir in the Yangtze Basin Water Resources Project (Ln 3874; Cr 2710) elected to move away to alternative resettlement sites, while others elected to move back onto hillsides adjacent to the reservoir. With time, most of those remaining in the area began to have difficulty making a living and decided they would like to join the ones who had moved away. Although measures required by the RP had

7

already been implemented, the project authorities agreed to help these families by identifying available land for their use and partially compensating them for their additional housing and moving expenses.

Once the RP has been finalized, it should once again be distributed to the same set of locations as the draft RP, including the Bank InfoShop and the host country PIC. Final resettlement policy frameworks and process frameworks follow the same distribution as that of their draft versions. The ISDS should also be finalized and sent to the Bank InfoShop.

Project Implementation

Step 7a: Participation in Committees

The quality of resettlement and rehabilitation depends on the quality of implementation, which in turn is often enhanced by supportive and responsive participation. A minimal step is to ensure that project agencies charged with implementing the RP systematically consult the affected communities throughout implementation. Another method to increase DP support and responsiveness is to ensure that the DPs are represented in formal committees established for land valuation or purchase, grievance redress, and other purposes.

Project example: In Brazil, the Nova Jaguaribara Project (a non-Bank project) authorities constituted a committee of project officials, DPs, and representatives from local and state agencies. The committee met quarterly and heard the reports of its technical subcommittees, which took up specific issues. The existence of the committee helped maintain institutional coordination, because representatives from the concerned agencies participated in the decisions. Also, participation of the state environmental control agency and the Public Works Minister made modifications possible in the original basic design, and these changes were implemented immediately.

Project example: In Cambodia, the Phnom Penh Power Rehabilitation Project (Cr 2782) team created local grievance committees composed of the legal authority in the municipality, a representative of an independent and reputable NGO, and a village elder. All grievances were referred to the committee, and the company based its subsequent negotiations with landowners on this committee's recommendations. The committee members received a small honorarium for each case.

Project example: In India, the National Highways Authority of India Project (Ln 4559) team established valuation and grievance committees whose members were government officers, Authority officials, and DP representatives.

Step 7b: Participation in Delivery of Assistance

In many projects, a good practice is to enlist DPs for the actual implementation, either directly or through NGOs. (As OP 4.12 suggests, local institutions and representative organizations can be used to represent the interests of DPs: "Experience has shown that local NGOs often provide valuable assistance and ensure viable community participation" [Annex A, endnote 4].) At the community level, local organizations, such as NGOs accepted by DPs, often have a deeper understanding of local social and environmental conditions and may already enjoy the support of the affected population. Using local institutions may also help preserve these institutions or help them adapt to new circumstances. At the level of individual DPs, incentives that enable DPs to reconstruct their own housing where they desire may ensure acceptance, and hiring DPs to assist in preparing resettlement sites or project infrastructure may help create a greater sense of local ownership. After resettlement sites have been prepared, a good practice is to provide incentives to encourage DPs to look after the maintenance of community services or facilities, including schools, water and sanitation facilities, and irrigation works.

Participating in implementation does not mean that DPs only contribute labor; they can also take control of decisionmaking through community contracting of necessary goods and services and other activities involving decisions and management tasks. (The DPs could be hirers as well as hirees in different situations, depending on their capacity and interest.)

7

> **Project example:** In Brazil, the project team of the Salto Caxias Hydropower Project (a non-Bank project) established residents' associations of 50–60 members for each of the 19 areas where the DPs were to be relocated. The associations participated in the construction of houses and communal buildings (for example, warehouses, recreational areas) and directly negotiated agreements with local supporting agencies. The residents' associations are also responsible for the management of each resettlement project once the project authority fulfills its obligations.

> **Project example:** Also in Brazil, the Urban Development and Water Resource Management Project (also referred to as the PROURB Project [Projeto de Desenvolvimento Urbano], a non-Bank project) sponsored residential house construction through community associations of DPs. Each family contributed 24 working hours a week over the course of 18 months to construct 200 houses. More than 80 percent of the future inhabitants participated in this work, and they were satisfied with their housing. Equally important is the fact that some inhabitants learned new skills, such as masonry, while others, especially the construction supervisors, were able to secure employment in other municipal or private projects.

Project example: Also in Brazil, the Nova Jaguaribara Project (a non-Bank project) established a development fund. The fund received income from each of the nine affected municipalities, which contributed 1 percent of the royalties they received from the power project. An NGO skilled in enterprise development used the development fund to support the creation of new companies and oversee their business program. The first small companies specialized in products previously imported into the area, such as brooms and cooking pots. The Nova Jaguaribara Project submitted various proposals to a vote by the DPs. Specifically, the project asked the DPs to vote on the delimitation of the area to be used for the new city to which they would be relocated, the architectural style for the new church, and the preferred style for the new cemetery. While the DPs showed no unanimity on any of these matters, a majority vote determined the decision, and all parties were bound to accept the democratic outcome.

Step 7c: Participation in Monitoring

Another good practice is to include mechanisms for systematic internal, as well as external, monitoring (see chapter 10). If monitoring teams include representatives of the DPs, then monitoring is more likely to accurately reflect DPs' reactions and perceptions. In phased resettlements, feedback from initial phases of relocation or income restoration can be used by project managers to improve subsequent phases.

Project Completion

Step 8: Participation in Evaluation

In many projects, post-implementation evaluation is likely to require consultation with DPs. Also, DPs may be directly involved in planning and carrying out this evaluation—their input is especially valuable in the areas of fundamental resettlement objectives (such as restoration of incomes and living standards) and follow-up plans or remedial actions.

The Role of the Bank in Supporting Participation

A critical aspect of an effective RP is the provision of an adequate budget to ensure compliance with its terms. Accordingly, the Bank frequently extends financing to cover many costs of resettlement. In terms of participation, the financing of technical assistance may be particularly relevant. Technical assistance is normally provided to improve the technical or administrative capacity of project agencies. Technical assistance can include direct assistance for incorporating participatory methods in resettlement planning. Technical assistance can also include financial

---

Box 7.1   Disclosure Requirements for Bank Resettlement Documents

The first document containing information related to resettlement is the Integrated Safeguards Data Sheet (ISDS). The ISDS should be made publicly available by sending it to the Bank InfoShop after the first formal review of the proposed operation is held by Bank management, generally the project concept review meeting.

The second document requiring disclosure is the draft resettlement instrument (RP, policy framework, or process framework). Making the draft resettlement instrument public is a precondition for appraisal. The draft resettlement instrument must be made available at locations that are convenient to the DPs and other local stakeholders in a form and language understandable to these groups. The draft resettlement instrument is also sent to the Bank InfoShop and the Bank project information center (PIC) in the project country. The ISDS should also be updated at this time and sent to the Bank InfoShop.

If the project requires a resettlement policy framework, it may not be possible to disseminate it at the local level because the location of the impacts is not yet known. The draft resettlement instrument should be made available at government offices within the administrative unit where the project is known to be located.

Once the resettlement instrument has been finalized, it should once again be distributed to the same set of locations as that of the draft RP, including the Bank InfoShop and the host country PIC. Final resettlement policy frameworks and process frameworks follow the same distribution as their draft versions. The ISDS should also be finalized and sent to the Bank InfoShop.

(See the World Bank's 2002 Disclosure Policy paragraphs 30 [ISDS] and 34 [RP] and Disclosure Handbook paragraphs 37 [ISDS] and 40 [RP] for official requirements and guidance.)

7

assistance for training in consultation and participation, stakeholder analysis, and related methodologies for resettlement staff, local NGOs, village leaders, the DPs' representatives, and others. (Additional financial resources may be available through trust funds, grant facilities, or special arrangements.)

The Bank can also help borrowers enhance consultation and participation by ensuring these issues are included in the policy, legal, and institutional frameworks for resettlement. This is particularly relevant for new member countries and for countries recovering from major conflicts or other forms of political or legal disruption.

Finally, the Bank supports participation through its disclosure policy and requirements for project processing. For easy reference and access, the various steps and requirements for disclosing resettlement documents are summarized in Box 7.1.

Note

1. For more detailed information on methods and tools for enhancing participation in Bank projects, consult *The World Bank Participation Sourcebook* (1996).

Annex: Consultation and Participation Matrix

Project cycle and steps	How	Output	Who	Remarks
Identification				
1. Identification of stakeholders; analysis	Identify stakeholders Inform borrower of Bank OP 4.12 and discuss borrower's policies, plans, or preliminary ideas for the resettlement sites, income restoration strategies, institutional and legal arrangements, and so forth Carry out field visits and preliminary assessment of potential impacts: sites, natural resources, economic and livelihood situations, and so forth Review demographic data and other references for additional information	List of stakeholders and potential impacts; assessment of the relative influence on the project of the following of stakeholders: • government • project beneficiaries • affected groups (DPs) • host communities • other interested groups (NGOs, private sector, and so forth) • Bank • other donors	*Borrower*—Is the responsibility mainly of government officials or team; local administration or government unit plays key role; local consultants under a trained social scientist can be hired to assist *Bank*—Advice for overall effort provided by TT, with assistance from regional social development unit, particularly as related to Bank OP 4.12 (TT should also have discussions with selected stakeholders and visit the field)	Undertake this exercise as part of preliminary project design in most cases Refer to "Step 1: Identification of Stakeholders and Analysis" in this chapter and *World Bank Participation Sourcebook* (pp. 195–196) for more information on stakeholder analysis

Project cycle and steps	How	Output	Who	Remarks
Preparation (Concept Paper)				
2. Preliminary dissemination of information; consultation	Share information on preliminary project design and resettlement-related impacts and explore alternatives through consultation to minimize resettlement and adverse social impacts; this can be done via • Meetings at town halls, village halls, community halls, schools, and places of worship • Smaller group meetings (groups of families, women, vulnerable groups, or door-to-door if the number of DPs is small; see also step 3) • Distribution of printed information in local languages; dissemination of information via other audiovisual media where appropriate	Informed borrower and Bank TT Documentation of information provided to stakeholders Documentation of information *obtained from* stakeholders (their feedback, concerns, recommendations) Informed stakeholders (regarding project objectives and likely positive and negative social impacts) Record of meetings and consultations with DPs, feedback (from community meetings and from small groups of households, women, other vulnerable groups, and so forth)	Borrower, through same consultants as above or a resettlement unit if it exists Project agencies (or their designees), who consult with local leaders and community representatives	Use local methods, avenues, and mechanisms for consultation as much as possible; ensure that as many people are reached as possible Make a special effort to include isolated and marginalized groups Ensure that participatory approaches fit the scale and nature of the project Be aware that representativeness may be a concern in consulting with local notables and NGOs Use the media as effective allies in information dissemination
	Send the ISDS to the Bank's InfoShop	Written material, visual material, and so forth	The task team	Update the ISDS as project preparation evolves

(continued)

7

(*continued*)

Project cycle and steps	How	Output	Who	Remarks
3. Gathering of information (census and socio-economic survey)	*Quantitative*—Determine location, number, and types of persons and assets potentially affected *Quantitative*—Carry out a socioeconomic survey • To determine the dynamics of communities that will be affected (use systematic data gathering, based on appropriate sampling techniques) • To determine the quantitative aspects (refer to survey requirements in chapter 10) *Qualitative*—Gather relevant social and cultural data, as well as socioeconomic information on people's attitudes, feelings, and preferences; methods include • Focus group discussions (semistructured interviews of small groups composed by gender, age, income levels, occupations, interests, and so forth); particular emphasis is given to responses of women and other vulnerable groups because in many cases they bear the brunt of the relocation • Interviews of affected people • Interviews of experts (including key informants) knowledgeable about the people and area • Observation of participants (can provide key information about the social, institutional, and power dynamics of a community) • Discussions with national and provincial government officials, local institutions, NGOs, religious groups, community groups, private sector, and so forth	Census of DPs (individuals and assets affected) Socioeconomic baseline survey (information pertinent to understanding the community; input needed for RP formulation) Preliminary resettlement options based on social information Preliminary entitlement options based on social information Assessment of most likely negative impacts	Same as above or a contracted team under the guidance and leadership of a trained team leader or social scientist	Integrate information gathering with social assessment where possible Consider using consultants from local universities, NGOs, and others to carry out focus group discussions and interviews with beneficiaries and DPs Refer to *World Bank Participation Sourcebook* (pp. 191–202) for more information on methods and tools for participatory rural appraisal, beneficiary assessment, gender analysis, social assessment, and so forth

Project cycle and steps	How	Output	Who	Remarks
4. Dissemination of information (socioeconomic surveys, social assessment, preliminary RPs, options, and entitlements); preparation for participation	Disseminate information to DPs on survey results; present options for project design, resettlement, and entitlement	Modifications in project design, resettlement, and entitlement based on DP feedback	Project management team and resettlement unit	Refer to "Step 4: Dissemination of Information and Preparation for Participation," in this chapter, for more information
	Consult with DPs, host communities, and other stakeholders to obtain responses, feedback, and preferences	List of feasible options for entitlement packages, resettlement sites, income restoration measures		Verify institutional and budgetary mechanisms for implementation
	Set up public information unit	List of DP choices from available options		Ensure wide coverage of the information and consultation program; document the results of consultations
	Establish concrete logistic and implementation arrangements through consultation	Stationary or mobile public information unit (using media, printed and visual material, oral presentations, and so forth)		

(continued)

7

147

7

(*continued*)

Project cycle and steps	How	Output	Who	Remarks
Preappraisal				
5. Preparation of the RP (exploration of site and income restoration options)	Prepare a draft RP based on the information collected in steps 1–4 In addition to the required information and data for an RP (census, plan, budget, timetable, institutional arrangements, and so forth), include the following: • Strategy or methods for DP participation during implementation of resettlement • Specific timing, location, and personnel for consultation during resettlement • Decisionmaking responsibilities and procedures • Mechanisms or procedures for changing plan provisions during implementation if corrective measures are required Establish mechanism for redressing grievances Send the draft RP and updated ISDS to the InfoShop and send the draft RP to the PIC of the project country	Draft of RP that reflects DP input and consultation (including sets of options, risks, and choices) Grievance redress mechanisms Informed stakeholders	Coordinated by the resettlement unit or the project team; usually prepared with the help of local consultants (as above) and with assistance from resident missions or regional social development unit	Depending on the nature of the project, prepare the RP as a complete document for the whole project from the beginning or as a *rolling RP*, which includes • a resettlement policy framework for the overall project • plans and implementation schedule for the first year of the project • schedule for the next phases of the RP Distribute the draft RP in an accessible place, form, and language for DPs, affected people, and local NGOs

Project cycle and steps	How	Output	Who	Remarks
Appraisal				
6. Finalization of the RP; dissemination of information	Consult and share draft RP with project management team, local officials, community leaders, and DPs to obtain any additional feedback	Verified record of DPs and their assets and losses	Project resettlement unit	Remember that submission of the RP and clearance by the Bank are conditions of appraisal
	Send RP to Bank's regional social development unit and Legal Department for review, discussion, and clearance	Informed DPs (regarding final options)	Bank TT, which is responsible for submitting a draft copy of RP to the Bank and discussing it with Bank reviewers	Inform the borrower that after the loan agreement incorporates the RP, it becomes a legally binding document between the borrower and the Bank and requires the borrower to meet the RP's contractual obligations
	Modify RP as necessary after discussions and resubmit for clearance	Each DP's choice of options		
	Send the final RP and the final ISDS to the InfoShop and send the draft final RP to the PIC of the project country	Informed stakeholders		

7

(*continued*)

(concluded)

Project cycle and steps	How	Output	Who	Remarks
Implementation				
7a. Participation in committees	Instruct project agencies to establish a systematic consultation process	Systematic client consultation to facilitate implementation of RP	Project resettlement unit, with DP committee	Consider using local institutions and NGOs for RP implementation and monitoring; however, these collaborating agencies are to be carefully screened and selected on the basis of experience, competence, and a local presence in the area
	Invite DPs to participate in management and land valuation committees:	Representation and participation of DPs in joint decision-making activities		
	Appoint community resettlement representatives			
	Provide training in RP implementation tasks			Ensure that surrogates are not allowed to make choices or receive or collect compensation (this is to protect women and other vulnerable DPs); exceptions will require strong justification
7b. Participation in delivery of assistance	Where appropriate and feasible, encourage DPs to implement and manage community development activities (construction of houses, schools, and water and sanitation facilities) and other programs	Community-based decisionmaking and management of development activities	Project resettlement unit, with DP committee and with community representatives	To ensure successful resettlement, transfer responsibility from the project resettlement unit to the settlers and local agencies in a timely manner
	Provide training in above	Physical facilities and services		

7

150

Project cycle and steps	How	Output	Who	Remarks
7c. Participation in process management and monitoring	Invite DPs to participate in the grievance and monitoring committees Provide training in above	Representation and involvement of DPs in monitoring and grievance resolution processes Grievances satisfactorily resolved Feedback from initial phases used to improve performance Mechanisms for corrective action functioning effectively	Project resettlement unit, with DP committee and with community representatives External agency periodically monitoring RP implementation	Consider using local institutions and NGOs for RP monitoring; however, these collaborating agencies are to be carefully screened and selected on the basis of experience, competence, and a local presence in the area

Project Completion

Project cycle and steps	How	Output	Who	Remarks
8. Participation in evaluation	Invite DPs to plan and participate in the evaluation of the RP component Provide training in above	Report and remedial action or follow-up steps, if needed	External evaluation team	

Note: The steps described in this matrix are guidelines for preparing and implementing a generic project resettlement action plan; specific steps and the order in which they are undertaken will be determined and affected by project type (for example, dam, power, transport, urban, rural) and the country in which they are being implemented. DP, displaced person; ISDS, Integrated Safeguards Data Sheet; NGO, nongovernmental organization; OP, operational policy; PIC, public information center; RP, resettlement plan; TT, task team.

7

Chapter 8

Income Improvement

This chapter identifies means for enhancing the effectiveness of measures to improve or at least restore incomes after resettlement. After stating the relevant parts of Operational Policy (OP) and Bank Procedure (BP) 4.12, it defines income restoration, discusses its importance, and reviews the issues commonly affecting it. This chapter outlines a generic approach to income restoration and briefly explores the issues of implementing land replacement options in rural areas, strategies for directing project benefits to displaced persons (DPs), other income generation strategies, monitoring, and the adequacy of income restoration measures. (The annex to this chapter discusses the role of microfinance arrangements in helping DPs assume responsibility for their own livelihoods.)

What OP 4.12 Says

OP 4.12 applies when the involuntary taking of land results in "loss of income sources or means of livelihood, whether or not the affected persons must move to another location" (para. 3[a]). In those instances, "displaced persons should be assisted in their efforts to improve their livelihoods and standards of living or at least to restore them, in real terms, to pre-displacement levels or to levels prevailing prior to the beginning of project implementation, whichever is higher" (para. 2[c]).

More particularly, "the resettlement plan or resettlement policy framework also include[s] measures to ensure that displaced persons are

(i) informed about their options and rights pertaining to resettlement;
(ii) consulted on, offered choices among, and provided with technically and economically feasible resettlement alternatives;
(iii) provided prompt and effective compensation at full replacement cost for losses of assets attributable directly to the project;
(iv) provided assistance (such as moving allowances) during relocation;
(v) provided with residential housing, or housing sites, or, as required, agricultural sites with a combination of productive potential, locational advantages, and other factors at least equivalent to the advantages of the old site;
(vi) offered support after displacement, for a transition period, based on a reasonable estimate of the time likely to be needed to restore their livelihood and standards of living; and

(continued)

8

(continued from p. 153)

(vii) provided with development assistance in addition to compensation measures, such as land preparation, credit facilities, training, or job opportunities" (para. 6).

Furthermore, "preference should be given to land-based resettlement strategies for displaced persons whose livelihoods are land-based. . . . [Where the DPs do not desire land or this is not a feasible option,] "non-land-based options built around opportunities for employment or self-employment should be provided in addition to cash compensation for land and other assets lost. The lack of adequate land must be demonstrated and documented to the satisfaction of the Bank" (para. 11).

"Payment of cash compensation for lost assets may be appropriate where (a) livelihoods are land-based but the land taken for the project is a small fraction of the affected asset and the residual is economically viable; (b) active markets for land, housing, and labor exist, displaced persons use such markets, and there is sufficient supply of land and housing; or (c) livelihoods are not land-based" (para. 12).

Whether land-based, non-land-based, or a mix of the two, the resettlement plan includes "a description of the packages of compensation and other resettlement measures that will assist each category of eligible displaced persons to achieve the objectives of the policy. . . . In addition to being technically and economically feasible, the resettlement packages should be compatible with the cultural preferences of the displaced persons, and prepared in consultation with them" (OP 4.12, Annex A, para. 11).

OP 4.12 also requires completion of resettlement activities before construction begins. "The implementation of resettlement activities is linked to the implementation of the investment component of the project to ensure that displacement or restriction of access does not occur before necessary measures for resettlement are in place. For impacts covered in para. 3(a) of this policy [land taking], these measures include provision of compensation and of other assistance required for relocation, prior to displacement, and preparation and provision of resettlement sites with adequate facilities, where required. In particular, taking of land and related assets may take place only after compensation has been paid and, where applicable, resettlement sites and moving allowances have been provided to the displaced persons. For impacts covered in para. 3(b) of this policy [restriction of access], the measures to assist the displaced persons are implemented in accordance with the plan of action as part of the project" (para. 10).

Where restrictions need to be imposed in legally designated parks and protected areas, "the borrower prepares a process framework acceptable to the Bank, describing the participatory process by which . . . measures to assist the displaced persons in their efforts to improve their livelihoods, or at least to restore them, in real terms, while maintaining the sustainability of the park or protected area, will be identified" (para. 7).

Furthermore, "during project implementation and before enforcing of the restriction, the borrower prepares a plan of action, acceptable to the Bank, describing the specific measures to be undertaken to assist the displaced persons and the arrangements for their implementation" (para. 31).

BP 4.12 mandates that the TT [task team] assess the likelihood of income restoration during supervision. Specifically, the TT is to examine "the plan of action to determine the feasibility of the measures to assist the displaced persons to improve (or at least restore . . .) their livelihoods with due regard to the sustainability of the natural resource" (para. 15).

8

Definition of Income Restoration in Operational Terms

Defining income restoration operationally depends on economic conditions in the project area. Most simply, "income restoration" can refer to reestablishment of income levels prevalent at the time of displacement. This narrow interpretation, however, is inconsistent with Bank policy objectives and insufficient for achieving these objectives for a number of reasons:

- Bank policy refers to "restoration of incomes" as the minimum acceptable outcome. Improvement in income is the policy objective. Resettlement plans (RPs) should therefore include income generation strategies to at least restore income and measures to yield *improved* incomes and living standards.
- Income restoration is often a fairly lengthy, dynamic process. Reestablishment of preproject income levels deprives DPs of any benefits of growth (or protection from inflation) generated in the intervening years. Conceptually, then, "income restoration" refers to recovery of income levels that would have prevailed in the absence of the project.
- *Income restoration strategies need to be sustainable.* Temporary employment in project construction and temporary living support, for example, may be desirable forms of short-term assistance, but they do not constitute long-term income restoration. They are necessary, however, if their absence would impede prompt income restoration. DPs cannot be made to suffer loss of income levels and living standards during the transition to income restoration.
- Income restoration needs to be based on productive income-generating activities. Although cash payment may be appropriate under certain circumstances, in other cases DPs may use cash payment for consumption, preventing the acquisition of productive assets.
- "Income restoration" refers to recovery of aggregate household resource flows. But livelihoods are often based on both the formal and the informal economic activities of all members of a household. To consider the impacts of income restoration activities on equity and the distribution of opportunity within the household is therefore also important (see "Gender Issues," below).
- Income-generating activities must be legal and culturally appropriate. Income restoration does not cover illegal or immoral activities, and it does not include the financial contributions of children if they have to discontinue schooling.

In view of these considerations, the objective of restoring livelihoods and standards of living "to pre-displacement levels or to levels prevailing prior to the

8

beginning of project implementation, whichever is higher" (OP 4.12, para. 2[c]) depends on the time frame and economic conditions. Generally, projects that take place within a short time frame pose little difficulty, because the income levels to be achieved are those the DPs had immediately before the project. However, projects with long gestation or implementation periods pose more difficulty, because the national or regional economy will have evolved in the interim. In countries where the economy has grown and incomes have risen, the objective of income restoration is to create conditions enabling people to achieve the higher income levels they presumably would have had without the project (Figure 8.1). In countries where the economy has contracted and incomes have fallen, the aim is to restore incomes to at least the predisplacement level, in real terms, even though this level is higher than the DPs would have achieved without the project (Figure 8.2). The rationale is that involuntary resettlement takes place in a development context, so projects incur the obligation to at least restore previous levels of livelihood and standards of living.

Compensation for expropriated assets is often not enough to restore livelihoods and standards of living, especially among poor and vulnerable groups. Compensation fails because of the inefficiencies that make markets unable to translate this compensation into income-generating assets. Therefore, in accord with the Bank's poverty alleviation objectives, its resettlement policy encourages the orientation of projects toward development, meaning additional assistance may be needed. In this perspective, people bearing the burdens of displacement are thought to deserve full benefit from the projects affecting them.

Accordingly, RPs should provide opportunities for DPs to restore or increase their incomes and living standards. In essence, Bank policy recognizes that the

Figure 8.1 Income Restoration Objective in Regions of Economic Growth

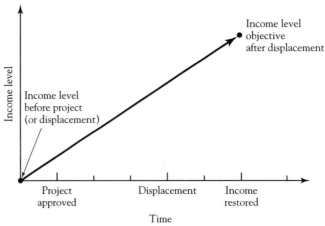

Figure 8.2 Income Restoration Objective in Regions of Economic Contraction

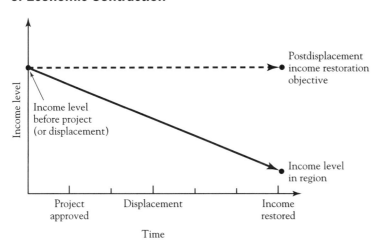

changes imposed by displacement frequently involve loss of more than physical capital. People affected also risk impoverishment because existing skills cannot be transferred to new circumstances (loss of human capital) or because institutionalized norms and relationships are dismantled or are inappropriate in the new circumstances (loss of social capital).

To meet the Bank's development objective, OP 4.12 mandates additional assistance to DPs who are compensated for assets but are still unable to restore incomes because replacement assets or alternative economic opportunities are not available or attainable. In addition, the policy extends protection to several categories of people whose hardships have often been overlooked: specifically, DPs who lose assets but are ineligible for compensation because they lack formal title; and DPs who do not lose assets but nonetheless lose access to income-generating opportunities, notably as a result of lost wages, sales, or rental agreements.

Issues in Income Restoration

Unlike compensation, income restoration is both complex and uncertain, unfolding over time and contingent on factors beyond the control of project agencies or the Bank (Table 8.1). These aspects of income restoration make planning difficult and the limits of project responsibility harder to determine.

The scale and extent of the resettlement operation magnify the difficulties of income restoration.

Lessening as much as possible the number of DPs and the degree of change imposed on them by displacement significantly increases the chances of restoring

Table 8.1 Comparing Compensation and Income Restoration

Compensation	Income restoration
Compensation is usually a single payment, often received before the move and before DPs fully recognize options or constraints inherent in new circumstances	Income restoration is usually conceived in more dynamic terms as plans or actions required to reestablish an income stream over time
If provided as a lump sum, no recurrent monitoring is likely to be provided	As income restoration involves a series of steps or stages over time, recurrent monitoring is essential
Compensation strategies assume the existence of replacement assets or appropriate substitutes, so DPs remain responsible for their own welfare	Supplemental-income strategies are necessary where markets are thin, replacement assets are scarce, or loss of human or social capital may be debilitating
Although valuation methods vary, the principle of compensation is normally enshrined in domestic law	Domestic law in many countries has no explicit provision for income restoration measures
In Bank projects, compensation is defined as the amount required to obtain equivalent assets *at the time of the expropriation*	In Bank projects, income restoration is operationally defined by reference to income streams over time, in comparison with incomes at the time of taking or at the time of project initiation, whichever are higher
Compensation is normally paid before displacement or the initiation of civil works	Income restoration may take many years and remain incomplete when the Bank project is formally completed
Because of the simplicity and timing of the compensation process, the Bank can effectively guarantee compensation at replacement cost	Because income restoration processes are highly contingent, the Bank can require income restoration strategies (and supervise their implementation) but cannot guarantee income restoration

Note: DP, displaced person.

income. Finding livelihoods for a handful of DPs, or even a few hundred, is vastly easier than finding income-generating strategies for tens of thousands. Furthermore, the extent of change required of DPs strongly conditions the prospect of success. This difficulty is the reason Bank policy gives preference to land replacement options for displaced rural agriculturalists. In such cases, direct asset replacement can return the DPs to familiar and productive livelihoods. In contrast, rural agriculturalists who are not provided options for replacement land may be forced to undertake unfamiliar activities in an alien or more competitive environment. Under these circumstances, the losses directly imposed by displacement may be compounded over time. The factors of scale and extent vary widely between and within sectors, accounting in part for differences in the resettlement success of various types of projects.

Resettlement has various degrees of specific impact on households and individuals.

Displacement does not necessarily have the same effects on different households or even on the different individuals in those households. These effects are determined both by changes brought on by displacement and by people's abilities to adjust to these changes. Although individuals and households may not have generic vulnerability, they may be especially vulnerable to certain types of change.

> *Project example:* In Thailand, the Pak Mun Hydropower Project (Loan [Ln] 3423) had widely differing impacts on different classes of people. People who lost houses generally benefited. They were given generous compensation to rebuild their houses; or they were given new, improved houses, usually along paved roads, which provided more economic opportunities for service-based livelihoods. People who lost land also received generous compensation, especially for land that had not been adjacent to the river and produced less than a ton of rice per hectare each year. People who did not lose houses or land but lost income or subsistence from fishing in the river received compensation only for the three years of lost income during dam construction. Most of these people were unable to restore their fishing livelihoods, as the fish population and reservoir fishery yield appear to be much lower than was predicted before construction of the dam.

Poorer, more vulnerable groups often face greater difficulties.

Because people's skills, aptitudes, resources, and preferences vary, their responses to displacement problems and resettlement opportunities also vary. Typically, some proportion of the affected population will have the skills, personal contacts, or other entrepreneurial attributes to adapt successfully. An unfortunate fact, however, is that displacement disproportionately affects the poor, the less educated, the unskilled, women, children, the elderly, and people not advantaged by political institutions or power structures. The people in these groups also bear a much more significant risk of severe impoverishment and are less likely to adapt without assistance (see also CD Appendix 14, "Assistance to Vulnerable People," for an example from a Bank project).

8

Project example: In Brazil, the Machadinho Hydropower Project (not a Bank project) team closely monitored the economic recovery of displaced families according to socioeconomic class. Families with little or no vulnerability were able to restore their livelihoods within a short period of several years. By contrast, the poorest families, categorized as the most vulnerable, encountered much more difficulty restoring their incomes, because their survival strategies depended on neighborhood groups and exchange systems broken up during the relocation process.

Project example: In India, in the Upper Krishna Irrigation II Project (Ln 3050; Credit [Cr] 2010) survey data show that men were more satisfied than women with the resettlement and that the young were more satisfied than the elderly. These results appeared to be largely related to who received the benefits of resettler assistance (men's losses were better recognized and compensated for than women's losses) and who was more able to adapt to changing circumstances caused by resettlement (young adults were starting off in life and were more flexible, having less invested in their former location and occupation).

A dynamic regional economy helps income restoration.

That a growing regional economy creates jobs and helps restore the incomes of DPs is axiomatic. Conversely, stagnant, typically remote, economies, with few new opportunities and with poor transportation and communications systems, make income restoration more difficult. Taking full advantage of the new opportunities created by the project and developing a wider menu of development options for DPs is important.

Project example: In China, Indonesia, and Thailand, the Operations Evaluation Department study of resettlement for large dams found that successful income restoration usually depends on a dynamic regional economy. China's Shuikou Hydroelectric Project (Ln 2775) deliberately based its income restoration strategy on the rapidly expanding economy of northern Fujian Province, to which the dam project made a significant contribution. Thailand's Pak Mun Hydroelectric Project (Ln 3423) did not deliberately build on the expanding Thai economy, but many resettler households had family members migrating, seasonally at least, to the provincial and national capitals, and that helped restore family incomes, as well as spurring more local economic growth. Indonesia's Kedung Ombo Multipurpose Project (Ln 2543) had a mixed record of income restoration, but the resettlers who migrated on their own to the cities and towns of Central Java had, on average, the greatest increase in incomes, presumably as a result of the rapidly growing Central Java economy.

Externalities can upset income restoration plans.

Even the most careful and elaborate income restoration strategies may be subject to uncontrollable external factors (for example, the general rate of economic growth; adverse shifts in trade). Moreover, the effectiveness of income restoration strategies is contingent on DPs' responsiveness to new circumstances. Bank experience shows that adversely affected people must become key participants in the process of restoring their own incomes and living standards. But precisely because it is involuntary, displacement can retard the risk taking and adaptation sometimes essential to restoring incomes. Consequently, the kinds of options DPs receive and the DPs' perceptions of the risks they face after displacement are crucial to the success of income restoration programs.

> *Project example:* In Togo, the Nangbeto Hydroelectric Project (Cr 1507, 1508) appeared to have implemented a successful resettlement program when relocation was completed in 1987. Conditions deteriorated precipitously after 1990, when the entire economy collapsed. The government ceased to provide many services, including subsidized fertilizer and improved seeds, and incomes fell dramatically. Because the situation deteriorated for nonresettlers as well as for resettlers, it is difficult to disaggregate the effects of resettlement from broader effects of Togo's economic decline. The RP implicitly assumed that resettlers would intensify their agriculture, but people are generally too poor to afford fertilizers, improved seeds, and other inputs to maintain productivity. This may have been possible earlier, but the combination of increasing population pressure, insecure land tenure, and economic crisis prevented an organized transition to more intensified agriculture. The situation is so bad in two of the resettlement zone villages that some resettlers returned to their old villages to find land to farm.

8

The limits of responsibility are difficult to establish early on.

Bank policy requires restoration of livelihoods and incomes and strongly recommends efforts to improve local conditions. However, just how long these efforts will need to continue can be difficult to establish in the planning and early implementation stages. Income sustainability is key to this issue. Technically, economically, and financially sustainable activities enable DPs to at least restore their livelihoods, thus limiting project responsibility. A thorough, multifaceted feasibility analysis is critical for success. A monitoring program that tracks the recovery of DPs, identifies problems, and crafts solutions is, therefore, crucial for assessing and facilitating the recovery process.

Income restoration strategies are more likely to be successful, then, if they do the following:

- Comprehensively and accurately identify existing income streams and the resettlement effects on them;
- Identify the DPs most vulnerable to risk (such as the poor, the landless, women);
- Allow the DPs themselves to select from a menu of options;
- Conduct a thorough analysis of feasibility, risks, and commitments before options are selected;
- Rely on economically, financially, and technically feasible income-generating activities;
- Avoid, or minimize as much as possible, the change required in new economic activities (for example, old farmers should not have to shift to jobs in industrial enterprises);
- Take advantage of an expanding economy;
- Anticipate external factors affecting the DPs and income restoration strategies; and
- Direct project benefits to the DPs, rather than concentrating solely on mitigation measures.

Risk Analysis

Resettlement practitioners and researchers have propagated a number of frameworks for analysis of risk. Apart from the risks perceived by the DPs, the following risks need to be assessed during the design of the resettlement program:

- *Institutional risks*—Do the agencies responsible for implementing the resettlement have the capacity to carry it out, including the capacity to coordinate the many activities involved in the resettlement program?
- *Financial risks*—Will adequate funding for all resettlement activities be available when needed? Will project delays result in escalating resettlement costs?
- *Technical risks*— Will changes in any of the underlying factors or assumptions on which the proposed mitigation strategies were based affect the technical aspects of the project? (For example, the assumption that irrigated agriculture is feasible may be proven incorrect by soil or drainage features discovered during implementation.)
- *Macroeconomic risks*— Will the goods and services to be supplied by the DPs find a market? Will the supply of inputs for production be reliable?

8

- *Implementation risks*— Will people's needs and preferences change during the implementation of resettlement? (Elaborate plans have been made on the basis of DPs' acceptance of replacement land, only to see people change their minds about the location during implementation.) Might the borrower fail to implement the project after completion of detailed planning and partial implementation?

One of the frameworks employed by resettlement practitioners and researchers is called impoverishment risks and reconstruction (IRR), which was applied in the Bankwide review of projects with resettlement conducted in 1993–1994 (Box 8.1).

Box 8.1 Impoverishment Risks and Reconstruction: A Framework for Resettlement Analysis and Planning

The essence of safeguarding in resettlement operations is not just to counteract the adverse affects of these operations, but—even more important—to anticipate possible risks and preempt or mitigate them before they become major adverse effects.

An analytical framework that enjoys consensus holds obvious appeal as a tool for resettlement planning and implementation. Many practitioners and analysts, inside and outside the Bank, report considerable success with the IRR framework advanced by Michael M. Cernea for preparing resettlement components and rapid appraisal processes. The IRR framework is empirically derived from previous project experiences and research and was applied in the 1994 Resettlement Review conducted by the World Bank. It helps project teams anticipate the common risks inherent in displacements and orient the RP toward preventing and managing these risks. The IRR framework identifies major categories of impoverishment risk. Practitioners maintain that using these categories can improve identification of the people most vulnerable to impoverishment, guide the design of effective mitigation measures, and provide a matrix for monitoring the resettlement process. The framework's nine major categories of impoverishment risk are the following:

- *Landlessness*—Loss of land by DPs, especially in agricultural areas, can be a source of the most severe form of lasting impoverishment.
- *Joblessness*—Loss of employment may be overlooked if planners focus solely on loss of land, but this risk affects many DPs, and creating new employment is one of the greatest challenges in resettlement.
- *Homelessness*—Replacement of housing is only one aspect of relocation. Relocating may also disrupt family and neighborhood relationships that are vital to restoration of living standards.
- *Marginalization*—Loss of economic power and of social status pushes families closer to the poverty line, or even further beneath it. Resettlement may similarly result in social marginalization.

(continued)

(continued from p. 163)

- *Increased morbidity and mortality*—Relocation tends to expose resettlers to new or more intensive sources of illness or debilitation, or it may deprive them of access to health services or traditional remedies.
- *Food insecurity*—Diminished self-sufficiency and disrupted food production and supply can cause or exacerbate chronic undernutrition (defined as calorie or protein intake below minimum levels needed for normal growth and work).
- *Interruption of education*—Schooling is often interrupted during displacement; furthermore, children are required to work to contribute to family income restoration and are not back to school, or they may lack access to schools at the relocation site.
- *Loss of access to common property*—The groups most vulnerable to impoverishment (especially the women in these groups) rely heavily on common property resources, such as forests, water bodies, grazing areas, and fuelwood. These resources are often lost in displacement, and rapid appraisal processes should counter such losses.
- *Social disarticulation*—Social capital can be lost through dismantling or debilitation of community-level networks and associations, kinship systems, and mutual help arrangements.

The timely use of the IRR framework for resettlement analysis serves several functions. As a *diagnostic* tool, the IRR framework can be used by the task team (TT) to accurately (and in a more timely manner) identify relevant risks and adverse impacts and to estimate their scope and intensity, which vary from project to project. As a *planning* tool, the IRR framework (which also shows in detail how to mitigate the identified risks through reconstruction [see the appendix on the CD] helps direct project resources to risk management. And as a *monitoring* tool, the IRR can be used to convert the relevant impoverishment risks into key performance indicators, thus increasing the likelihood that resettlement agencies will be reliably informed about key implementation results or constraints.

Note: Ongoing research and practical experimentation in many projects provide more information on the use, reliability, and effectiveness of the IRR framework in practice. CD Appendix 16, "Risk Assessment," contains "Risks Diagnostic and Risk Management in Involuntary Resettlement," Michael Cernea, 2002, and is a more complete explication of the IRR framework, written by Cernea. This will be of interest to TT leaders and agencies interested in applying the IRR framework in project preparation and management.

Design of Income Restoration Strategies

As a generic process, designing income restoration strategies involves three stages. The first is to analyze existing sources of income. The productive activities and existing income sources of DPs are identified, and this information is used to assess the DPs' capabilities and to establish a baseline for subsequent comparison. The second stage is to survey and analyze existing economic conditions to identify resource bases and assess market conditions. The third stage is to identify new opportunities, matching DPs with appropriate opportunities,

8

in consultation, of course, with the DPs; and identifying implementation requirements, such as training, financial support, and other needs. Each stage is considered in turn in the following subsections.

Stage 1: Analyzing Existing Sources of Income

The first step in devising income restoration strategies is to identify the precise parameters of the problem. Census data, surveys, and social assessments are the most useful sources of demographic and socioeconomic information. In both urban and rural areas of many developing countries, much of the economic activity is informal. Identifying existing income sources thus requires a focus on informal trade, subsistence production, and barter activities, in addition to a focus on the payroll records, tax payments, and sales receipts of the formal economy. It also requires that attention be paid to the economic activities of women, children, casual workers, the elderly, and others who may be overlooked in standard employment surveys (see CD Appendix 10, "Household Income Stream Analysis," for an example of analyzing income sources).

Based on broad categorization, the data required for analyzing existing sources of income are the following:

- Primary income or subsistence from the DPs' own agricultural land;
- Supplementary income from the DPs' own agricultural land;
- Employment by others for agricultural production;
- Subsistence or income through tenancy or share-cropping arrangements;
- Subsistence or income from community property;
- Subsistence or income from exploitation of open-access resources;
- Subsistence or income from encroachment on public land;
- Income from rent for housing;
- Income from marketing, sales, or provision of services;
- Income from regular or irregular wage employment;
- Subsistence or income from barter activities;
- Formal or informal community or government support; and
- Remittances.

To establish a baseline to gauge the success of income restoration strategies, the project agency needs to measure or estimate actual incomes or the equivalent economic value of DP productive activities (see CD Appendix 8, "Baseline Survey Data," for a sample list of the data to be included in this survey):

- For regular employment in the private or public sector, payroll records are likely to provide an accurate basis for establishing incomes;
- For subsistence and informal economic activities, income must be estimated;

- For subsistence activities, estimating the consumption value or fair market value of products raised or gathered may be possible; and
- For informal economic activities, relying on surveys inviting the people affected to report their own incomes may be necessary.

Three general points are important. First, subsistence activities and informal economic activities are considered sources of income that require restoration under Bank policy. Second, surveyors and analysts must be alert to incentives that encourage underreporting or overestimation of incomes. Third, where objective determination of incomes is impossible, enabling DPs to choose among resettlement options may circumvent controversies and accelerate the pace of rehabilitation, which remains the fundamental objective.

Stage 2: Surveying and Analyzing Current Economic Conditions

A thorough, accurate analysis of current economic conditions is essential for fitting income restoration measures to the needs of DPs. Although no single, proven method is available for identifying viable income-generating activities, economic analysis should include the following considerations:

- An inventory of prevalent economic activities, specifying existing demand for products and services, general availability of labor and other resources, profitability, and present marketing practices and relationships;
- An assessment of support services, such as credit facilities, technical assistance, and marketing; and
- A profile of the labor pool, comparing skills and training of DPs with those of the general population and matching these with any expressed labor needs.

The first step in assessing economic opportunities is to make an inventory of the economic activities prevalent in the area. This inventory covers all economic activities in each place, including shops and stores, artisans and crafts people, and markets. The number of activities—and the number of practitioners of each activity—will vary systematically with the importance of the village or town. Moreover, the number of activities and practitioners of each activity will increase predictably with demand. Therefore, the enterprise inventory should be location specific, and the work should be supervised by a social scientist with expertise in economic geography or regional analysis.

The second step in the economic assessment is to examine the adequacy of support services, particularly financial institutions and development collaborators. A good practice is to inventory existing banks, savings and credit organizations, and any informal institutional arrangements for encouraging savings. The inventory details the conditions imposed by each agency for start-up or

8

expansion capital or for spreading of financial risk. It is also useful to assess project agencies', nongovernmental organizations' (NGOs'), or other entities' current capacity to develop economic opportunities, training, or other aspects of income restoration, because such organizations often become involved in the income restoration programs.

> *Project example:* In Indonesia, the Kedung Ombo Multipurpose Project (Ln 2543) invested in a massive, expensive, three-year, university-based agricultural research and extension effort that was largely ignored by the resettlers as being too academic and impractical. A modest, nine-month microenterprise program developed and funded by a local NGO much more effectively and sustainably produced income-generating activities. When visited three years after the programs, resettlers remembered, appreciated, and were still using the facilities of the NGO program, but not those of the university-based program. Assessing the resettlers' demand for the university-based program might have saved significant resources, which could have been used to fund activities preferred by the resettlers.

The third step in the economic assessment is to determine the number of economically productive DPs and their capabilities and interests. This information is usually collected in the course of the socioeconomic surveys, which include basic demographic information on primary and secondary occupations, education, and labor migration.

This stage provides an estimate of the type and number of opportunities, information on the availability of support services, and an estimate of the number of DPs who will require assistance to restore income.

Stage 3: Identifying New Opportunities

Identification of potential income restoration measures and assessment of their feasibility are the first steps in the process of fitting the identified needs and aspirations of DPs to existing and potential economic opportunities. Additional steps for identifying new opportunities may include the following:

- Consult NGOs, DPs or their representatives, and other relevant parties to solicit ideas and preferences. Coordinate information exchanges or meetings of DPs, NGOs, industry groups, or other entities with complementary interests.
- Assess potential demand inside and outside the region for new or expanded products and services. If the plan proposes the export of goods, for example, gauging international supply and demand is important.
- Assess possibilities for reducing market obstructions or for strengthening or diversifying market channels, to lower transaction costs.

8

- Identify constraints and other reasons why certain economic activities are not provided or are undersupplied. Maybe the RP or the project can address these constraints and provide new opportunities.
- Assess possibilities for improving access to credit by providing incentives for financial agencies to participate or by promoting NGOs, self-help schemes, or other measures.
- Assess the potential sustainability of suggested or identified income-generating activities, including assessment of risk of failure that might arise because of environmental externalities, climate change, shifts in terms of trade, or other factors beyond the control of DPs.
- Assess how well proposed activities will generally conform to regional and national laws and development plans. Consult with local and, if relevant, regional governments to assess the feasibility of the proposed activities and obtain relevant information.

All opportunities identified should be technically, economically, socially, culturally, and financially feasible. Individual DPs must have the skills or aptitudes to produce the goods or services. In fact, the effectiveness of income restoration measures largely depends on the responsiveness of DPs. Thus, income restoration strategies need to address the incentives (and disincentives) that condition DP behavior. This assessment is especially important if displacement is likely to make DPs risk-averse, to affect vulnerable groups, or to impose major shifts in income-earning activities. To achieve sustainable results, income restoration programs must, for example, guard against placing too many DPs into the same activity. Restoration programs cannot be allowed to contribute to oversupply of labor or to market saturation of DPs' products. Program planners must also assess market specifications, consumer preferences, transport, jobbers and wholesalers, and other marketing issues.

> **Project example:** In China, a non-Bank highway project planted excessive quantities of apple trees, which drove the price down from $0.22 to $0.08 per kilogram (all dollar amounts are current U.S. dollars). In India, in the Upper Krishna Irrigation project (Ln 3050; Cr 2010), too many DPs used their income-generating grants to purchase ox teams and carts, grain-milling machines, and herds of goats, thus reducing the economic return on each of these options (as supply exceeded demand).

Not all DPs are tradition bound or risk-averse. In many cases, resettlement proves to be a catalyst for change. In some East Asian regions, for example, displacement quickly spurred people to entrepreneurial behavior, especially in peri-urban areas or areas characterized by economic expansion. Provided options to do so, thousands of DPs in many countries have chosen to leave behind agricultural lives for productive and sustainable urban employment. DPs vary—by country, by project, and even within the same project—in their reaction to displacement and in the pace at which they adapt to new circumstances.

Although incentives can be adjusted by various means, general considerations include the following:

- *Participation*—Involvement of DPs in the design and implementation of displacement and resettlement processes can reduce passivity and quicken the pace of adaptation.
- *Choice*—Providing DPs with options increases the likelihood of fit with their own preferences and aptitudes.
- *Security of tenure*—Clear title to assets, assurances of long-term access to resources, and guaranteed periods of employment are among mechanisms that lengthen the time perspective of DPs, promoting investment and reducing risk aversion.
- *Development of human capital*—Small-business training, job skills development, and internships are among mechanisms that encourage entrepreneurial activities or build confidence in alternative occupations.

Income Restoration through Land Replacement

Matching the DPs' capabilities and interests to productive opportunities is premised on taking advantage of existing knowledge and expertise. For this reason, Bank policy gives preference to land replacement for those who depend on the land and want to continue doing so.

Land replacement is the preferred option for DPs who rely on, and wish to continue with, land-based livelihoods.

Land replacement is the preferred option for DPs earning their living from the land and wanting to continue doing so. When only a few people are displaced, finding an equivalent amount of replacement land of similar quality nearby is usually possible, either by accessing the private market or releasing otherwise unused public lands. When large numbers of people are displaced, however, finding equivalent land nearby for all the DPs may be difficult.

Various approaches have been used successfully to locate and acquire replacement land:

- Individual DPs may locate plots themselves, and then a land committee (composed of project officials and DPs) verifies the suitability and price of the land before authorizing release of the funds;
- The project or the responsible government agency identifies areas for the DPs to move to and work in. The DPs select the area they prefer, and lots are allocated, often on a lottery basis; or

8

- The project can purchase agricultural land acceptable to DPs in the open market.

Regardless of approach, DPs should be encouraged to visit the relocation sites so that they personally see the land, its qualities, and the need for improvements.

The land usually needs to be developed to bring it up to the standards of the plots taken. In this regard, income restoration in resettlement projects resembles regional agricultural development. The same amount of effort is needed to prepare either agricultural development projects or resettlement projects with a land development component. A target area is delimited, the soils are tested, improvements are decided on, and a work program is defined. The DPs must not bear the cost of this preparation. But if the DPs do this work they should be compensated. This compensation can take the form of short-term assistance to support DPs while they restore their assets to production. Projects where land-based options are included without thorough feasibility analyses are likely to fail.

> *Project example:* In the Brazil Itaparica Resettlement and Irrigation Project (Ln 2883), land-based resettlement was accepted by the project authorities without a rigorous feasibility analysis, as a result of strong pressure by Polo Sindical, an NGO claiming to represent the interests of the DPs. Developing substandard lands for irrigated agriculture proved to be difficult and expensive (almost $250,000 per household), as a result of inherent deficiencies in soil quality. Incomes from irrigated plots were still insufficient and had to be supplemented with additional income assistance and with subsidies for irrigation water.

Finally, land is a scarce resource. By taking land and relocating the population, involuntary resettlement inherently increases the population density in the receiving areas. Unless the population in the receiving area is unusually sparse, accommodating all DPs with land-based options may not be possible. Other non-land-based alternatives will likely be necessary, especially in large operations. It is, therefore, incumbent on the project team to determine as closely as possible the number of people who would be willing to move into non-land-based occupations.

> *Project example:* In China, the Shuikou Hydroelectric Project (Ln 2775) took full advantage of the agricultural opportunities in the area. The project team used the drawdown area and outlying marginal lands to redevelop agricultural production, including integrated fish, duck, and hog farming near the lake; pig raising and mushroom cultivation in confined spaces next to the houses; orchard growing on terraced slopes; bamboo and tea cultivation on the steeper slopes; forestry on the steepest slopes; and goat herding on the drier hills. Each activity was costed

8

out and scheduled, and development of the plantations and orchards began several years before relocation so that by the time the DPs arrived the enterprises would be almost in production.

Project example: Also in China, the Inland Waterway Project (Ln 3910) fostered DP participation in livelihood planning. County and township resettlement officers worked together with the affected villagers to develop specific measures for each farmer group. The collaborative planning covered adjustments to agricultural land; land reclamation; improvement of low-yielding land; and development of orchards, fish ponds, and reservoir fishing. Various resettlement agencies also organized study tours and other training to assist villagers in their economic recovery.

Project example: Also in China, the project team of the unusually isolated Yantan Hydroelectric Project (Ln 2707) found that local resources were too limited to accommodate the income restoration of all DPs. Therefore, 3,600 people were relocated to two sugar estates near the rapidly developing coastal zone. These resettlers' incomes more than tripled. Another 11,500 people were relocated to another state farm near the provincial capital.

Strategic Use of Project Opportunities

More and more today, DPs prefer options other than land when they must restore their livelihoods and incomes. For this reason, Bank experience shows that the most effective resettlement programs provide DPs with a range of opportunities, whether those opportunities are directly related to the project or developed separately from the project but under its aegis.

Project-related benefits typically include access to resources, employment in the project, or a share of its revenues. Such opportunities can directly restore income streams or at least contribute to restoring them. Sharing project-generated benefits with DPs is consistent with general development planning, and it may further the aim of social equity.

Project example: Between 1989 and 1991, Brazil, China, and Colombia adopted national laws requiring hydroelectric projects to share revenues with local communities, including DPs. The projects that have shared 1–6 percent of their revenues with DPs and local communities include the Yantan (Ln 2707), Ertan (Ln 3387), Shuikou (Ln 2775), and Lubuge (Ln 2382) hydroelectric projects, in China; the Rio Grande Hydroelectric Project (Ln 2449), in Colombia; and the Leyte Cebu

(Ln 3700) and Leyte-Luzon (Ln 3702) geothermal projects, in the Philippines.

Providing access to resources, such as irrigation, is often a workable strategy.

Hydroelectric and irrigation projects can often direct project benefits to the people they adversely affect. Bank reviews of water control projects, for example, recount many cases of DPs' being the targeted beneficiaries of irrigation works, often leading to a doubling or trebling of their agricultural incomes. In several reservoir projects, DPs have been among those people given aquaculture opportunities capable of yielding incomes substantially higher than those derived from their previous, land-based activities. Hydroelectric projects hold additional promise as sources of residential or commercial electricity for resettlement areas, as sources of employment, or as sources of revenue earmarked for development activities in affected communities.

> *Project example:* In China, the Shuikou Hydroelectric Project (Ln 2775) introduced oyster beds and fish cages in the reservoir. Other examples of hydroelectric projects developing reservoir fisheries as a means of restoring resettlers' incomes are Cirata (Ln 2300) and Saguling, in Indonesia; Aguamilpa (Ln 3083), in Mexico; Pak Mun (Ln 3423), in Thailand; and Yantan (Ln 2707), in China.

> *Project example:* Many projects provide irrigation benefits to the people they displace. Examples are the Orissa Water Resources Consolidation (Cr 2801), the Andhra Pradesh II (Ln 2662; Cr 1665) and III (Ln 4166; Cr 2952), the Gujarat Medium II (Cr 1496), and the Maharashtra III (Cr 1621) irrigation projects, in India; the Daguangba Multipurpose (Cr 2305) and Lubuge Hydroelectric (Ln 2382) dam projects, in China; and the Ceará Integrated Water Resources Management Project (Ln 4531), in Brazil.

Giving DPs hiring preference during construction provides them with short-term income.

Giving DPs hiring preference in construction jobs provides income for some families during the difficult time when their livelihoods are disrupted. If properly managed, the hiring program can also impart job skills that DPs can continue to use after construction ends. Temporary employment is not a substitute for complete, long-term reconstruction of livelihoods, but it should be offered to DPs during the critical reestablishment phase, if possible.

> *Project example:* In Brazil, the Urban Development and Water Resource Management Project (referred to as the PROURB Project [Projeto de

8

Desenvolvimento Urbano], a non-Bank project) supported DPs' construction of new urban housing. Over the course of the project, some of the women and men learned masonry, and they plied that trade after the project ended. In addition, one community member was designated as supervisor for each construction project. These individuals later secured jobs in the private sector or in other municipal projects.

Project example: In Turkey, contractors gave hiring preferences to local residents, matching skills and aptitudes with job requirements. The hiring preferences were not only for construction, but also for mechanical repair and office work. Over time, several thousand local people gained employment, and many of these people were later able to ply their new trades in the area as mechanics, painters, bookkeepers, and the like.

Project example: In India, the Upper Krishna II (Ln 3050; Cr 2010) and Maharashtra III Irrigation (Cr 1621) projects employed DPs as laborers in the construction of the canals in the command area, where DPs were being resettled. The project directed its benefits toward resettlers in two ways and linked their temporary and permanent livelihoods.

Project example: Projects that require the preparation of relocation sites often allocate that work to DPs. The Karnataka Power Project (Ln 2827), in India, and the Ertan Hydroelectric Project (Ln 3387), in China, are two examples of projects that paid DPs to prepare resettlement sites. This employment had the double benefit of paying DPs during a particularly vulnerable period and helping ensure that resettlement sites reflected their preferences.

Direct employment is a common way of delivering project benefits.

Projects have given employment to DPs in sectors ranging from forestry to mining to urban improvement. Such employment can quickly resolve income restoration problems if labor is in demand and the number of people requiring income restoration is not unmanageable. More typically, however, projects can offer only a few jobs and cannot employ all, or even most, of the people they displace. Whether extensive or limited, however, employment in the project typically increases human capital, as workers gain skills and experience.

When conditions are less favorable, employment measures can place severe burdens on either the project or the DPs. The DPs may be promised jobs that fail to materialize, jobs they lack the skills to perform, or jobs that disappear for any number of reasons before their recovery can be said to be complete. Also, because jobs in projects often provide both security and fairly high incomes, they are often highly desired, but the focus on this type of employment impedes other income restoration initiatives.

8

Project example: In Pakistan, the Ghazi-Barotha Hydroelectric Project (Ln 3965) and, in China, the Sichuan Power Transmission Project (Ln 3848) offered DPs temporary construction jobs and gave them priority for permanent employment with the company.

Project example: Many projects in China have allocated jobs to DPs. Most of these projects displaced small numbers of people. China's rapid economic growth and the shift in the labor force from agriculture to industry also helped in hiring DPs. The Shanghai Environment Project (Ln 3711) recruited DPs as operators and maintenance staff at the pumping station that displaced them. The Southern Jiangsu Environmental Protection Project (Ln 3582) retrained farmers to work at the wastewater plants displacing them. The Second Red Soils Area Development Project (Cr 2563) offered DPs jobs in the agro-processing enterprise acquiring their land. The Lubuge Hydroelectric Project (Ln 2382) assigned DPs to reservoir maintenance and other development activities conducted by local government.

Project example: In India, the practice at various coal projects, until several years ago, was to offer employment to DPs. This strategy, however, encouraged overemployment, low productivity, and resistance to displacement among those who were not provided the opportunity for employment. The practice also created dissension within the family because the DPs who gained jobs with the company might not share their salaries with their relatives. And, in the longer run, the strategy led to extraordinary demands on the coal company, such as demands for employment for all the sons when the father died.

Contracting services out to DP groups is a preferable option.

Besides offering direct employment with the company, a project can contract out the services and products it needs to DP groups.

Project example: In India, the National Thermal Power Corporation (Ln 3632) contracted services from DP groups. Office cleaning and gardening contracts were let annually. In addition, the corporation contracted with auto-rickshaw drivers to ferry school children between home and school and directed its staff to purchase office supplies from DP shops, whenever possible.

Project example: Also in India, the Coal India Sector Environmental and Social Mitigation Project (Cr 2862) developed an innovative approach in the Singrauli region. Coal India, Ltd., contracted with a local NGO to identify material the company normally purchased that could be made locally. DP groups, if provided the raw materials and guided in production (to ensure quality), could locally produce such goods as shovels, gloves, helmets, and baskets.

Project example: In China, the Asian Development Bank Shaanxi Roads Project hired DPs for unskilled labor in construction and also contracted them to provide materials, such as sand and stone; food and lodging services to the non-local construction labor force; and other needed supplies and services. The value of all labor and services hired or contracted from DPs was equal to the resettlement budget, each about $75 million, out of a total project budget of $750 million.

The project opportunities depend on the investment and sector.

The effectiveness of using project opportunities is often limited by the nature of the project. Many transport projects, for example, can deliver primarily general benefits to the economy, benefits that are fairly difficult to divert to any specific target group. Even in this sector, however, imaginative design can open up new possibilities. Design of corridors, placement of expressway ramps or rail stations, and regulatory or zoning practices, for example, can often direct commercial or service opportunities to resettlement areas.

Project example: In China and Thailand, DPs in the Shuikou (Ln 2775) and Pak Mun (Ln 3423) hydroelectric projects took advantage of their new locations along new roads to develop roadside businesses, both retail and services, related to the new traffic flows. In China, DPs at several dam projects—including Shuikou, Yantan (Ln 2707), and Wanjiazhai (Ln 4179)—have taken advantage of newly created reservoirs to develop ferry and other water transport services.

8

The effectiveness of strategies for directing project benefits to DPs and the frequency with which such strategies are used are likely to increase as additional lessons are drawn from Bank experience. In the interim, however, a few cautionary notes warrant mention:

- General benefits to the economy are not an acceptable substitute for compensation or rehabilitation of project-affected persons. Those benefits are desirable, of course, and are fundamental to project purposes. But OP 4.12 is based on the recognition that aggregate growth or other forms of improvement do not necessarily protect project-affected people.
- Project benefits, such as short-term employment or the promise of irrigation, are not by themselves a solution. For short-term employment, the problem is its duration. For irrigation, the problem is whether irrigation will actually be delivered and translate into higher incomes. Irrigation

systems can be built, but the benefits may not materialize for a number of reasons, including DP unfamiliarity with irrigation practices and lack of a market for irrigated crops. RPs and project documents establish the fact that the borrower's resettlement obligations are not considered fulfilled until such benefits are delivered.

Other Income Restoration Strategies

The size of the project and the scope of its impacts are key elements in preparation of income restoration plans. If only a few individuals require economic rehabilitation, a simple statement detailing arrangements for employment or other forms of assistance may suffice. But if groups of people in different areas require rehabilitation, especially if their current socioeconomic situations differ substantially, separate plans may be required for each area. If whole communities are to be adversely affected or new resettlement areas are to be established, income restoration measures dealing with community-based planning or with collective activities may be needed. With project circumstances differing so widely, a good practice is to discuss the scope of income restoration planning with the project agencies, local government, the Bank Task Team Leader, and the resettlement specialist or consultant, but in consultation with DPs or their representatives and NGOs. Whatever the context, feasibility analyses of the technical, financial, economic, and institutional issues are fundamental in planning future activities (see CD Appendix 15, "Income Restoration Measures," for an example from a Bank project).

Requirements for Reporting and Review of Income Restoration Plans

Income restoration plans are detailed in the RP and summarized in the Project Appraisal Document. In complex projects (for example, those with large numbers of DPs requiring rehabilitation or those requiring several separate plans), detailed plans are appended to the RP. The purpose of the plan, of course, is to propose concrete actions for income restoration, including budgets, timetables, responsibility for implementation, economic assumptions and risks, and contingency arrangements to be used in the event of failure or significant change in the socioeconomic environment. In all cases, the list of income restoration options includes only activities that meet the test of overall feasibility and sustainability. Arrangements for piloting interventions may therefore be necessary.

Components of an income restoration plan are likely to include the following:

- A review of current socioeconomic conditions, including summary of income baselines;

- A summary of DPs' preferences for income restoration (including description of methods used to elicit DPs' views);
- Detailed feasibility studies of the technical, economic, financial, and institutional viability of the proposed economic activities, including realistic estimation of incomes to be received by participating DPs and of the numbers of DPs each activity can absorb (the adequacy of a list of activities cannot be judged without these numbers);
- A summary of options available to DPs and of the process for matching DPs to particular programs or activities;
- A review of supplementary economic activities available to household members;
- A summary of specific programs (not the details) of assistance available to vulnerable groups;
- A plan for development of human capital (for example, outreach, education and training);
- A plan for provision of financial credit, as needed;
- Plans to promote marketing of local products or services or to enhance the functioning of markets, as needed;
- Arrangements to establish institutions and infrastructure as needed (for example, provision of infrastructure; creation of local cooperatives, collective enterprises, or self-help organizations); and
- Arrangements (and indicators) for monitoring the effectiveness of income restoration measures and for modifying plans found to be ineffective.

Where income restoration measures are not feasible, flat annuities with a yield sufficient to maintain equivalent living standards may be provided as a substitute for productive economic activity. No matter how difficult the economic circumstances, the Bank cannot accept an RP without realistic plans for restoring the incomes of all categories of affected persons.

Monitoring and Supervision of Income Restoration Measures

In Bank policy, income restoration is the least acceptable outcome—improvement of incomes is the objective. Monitoring of income restoration programs therefore focuses on income levels and socioeconomic factors, especially the responsiveness of DPs to new opportunities, the number of DPs undertaking each activity, the success of each type of endeavor, and the difficulties encountered. In addition, an independent monitor with social and economic experience may be appointed to provide a comparative overview of project activities.

The focus on monitoring income restoration is distinct from much monitoring of projects, which primarily concerns monitoring of administrative performance, such as construction of facilities or delivery of compensation.

The dynamic and contingent nature of income restoration makes monitoring especially important. To be effective, monitoring programs need to pay close and frequent attention to identified problems and potentially problematic circumstances. Furthermore, because of the contingent nature of income restoration processes, DPs are likely to adjust at widely varying paces and have unforeseen forms of adaptation. The variability of DPs' adaptation strategies makes careful monitoring critical for achieving policy objectives. Close monitoring is needed especially in the early stages, to assess whether the proposed measures are working. Monitoring systems provide the early warning necessary to correct deficiencies in any aspect of the income restoration program.

A common practical difficulty in monitoring income restoration is that this activity frequently extends beyond the normal construction project cycle. For projects requiring income restoration programs, making arrangements during project preparation for a midterm resettlement review is advisable. This review provides a mutually agreed-on mechanism for assessing the effectiveness of implementation fairly early in the process and for appropriately revising income restoration strategies to resolve problems or capitalize on new opportunities.

The monitoring system is basically the same, regardless of the scale of income restoration activities.

The nature of the monitoring system is basically the same for every project, regardless of the scale of the income restoration activities. The monitors periodically interview a sample of DPs about a series of critical indicators:

- Remunerative activities for each member of the household, including information on income and seasonality and any costs or savings associated with each activity (such as transport and subsistence costs related to new job locations; capital purchases);
- Types of problems encountered;
- Perceived need for additional assistance (and type);
- Individual satisfaction with current economic activities;
- Household furnishings (sales may indicate impoverishment; purchases indicate buying power); and
- Agricultural equipment and animals (sales of either may indicate impoverishment).

Large programs involving numerous DPs and changes in occupation require a systematic sampling of DPs. A good practice is to stratify the sample so that the poor and vulnerable groups are overrepresented and included in sufficient numbers

8

to permit statistical analysis. Over time, groups that have already restored their incomes can be monitored less frequently or dropped from the sample. Attention would then focus on the groups encountering more difficulty.

> *Project example:* In China, the Ertan Hydropower Project (Ln 3387) tracked the incomes of DPs for several years after relocation. In the first years, the project monitored all groups; in the later years, it followed only those DPs whose incomes had still not been restored. Finally, only a handful of families had yet to achieve their earlier economic status, and a case-by-case analysis documented that each instance involved some specific factor, such as the death of a breadwinner.

The borrower must verify income restoration before project closing.

For projects with large-scale or complex resettlement, the independent monitoring unit (or consultants hired for the purpose) should conduct a follow-up socioeconomic survey before the scheduled project closing (see Appendix 8, "Baseline Survey Data," for an example of the data that should be monitored in the follow-up socioeconomic survey; see Appendix 9, "Terms of Reference for a Socioeconomic Study," for guidance in scoping the survey).

OP 4.12 states that the borrower has "obligations to carry out the resettlement instrument and to keep the Bank informed of implementation progress" (para. 23).

Furthermore, "the borrower is responsible for adequate monitoring and evaluation of the activities set forth in the resettlement instrument. . . . Upon completion of the project, the borrower undertakes an assessment to determine whether the objectives of the resettlement instrument have been achieved. . . . If the assessment reveals that these objectives may not be realized, the borrower should propose follow-up measures that may serve as the basis for continued Bank supervision" (para. 24). In that case, project closing arrangements will ideally include continued income restoration, along with continued independent monitoring and Bank supervision.

8

When does the income restoration process end?

The Bank operationally concludes that income restoration requirements have been met if the following conditions apply:

- Subsequent household surveys show improvement or restoration of income streams, as formulated above.
- Productive assets have been replaced in kind, under roughly equivalent social, economic, and environmental conditions, and have started yielding anticipated income levels.

All of the above indicate conditions for restoring income to DPs through productive activities. Under special circumstances, other conditions may be acceptable:

- Some projects provide DPs with annuities equivalent to previous incomes, without necessarily giving them opportunities to engage in productive work. This alternative may be appropriate if other income-generating activities are especially scarce and the annuities provide a reliable income flow.
- DPs have chosen early retirement or accept alternatives provided for others within the same household.
- When resettlement is based on participatory approaches, some DPs may choose to place more emphasis on locational or cultural advantages than on income restoration. Ideally, the project provides a range of options so that DPs do not need to make this kind of a choice, but governments cannot create solutions to meet all the preferences of each individual. In effect, DPs opting out of opportunities assume responsibility for their own choices.

Remedial action may be recommended for income restoration.

The Bank can offer assistance to projects where income restoration and other resettlement activities are incomplete, whether or not the Bank has been involved in the original project. In some instances, agencies implementing non-Bank projects while preparing new projects with the Bank have agreed to such a remedial program to address unresolved resettlement issues. In such instances, if the Bank provides technical or financial assistance, monitoring and supervision are required. But in general, progress on remedial programs for non-Bank projects should not be a condition for approval of funding for Bank projects unless the non-Bank project is integrally linked to the Bank project's design or performance.

Remedial programs of this type are difficult under any conditions and become increasingly difficult with the passage of time. Without RPs or baseline surveys in many cases, tracing DPs who have migrated from the area is often difficult or impossible, and determining the present value of compensation for land acquired in the past is also difficult. An additional difficulty stems from a lack of sufficiently detailed project information within the Bank. Given these constraints, this section provides guidance for determining whether a remedial program is necessary or desirable.

Project example: In Pakistan, Bank preparations for the Ghazi-Barotha Hydropower Project (Ln 3967) led to the discovery that 1,440 households were awaiting allocation of replacement lands roughly 20 years

8

after their displacement for the Bank-supported Tarbela Dam. The Bank required preparation of an acceptable action plan to resolve outstanding claims as a condition of effectiveness.

Project example: In India, for the Andhra Pradesh III Irrigation Project (Ln 4166; Cr 2952), the Bank required rectification of inadequate compensation under the preceding project. The Government of Andhra Pradesh also undertook to rectify inadequate compensation under the non-Bank-funded Srisailam Dam, which would be linked to the performance of Andhra Pradesh III.

Community-based initiatives are appropriate in projects lacking RPs or baseline surveys.

In some projects, adequate data are available to determine retrofit objectives. Where RPs or baseline surveys are incomplete or do not exist, however, establishing appropriate levels for income restoration may be impossible. Under such circumstances, the appropriate remedial strategy would be to undertake community-based poverty initiatives or other improvements in resettlement areas (such as credit programs; the improvement or construction of schools).

Project example: In India, the Coal India Environmental and Social Mitigation Project (Cr 2862) included a remedial program for earlier Bank-funded coal mines. Tracer studies were carried out to assess incomes and living standards of people affected by land acquisition in past projects. Rehabilitation assistance was provided for people whose incomes were below the official poverty level. In addition, improvements in public infrastructure were made in previously established resettlement sites.

Annex: Microfinance as a Tool for Income Restoration

For DPs ready to take entrepreneurial risks, microfinance can be an effective means of spurring income improvement. Microfinance is the provision of financial services through formal organizations (for example, commercial banks, government development banks, credit unions, finance companies) or informal arrangements (moneylenders, pawnbrokers, neighborhood savings or credit pools, and so forth).

Microfinance clients are similar to those displaced by Bank-supported projects: both groups consist of disproportionately low-income people. One significant difference, however, is that microfinance clients are already entrepreneurs, voluntarily taking risks, whereas displacement is involuntary and tends to promote at least short-term risk aversion.

Box 8.2   Microfinance and Market Failure

To help households or microenterprises recover from the shocks associated with displacement, microfinance strategies implicitly or explicitly address four potential sources of market failure:

- *Resource failure*—DPs do not have the resources (including raw materials, financial reserves, skills, and technology) to function productively under changed circumstances.
- *Information failure*—DPs are unaware of prevailing market arrangements, seasonality or soil conditions, customs and taste preferences, or other valuable forms of local knowledge.
- *Services failure*—DPs lack access to financial, technical, or commercial support services, even though such services may exist for others. Minimum residency requirements, formal licensing requirements, and insufficient collateral, among others, are barriers to access.
- *Environmental failure*—Poor or predatory regulatory practices or thin or nonexistent markets may create abnormally high transaction costs.

Microfinance strategies are likely to be inappropriate as long as DPs are not ready to manage financial risk. Such situations may require grants or subsidies to help DPs build a new asset base or obtain new skills that microfinance alone cannot provide. Moreover, many DPs will not have the marketable technical skills needed to secure employment, or they simply will not be willing to accept the risk of starting a business. But microfinance may be useful to more entrepreneurial DPs as they adapt to new circumstances and become informed, perhaps through limited experimentation, acquisition of new skills, or observation of others. Use of credit and compensation is more likely to be effective under such conditions.

What microfinance can provide is limited, however, even for business-oriented DPs (Box 8.2). In some cases, relocating a small business close to its customers or suppliers may not be possible. In other situations, community dispersal may lead to the collapse of the neighborhood associations that previously provided financial assistance. But under more favorable circumstances, microfinance can tap into, or increase, self-reliance, accelerating the income restoration process while reducing dependence on often ineffectively administered programs.

Microfinance as an Income Restoration Strategy

To reach DPs accustomed to taking business risks, microfinance offers several strategies:

- Loans with nontraditional forms of collateral or no collateral requirement;
- Use of social networks to create a collective collateral substitute;

- Savings schemes with minimal initial deposit or balance requirements;
- Informal neighborhood rotating savings and credit associations; and
- Guarantee or pilot schemes, linked to formal financial institutions.

As DPs intent on entrepreneurship enter the transition stage, they may need to be assisted in finding affordable and reliable sources of financing. Formal financial institutions tend to evaluate potential clients in terms of the "three Cs": collateral, creditworthiness, and character. Income restoration planners can help create more positive evaluations in concrete ways:

Collateral

- Link DPs to programs (existing or created) that offer guarantee funds, collective risk, or other collateral substitutes.
- Encourage new forms of collateral linked to smaller loans for lower-cost productive assets, such as sewing machines or kitchen equipment.
- Block part of the compensation package and direct it to forced savings, which can be accepted as temporary collateral for a loan.
- When replacement land is provided, make sure that land titling is timely and unencumbered.

Creditworthiness

- For fairly sophisticated investments (such as purchases of major equipment), find an agency to review the feasibility of proposed activities in light of local market conditions.
- Conduct participatory market studies to help DPs choose productive activities.
- Discourage DPs from all taking up the same activity if this would lead to oversupply and diminishing prices.
- Provide ongoing training and advice in managing and operating a small business. Often this training and advice can be provided by local NGOs with expertise in microenterprise development.

Character

- Document the credit experience of DPs, including informal credit histories with store owners, suppliers, or others.
- Create links between DP groups, other neighborhood groups, and leaders of financial institutions at the new site. These leaders are in a position to provide character references for DPs seeking access to market-priced credit.

8

Promotion of Favorable Practices among Financial Institutions

Project agencies and RPs can also encourage financial institutions to adopt practices favorable to DPs' microenterprises. These practices include the following:

1. Offer services that fit the needs of small businesses.
   - Offer short-term loans.
   - Offer small loans for working capital.
   - Provide easier access to repeat loans on the basis of repayment performance.
   - Relax restrictions on use of loans tied to productive investment.
   - Make sites and schedules convenient for microenterprise operators.
2. Streamline operations to reduce unit costs for loans.
   - Decentralize loan approval for small loans.
   - Decentralize loan approval for repeat loans.
3. Provide incentives to encourage loan repayment.
   - Give guaranteed access to future loans, increased loan limits, or lower interest rates for timely repayment.
   - Link staff incentives to a high rate of on-time repayment.
   - Establish credible sanctions to discourage late repayment or default.
4. Charge full-cost interest rates and fees.
   - Note that poor microenterprise operators, including DPs, are usually more concerned with access to loans than with the cost of loans (the interest rate).
   - Set interest rates and fees high enough to cover operating and financial costs if the relationship between financial institutions and DPs is to be sustainable (project subsidies cannot continue indefinitely).

8

Chapter 9

Costs, Budgeting, and Financing

This chapter summarizes basic financial and budgetary requirements for resettlement operations. It summarizes the relevant sections of Operational Policy (OP) and Bank Procedure (BP) 4.12, outlines categories of costs that require identification and estimation, and provides guidance on estimating and budgeting resettlement costs and on Bank disbursement issues.

What OP 4.12 Says

Bank policy requires project budgets to reflect resettlement costs as accurately and as transparently as possible. "The full costs of resettlement activities necessary to achieve the objectives of the project are included in the total costs of the project. The costs of resettlement, like the costs of other project activities, are treated as a charge against the economic benefits of the project; and any net benefits to resettlers (as compared to the 'without-project' circumstances) are added to the benefits stream of the project. Resettlement components or free-standing resettlement projects need not be economically viable on their own, but they should be cost-effective" (OP 4.12, para. 20).

OP 4.12 further specifies that the resettlement plan will present the detail on costs and financing sources: "Tables showing itemized cost estimates for all resettlement activities, including allowances for inflation, population growth, and other contingencies; timetables for expenditures; sources of funds; and arrangements for timely flow of funds, and funding for resettlement, if any, in areas outside the jurisdiction of the implementing agencies" (Annex A, para. 20)

Two basic principles of Bank policy affect resettlement costs: resettlement must be minimized; and those affected by Bank projects should not bear the resettlement costs.

OP 4.12 states that "where it is not feasible to avoid resettlement, resettlement activities should . . . [provide] sufficient investment resources to enable the persons displaced by the project to share in project benefits . . . [and] to improve their livelihoods and standards of living or at least to restore them, in real terms, to pre-displacement levels or to levels prevailing prior to the beginning of project implementation, whichever is higher" (para. 2).

In principle, these objectives burden the project—not the people displaced by the project—with the financial responsibility for resolving issues. Displaced persons (DPs) are entitled to compensation at replacement cost or to other forms of agreed assistance. In practice, however, underestimation of resettlement costs and insufficient resettlement funding sometimes create severe burdens for DPs and undermine other project objectives as well. Therefore, it is especially important that resettlement costs be comprehensively identified, accurately estimated, and fully internalized within the project and not be transferred to DPs, either intentionally or unintentionally.

Bank projects now routinely include estimates of resettlement costs.[1] The quality of those estimates still varies, however. Because of poor planning, underestimation of resettlement costs often leads to cost overruns. Unanticipated impacts or obligations in later subprojects may outstrip the original estimates of resettlement costs. Other financial problems may arise only during implementation, so assuring adequate contingency funds is especially important for resettlement. And even the best budgets may be of little value if funds are unavailable or financial responsibility is not clearly assigned.

Identifying and Reporting Resettlement Costs

Since the advent of the Bank's first resettlement policy, in 1980, recognition of commonly recurring costs associated with land acquisition and resettlement has grown, and similar policies have been adopted by other development agencies. Resettlement costs are now more broadly recognized and accepted in general terms, but actual resettlement costs associated with particular projects quite frequently remain unidentified in the planning stages.

Standard cost reporting provides a framework for identifying resettlement costs. Most resettlement-related costs incurred in implementation can be placed in four budgeting categories: compensation, relocation costs, income restoration or costs, and administrative costs. Within these four broad categories of costs are some further distinctions. The costs of replacement of community infrastructure, provision of community services, and development of resettlement sites are related to compensation, relocation, and income restoration and improvement, but are distinct categories in themselves. The categories are briefly defined below (see Appendix 7 and CD Appendix 17, "Resettlement Budget," for sample budgets from Bank projects) and include suggestions for reducing costs in each category.

Compensation

"Compensation" refers primarily to the cost of payment for expropriated land (including trees and crops that cannot be harvested), housing, structures, and other fixed assets, including assets acquired for temporary project use. It includes the costs incurred to help directly acquire substitute properties. Compensation costs also include the cost of acquiring resettlement sites. Compensation applies to vendors, enterprises, and other commercial operations, as well as residential units (households).

Community Infrastructure and Services Costs

Expropriated public land, buildings, structures, and other fixed assets are more often replaced than compensated per se. These costs can include those for replacing or restoring community facilities (for example, community centers, religious facilities) and public infrastructure (roads, bridges, sewerage, irrigation works, utility lines, and so forth) and for providing access to potable water, fuelwood, grazing areas, or other resources needed to restore living standards. These costs include not only the infrastructure to be replaced, but also the associated services provided. For example, schools and health centers require teachers and health workers.

The Bank requires compensation at replacement cost. Project planners have limited scope to minimize compensation costs. The best way, of course, is to avoid expropriation or at least minimize the adverse impacts of land taking by using, if feasible, less valuable land and avoiding expropriation of structures and other fixed assets to the extent feasible. Once the options regarding location and extent of land taking have been finalized, little flexibility is left in costing compensation. Attention to the timing of land acquisition, for example, may permit a harvest, alleviating the need for crop compensation, but such compensation is usually a small cost in any resettlement operation. Timely payment of compensation can help avoid cost escalation resulting from inflation.

Relocation Costs

"Relocation costs" refers to the costs associated with the physical relocation of people, businesses, livestock, and moveable assets. These include the cost of developing agricultural and residential resettlement sites; cost of transporting affected people and their assets to the resettlement sites; any transfer fees, taxes, or other administrative costs; the costs of identifying new housing or land; and other costs, such as any expenses for shelter for DPs between the time of displacement and the time of relocation. Temporary housing can be a major charge to the project, especially when delays in construction create pressure for several relocations in a short period.

9

Resettlement Site Preparation Costs

In projects involving physical relocation of affected people or allocation of replacement lands, costs associated with the preparation of the resettlement site are a substantial part of the overall relocation costs. Resettlement site preparation costs include the costs of acquiring the land and preparing or improving the sites to fully replace all lost private and community assets. Site preparation costs for agricultural land can include the provision of irrigation infrastructure, soil enhancement, and access, including roads, bridges, and over- or underpasses.

Relocation costs can be kept at a reasonable level through timely preparation of replacement sites and provision of services. But failure to promptly execute the relocation operation can add appreciably to project costs—if project implementation is speeded up before the relocation site is ready, temporary housing will be needed; or if the entire project is much delayed, costs may rise with inflation. In the latter instance, the contingent liability, which is usually not a major issue, can become important if the amounts budgeted fall short of actual needs.

> *Project example.* In China, the Shanghai Environmental Project (Ln 3711) experienced delays in project initiation that increased the pressure to complete civil works and shortened the notification period to less than a month. Many households had no choice but to stay in temporary housing. They either rented from or shared housing with relatives. Each household was paid an additional 60–150 yuan per month, normally for four months, to cover the costs of temporary housing (in 2003, 8.2872 Chinese yuan renminbi = US$1.00).

> *Project example:* Also in China, the Shanghai Sewerage Project (Ln 2794; Credit [Cr] 1779) offered special inducements to displaced families because the notification period was unduly short. Various bonus schemes were designed and implemented to encourage the DPs to relocate from their land and houses as quickly as possible. The bonus packages were generous, and in all cases the relocated households accepted the package, including the provision of government-paid rent. The scale of temporary relocation was substantial and had an appreciable effect on the project budget.

Income Restoration and Improvement Costs

"Income restoration and improvement costs" refers to the costs of ensuring opportunities for DPs to restore or improve their incomes, as well as the costs of providing temporary income support if required. Costs may include purchase of alternative income-generating assets, measures for training, agricultural

9

extension services, identification of employment opportunities, and start-up capitalization for microenterprises. Costs in this category tend to be more contingent, because income recovery depends in part on the skills and attitudes of those affected. However, careful resettlement planning can lower costs by encouraging the DPs' acceptance and adaptation. Conversely, poor planning can increase costs by exacerbating their uncertainty and vulnerability.

Administrative Costs

"Administrative costs" refers to operating costs incurred in preparing and implementing resettlement operations. These include the following:

- *Staff costs*—Staff costs include the salaries and benefits of resettlement staff.
- *Fuel and equipment costs*—Fuel and equipment costs include office expenses, equipment, vehicle, and other costs incurred to operate the resettlement agency.
- *Resettlement preparation costs*—"Resettlement preparation costs" refers to costs incurred to develop and prepare a resettlement budget and plan, including the cost of obtaining the necessary information and conducting various studies (such as census, surveys, and soil-quality and irrigation surveys). These costs are incurred before the budget is prepared, but they may be eligible for Bank financing through the Project Preparation Facility.
- *Technical assistance costs*—"Technical assistance costs" refers to the costs of personnel training, institutional capacity building, and consultancy services.
- *Monitoring and evaluation costs*—Monitoring and evaluation costs cover periodic monitoring of the resettlement program by the resettlement implementation unit and by external agencies.

Estimating Resettlement Costs

Because resettlement involves complex and contingent processes, developing cost estimates and budgets is not always easy. Nonetheless, adequate estimates and budgets need to be prepared based on the best information available at the time of resettlement preparation. In essence, adequate budgets require (a) estimates that, on balance, fall within a reasonable margin of error; and (b) reasonable contingency arrangements.

Resettlement budgets for specific projects will vary according to the scope and complexity of the resettlement measures needed. Nonetheless, for the purposes of preliminary planning, average resettlement expenses for other projects may be useful. On average, according to one review, Bank-supported hydropower project

9

teams estimated at appraisal that resettlement costs would amount to 8–9 percent of overall project costs, whereas their project completion reports indicate an average of roughly 11 percent.[2] From another perspective, current resettlement costs average three to five times per capita gross national product (GNP) for each DP subject to actual physical relocation. Moreover, projects budgeting more than three times per capita GNP have been reasonably free of major resettlement problems, whereas virtually all those budgeting less than two times per capita GNP have experienced significant difficulties.[3] Of course, these are average costs, with a wide range of variation: projects requiring relocation and rehabilitation may cost a lot more, and projects requiring only partial asset acquisition and no actual relocation may cost a lot less.

The basic tools for identifying and estimating resettlement costs are the following:

- A legal *framework* to establish eligibility criteria for entitlements and other forms of assistance;
- A *census* to establish the number and identity of individuals, households, or communities that will be affected;
- An *asset inventory* to detail all of the property (for example, land, buildings, other improvements) that will be affected, usually carried out at the same time as the census;
- A *socioeconomic survey* (or surveys) to determine household incomes and estimate the impacts of resettlement on incomes and living standards (such surveys often uncover costs not previously recognized by planners); and
- *Project technical designs*, including designs for relocation sites, to determine the full range of resettlement facilities and services that will need to be constructed or provided.

Socioeconomic studies can identify costs that may otherwise be overlooked.

The failure to identify the people affected, to inventory affected assets, even temporarily, or to recognize adverse impacts on income sources can lead to cost increases for which financial resources have not been allocated. Bank reports indicate that resettlement cost overruns remain pervasive and generally exceed overall project cost increases.[4] Moreover, because resettlement is typically on the "critical path," underestimation of costs through poor resettlement planning can undermine the performance of the project itself. Socioeconomic studies often provide information that can help planners avoid these errors and their consequences.

Project example: In Thailand, fishers affected by the construction of the Pak Mun dam (Ln 3423) were not covered in the census and

9

socioeconomic surveys carried out at the beginning of the project. Total resettlement cost estimates were, therefore, significantly underestimated, and the project had to allocate significant additional resources to compensate those affected by the decline in incomes from fishing.

Project example: In India, socioeconomic surveys for the Andhra Pradesh Irrigation III Project (Ln 4166; Cr 2952) identified a category of people that would be more severely affected than acknowledged in plans. Although only some of their lands were to be affected, the remaining holdings were not economically viable for agricultural use. The government created another category for functionally landless DPs and revised the resettlement entitlements accordingly.

Project example: In Pakistan, the Left Bank Outfall Drainage Project (Cr 1532) team conducted a socioeconomic survey for Chotiari Reservoir resettlement. The team found that many of the people to be displaced would be unable to move to designated replacement land because they were bound by debts to local *zamindars*. The government decided to pay off the debts to the *zamindars*, thus freeing those affected from this bondage and allowing them to claim their entitlements and restore their livelihoods.

Project example: In Tajikistan, the Pamir Energy Project (Cr 3862) expanded an existing run-of-the-river hydroelectric project. The expansion reduced the volume of a high-altitude natural lake during the two-year construction period. The reduced water levels would affect the growth of lakeshore grasses on which the local people depend for cattle grazing and winter hay production. The project company therefore developed a program to monitor annual lakeshore grass production so that the company could compensate the people, in cash, for lost production. The company budgeted for this expense, and it made arrangements to pay locally nominated representatives for the purchase of hay for the two winters of lower production.

Planning Costs

The costs of preparing resettlement plans (RPs) depend on the complexity of the project and on who is doing the planning. If project agencies have skilled personnel, part of the preparatory costs are likely to be absorbed in existing budgets. Consultants, by contrast, typically obtain flat-rate contracts to perform preparatory work. Contract rates typically reflect the scale of land acquisition and the complexity of resettlement. In some cases, hiring consultants on a contract basis may be more cost-effective than developing internal planning capacity.

For project agencies likely to be involved with more than one Bank project, however, the Bank recommends that agencies develop their own resettlement planning capacity. This is likely to reduce both planning costs and implementation costs over time.

> *Project example:* In China, project agencies often contract with regional design institutes to develop the technical plans for their investments. The design institutes have developed expertise in resettlement planning so they can provide the agencies with a technical proposal that includes the social aspects of the program.

Compensation Costs

In principle, compensation refers to a fairly simple financial transfer in return for expropriated assets. Many costs in this category can be determined with a fair degree of precision, especially where active markets provide prices approximating net present value. Moreover, as a single transaction, compensation is generally free of recurrent costs. Nonetheless, estimation of compensation at replacement cost can be complex, especially where markets function poorly, property values change rapidly, or property rights are uncertain (see "Calculation and Application of Replacement Cost," in chapter 4).

> *Project example:* In India, in the Upper Krishna II Irrigation project (Ln 3050; Cr 2010), compensation rates for land increased from $380 per acre in 1978 to $1,500 for dryland and $2,300 for irrigated land in 1997 (all dollar amounts are current U.S. dollars). The long gestation period significantly increased resettlement costs.

> *Project example:* In Thailand, the Pak Mun Hydropower project (Ln 3423), compensation rates for land increased from between $1,440 and $1,920 per hectare in May 1990 to $8,750 per hectare in December 1991, that is, 7–10 times the market value of the land. This increase was to reduce DP resistance to the project, although by April 1993 land prices had already escalated to $6,560 per hectare, 75 percent of the compensation rate. Resettlement, together with compensation for expropriated land, often leads to severe inflation in land prices.

Community Infrastructure Costs

Community infrastructure costs should not be too difficult to estimate, as they do not suffer the inflationary pressures of land compensation and other aspects of compensation costs. Unfortunately, some projects have failed to identify all the community infrastructure that needs replacement and therefore have underestimated this cost. For example, common property resources—such as land for grazing and gardens, forests for fuelwood and nontimber forest products, and other resources—may be neglected in the inventory of lost assets. In some projects the same infrastructure is provided, such as water supply and schools, but at greater distances from houses, thus imposing additional costs in terms of the time DPs must spend to reach this new infrastructure. If distances are too great, as with schools that are located in another village, DP children may drop out of school. Once again, consulting DPs is very useful in comprehensively identifying community infrastructure and services and therefore contributing to more accurate estimates of the costs to replace them.

Relocation and Resettlement Site Preparation Costs

Most relocation costs are one-time expenses. Packing household effects and business inventories, transporting the goods to the new site, and unpacking are the major expenses. People also need help with meals for the first several days, until they have their kitchens back in running order; and the need for social workers tends to be high during the initial relocation. Costs of relocation may escalate appreciably if facilities in the relocation area are incomplete, making temporary accommodations necessary.

Resettlement site preparation costs can vary a great deal, depending on the extent of preparation required. Additional complexities attend the estimation of site preparation costs until technical designs, timetables, and possibly other resettlement activities are finalized. Such costs may also depend on the choices the DPs make regarding alternative sites or compensation options. Resettlement site development is also a recurring source of cost underestimation, because estimates are often not based on technical expertise, scheduled construction rates, examples from similar projects, or other appropriate sources of guidance. Consultation with the DPs to identify their needs and preferences helps to reduce site preparation costs. Inadequate consultation has even led to resettlement sites being abandoned or requiring far greater investments than originally anticipated. That is why the feasibility analysis described in chapter 8, "Income Improvement," is so important. Proper feasibility analysis can lead to major savings.

> *Project example:* In Pakistan, in the Left Bank Outfall Drainage Project (Cr 1532), irrigation engineers made cost estimates for on-farm irrigation works. They based their estimates on designs and layout maps for the Chotiari Reservoir resettlement. These estimates were 10-fold higher than those in the RP, which had been prepared without the input of technical expertise.

9

193

Project example: In Brazil, in the Itaparica Resettlement and Irrigation Project (Ln 2883), resettlement site preparation costs were based on normal, canal-fed irrigation systems. When these proved insufficient for the substandard lands next to the reservoir, they were replaced with sprinkler irrigation systems, with total land development costs up to $54,000 per hectare, at least triple the norm, and the farmers continue to require water subsidies. Better feasibility analysis of the soils and their irrigation potential would have made clear the economic irrationality of this rehabilitation strategy.

Project example: In Thailand, the Pak Mun Hydropower project (Ln 3423) began to develop a resettlement site 15 kilometers away that would be irrigated by an older dam. None of the DPs was willing to move to the resettlement site, and instead they were all resettled within a kilometer of their former location, usually moving back from along the river to along the newly improved roads to each village. Better consultation with the DPs would have revealed their unwillingness to move to the proposed resettlement site, before resources were wasted developing a site that would never be used.

Income Restoration or Improvement Costs

Estimates of income restoration or improvement costs are typically based on proxies, such as training costs or the costs of providing credit. Alternatively, projects may typically assign a standard unit cost to income restoration or improvement activities. Although these approaches provide preliminary estimates for probable costs, actual costs are highly variable and can include subsidies and maintenance payments during the transition period. The socioeconomic surveys provide enough information to allow a more accurate estimation of costs. If surveys are not available for this purpose, budgets should earmark substantial contingency funds for these costs.

Sometimes the income restoration strategy falters during implementation. Alternative income-generating strategies need to be developed, and this increases costs. If the failure of the initial strategy was the fault of inadequate planning and not the fault of DP implementation, then the costs of designing and implementing an alternative income restoration strategy should be borne by the project, not the DPs.

Project example: In China, the Shuikou Hydroelectric project (Ln 2775) planted orange-tree orchards, but they were unsuitable for that microclimate. Furthermore, too many fruit-tree orchards were planted, and local markets were saturated with certain varieties of fruit. Technical and economic feasibility had been insufficiently analyzed. The orange trees had

9

to be dug out and replaced with more suitable fruit trees and other tree crops, thus increasing costs.

The costing of income restoration and improvement measures is often inexact, because the scope of project assistance necessary is often unclear. In principle, DPs should be fully informed of their livelihood options, make rational economic choices among the possibilities, and succeed in restoring their livelihoods in their first endeavor. In practice, people may choose from a menu of untested options—or may decide on the basis of their short-term interests and concerns—and fail to even restore their previous standard of living, thus making additional assistance necessary. Because Bank policy promotes provision of assistance to DPs to restore their livelihoods as the minimum acceptable outcome, no clear rule can be given for determining the limits of liability. Rather, project agencies must inform DPs as fully as possible about feasible income options and counsel them about the possible consequences of deciding on the basis of their short-term issues and concerns about relocation.

> *Project example:* In China, in the Yangtze Basin Water Resources Project (Ln 3874; Cr 2710) some DPs chose the option of moving back up the slopes surrounding the reservoir, while others chose to move out to lands elsewhere. Over time, those who moved away fared much better than those who had remained in the project area, many of whom now wanted to move out. But the funds allocated had already been spent on housing and other forms of assistance. To resolve the issue, the government has offered only half of the original resettlement package to people who now want to move out, on the grounds that the DPs have to accept responsibility for their own choices.

Administrative Costs

Administrative costs will vary with the scope and complexity of the project. In projects with severe resettlement impacts, for example, a social worker may be needed for each group of 50 families, so the number of administrative staff increases significantly with the size of the resettlement operation. Costs associated with office space, equipment, and vehicle requirements increase similarly. In addition, administrative costs will vary with the institutional arrangement for project implementation. Employing resettlement agency staff specifically for resettlement or distributing resettlement-related tasks among existing agencies and staff may cost the project less than contracting resettlement tasks to consultants, NGOs, or others. However, project decisionmakers also need to take into account the relative effectiveness of different institutional arrangements to achieve resettlement objectives, and costs should not be the only criterion for selecting institutional mechanisms for delivery of resettlement entitlements.

9

Project authorities have run into difficulties with the administrative costs budgeted for resettlement. In some projects, many approved staff positions have been left vacant because funds had not been allocated for hiring. In other instances, office space, equipment, and vehicles have frequently not been on procurement lists, resulting in either poor performance or cost increases in implementation.

Project example: In Bangladesh, only one person was to be assigned full-time to resettlement in initial plans prepared by the Jamuna Bridge Authority (Cr 2569). Over time, the complexity of the operation led to an increase in the resettlement staff to 60 people, even before loan approval.

Financial Flows, Arrangements, and Contingencies

Key Issues

Like RPs in general, resettlement budgets should be viewed as guidelines, not as rigid blueprints. A thorough budgeting process can reduce uncertainty. But even the most elaborate budgeting exercise does not guarantee that adequate funds will be available when needed. RPs should build in mechanisms for financial flexibility, ensuring that funds flow for anticipated resettlement activities when needed and that funds are reserved for unanticipated contingencies as they arise (see CD Appendix 18, "Flow of Resettlement Funds," for diagrams of resettlement financial flows from two Bank projects).

A good practice is to budget by the year as well as by the item.

A partial corrective involves linking the flow of financial resources to the resettlement timetable. Funds may be sufficient but released too late, generating delays, losses to inflation, or other difficulties. Given the fact that most countries have rigid budgetary procedures, timely financial allocation in the government's annual budget is important. Therefore, a good practice is to set up the resettlement budget according to year-by-year spending requirements. Similarly, a good practice is for supervision missions to review future financial requirements in light of past resettlement performance, at least annually.

Earmarking is important if financial management is weak.

In projects with weak financial management or scarce financial resources, it may be advisable to establish financial earmarks or escrow accounts, designating funds that can be used for resettlement purposes only.

Adequate contingency funds are essential.

Imprecise budget estimates are by no means unique to resettlement; all projects assign contingency funds, because virtually all project-related activities involve

9

price or physical contingencies. In resettlement, the sources of contingency are much more diverse, and OP 4.12 seeks to ensure that the project bears any contingent costs, not the DPs.

Like other aspects of the project, establishing adequate contingency funds involves judgment. As a general principle, as resettlement becomes more complex, the potential need for contingency funds increases. Similarly, resettlement is often time sensitive: the longer the interim between identification of resettlement and completion of resettlement activities, the greater the potential need for contingency funds. Thus, projects with multiple subprojects for which resettlement frameworks are prepared at the time of project appraisal need higher levels of contingency funds, because the scope and scale of resettlement may increase significantly during project implementation, when specific subprojects are identified. If contingency is assigned as a flat percentage of estimated resettlement costs, the percentage will logically be higher for projects requiring income restoration activities on any significant scale.

Following standard project practice, both price and physical contingencies are provided for resettlement. If resettlement is phased over a number of years, price contingency is essential to counteract inflation so that payment of compensation and other expenses can be maintained in real terms. (In some projects, the project itself may have a significant impact on land values through land acquisition.) Price contingency is to be estimated according to Bank guidelines and budgeted separately from physical contingency.[5] In principle, physical contingency covers incremental costs of implementation and now is provided for resettlement in many projects. However, the stage of technical preparation affects budgeting for physical contingency. If detailed designs are not available at appraisal, resettlement costs will have to be reassessed when designs are completed.

9

Failure to provide adequate contingency funds can jeopardize timely compensation.

When resettlement budgets lack adequate contingency funds, shortfalls in financing might be passed from the project agency to local governments or the displaced population. Underbudgeting has many causes, such as inflation or design changes that increase the amount of land taken. In either case, the displaced population is likely to bear the burden of the financial shortage as project authorities or administrative officials strive to keep the project on schedule and contain costs.

Project example: In China, the Shanghai Environment Project (Ln 3711) experienced significant increases in the amount of land to be taken, the number of households to be moved, and the number of workers to be assigned new employment. A solution had to be found, and in this case the municipal government decided that resettlement costs would be borne by the respective district governments, instead of the municipal government. This decision shifted the financial responsibility for resettlement to the lower level administrative units and exerted pressure on them. The shift also created difficulties in resettlement financing, such as a delay in disbursement of the transfer subsidy for laborers.

The RP must establish financial responsibility.

The ultimate safeguard in resettlement budgeting is ensuring that financial responsibility is clearly assigned in RPs and loan agreements. Of course, the Bank views the sovereign borrower as ultimately responsible for meeting financial obligations. In projects where resettlement issues span regional or municipal jurisdictions or require action from multiple agencies, however, RPs must delineate sources of funds and mechanisms for timely delivery. When borrower governments commit to financing resettlement, the internal sources of funding may actually come from lower levels of government, local communities, or elsewhere. Where borrowers contract with other agencies to implement resettlement, the task team should review the contract terms to make sure responsibility for contingencies and overruns is established.

> *Project example:* In China, the Second Henan Highway Project (Ln 4027) team implemented a strong financial management system. The village compensation received and the expenditure of resettlement funds were posted regularly within the villages. All city and county resettlement offices established financial sections and maintained separate accounts for resettlement funds. Resettlement funds were included in the annual project auditing exercises. And the city and country resettlement offices conducted internal auditing exercises to verify the appropriate use of funds.

Resettlement entitlements are financial liabilities that can rise and fall without regard to budgetary allocations. Inadequate funding cannot be accepted as an excuse for nondelivery. When income restoration costs are partly contingent on the responsiveness of DPs, the limits of liability are less clear. In terms of financing, good practice is to ensure that adequate funds are provided to create realistic opportunities for restoration or improvement of incomes; some people may need repeated assistance. To reduce costs during implementation, plans need to assess the likelihood that training programs, replacement jobs, or other measures will be sufficient to return DPs to productive lives.

Financial Arrangements for a Resettlement Policy Framework

Stating basic principles is a necessary first step in estimating the cost of resettlement for any project. This policy framework includes eligibility criteria that establish who will be entitled to what forms of compensation, income restoration measures, or other forms of assistance (OP 4.12, Annex A, para. 24[e]). Eligibility criteria also establish the range of impacts directly attributable to the project.

That first step may be all that can be taken for multiphase projects, in which determining the eventual scale or complexity of resettlement is impossible at appraisal. In some multiphase projects, whether *any* resettlement would occur may not be clear. For such projects, the following financial principles would apply.

If resettlement is a possibility, a framework establishing financial responsibility is required.

Unless project documents state categorically that the project will not require involuntary land acquisition, a resettlement policy framework is required. The framework must clearly establish financial and implementation responsibilities and clear arrangements for coordinated delivery of funds and services if more than one jurisdiction or line agency is involved.

RPs with resettlement budgets are required for all components for which final designs can be prepared by the time of appraisal.

Standard procedures for establishing financial arrangements apply to all components for which final designs can be prepared by the time of appraisal. These standard procedures also apply to all components for which civil works are to begin in the first year of the project.

RP approval for subsequent components is required as a condition of approval of the subproject.

To ensure the adequacy of financial arrangements (and other aspects of resettlement planning), Bank approval of a subcomponent or subproject RP is required for initiating civil works.

9

> OP 4.12 states that "for each subproject . . . that may involve resettlement, the Bank requires that a satisfactory resettlement plan or an abbreviated resettlement plan that is consistent with the provisions of the policy framework be submitted to the Bank for approval before the subproject is accepted for Bank financing" (para. 29).

Generally, RP approval is to occur before letting of contracts for civil works, and payment of compensation to DPs and activities related to physical relocation are to be completed before actual construction begins. In some instances (especially if resettlement is identified late in the preparation process), Bank disbursement may be used as a condition for submission of an acceptable RP.

Allocations for contingency funds increase with uncertainty.

When subprojects or components are not identified or their design characteristics are unknown, cost estimates are likely to range from grossly uncertain to nonexistent. Furthermore, such circumstances create a much greater likelihood that entirely unanticipated categories of resettlement impacts will be discovered after the resettlement framework has been agreed to. A good practice is to adjust contingency accordingly and to establish earmarking arrangements if financial management appears weak or complex.

Financial Arrangements for Income Restoration

Eligibility criteria establish who will receive compensation for affected assets and other forms of assistance. One-time costs (relocation expenses) are fairly easy to estimate. But estimating the cost of providing opportunities for income restoration is highly uncertain, especially when DPs are required to shift to unfamiliar productive activities. Although project responsibility for compensation for, or replacement of, expropriated assets is defined, the limits of responsibility for income restoration are less clear.

Income restoration is one of the most problematic aspects of resettlement operations. Bank policy is to minimize all displacement impacts; because of cost, impacts that require income restoration measures especially need to be minimized. Efforts are needed to minimize the number of DPs whose livelihoods are disrupted, and where disruption is unavoidable, efforts are needed to minimize the number of DPs shifting to new occupations. Wage employment is a poor substitute for agricultural land, for example, if the affected DPs lack the requisite skills and some assurance of job security in exchange for labor. When shifting livelihoods is involuntary, the issues of adaptability and job security frequently make income restoration more costly and more complex than providing replacement agricultural land.

When income restoration measures are necessary, a good practice is for financial arrangements to ensure that

- Income support is provided for a reasonable transition period, allowing restoration of income streams;
- Sufficient funding is provided for employment training or start-up capitalization for microenterprises; and
- Contingency funds for secondary income restoration efforts, if initial measures prove unsuccessful.

Bank Disbursement for Resettlement

Current practice shows that borrowers pay most resettlement costs. Few projects with resettlement include any direct Bank disbursement for resettlement activities.[6] Many borrowers have requested that the Bank increase its disbursement to cover these expenses. A common refrain is that the project agencies are committed to satisfactory resettlement but simply lack the funds to provide it.

The Bank has two strong justifications for expanding financial support for resettlement. First, making Bank funds available can alleviate a shortage of funds. Even if a borrower is initially reluctant to borrow for resettlement, supplemental Bank financing could help the borrower take care of resettlement contingencies, and it would negate claims that financial resources are simply unavailable. Second, increasing the Bank's role may be just as important as increasing the flow of Bank funds. Bank disbursement categories typically enjoy greater and earlier attention in planning and implementation among borrower agencies. Bank supervision, too, is typically more intense in project areas subject to Bank disbursement. In effect, tying resettlement performance more closely to disbursement would allow the Bank to set appropriate earmarks for resettlement purposes.

The range of resettlement costs subject to Bank disbursement has expanded. Bank disbursement can now cover virtually all resettlement costs except direct transfer payments for cash compensation, land acquisition, purchase of existing replacement housing, and taxes and legal transfer fees (see CD Appendix 19, "Resettlement Costs Eligible for Bank Financing"). Costs that are covered include all costs associated with land improvement, construction of new housing and community infrastructure, and income-generating measures. In exceptional circumstances, disbursement for land purchase may even be possible (with the explicit agreement of Bank management) if such an action is likely to contribute to poverty reduction and security of tenure of small landholders. So the major constraint to Bank disbursement is not categorical exclusion but that available disbursement options are not being used. In part, this lack of use reflects both a lack of familiarity with various lending mechanisms and the reluctance of some governments to borrow on International Bank for Reconstruction and Development terms for resettlement expenses. In part, this lack of use of disbursement options appears to reflect a shortage of collaborative searches for solutions to problems of resettlement design.

Resettlement activities may be contracted locally, to support the utmost involvement of affected communities. Many resettlement activities are small-scale and often require the involvement of the affected people in actual implementation, to achieve satisfactory results. Competitive bidding in such circumstances is often out of the question. Therefore, these goods or services can be procured through force account or direct contracting with villages or community-based organizations.

Project example: In China, the free-standing Xiaolangdi Resettlement Project (Cr 2605) financed house construction in the new resettlement villages through force account contracts with the resettlement villages

9

(as collectives). Resettlers either hire contractors or employ villagers to build their individual houses.

Project example: In India, the Tamil Nadu Water Resources Consolidation Project (Cr 2745) financed small civil works for on-farm works through direct contracting with community organizations, to maximize local participation.

Project example: In Pakistan, the Left Bank Outfall Drainage Project (Cr 1532) financed small civil works for on-farm works through direct contracting with community organizations, to maximize local participation.

Financial monitoring assesses effectiveness of input use.

A good practice is to use financial monitoring to assess the effectiveness of expenditures. In resettlement, "effectiveness" necessarily depends on whether compensation and resettlement services reach intended recipients and have the intended effect.

Two common complaints in the field are payment delays and insufficient payment. In some countries, as compensation passes through the bureaucratic approval process various government agencies may divert a portion of the funds for other purposes, public or private. In China, for example, land compensation funneled through township or county governments might be used for development activities that do not adequately benefit the villages or individuals directly affected. In some countries, local government officials allegedly demand commissions for delivery of compensation or other benefits. In areas with such alleged practices, a good practice would be to have the implementation plan include mechanisms to ensure delivery of compensation and other benefits. Such mechanisms include the following:

- A *revolving fund*, to ensure prompt payment if budget constraints or bureaucratic processes are likely to cause delays;
- *Public disclosure of compensation amounts and public payment*, to enhance transparency and discourage exploitative practices;
- *NGO involvement*, to deliver the payments or monitor the compensation procedures;
- *Payment of compensation by check or by direct deposit into a bank account*, to reduce immediate opportunities for extortionate practices;
- *Conditional provisions in the RP*, to prevent people from being evicted from their land or house before they have received full compensation; and
- *Grievance procedures in the RP*, to give DPs a remedy when they believe they have been treated improperly.

9

In some projects, community-based entitlements may be provided for loss of common property or other community facilities. In such cases, monitoring agencies must determine whether all project-affected individuals enjoy access to community-based remedies and benefits.

Notes

1. "Less than half of the FY86–FY91 projects include resettlement budgets, followed by a sudden jump to 85 per cent in FY92 and approaching 100 percent in FY93–FY94." World Bank. 1996. *Resettlement and Development: The Bankwide Review of Projects Involving Involuntary Resettlement 1986–1993*. Environment Department, Washington, D.C., SDP 13, p. 142.

2. World Bank. 1993. *Involuntary Resettlement in Hydropower Projects*. Industry and Energy Department, Washington, D.C., pp. 44–45.

3. If per capita cost measures are calculated and used, they should refer only to costs of providing resettlement benefits and services to the affected population and not to costs associated with replacing public infrastructure or restoring public services that benefit a much broader population. If the latter costs are included, the per capita costs reported would likely be very high, while actual expenditures on DPs may be far from adequate. See *Resettlement and Development*, pp. 145–46.

4. *Resettlement and Development*, p. 145.

5. See OP 6.50, Annex B (Expected Price Increases and Interest Rates).

6. The review of projects for *Resettlement and Development* (p. 47) revealed that fewer than 15 percent included direct Bank financing for resettlement. It can be seen that the Bank indirectly finances resettlement, however, whenever the Bank's financial contribution is figured as a proportion of overall project costs, including resettlement costs.

9

Chapter 10

Surveys, Monitoring, and Supervision

This chapter first describes the survey information required for resettlement planning and the instruments used for information gathering. This information gathering is essential for determining the applicability of Operational Policy (OP) 4.12, identifying displaced persons (DPs) and those that are especially vulnerable among them, establishing baselines for measurement of income restoration and other objectives, and designing technically feasible and socially acceptable alternatives.

The chapter also describes methods that project agencies, independent monitors, and the Bank can use to gather information during implementation. Monitoring and supervision are critical for successful resettlement. For many Bank projects in general—and many resettlement components in particular—sophisticated planning does not reliably generate desired project outcomes. Accordingly, Bank studies and resettlement reviews now emphasize improving results on the ground. Because of the myriad social and economic contingencies that arise during project implementation, resettlement is better conceived not as a rigid blueprint, but as a learning process in which tentative plans are adapted responsively to unfolding obstacles and opportunities. The chapter also considers issues of discretion and responsibility when agreed plans are subject to change during implementation.

What OP 4.12 Says

10

OP 4.12 (including Annex A) and Bank Procedure (BP) 4.12 provide detailed guidance on the studies needed for developing a detailed resettlement plan (RP). As stated in OP 4.12, the studies, conducted in the early stages of project preparation and with the involvement of potential DPs, include the following:

"(a) The results of a census survey covering
   (i) current occupants of the affected area to establish a basis for the design of the resettlement program and to exclude subsequent inflows of people from eligibility for compensation and resettlement assistance;
   (ii) standard characteristics of displaced households, including a description of production systems, labor, and household organization; and baseline

(continued)

(continued from p. 205)

information on livelihoods (including, as relevant, production levels and income derived from both formal and informal economic activities) and standards of living (including health status) of the displaced population;

(iii) the magnitude of the expected loss—total or partial—of assets, and the extent of displacement, physical or economic;

(iv) information on vulnerable groups or persons as provided for in OP 4.12, para. 8, for whom special provisions may have to be made; and

(v) provisions to update information on the displaced people's livelihoods and standards of living at regular intervals so that the latest information is available at the time of their displacement.

(b) Other studies describing the following:

(i) land tenure and transfer systems, including an inventory of common property natural resources from which people derive their livelihoods and sustenance, non-title-based usufruct systems (including fishing, grazing, or use of forest areas) governed by local recognized land allocation mechanisms, and any issues raised by different tenure systems in the project area;

(ii) the patterns of social interaction in the affected communities, including social networks and social support systems, and how they will be affected by the project;

(iii) public infrastructure and social services that will be affected; and

(iv) social and cultural characteristics of displaced communities, including a description of formal and informal institutions (e.g., community organizations, ritual groups, nongovernmental organizations . . .) that may be relevant to the consultation strategy and to designing and implementing the resettlement activities" (Annex A, para. 6).

Furthermore, OP 4.12 specifies that "the borrower's obligations to carry out the resettlement instrument and to keep the Bank informed of implementation progress are provided for in the legal agreements for the project" (para. 23).

Moreover, "the borrower is responsible for adequate monitoring and evaluation of the activities set forth in the resettlement instrument. The Bank regularly supervises resettlement implementation to determine compliance with the resettlement instrument. Upon completion of the project, the borrower undertakes an assessment to determine whether the objectives of the resettlement instrument have been achieved. The assessment takes into account the baseline conditions and the results of resettlement monitoring. If the assessment reveals that these objectives may not be realized, the borrower should propose follow-up measures that may serve as the basis for continued Bank supervision, as the Bank deems appropriate" (para 24).

BP 4.12 reiterates the importance of fulfilling the terms of the resettlement plan. "A project is not considered complete—and Bank supervision continues—until the resettlement measures set out in the relevant resettlement instrument have been implemented. Upon completion of the project, the Implementation Completion Report (ICR) valuates the achievement of the objectives of the resettlement instrument and lessons for future operations and summarizes the findings of the borrower's assessment. . . . If the evaluation suggests that the objectives of the resettlement instrument may not be realized, the ICR

(continued)

(continued from p. 206)

assesses the appropriateness of the resettlement measures and may propose a future course of action, including, as appropriate, continued supervision by the Bank" (para. 16).

For a process framework, the baseline census and subsequent monitoring program are determined during the initial consultative processes. The baseline census determines, among other matters, the number of people that will be affected by the project and their bases of livelihood.

According to OP 4.12, a process framework describes how the "project components will be prepared and implemented," the "criteria for eligibility of affected persons," and "measures to assist affected persons in their efforts to improve their livelihoods or restore them, in real terms, to pre-displacement levels, while maintaining the sustainability of the park or protected area" (Annex A, para. 27).

The information required for a resettlement plan (RP) or a process framework, when elaborated by the DPs, falls into four general operational categories. These categories are as follows, although the sequence in which information becomes necessary for project preparation may differ from case to case.

1. Identification of general impacts of a proposed project:
   - Determining whether OP 4.12 applies;
   - Estimating magnitude of displacement and asset losses;
   - Searching for alternatives to avoid or minimize displacement; and
   - Gathering information on affected public infrastructure and community services.
2. Census to establish eligibility for entitlements:
   - Enumerating all affected persons and structures, to prevent fraudulent claims for compensation from inflows of people;
   - Categorizing all affected assets; and
   - Determining standard household and demographic characteristics (as the basis for resettlement data management).
3. Baseline information for restoration of incomes and living standards:
   - Gathering information on the full resource base and other socioeconomic indicators of the affected population, including income derived from the informal sector and from common property.
4. Information for design of feasible resettlement program and entitlements:
   - Identifying local organizations and social institutions capable of helping to design and implement resettlement provisions; and
   - Determining perceptions of, and preferences for, potential resettlement options.

10

Table 10.1   The Project Cycle and Information Requirements

Project cycle	Information required
Identification	Land acquisition assessment
Project concept definition	Census of DPs
	Inventory of assets to be acquired
Preappraisal and RP preparation	Socioeconomic surveys and consultations
	Socioeconomic baseline studies
	Assessment of institutional capacity of
	implementing agency
	Entitlement policy
	Land market survey
Implementation	Reporting by implementing agency
	Internal monitoring and supervision
	External monitoring and diagnostic studies
	Bank supervision
	Midterm review (interim evaluation)
Project completion	Evaluation of income restoration

Note: DP, displaced person; RP, resettlement plan.

Depending on the specific context and processing timetables of the project, these studies can be combined or undertaken in separate exercises. In countries with poor residential or property registration, conducting a census early on to establish eligibility and discourage land invasions or fraudulent claims for compensation makes sense (see OP 4.12, para. 16: "Persons who encroach on the area after the cutoff date are not entitled to compensation or any other form of resettlement assistance"). Elsewhere, the census and inventory of assets are frequently combined in one survey to establish basic data on the magnitude of impact. The time and resources required for gathering information will vary significantly, depending on the project and the complexity of its impacts. In projects with large-scale or complex resettlement operations, information gathering not uncommonly continues for 6 months or more (Table 10.1).

Identification: Land Acquisition Assessment

If land is to be acquired or sovereignty to be exercised over occupied public lands, further assessment to determine the magnitude of socioeconomic impacts is mandatory. The land acquisition assessment should be undertaken as early as possible so that sufficient time is available to prepare the RP. For projects requiring an environmental impact assessment or where a social impact assessment is being conducted, the land acquisition assessment can be incorporated as one of

10

Table 10.2   Land Acquisition Assessment

Land acquisition assessment	Information sources
Quantity of land required	• Planning documents, including engineering designs and maps
Location of land required	• Field verification
Use of land required	• Field verification • Consultations with DPs and technicians
Productive use (e.g., agricultural or commercial), including present use of public lands designated for the project and seasonal or periodic uses; estimated number of households affected in each category	• Local records • Field verification
Estimated number of residential households affected	• Field verification
Tenure status of present users	• Local records • Field verification
Presence of public or community infrastructure	• Land records • Local verification

Note: DP, displaced person.

their elements. The terms of reference for the environmental impact assessment would then require socioeconomic analysis as well. In projects expected to have minor impacts only, the land acquisition assessment would normally be a low-cost, short-duration exercise, undertaken by the borrower, with assistance from a Bank mission member.

The information needed for land acquisition assessment and the likely available sources of these data are outlined in Table 10.2 (see also CD Appendix 4, "Guidelines for Land Acquisition Assessment," for more detailed guidance on land acquisition assessment).

Census of DPs and Inventory of Assets

A census of DPs and their households and the inventory of assets to be acquired serve two vital functions. The primary function is to identify DPs eligible for resettlement entitlements, which is especially important if disclosure of project plans is likely to encourage land invasion and fraudulent claims for compensation. The census and inventory also supply an important part of the resettlement database to be used for project monitoring and supervision (Table 10.3)

10

Table 10.3   Elements of a Census

Census and asset inventory	Information sources
Determining eligibility for entitlements	• Property registration records, with on-site verification
Determining categories of entitlements	• Information from surveys regarding the type and extent of impacts
Providing (partial) basis for valuation and compensation	• On-site assessment of quantity and quality of assets

(see also Appendix 2 and CD Appendix 5, "Checklist for Census Information"; Appendix 6, "Census Forms"; and CD Appendix 7, "Asset Inventory").

The census and the inventory of assets can be done separately. As each requires visits to all affected households, however, doing them together is generally more efficient. Where establishing ownership or length of residency is difficult, the census should be conducted as soon as possible, to determine a cutoff date for eligibility for entitlements. In such situations an immediate partial inventory, sufficient to establish the number and general size of structures and other assets to be taken, may be advisable to supplement the census. The precise attributes of structures and an inventory of remaining fixed assets (such as boreholes) acquired or affected can be determined later.

Census data are time sensitive.

Establishment of baseline data is time sensitive. The census needs to be undertaken as soon as possible to ensure accurate determination of eligibility for entitlement. The accuracy of census information falls over time. Lengthy delays or major redesigns between the time of the census and the beginning of implementation may necessitate a new census, not merely adjustment of an existing one.

Generally, if a lag of 3–5 years or more occurs between the census and actual acquisition, demographic and socioeconomic factors may change significantly, diminishing the validity of census data. Children are born; some people die; some come of age, marry, or move away. A good practice is therefore to hold the census within 1 year of the scheduled date of land acquisition, if possible. If acquisition of land does not occur for at least 2 years after gathering of baseline data, the data can usually be updated. If an early census has been necessary to establish eligibility but implementation is delayed, a reasonable solution may be to redo the earlier census before implementation, using agreed procedures for handling transfer of entitlements through inheritance, maturation, or property transactions.

Project context influences duration of census and asset inventory.

The project context may also affect the timing of census and inventory exercises. In rural settings, where impacts are generally less diverse, the census may be less complicated. However, the affected population can be more dispersed, particularly in the case of linear projects. In urban projects, in contrast, impacts are often more complex but the population is spatially concentrated. If the project is expected to have more than 1,000 DPs, at least 8 months before appraisal is commonly needed for census and survey work and resettlement planning, and this estimate assumes organizational competence in taking the census.

Sometimes resettlement planning is phased, posing additional challenges for the census. In linear projects, implementation may begin in one location, while engineering and siting specifications (such as precise alignments for highways or transmission lines; or the site for a future component of the project) remain unknown farther along the route. When the approximate location and land requirements are known, Bank practice is to establish a maximum corridor of impact. This corridor is based on the area included in preliminary designs and takes in the entire population of this area as determined by census. Although this population is likely to be larger than that actually to be affected, this procedure basically identifies those potentially eligible for entitlements. In addition, this census information may be useful in choosing precise sites and alignments to minimize negative impacts. If siting of a component cannot be even roughly determined, this component is to be formally treated as a subproject, for which a separate census and RP must be prepared once site details are determined.

Data Collection Formats

The formats for the census and the asset inventory must be adapted to the specific context and informational requirements of the project. Large infrastructure projects in rural areas generally need the most extensive information, because entire communities must be moved. In rural areas, a wide range of temporary and seasonal impacts may have to be carefully recorded. Many urban projects, by contrast, collect more limited information if these projects involve little or no income restoration. Here, the difficulty often lies in operationalizing the concept of household, as many living arrangements can be found in poor urban areas. Finally, linear projects, such as rural roads, that take small portions of agricultural plots may need only particulars about the landowner and the percentage of the plot to be taken. In any case, the format needs to be field-tested, to ensure that the questions and the phrasing of them elicit the required information.

Staffing

Project agencies seldom have the in-house expertise to conduct a census of DPs or an inventory of assets to be acquired. Therefore, a qualified government agency or a consultant group experienced in census and survey work is usually

10

Table 10.4   Topics of a Week-Long Training Program

Day	Topic
1	Introduction: development programs
2	Census questionnaire (and vocabulary)
3	Enumerator interviews: practice
4	Interviewing techniques: field test
5	Review: issues in questionnaire and interviewing

contracted to prepare and carry out the studies. Whether the work is done in-house or contracted out, personnel are selected for cultural and cross-cultural compatibility. For example, female enumerators may be more acceptable to women in many settings than male ones would be. Also, enumerators need to be familiar with the local area and fluent in local languages. Even skilled enumerators will benefit from a week-long training program on the use of the census and inventory formats in the field and on coding and filing procedures (Table 10.4). Such courses will improve the accuracy of the census.

If a project resettlement office is to be established, the office staff should also attend these training sessions, to learn how to maintain and update the census and survey data during implementation and monitoring.

Field Operations

The number of DPs, the size of the project area, and the time available determine the logistics of data collection. One supervisor can oversee about eight enumerators. Generally, enumerators can conduct only two or three interviews, each an hour long, per day. Their time is also spent on transport, repeat visits, and reviewing and coding of information.

The first few days of the interview process are usually the most problematic. The field supervisor must go over each form from each enumerator each day and discuss any systematic difficulties. (For practical reasons, the supervisor can only review the questionnaires in the evening and discuss them with the enumerators the next morning, before work begins.) Any unacceptable questionnaires must be redone. In areas where the DP population is literate, the DP can review the completed interview form and certify its accuracy by signing the form.

Data and Records

The usual practice is for enumerators to code information while the teams are in the field. This way, incomplete or obviously incorrect information can be corrected on repeat visits. The information is then sent to the project office for data entry and filing. Whether data are recorded manually or on a computer (Box 10.1), the standard practice is to check all interviews for consistency and accuracy.

Box 10.1 Censuses, Surveys, and Computer Technology

For projects producing only small-scale displacement, census data can be collected and managed manually, and customary procedures can be used. But if large numbers of DPs are involved (for example, more than 500 households), manual processing of census and survey data may delay the project. Or if RP implementation requires the coordination of several agencies, inconsistent data management can create confusion. Both of these unwelcome prospects can be avoided with computer technology.

Keeping data in electronic form helps ensure rapid and effective maintenance and simplifies merging of accumulating data sources. The computerized resettlement database also serves as the backbone for both internal and independent monitoring.

If computer technology for data management is not available at the local level, the project resettlement office (or other designated data management agency) can supply implementing agencies with the necessary technology and training. (Bank financing and technical assistance may also be available for establishing a computerized resettlement data management system.) Independent monitoring consultants or organizations should be encouraged to participate in training programs, to ensure compatible data and computer methodologies.

Census and baseline survey data may be of use to several implementing agencies, project resettlement officers, and independent project monitors. A good practice is therefore to design data collection formats to treat only the main objectives of the project and resettlement program, while accommodating the resettlement needs of all users. Standardizing formats for data recording, codes, and software (if data are processed electronically) requires coordination among all concerned institutions. The data can then be transmitted to the project resettlement office (or another designated data management agency) to be checked for accuracy, updated as implementation progresses, and eventually shared with collaborating agencies. Security procedures may be necessary, both to maintain the accuracy of the information and to ensure the privacy of the DPs.

RP Preparation: Socioeconomic Analysis

A land acquisition assessment provides preliminary information about the socioeconomic impacts of the project. Additional socioeconomic analysis may be necessary, however, to minimize displacement, to enable the project team to design appropriate and acceptable economic rehabilitation measures, and to enlist the participation and cooperation of the people to be affected by the project. This analysis is especially important if no entitlement policies are already in place, if some groups (for example, indigenous peoples, women, the poor) are vulnerable to severe risk or hardship, if whole communities will be displaced, or if host communities are likely to be adversely affected by a sudden population influx.

10

As is the case with the land acquisition assessment, much of the socioeconomic information can be gathered soon after project identification, even before the scope of the project is determined. Although preliminary information can be gathered from secondary data sources, it usually needs to be supplemented with information obtained from a socioeconomic survey, conducted in tandem with, or following, the census. Focus-group discussions and various participatory rural appraisal methods can be used (see chapter 7, "Consultation and Participation," for further detail) (see CD Appendix 8, "Baseline Survey Data," and Appendix 4 and CD Appendix 21, "Terms of Reference for a Socio-Economic Study," for an outline of the content of a socioeconomic analysis of resettlement in a Bank project).

The census and inventory—supplemented, as necessary, with data from socioeconomic surveys—are used to establish baseline information on household income, livelihood patterns, standards of living, and productive capacity. This baseline information constitutes a reference point against which income restoration and the results of other rehabilitation efforts can be measured (see also CD Appendix 10, "Household Income Stream Analysis").

In addition to information on productive activities, sources of income, and property rights, the socioeconomic analysis, particularly in rural areas, usually provides information on local social and economic organization, potential risks, and local forms of cooperation. OP 4.12 (Annex A, para. 6[b]), as noted earlier in this chapter (see "What OP 4.12 Says"), lists other areas of socioeconomic analysis: land tenure and transfer systems; the patterns of social interaction in the affected communities; public infrastructure and social services that will be affected; and social and cultural characteristics of displaced communities.

Interviews are conducted with a systematic sample and using uniform questionnaires. In small projects, such as a rural road widening and upgrading project that affects a limited number of people, everyone affected may be interviewed. In large projects, such as a dam and reservoir or urban upgrading project, the number of people affected may run into the tens of thousands, and only a sample survey would be feasible. Although all DPs must be enumerated in the census, the DP population can be sampled for the socioeconomic surveys. Stratifying the sample—that is, ensuring that small, vulnerable groups (the very poor, female heads of household, the elderly, and minority ethnic or religious groups) are overrepresented—should provide a sufficient number of cases for statistical analysis. This approach is necessary because the initial socioeconomic survey will provide the baseline for future monitoring and evaluation (Table 10.5). Because monitoring and evaluation will focus on the situation of vulnerable and poor groups during project implementation, their statistical representation in the original survey is critical.

Table 10.5   Elements of a Socioeconomic Analysis

Socioeconomic analysis	Information sources
What forms of social organization (family or kinship, caste, patron–client relations, informal institutions, and so forth) structure group relations and decisionmaking?	• Field observation • Household surveys, focus-group discussions, PRA methods
What forms of property (including common property), social specialization, or division of labor forms the basis of economic activities?	• Key-informant interviews • Focus-group discussions
What risks does the project present, and which groups are vulnerable to them?	• Key-informant interviews • Household surveys, focus-group discussions, PRA methods
Whose cooperation (village heads; leaders of professional groups, women's groups, cultural groups, and so forth) is essential to effective resettlement design and implementation?	• Key-informant interviews

Note: PRA, participatory rural assessment.

Implementation: Monitoring

The objective of monitoring is to identify implementation problems and successes as early as possible so that the implementation arrangements can be adjusted. Monitoring of RP implementation is important in all projects involving involuntary resettlement, for several reasons. Resettlement is often on the critical path and if not implemented adequately can cause severe delays in the project. Resettlement affects people's lives directly and can cause them severe hardship. Monitoring is the main mechanism for alerting management to delays and problems in implementation, and early identification often makes it easier to adjust programs and fix problems.

Monitoring and supervision are related but distinct activities. Monitoring is the responsibility of the borrower and can be divided into internal (or project administration) and external (or independent) monitoring. Monitoring primarily involves the systematic use of information to determine the extent to which plans are being implemented effectively. This information also helps in identifying problems requiring adjustment in the RP itself. Meanwhile, supervision is a Bank activity and is used to verify the findings from project monitoring.

The basis of any monitoring system is regular reporting within the project. One monitoring system, the Management Information System, usually covers

Table 10.6   Elements of a Monitoring System

Management information system[a]	Source of information or data collection method	Responsibility for collection and analysis
"(a) Procurement and physical delivery of goods, structures, and services, and the costs incurred"	Internal, monthly, or quarterly physical and financial reporting	Implementing agency; resettlement unit, if existing
"(b) Use of the structures and services by the project beneficiaries and their initial reactions"	Monitoring, DP contact	Project resettlement unit and contracted external monitoring agency
"(c) Reasons (social, economic, or environmental) for unexpected reactions by the project beneficiaries, when these are revealed by the information obtained in (b) or through other sources"	Diagnostic studies and other special studies	External monitoring agency or other agency contracted to study the issue (academic institution, NGO, consultants)
"(d) Measurement of output indicators such as productivity gains, to the extent that these can be measured during implementation"	Internal reporting and external sample surveys	Project resettlement unit or external agency (academic institution, NGO, consultants)

Note: DP, displaced person; NGO, nongovernmental organization.

[a] According to Operational Directive 10.70 (Project Monitoring and Evaluation) (para. 14).

the areas shown in Table 10.6 (see CD Appendix 30, "Monitoring Programs and Forms," for examples of monitoring systems in several Bank projects).

The importance of regular reporting on financial and physical progress—the basic functions of project management—cannot be overemphasized. Responsible project managers rely on timely feedback on availability of inputs, flow of finances, and delivery of services. Progress is usually reported against time-bound action plans (normally expressed in the project implementation plan as bar charts, Gantt charts, or Microsoft Project tables). Quantitative indicators provide an efficient tool for monitoring many aspects of project performance. In the case of socioeconomic impacts, however, supplementary qualitative assessment is likely to be necessary.

Table 10.7 Process Model for Tracking Project Performance

	Inputs	Activities	Outputs	Effects or outcomes	Impact
Internal monitoring	—————	—————	————		
External monitoring		—————	—————	—————	
Supervision	—————	—————	—————	—————	
Evaluation			—————	—————	—————

Table 10.7 provides a simplified overview of who monitors which activities.

Table 10.8 provides a set of generic monitoring indicators for resettlement. No single set of indicators is universally sufficient, however, and project-specific indicators are likely to be needed to reflect project-specific activities and implementation arrangements.

Close monitoring of DPs is helpful to project management.

The monitoring of DPs is essential to successful overall project monitoring. A direct channel for DPs to use to voice their concerns, perceptions, and acceptance or rejection of project interventions is critical to successful implementation. DP contact and monitoring are often linked to a strategy for participation. Periodic meetings, focus-group discussions, or other such participatory venues are usually part of the implementation strategy and are thus the responsibility of the implementing agency. To augment line agency interaction with DPs, external or outside consultants should be engaged to work with DPs and to verify the internal project (that is, administrative) reporting. As is well known, DP interview responses depend both on the questions asked and on who is asking the questions. DP monitoring can be reported in both quantitative and qualitative terms. A good practice is to record the minutes of meetings and to communicate the major issues raised to project management as part of the regular review process. More systematic surveys may be used, perhaps on an annual basis, to obtain quantitative information about the initial effects of project interventions.

Special studies may be necessary, especially in large-scale projects.

Special studies may be commissioned specifically to address problems identified through regular reporting or DP monitoring. For example, market surveys may be necessary to assess changes in regional demand patterns that affect the feasibility of economic rehabilitation options considered workable during resettlement preparation. Similarly, studies may be needed to examine why DPs refuse to accept certain options or fail to adapt to resettlement. Such studies recommend actions to remedy any deficiencies, many of which cannot be anticipated

10

Table 10.8   Suggested Generic Indicators of Resettlement Performance

Sequence	Dimensions of the resettlement process	Indicators	Means of verification
Inputs	Establishment of project management unit	Qualified staff in place / Equipment available / Finance on deposit	Quarterly internal monitoring reports
Process	Information to DPs	Information disseminated	Internal and external monitoring
	Capacity building	Training of DPs	Internal and external monitoring
	Consultation and participation	Meetings held and committees formed	Internal and external monitoring
	DP opinions and attitudes	Qualitative information on DP reactions	Internal and external monitoring of complaints heard by community leaders
Outputs	Compensation	Compensation paid for acquired assets	Internal and external monitoring
	Acquisition	Assets acquired	Internal and external monitoring
	Compensation	Community assets replaced and relocation site prepared	Internal and external monitoring
	Relocation of DPs	Relocation completed and grants paid	Internal and external monitoring
	Rehabilitation	Jobs, businesses, or incomes provided (including DP satisfaction)	Internal and external monitoring
Impact	Results	Incomes restored / Living standards restored	External monitoring

Note: DP, displaced person.

at the planning stage. Another good practice is to conduct these studies as early as possible, as part of the early review of resettlement implementation required under the Bank's policy for all projects with significant resettlement, so they can be concluded in time to adjust plans and procedures and benefit the most DPs.

Internal Monitoring

During project preparation, and as part of the RP, the implementing agency develops a monitoring and reporting framework for resettlement activities. Central to this framework are the census of DPs, the inventory of assets, and the eligibility criteria and description of resettlement entitlements constituting the basis for the agreed RP. The organizational unit responsible for project reporting on resettlement (project resettlement unit, where it exists) will oversee the progress in resettlement preparation and implementation. The unit will review the regular progress reports on key indicators of finance, inputs, and activities.

The overall monitoring and reporting framework provides a routine flow of information from the field to the headquarters of the implementing agency. Monitoring is based on predefined indicators and includes periodic supervision and verification by the resettlement unit or those in charge of resettlement operations.

Monitoring reports must be submitted to the Bank, although this can be done after the project agencies have had a chance to review and comment on drafts provided by the monitoring agencies. The spatial concentration of urban and other projects in a well-defined area makes it feasible for the project agencies to directly participate in land acquisition and resettlement. The dispersed nature of linear projects, by contrast, often leads project agencies to contract land acquisition and resettlement out to local officials, and the project agency often considers the activity complete once the contract with local officials is written. The monitoring of actual progress, too, is often left to local officials who do not forward their reports to the project agency. The project agency, however, remains ultimately responsible for land acquisition and resettlement, even if the actual work is contracted out, so internal reporting from localities to project offices needs to be established.

> *Project example:* In China, the Third Xinjiang Highways Project (Ln 7143) paid compensation to county land administration bureaus, but the project authority did not track subsequent distribution of compensation. No regular reviews of the resettlement activities were conducted. In consequence, little or no flow of information occurred between the local government and the project authority, which basically considered resettlement the responsibility of local officials.

External Monitoring

External (or independent) monitoring is often needed to periodically assess resettlement implementation and impacts, verify internal reporting and monitoring, evaluate qualitative aspects of the resettlement program, and suggest

10

adjustments to the delivery mechanisms and procedures, as required. Integral components of this monitoring activity include a social and economic assessment of the results of entitlements and a measurement of the income and standards of living of the DPs before and after resettlement (see CD Appendix 31, "Terms of Reference for Impact Assessment," for an outline of the content of a resettlement impact assessment from a Bank project). The following activities are the standard functions of the external monitors:

- Verifying internal reports by field-checking delivery of compensation to intended recipients, including the levels and timing of the compensation; readjustment of land; preparation and adequacy of resettlement sites; construction of houses; provision of employment, the adequacy of the employment, and income levels; training; special assistance for vulnerable groups; repair, relocation, or replacement of infrastructure; relocation of enterprises, compensation, and adequacy of the compensation; and transition allowances;
- Interviewing a random sample of DPs in open-ended discussions, to assess their knowledge and concerns about the resettlement process, their entitlements, and the rehabilitation measures;
- Observing the functioning of the resettlement operation at all levels, to assess its effectiveness and compliance with the RP;
- Checking the type of grievance issues and the functioning of grievance redress mechanisms by reviewing the processing of appeals at all levels and interviewing aggrieved DPs;
- Surveying standards of living of DPs (and people in an unaffected control group, where feasible) before and after implementation of resettlement, to assess the effects of the resettlement on their standards of living; and
- Advising project management regarding possible improvements in the implementation of the RP.

Regular external monitoring begins about the same time as implementation activities and continues until the end of the project. It sometimes continues even beyond project completion if the standards of living of all DPs have not at least been restored and the Bank and the borrower agree that the situation needs continued follow-up. In projects with large-scale resettlement impacts, a good practice is to conduct standard-of-living surveys before beginning resettlement (baseline survey) and then to repeat them 3 years after resettlement and thereafter, as required, to assess the effectiveness of remedial measures.

Project example: In China, the Second National Highways Project (Ln 4124) carried out exemplary monitoring in its Guangdong Section.

10

Researchers from the independent monitoring agency personally inspected infrastructure, visiting rebuilt houses and monitoring reclamation sites. They participated in both village meetings on resettlement issues, such as land adjustment and selection of resettlement sites, and township- and county-level meetings on land reclamation. They interviewed DPs on their general level of welfare and heard grievances, when on-site, from DPs. They reviewed the annual reports on the economic and social development of the villages, and then they conducted periodic sample surveys of living standards to verify the findings of those reports.

Project example: Also in China, the Inland Waterway Project (Ln 3910) hired an independent agency to oversee resettlement implementation. The institute monitored the construction of protective works and livelihood restoration. It set up three stations in the project area and produced monthly reports for the project authority.

Bank Supervision of Resettlement Operations

"Recognizing the importance of close and frequent supervision to good resettlement outcomes, the Regional vice president, in coordination with the relevant country director, ensures that appropriate measures are established for the effective supervision of projects with involuntary resettlement. For this purpose, the country director allocates dedicated funds to adequately supervise resettlement, taking into account the magnitude and complexity of the resettlement component or subcomponent and the need to involve the requisite social, financial, legal, and technical experts. Supervision should be carried out with due regard to the Regional Action Plan for Resettlement Supervision" (BP 4.12, para. 13).

Further, "throughout project implementation the TL [team leader] supervises the implementation of the resettlement instrument ensuring that the requisite social, financial, legal, and technical experts are included in supervision missions. Supervision focuses on compliance with the legal instruments, including the Project Implementation Plan and the resettlement instrument, and the TT [task team] discusses any deviation from the agreed instruments with the borrower and reports it to Regional Management for prompt corrective action. The TT regularly reviews the internal, and, where applicable, independent monitoring reports to ensure that the findings and recommendations of the monitoring exercise are being incorporated in project implementation. *To facilitate a timely response to problems or opportunities that may arise with respect to resettlement, the TT reviews project resettlement planning and implementation during the early stages of project implementation.* On the basis of the findings of this review, the TT engages the borrower in discussing and, if necessary, amending the relevant resettlement instrument to achieve the objectives of this policy" (BP 4.12, para. 14; emphasis added).

10

Supervision

Supervision is closely linked to monitoring, because in projects with significant resettlement impacts, supervision relies to a large extent on monitoring data and information generated by the implementing agency. Supervision is also distinct from monitoring, however, both because it is a Bank responsibility and because supervision implies attention to problems at a higher level of authority. Supervision is a critical activity during implementation, as circumstances may change after the RP has been prepared, which in some projects could have been several years earlier. Without effective supervision and necessary midcourse correction, the implementing agency may continue to implement an outdated or infeasible RP. With the shift in emphasis from the blueprint approach to the process approach and practical results, supervisory arrangements become more important.

Supervision of resettlement serves both control and support functions. The supervisory team assesses the extent to which Bank financing is used for the intended purposes, and this process enhances public accountability. Bank supervision is also a management function. The supervision team can make recommendations based on multiple sources of information, including internal reporting, external monitoring, supervision field visits, and interaction with frontline staff, DPs, and local NGOs.

According to OP 13.05 (Project Supervision), supervision is one of the Bank's most important activities. One of the objectives of Bank supervision is "to identify problems promptly as they arise during implementation and recommend to the borrower ways to resolve them; [and] recommend changes in project concept or design, as appropriate, as the project evolves or circumstances change" (para 2[b, c]) (see Appendix 9 and CD Appendix 29, "Resettlement Supervision," for generic resettlement supervision guidelines and a supervision plan for a Bank project).

Resettlement operations need appropriate supervisors.

To provide the best quality technical assistance to the borrower, the supervision team must have the appropriate expertise. Until recently, resettlement operations often went unsupervised, were supervised from afar (without field-checking), or were supervised by personnel unfamiliar with resettlement nuances and complexities. Identifying the appropriate person to supervise resettlement depends in part on the nature of the project, the phase of the project, and local or country characteristics. Urban planning expertise, for example, is obviously appropriate for an urban development project. Legal expertise may be more important in initial stages. When projects affect indigenous peoples, supervision should include attention to the cultural setting. In general, however, supervision is conducted by people with some blend of expertise, including applied social

10

science, project management, physical planning, and microenterprise development. The supervision team may include Bank personnel, or consultants may be hired for this purpose.

Supervision can be adapted to the resettlement process.

Three factors are especially important in devising an effective plan for resettlement supervision:

- *The demonstrated capacity (and commitment) of the implementing agency or agencies*—To enhance the efficient use of Bank resources and further the goal of client ownership, project agencies with proven ability are to be encouraged to work with a minimum of supervision. In contrast, project agencies with a poor or unproven resettlement record are likely to require intensive supervision, at least in the initial phases of implementation.
- *The complexity of the project*—As a general rule, projects affecting few people or producing minor impacts require limited supervision. In contrast, projects generating large-scale displacement and likely to significantly affect the vulnerability of DPs require more, and more specific, supervision.
- *The timing of the resettlement impact within the project*—Projects requiring the resettlement of rural agriculturalists within a rural agricultural setting, for example, are likely to require greater supervision in the early phases of relocation and site preparation than later on. In contrast, projects requiring rural agriculturalists to make a transition to wage employment are likely to require prolonged supervision of income restoration measures.

Supervision reports result in action.

Identification of resettlement inadequacies through supervision is pointless unless supervision reports result in action. Ideally, translating these reports into effective action will require a collaborative effort between the Bank and borrower. A good practice is for project agencies to participate in the supervision process, increasing the likelihood that supervision will have the desired consequences. Also important is discussing the key findings and recommendations of this process with the project decisionmakers at the end of each supervision mission. Significant recommendations, especially those related to unresolved problems, can be reiterated by senior management in the official communication that follows the supervision mission. Most implementation problems can be resolved with prompt identification and timely discussion of possible solutions with the borrower. Where a shared commitment to resettlement objectives is

10

lacking, however, effective Bank supervision may require a clear and firm demonstration of the Bank's willingness to invoke suspension of the project or to take other measures to enforce remedial action.

For collaborative supervision to be effective, the project officials reviewing the supervision reports need to be of sufficient rank or status to take action. They also need the support of project management. Bank supervision teams similarly require a commitment from country and regional management. When problems are not alleviated through normal supervision processes, issues may be brought to the attention of higher levels of management and, if necessary, resolved by invoking the available legal remedies, such as threat of suspension, suspension, and loan cancellation.

Projects are not considered complete unless the RP is implemented.

A question has often arisen about how to address the outstanding resettlement issues after the completion of the project. To answer this question, it is important to delineate two phases of resettlement implementation:

- The first phase is when the borrower implements the actions described in the agreed RP. These are typically input-oriented activities, such as paying compensation, preparing resettlement sites, moving people to new sites, providing inputs for various income improvement strategies, and implementing transition arrangements. Because the resettlement program is one of the components of the project, the project cannot be considered complete until the RP agreed on with the borrower is fully implemented.
- The second phase is when the inputs provided as part of the RP help meet the key economic objective of the resettlement program: to improve or restore the incomes and livelihoods of DPs. This phase can sometimes take a long time and depends on many variables beyond the quality and timelines of the inputs. Although this phase starts as soon as inputs are administered, it often continues beyond project completion.

The Bank's resettlement policy requires that at the time of project completion, after the RP has been fully implemented, an assessment be made of the extent to which DPs have been able to improve or restore their standards of living. This assessment is usually based on the results of a follow-up socioeconomic survey conducted by the borrower at the time of project completion. If the assessment reveals that most DPs have already improved or restored their standards of living and the remaining ones are on track to doing so in the near future, no further supervision is needed. However, if the assessment reveals that a significant portion of DPs have not been able to improve or restore their incomes and are also unlikely to do so in the near future, the task team should discuss additional measures with the borrower to address this situation. The task team may (in consultation with the borrower) decide to continue the supervision of the resettlement program after the formal completion of the project, as necessary (see CD Appendix 33, "ICR Section on Involuntary Resettlement," for the section of a Bank project Implementation Completion Report covering involuntary resettlement).

> *Project example:* In the Upper Krishna Project, in India (Ln 3050; Cr 2010), and in the Itaparica Irrigation and Resettlement Project, in Brazil (Ln 2883), the Bank and the borrowers agreed that Bank supervision of resettlement should continue after formal project completion.

The Project Supervision Report can be an effective supervisory tool.

The revised format of the Project Supervision Report (PSR) requires the task team to rate implementation performance in terms of all safeguard policies triggered by a project. Thus, if the policy on involuntary resettlement has been triggered at project entry, each PSR comments on the progress of resettlement implementation. To check "not applicable" or "not rated" during supervision is not possible in such cases. A rating on resettlement must be provided, along with an explanation for the rating. When the relevant sections of the rating section are being filled out, a "compliance matrix" opens up in the PSR, describing the indicators of compliance with the resettlement policy during implementation.

Early Review of Resettlement Implementation

A recurring concern in resettlement operations, as in Bank operations more broadly, is effective implementation of plans, to achieve improved results on the ground. In environments with considerable uncertainty, such as those common to resettlement operations, implementation must be responsive to actual conditions and the people whose efforts actually determine outcomes. Consequently, plans are subject to revision or adaptation.

The midterm project review, which is normally a midcourse evaluation of project implementation and may result in corrections, is generally done at too late a stage for resettlement corrections. Resettlement is a front-loaded activity—among the first activities to be undertaken before the start of project construction. Therefore, resettlement implementation requires an early review so that the project team still has time to undertake corrective action (see CD Appendix 32, "Resettlement Mid-Term Review," for an example of a mid-term review report from a Bank project).

10

Bank operational policies and procedures support an institutionalized process of early resettlement review. "To facilitate a timely response to problems or opportunities that may arise with respect to resettlement, the TT reviews project resettlement planning and implementation during the early stages of project implementation" (see BP 4.12, para. 14, quoted earlier in this section, "Project Completion: Bank Supervision of Resettlement Operations").

Furthermore, the Bank policies on monitoring (OD 10.70) and on supervision (OD 13.05) insist on early identification of implementation obstacles and necessary adjustments to overcome them. Indeed, in the Africa Region, midterm reviews are now mandatory for all investment projects, and they are becoming increasingly common in other regions. This trend has been encouraged by inclusion of midterm reviews in Bank project status reporting (Form 590).

An early review of resettlement is also desirable in uncertain or complex situations.

Early review of implementation is required for projects involving significant resettlement. The review is also critical in projects burdened by high levels of uncertainty or complexity, when any of the following conditions hold:

- RPs are not fully specified by appraisal;
- RPs involve untested rehabilitation measures or compensation arrangements;
- Resettlement may expose groups to impoverishment, social disintegration, or other sources of vulnerability; or
- The borrower's capacity to implement an RP is unproven or believed to be weak.

The timing of the early review of implementation is important.

The best time to conduct the review is after early experience offers evidence of the effectiveness of plans but time remains to make adjustments to benefit as many DPs as possible. The temptation is often to wait until more information is available, but the cost of waiting can be a loss of leverage over events. Because the resettlement review assesses the resettlement process, and much of the resettlement process occurs at an early stage, the resettlement review is likely to precede any midterm review of the overall project.

A formal review is an opportunity to resolve issues.

Regular project monitoring and periodic Bank supervision are likely to identify problems in implementation. Many such problems may be correctable through minor adjustments to routine, marginal acceleration of service delivery, or other adjustments within agreed plans. A formal review, by contrast, provides an

10

opportunity to resolve issues arising out of the plan or design, changes in the project environment, or failure to correct problems found in regular monitoring and supervision processes.

Changing RPs may raise issues of responsibility and authority, however. Where changes related to basic resettlement policies or entitlements are necessary, task team leaders may need to seek legal and technical guidance. BP 13.05 (Project Supervision) states that, "During project implementation, if priorities or circumstances surrounding the project change, it may be desirable to introduce corresponding changes in the project, its design, or the implementation arrangements. The TL [team leader] discusses any proposed change with the borrower and consults with the lawyer to determine how to effect the change, including any required modifications to the legal agreements. If the change may involve Bank policies such as those concerned with financial management, procurement, or environmental and social safeguards, the TL consults with the responsible specialists in the Region." (para. 16). As a general resettlement principle, plans can be adjusted to add overlooked persons to the census of DPs or to enhance entitlements, as needed, without formal Bank approval. But elimination or reduction of entitlements will likely require both formal approval to ensure legality and reappraisal to ensure appropriate arrangements for entitlements and implementation. An aide-mémoire (and the PSR) reflects agreement with the borrower on actions to be taken, along with financial arrangements and designation of responsibility.

10

Chapter 11

Organizations for Planning and Implementation

This chapter focuses on the agencies and organizations involved in resettlement operations and on the design of measures for capacity building. After discussing the specific steps in organizational assessment and capacity building, the chapter reviews the strengths and weaknesses of various organizational models and suggests mechanisms to make the functioning and coordination of the agencies across political and administrative divisions more effective. Organized according to the project cycle, the chapter looks first at the organizations involved in resettlement planning and preparation, then at those involved in resettlement implementation, and finally at those involved in monitoring and evaluation.

What OP 4.12 Says

All resettlement plans should include an analysis of the institutional framework for the operation and the definition of organizational responsibilities (Operational Policy [OP] 4.12, Annex, paras. 8 and 18).

Specifically, OP 4.12 states that the analysis of the institutional framework will cover the following areas:

"(a) the identification of agencies responsible for resettlement activities and NGOs [nongovernmental organizations] that may have a role in project implementation;

(b) an assessment of the institutional capacity of such agencies and NGOs; and

(c) any steps that are proposed to enhance the institutional capacity of agencies and NGOs responsible for resettlement implementation" (Annex A, para. 8).

The organizational framework for implementing resettlement is also outlined in OP 4.12. The framework includes the following elements: "identification of agencies responsible for delivery of resettlement measures and provision of services; arrangements to ensure appropriate coordination between agencies and jurisdictions involved in implementation; and any measures (including technical assistance) needed to strengthen the implementing agencies' capacity to design and carry out resettlement activities; provisions for the transfer to local authorities or resettlers themselves of responsibility for managing facilities and services provided under the project and for transferring other such responsibilities from the resettlement implementing agencies, when appropriate" (Annex A, para. 18).

11

Effective resettlement depends on the commitment and capacity of organizations responsible for resettlement preparation and implementation. Bank project supervisory reports and Operations Evaluation Department (OED) evaluations show a close correspondence between institutional commitment and the success of a resettlement program. Indeed, one recent OED study concluded that a main lesson is that "genuine borrower commitment to doing resettlement well is the key to success."[1] Borrower commitment is needed to ensure the close coordination of all the organizations involved in resettlement activities, as explicit and effective coordination requires adequate funding, staff, and equipment.

Organizational Responsibility for Resettlement Preparation and Planning

Soon after finding that a project involves involuntary resettlement, the borrower determines which agency is responsible for resettlement planning and implementation. Existing units or agencies often have experience with resettlement and Bank requirements and can be expected to implement resettlement effectively. Even if the project authority has no dedicated resettlement unit, the resettlement arrangements can be discussed with those responsible for preparation and planning. Indeed, a senior official must have responsibility for resettlement preparation and planning and sufficient authority to coordinate activities of various agencies or ministries. In that case, however, some or all of the resettlement preparation activities will likely be contracted to consultants.

The responsible agency or person will have to call on a wide range of experts to prepare and implement the resettlement operation. Preparation of the resettlement component has two phases: (1) activities and studies to investigate resettlement impacts and the feasibility of remedial measures; and (2) preparation of the resettlement plan (RP) on the basis of those findings. Resettlement often involves diverse activities that require specialized expertise. The organizational assessment ascertains whether appropriate expertise has been used in determining the range of activities required and whether qualified people will conduct each of these activities. For example, inexperienced surveyors may assume that areas surrounding a village are uncultivated when what looks like uncultivated bush is in fact manioc fields. In land-based resettlement programs, a project agency lacking qualified personnel for objective assessment may assume that replacement land consisting of hills, forest, or even parched wasteland is cultivable. But slope, soil, water availability, climate, and other variables can have a tremendous impact on crop selection, output, and the applicability of displaced persons' (DPs') existing skills. For this reason, good practice is to have a qualified agent undertake technical feasibility studies *before* replacement lands, if any, are included in a resettlement strategy.

11

Key preparation activities and the most suitable organizational arrangements for each are outlined in Table 11.1 and described in the next subsections.

Project example: In Cambodia, the land acquisition and compensation plan for the Phnom Penh Power Rehabilitation Project (Credit [Cr] 2782) contained a chart that detailed the required activities, the agencies responsible, and the agencies charged with carrying out each activity:

Activity	Agency responsible	Agency for implementation
Physical surveys	Électricité du Cambodge (EDC)	Planning Department (national) Department of Cadastre and Geography (municipal)
Loss assessment	EDC and municipality	Planning Department
Negotiation with owners on compensation	EDC and municipality	Planning Department District land office Village head
Notification	Municipality	District land office
Establishment of appraisal	EDC	Project implementation unit (PIU)
Transfer of land ownership	Municipality	District land office
Payment of compensation	EDC and municipality	PIU District land office Village head
Supervisory visits	EDC	PIU deputy director
Progress reports	EDC	PIU
Monitoring and evaluation	EDC-contracted nongovernmental organization (NGO)	NGO social scientists

11

Land Acquisition Assessment

Resettlement preparation cannot begin in earnest until a preliminary estimate of the scope and severity of adverse impacts is available. A land acquisition assessment (or similar exercise) establishes the extent, location, and current use of lands required for the project. Where land records are accurate and up to date, the project office may work directly with the land registry office to determine ownership and use of the plots to be acquired. Where land records are incomplete or inaccurate, the project office may need to hire a consulting firm

Table 11.1 Preparation Activities and Agencies Responsible

Activity	Actions	Agencies involved
1. Land acquisition assessment	• Conduct detailed land survey of plots to be acquired and confirmation of ownership	• Project resettlement unit • Land registry office • NGO (field verification)
2. Census and socioeconomic surveys		• Project resettlement unit • Local administrative officials • NGOs
3. Determination of eligibility criteria and resettlement entitlements	• Determine legal obligations for compensation and resettlement • Agree on additional assistance for compensation and resettlement	• Project agency or resettlement unit • Government agencies (legal, financial, technical, and administrative)
4. Consultations	• Inform DP population • Discuss project area or route and extent of land acquisition • Discuss valuation and grievance procedures • Establish committees	• Project resettlement unit • NGOs
5. Feasibility study of resettlement sites	• Determine viability of residential, commercial, and agricultural relocation sites	• Project resettlement unit • NGOs • Relevant government agencies (land survey, soils, irrigation, urban development, water and sanitation, and so forth)
6. Feasibility of income improvement measures	• Determine the technical, economic, and financial feasibility of each of the proposed income improvement strategies before they are included as options to be made available to affected people	• Project resettlement unit • Relevant government agencies for land-based income improvement strategy (land survey, soils, irrigation, geological, urban development, water and sanitation, etc.) • Labor agency • Employment agency • Welfare agencies • Finance agency • Consulting firms to conduct the economic feasibility studies of the proposed strategies • NGOs

Note: DP, displaced person; NGO, nongovernmental organization.

11

or nongovernmental organization (NGO) to verify ownership and use. Where land records do not exist, the project office or a contracted agency will have to hold meetings with residents to ascertain ownership and use. A resettlement specialist can assist the assessment team or review its results to ensure that the project takes the least amount of land consistent with its requirements.

> *Project example:* In India, the National Thermal Power Corporation (Loan [Ln] 3632) reassigned three staff to work in the land registry office in one state to help process the land records of the plots to be acquired. During this experiment, record processing took a little less time.

Census and Socioeconomic Surveys

The project agency generally conducts the census of DPs and inventory of assets, in close coordination with local government officials. If the implementation capacity of the project agency is weak or the impacts are complex or diverse, specialized NGOs are contracted to carry out this work. Project staff and local government officials are nonetheless involved, because appropriate government authorities must validate the census results. To prepare for the census, good practice is to verify that the census instruments are reliable; personnel are well trained and speak the appropriate languages; and in areas where opportunistic land invasion may be a problem, enough personnel and resources are available to conduct the census quickly. The project office is also responsible for ensuring that skilled personnel and equipment are available for tabulation.

> *Project example:* In Zambia, under the Power Rehabilitation Project (Cr 3042), the national power company established an environmental and social affairs unit to conduct the baseline census for prospective land acquisition and rights-of-way. The unit conducts the initial census of affected properties, but it contracts with certified valuators to establish the undepreciated replacement value of these properties and works through local authorities to identify alternative plots of land acceptable to DPs.

Socioeconomic surveys often involve both quantitative (statistical) and qualitative (participatory) methods, so usually they are also best conducted by an experienced and qualified NGO or research organization. Some areas may simply lack local organizations with the potential to conduct surveys. If an external organization is hired to conduct the survey, it should work together with local organizations or representatives of the project-affected people. This arrangement is mutually advantageous, as survey teams obtain invaluable knowledge of local conditions while giving local groups experience with survey methods.

11

Eligibility Criteria and Resettlement Entitlements

Ideally, the unit or people responsible for resettlement preparation are authorized to recommend criteria for determining eligibility for resettlement entitlements. They are also authorized to determine the kinds and amounts of assistance needed. Some projects give an experienced and qualified resettlement unit the authority to develop eligibility criteria and assistance packages, subject to established guidelines and managerial oversight. For other projects, establishing a resettlement oversight committee, with representatives from relevant legal, financial, technical, and administrative agencies, may be advisable.

Project staff dealing with resettlement preparation may have no authority to determine eligibility criteria, and or they may lack support for their decisions from higher level policymakers. Such situations can cause costly delays if disagreements over eligibility criteria or forms of entitlements subsequently arise. Both the task team and the resettlement specialist need to assess this aspect of resettlement preparation and make appropriate arrangements to prevent loss of valuable time.

Consultations

The resettlement program should be designed on the basis of consultations with the DPs and their representatives. Capable (and available) NGOs or other nonproject institutions can be given the primary role of conducting consultations with the DPs, as long as the organizations have credibility and are accepted by the DPs. Also, DP committees, comprising representatives of the affected people from each impact category, can improve the quality of consultations.

Consultation with DPs is fundamental, but project and local government officials are still involved in the process because they have substantial influence on the design of the resettlement program. In practice, joint consultation with DPs and officials is a delicate matter. If government officials are not present, the project has no "ownership," and no dialogue occurs between the project authority and the DPs. If government officials attend DP meetings, they may unduly influence the communication process. Consultation, therefore, involves a mix of methods to ensure that the various DP groups have the opportunity to speak freely. Typically, government or project officials who are present at village meetings are there to hear concerns and answer questions, but they do not assist in individual household interviews or focus-group discussions.

Summaries of the consultations are a good mechanism to preserve institutional memory of attitudes and preferences.

11

Feasibility Study of Resettlement Sites

The feasibility of relocation sites must be closely reviewed before any are accepted in a resettlement program. These feasibility reviews are of two types: (a) technical studies of the adequacy of the sites to support the development activities planned for them; and (b) an analysis of site acceptability to the DPs, who may have reasons other than technical ones to reject (or accept) proposed sites. Because both forms of analysis require considerable expertise, an assessment of the organizational capacity of many service agencies is often necessary. Agencies typically involved in technical feasibility studies may include the following:

- Land survey agency, to determine topographical features, slope, contour mapping, and so forth;
- Soil survey agency, to determine the type of crops that can be cultivated at the resettlement sites;
- Irrigation agency, to establish the irrigation potential of the site;
- Groundwater agency, to establish the availability of water and the extent to which it can be harnessed;
- Site planning agency, to conduct urban or rural planning, depending on the type of resettlement site; and
- Urban development agency, to develop housing plans and neighborhood infrastructure.

In most cases, these activities can be conducted by local infrastructure agencies. Where local capacity is weak or the relocation involves complex interventions, external consultants or agencies from other parts of the country can be engaged. Wherever possible, site planning also includes local NGOs specializing in this field. They often have a deep understanding of local opportunities and constraints, as well as of the needs and priorities of the people.

The project resettlement unit can do the consultations on site acceptability with the help of local officials, especially if the latter have a good rapport with project-affected people and the project agency enjoys a reputation for fair treatment. If these conditions do not apply, engaging a local NGO or other intermediary is advisable.

Feasibility Study of Income Improvement Measures and Formation of DP Committees

Income improvement is the core objective of any resettlement program affecting livelihoods, so competent consulting firms or agencies must be contracted to evaluate the feasibility of income proposals. Experience shows that if this evaluation is omitted, the measures advanced by project resettlement agencies or

11

local governments alone are likely to be seriously deficient, and DPs often bear the costs of failure. To increase the fit between income improvement strategies and DPs' needs and preferences, good practice is to promote frequent consultations with DPs and provide them with opportunities to make informed choices.

Because the same project can have many different kinds of rehabilitation programs, getting the right organizations to assess the feasibility of each program can help prevent improper selection of program elements. The assessment of land-based measures requires agricultural expertise. A different mix of expertise is required to assess technical, economic, and financial feasibility of non-land-based measures, such as employment programs or microenterprise development. The agencies typically involved in these analyses are the following:

- Labor agency, to inventory skills and assess the existing labor pool and its training needs;
- Employment agency, to identify current vacancies and opportunities for job creation and to assess the viability of enterprises hiring DPs;
- Marketing agency, to assess existing market conditions and competition and the economic feasibility of activities to promote new products or services;
- Welfare agencies, to strengthen or create a safety net for unemployable DPs or for DPs who subsequently lose their jobs; and
- Finance agency, to inventory existing sources of credit for business creation or expansion.

The involvement of other planning and administrative agencies may be required if income improvement measures hinge on market restructuring or regulatory change. The critical requirement here is that the organizations that are responsible for designing and implementing resettlement strategies should also be involved in determining their feasibility. For example, if the program provides jobs to DPs, potential employers can be involved in determining the number of jobs available, the skills that are necessary, and the general terms of employment. Similarly, if microenterprise development programs are to rely on existing banks or credit agencies, the implementing agency needs to consult these banks or credit agencies to determine eligibility criteria and lending and repayment rules and, if necessary, to devise mutually acceptable incentive schemes or subsidies.

Giving all agencies in the resettlement operation an opportunity to review and approve the draft RP before final approval is strongly recommended. RPs need to be approved by authorized agencies, even though some detailed preparation may have been done by consultants or other specialist agencies. Consulting the provincial and local agencies responsible for implementing the RP helps ensure both the technical feasibility of the program and the necessary administrative support.

11

Implementation

The RP serves as a guideline for implementation. As Bank reviews have noted, the failure of many resettlement operations is due less to the quality of the planning than to an inability to implement them adequately to attain project objectives in practice. Implementation fails to keep pace for a number of reasons:

- Organizations responsible for implementation may not understand the RP. They may not have been involved in its preparation and may lack an understanding of its objectives.

Project example: In China, project senior management negotiates the loan agreement, but field officers may not be aware of the conditions agreed to or the requirements of Bank resettlement policy. In exemplary good-practice cases, the project office informally translates the relevant sections of the project agreement into Chinese for distribution to local officials.

Project example: In Vietnam, the project authority of the First Highway Rehabilitation Project (Cr 2549) had agreed that anyone living in the rights-of-way was included in the resettlement program. Subsequently, the government issued a road-safety decree allowing for eviction, without compensation, of anyone living along the national highways without a permit. The Provincial People's Committees, who were responsible for implementing the RP, had no information on what had been agreed to in the RP and started evicting people, including those entitled to resettlement under the project. Protracted negotiations were needed to rectify the situation.

- Project agencies may lack the flexibility or adaptability to depart from conventional modes of operation or to respond to shifts in the project environment.

Project example: In India, Coal India, Ltd. (Cr 2862) has a standard set of procurement regulations, which necessarily apply to resettlement operations as well. The procurement regulations for competitive bidding, among other matters, made it difficult for the company to purchase local products made by DP groups.

- Coordination mechanisms may be weak, leading to delays or breakdowns if resettlement activities require the cooperation of various agencies. Usually, such a situation occurs when the central resettlement unit is weak or ineffective.

Project example: In China, the project authority for the Shanghai Second Sewerage Project (Ln 3987) had a change in resettlement management,

11

and this change weakened its capacity to manage and coordinate resettlement. The responsibilities for resettlement were effectively split between district governments. Without central coordination, resettlement implementation varied in quality, and serious difficulties arose in resettlement management.

- Project agencies may have a technical bias, focusing more on relocation and physical development and less on income restoration measures and socioeconomic factors in resettlement outcomes.

Project example: The National Highways Authority of India (NHAI) (Ln 3632) is largely staffed by civil engineers, many of whom see their job as road construction. The need to consult with local populations and work with DPs to define alternatives and other such matters has not been part of their perspective. The Bank has found it useful to collaborate closely with NHAI on social awareness training of NHAI staff. Staff thus broaden their view of their jobs to include consideration of the social consequences of road construction.

- Bank attention may be front-loaded, dedicating a lot of time and resources to project preparation and approval but giving little attention to supervision during implementation.

Project Launch Workshop

The project launch workshop initiates most Bank projects and provides a valuable opportunity for the workshop leaders to summarize preparation, recapitulate the main provisions of the RP, and review the benchmarks for assessing implementation. A good practice is for workshop organizers to consider the following issues:

- Participation of the Bank resettlement specialist assigned to the project.
- Participation of internal and external monitoring agents in discussions of implementation.
- Participation of the field staff to be involved in implementation, as well as the staff involved in preparation. (Confusion can result during implementation if the implementers do not understand the RP provisions or the agreements reached during resettlement planning. In extreme cases, the field staff of implementing agencies do not even have copies of the RP and continue to work according to local guidelines and practice.)
- Participation of project resettlement staff, who will discuss eligibility criteria, entitlement policy, organizational responsibilities, and other RP provisions.

11

- Agreement on key benchmarks that the resettlement specialist, monitoring agencies, and project resettlement staff will use in assessing progress during implementation.

Organizational Units

Organizational capacity and interorganizational coordination are vital to improving resettlement implementation. But the capacity of an organization cannot be assessed without consideration of its resettlement role and responsibilities. Normally, some combination of the following organizations is key to a well-implemented resettlement program:

- Project resettlement unit;
- Field offices of the project resettlement unit;
- Resettlement steering committee;
- Grievance redress committee; and
- Other service agencies (responsible for delivering entitlements and conducting activities specified in the RP, such as relocation, income restoration, and monitoring).

Project Resettlement Unit

A central project resettlement unit in the project agency provides a necessary core office for coordinating resettlement. The size, skills, and organizational structure of the project resettlement unit depend on the functions it has to perform. In projects with only minor resettlement, the unit's basic functions are to distribute funds to local offices, serve as a secretariat to the steering committee, and coordinate the work on internal monitoring reports. In such cases, the unit needs to be only large enough to handle financial management and secretariat functions and may be, for example, a section of the agency's environmental unit. In projects with major resettlement responsibilities, the project resettlement unit itself implements resettlement, either centrally, if the project is areally compact, or through its own network of field offices, if the project is dispersed. Typically, projects with major resettlement responsibilities require a much larger unit and more diverse skills and equipment than projects with minor resettlement responsibilities.

> **Project example:** In China, project agencies contract local government to acquire land and undertake any required relocation and income restoration. Most road projects have small project management units responsible for contracting with local authorities. By contrast, reservoir and other large-area projects usually establish separate project management units to coordinate the many tasks that have to be undertaken.

11

Project example: In India, NHAI (Ln 3632) established a small, four-person social and environmental unit at headquarters to coordinate the activities of the field unit at each project site. The headquarters unit was responsible for providing guidelines on terms of reference, selection of contractors, and compilation of periodic monitoring reports.

Project example: In Bangladesh, the Jamuna Bridge Project (Cr 2569) established a large resettlement office to manage surveys, process information, and assist DPs with relocation and income restoration, when necessary.

The project management unit requires its own budget.

When a project management unit is established in a new project, it usually has its own budget for purchases and operational expenses. When this unit is established within an existing agency, it may not have a separate budget, especially within the first year or two. The lack of a separate budget and of delegated authority to spend funds usually forces the unit to petition the existing agency for every request. These institutional procedures may be time-consuming and inefficient.

Project example: In India, NHAI (Ln 3632) established a separate environmental and social unit to coordinate land acquisition and resettlement in its many projects. Because the unit was established in the middle of the fiscal year, it did not have its own budget line and therefore had to present all its requests through the usual organizational channels. In consequence, the unit limited its requests and operated with minimal staff and facilities for its first year.

A good practice is for the headquarters unit to participate in performance evaluations of field staff.

Resettlement is almost always a component of the main project investment. In consequence, resettlement staff work under the supervision of the overall project manager, who is responsible for performance evaluations. Good practice suggests that if headquarters and field units are far apart, responsibilities for performance evaluation should be shared between the field project manager and the headquarters resettlement unit.

Local Field Offices of the Project Resettlement Unit

Differences in capacity of local field offices explain much of the uneven character of resettlement implementation sometimes seen in a project. Establishing local offices to promptly respond to DP concerns is important. Population density,

11

variations in language, and distance between locations, among other factors, help determine the appropriate levels of decentralization for resettlement. Smaller or more remote offices, however, sometimes lack skilled personnel, operating funds, or resources (such as vehicles or equipment) needed for their work. Because field offices are primary contact points for DPs, designated personnel should be familiar with participatory methods and consultations.

A checklist of issues to be addressed in the design and functioning of field offices includes the following:

- Locations that allow DPs easy access to project-affected areas and resettlement sites.

Project example: In India, until 1995, the offices of the Upper Krishna Project (Ln 3050; Cr 2010) were in the state capital. As a result, DPs had to travel several hundred miles to raise issues with project authorities. A reorganization of the resettlement unit in that year moved the project management unit to the project area, moved the head of the unit to the relocated headquarters, and established local field offices. Under the new regime, DPs had much easier access to project officials.

- Adequate incentives for qualified staff to work in field offices. Ideally, staffing and promotion patterns indicate that resettlement is important and will be rewarded, although this may be difficult to arrange in many project agencies. Financial and nonfinancial incentives may be needed to motivate staff assigned to remote locations.

Project example: In India, Coal India, Ltd. (Cr 2862), established a new cadre—resettlement officers—to the existing cadres of mining engineers, human resources officers, and accountants within its personnel system. The addition of the new cadre provided the possibility of promotion within its ranks and organizational support for the practitioners, as well.

- Structured communications between the project resettlement unit and field offices. Good communication channels are needed so that information can flow from the field to the project officials and field staff can obtain support or guidance for contingencies.

Project example: In India, NHAI (Ln 3632) implemented an electronic communications system between headquarters and its many field offices. Previously, headquarters staff could communicate with field staff only by telephone, which was difficult because field officers were often out of the office. Neither headquarters nor field staff had mobile telephones. Although the electronic communications system required staff training, especially for senior managers, it greatly helped project communications.

11

- Devolution of financial power to field offices, to allow problem solving without involving central project officials. Local offices need to be financially accountable, but to function effectively they also need to be responsive to requests and claims from DPs, and they need the authority to disburse funds for routine resettlement activities.

Project example: In India, the chair of NHAI (Ln 3632) alone approved all headquarters purchases and travel. In consequence, expenses outside the budget could not always be approved promptly.

- Adequate transportation and office facilities. The work of field offices can be stifled by lack of vehicles, office equipment, and other facilities. Without vehicles, staff may be unable to visit DP areas; without office equipment, staff may find it difficult to maintain information files, prepare reports, or communicate with headquarters. A separate budget line for field office expenses can help lessen such difficulties.

Project example: In India, the Environmental and Social Mitigation Project (Cr 2862) of Coal India, Ltd. made specific allocations for vehicles and office equipment, such as computers and telephones, for the social field units at its mines. In addition, the vehicles were ordered in a specific color so that they would be used by only the social unit staff.

Resettlement Steering Committee

RPs describe the various components of the resettlement program and the organizations responsible for their implementation. Each of these components typically requires coordination between and within various organizations. The typical RP assumes that these activities will take place as planned and that coordination will not be an issue. However, even the best of RPs—those with seemingly adequate institutional mechanisms—may fail to deliver their objectives if coordination is lacking. Thus, coordination is a critical part of resettlement design.

If several organizations are involved in resettlement implementation, they are not likely to be under the administrative control of the project agency. Some may be agencies affiliated with other ministries, some may be autonomous state agencies, and others may be NGOs or private firms. Civil works and resettlement in some projects cross provincial or regional boundaries and therefore involve agencies in various jurisdictions. A fairly small resettlement operation may need only a coordination unit inside the project agency itself; the unit would be headed by a senior official. In more complex situations, coordination groups or steering committees above the level of project management may be needed to integrate the activities of multiple agencies across multiple jurisdictions. Such a group is often interministerial and interjurisdictional, representing all agencies

11

responsible for resettlement funding and implementation and enjoying a mandate to make binding policy decisions. The responsibilities of a steering committee might include the following:

- Coordinating effective and timely inputs into RP preparation;
- Resolving problems related to coordination of several implementing agencies;
- Monitoring other development activities in the project, to reconcile project and nonproject activities;
- Responding to implementation problems identified in internal and external monitoring reports; and
- Ensuring adequate consultations with all stakeholders, including DPs or their representatives.

Project example: In Pakistan, the Ghazi-Barotha Hydropower Project (Ln 3965) established an independent development organization to help bring about participation and oversee resettlement activities. The board of the Ghazi-Barotha Development Organization comprised 13 members, including 6 community representatives divided evenly between men and women. The organization was also responsible for maintaining ongoing consultations with DPs and the community organizations of all the villages.

Another good practice is to translate key documents into the language of the project area.

Translating key documents—or parts of documents—into the language used in project implementation is one simple but often overlooked aspect of project coordination. All agencies need to be informed about project commitments and obligations. Often, though, the project agency senior staff negotiate the agreements but neglect to inform the staff responsible for implementing those agreements. Translating at least key sections of the project agreements into the language used in implementation helps to ensure awareness of project agreements at all levels. The translated brochures can be developed for the project launch workshop, and then additional copies can be distributed to other project agencies and their staff.

11

Grievance Redress Committee

Effective organizational design and coordination substantially decrease the probability of problems in implementation. Nevertheless, some DPs are still likely to believe they have been treated inadequately or unfairly. Providing an accessible and credible means for DPs to pursue any grievances may decrease the likelihood of overt resistance to the project or of protracted judicial proceedings that can halt implementation. For such reasons, the Bank requires that RPs specify grievance procedures available to DPs. A checklist of issues to be considered in design of grievance procedures includes the following:

- An inventory of any reliable conflict mediation organizations or procedures in the project area and an assessment to determine if any can be used instead of having to create new ones.
- A review of grievance redress mechanisms for simplicity, accessibility, affordability, and accountability. Good practice is to ensure that DPs can apply orally and in the local language and to impose explicit time limits for addressing grievances. Appeal procedures need to be specified, and that information needs to be made available to the DPs.
- Any new committee created to address grievances will need to be given the authority to resolve complaints. Such committees normally include representatives of DPs or NGOs, as well as project officials and staff from other agencies with a substantial role in resettlement activities.

Other Service Agencies

The number and type of agencies involved in a resettlement operation depend on the complexity of the activity. A small operation with only minor land acquisition may involve the project authority, local government, land office, DPs, and possibly NGOs. A large-scale operation, in contract, requires a wide variety of activities to be performed during the resettlement operation, so the number of agencies involved can be much greater than in small projects. The following checklists indicate the activities and types of agencies involved in each of the major resettlement activities:

Land and asset acquisition

Action	Agencies involved and comments
Obtain permission for land use	The project resettlement unit usually must work with regional planning agencies or land administration bureaus, often in more than one administrative jurisdiction.
Complete land acquisition	Land acquisition is usually completed by local governments following a request from the project agency. This time-intensive process is most likely initiated in the preparation stage but is often completed in implementation. Because land acquisition must be completed before civil works can begin, a good practice is for the project resettlement unit to closely monitor local governments' performance in the process.

Action	Agencies involved and comments
Confirm census and survey results	Even when the census and socioeconomic surveys are carried out by authorized institutes or local governments, formal project acceptance of the validity and accuracy of results is a prerequisite for calculating DPs' compensation or other assistance. Project resettlement agents usually find that working closely with local governments and DP representatives during this process is helpful.
Calculate and pay compensation	The project resettlement unit usually calculates and pays compensation if compensation is being paid directly by the project agency. Sometimes local governments manage the compensation process only, and the project agency provides the funds. In these instances, a good practice is for the project resettlement unit to ensure that valuation procedures and compensation rates are disclosed and observed. If collusion or extortion is at all likely, local resettlement offices and NGOs or DP groups can be enlisted to certify payment of compensation to affected households.

Physical relocation

Action	Agencies involved and comments
Acquire land for resettlement sites	If additional land is required for resettlement sites, it too must be obtained by the responsible government agency. The project resettlement unit negotiates compensation rates and ensures that required funds are promptly transferred to the acquiring government.
Determine technical feasibility of resettlement sites	Feasibility studies of resettlement sites for residential, agricultural, or commercial use follow terms of reference provided by the project resettlement unit. Of course, as mentioned previously, DPs' acceptance of proposed sites is an important factor in determining feasibility.
Develop resettlement sites	The project agency and local government agencies, with the help of qualified contractors, generally handle site development activities (for example, road building, infrastructure development, water supply, irrigation). NGOs active in areas such as

(continued)

11

(*continued from p. 245*)

Action	Agencies involved and comments
	housing design, spatial planning, or water management can also be involved in site development. Local governments should integrate new sites into local administrative regimes. When sites are developed away from existing communities, a good practice is to encourage DPs to form local organizations to assist in site development and prepare the local organizations for management and routine maintenance functions.
Relocate to resettlement sites	The project resettlement unit usually contracts with transport firms for relocation assistance. As this activity is almost exclusively logistical, the project team generally has little need to involve local governments, beyond keeping them informed of the operation. Where implementation capacity or funding is inadequate, however, assistance may be needed from local government to support this activity.
Reconstruct project-affected businesses	If new sites are well selected and developed, adequately compensated private and public enterprises can usually manage their own reconstruction efforts. The project resettlement unit may need to coordinate with local governments to provide business licenses or permits.
Allot residential and agricultural land	Determining and applying allotment mechanisms and procedures is commonly a joint effort involving local project resettlement offices, local government administrators, DPs, and perhaps representative NGOs.
Reconstruct project-affected houses	Unless the project builds or sponsors new residential construction, the reconstruction of houses is usually undertaken by the DPs themselves, according to their own preferences. They may wish to use materials salvaged from their old houses, use savings to supplement cash compensation to improve their accommodations, or use part of their compensation for other household purposes. To ensure that replacement housing is built, however, some projects withhold a portion of compensation until housing is complete or nearly complete.

11

Income restoration (or improvement)

Action	Agencies involved and comments
Implement income restoration measures	Various organizations are involved in implementing income restoration measures. Support from project agencies would usually be only in the form of adequate funding, detailed planning, and coordination of all stakeholders. A good practice is to have all agencies involved in developing aspects of the income restoration programs (credit, marketing, procurement of raw materials, and so forth) participate in the dialogue on income restoration. As far as possible, capable NGOs should be involved in the process, as well as private sector and local cooperative agencies. Where institutional arrangements or specialized programs are similar to those planned under the project, the project agencies do well to try to establish connections with them, rather than creating new organizations or programs.
Prepare job programs	If jobs are to be provided for DPs, the public agencies, enterprises, and other organizations responsible for job creation need to be involved from the early stages of RP preparation. The RP assesses the feasibility of job programs and includes clear, agreed benchmarks for determining whether the job programs are improving or restoring incomes. At the earliest stages of project preparation, the project agencies should also initiate discussions with local governments and the agencies likely to provide jobs.[2]
Ensure availability of credit	If some income-generating activities depend on the availability of credit, banks and other credit agencies will need to be involved in program design.
Send out information	Local NGOs, project field offices, extension workers, and media can help distribute timely and reliable information to DPs.
Deliver assistance packages	Agencies responsible for extension services, delivery of raw materials, transfer of processing skills, market analysis and support, or other forms of assistance need to be involved in projects requiring either agricultural or nonagricultural development packages.

(continued)

11

(continued from p. 247)

Action	Agencies involved and comments
Ensure availability of premises	The project agency, in coordination with local government agencies, is responsible for ensuring the availability of adequate premises for businesses and communities.
Obtain permits and licenses	The project resettlement unit needs to coordinate with government departments responsible for issuing permits and licenses. A good practice is to give these permits and licenses to DPs, free of charge, even if licensing charges must then be borne by the project.

Monitoring

Action	Agencies involved and comments
Monitor implementation	Adequate and reliable arrangements for internal and external monitoring are basic to tracking project achievements. The project resettlement unit (or resettlement steering committee) needs to ensure that the external monitoring agency obtains access to necessary information. This unit should also ensure that implementing agencies are responding to the issues identified. If an internal monitoring unit is to be established, it can be housed in the project agency, at a level that allows reporting to high-level decisionmakers. If existing monitoring arrangements are to be used for the project, a review of the effectiveness of previous reporting and the extent to which decisionmakers have responded to monitoring reports is important.

Organizational Models for Resettlement Implementation

Because organizational context differs from country to country, and usually from sector to sector within a given country, an assessment of organizational capacity must always be attuned to the unique circumstances of the project. Nonetheless, a general review of organizational models and coordination methods may suggest approaches better suited to particular sectors, political-administrative conditions, and operational constraints found in a given project setting. The scale of resettlement, the structure of the project agency, and the political-administrative structure of the country determine which of three main organizational models for resettlement implementation would be most appropriate. The features of each of these models and their strengths and weaknesses are discussed in the following subsections.

11

Resettlement Carried Out by the Project Agency

The "resettlement carried out by the project agency" model is generally used if the project agency is fairly capable and has the required authority to perform resettlement tasks. This model is also likely to be used if government capacities are otherwise weak, especially in remote areas; if the project agency is a parastatal with wide-ranging authority; or if the project is a private sector one involving small-scale resettlement.

Because the project agency's resettlement unit and field offices carry out most resettlement activities, interaction with other government agencies mainly involves regulatory issues (for example, official land allotment, development permissions, licenses). Private contractors, NGOs, and external monitoring agents are hired on a contract basis, as necessary. The advantage of this model is reduced dependence on the coordinated activities of many agencies. However, the mandate of the project agency needs to be broad enough to encompass all the functions generally in the government's domain.

> *Project example:* In India, parastatals with activities throughout the country, such as the National Thermal Power Corporation (Ln 3632) and Coal India, Ltd. (Ln 2682), carry out their own resettlement activities, in collaboration with the responsible government agencies and local organizations. In both of these instances, the parastatals coordinate their field activities through a central resettlement office.

Resettlement Implemented with Major Support from Local Governments and NGOs

The "resettlement implemented with major support" model is commonly used when the project agency lacks the capacity or authority to implement all aspects of resettlement. In such cases, the project agency relies on support from local governments or NGOs for some physical works and delivery of services, as well as regulatory matters. Local governments, for example, would usually retain authority for effecting changes in land use and designation of resettlement sites within their jurisdictions. The project generally maintains strong field offices to coordinate with the local governments or NGOs. This model can be advantageous if local governments are strong and already have sufficient capacity and expertise.

Resettlement Implemented Mainly by Local Governments with Funding Provided by the Project Agency

The "resettlement implemented mainly by local governments" model is more likely to be used if local governments are capable and experienced and have strong grassroots institutional networks. The project agency usually remains

11

responsible for resettlement planning, funding, and monitoring, but most other activities are contracted to others. A concern arises with this model if the project agency is disconnected from implementation altogether. Because the Bank's relationship is with the borrowing agency but not usually with others contracted to do the actual implementation, the RP and project agreements should include a review of contractual terms designed to ensure compliance with RP provisions. Involving the local governments in resettlement planning is important in this model.

> *Project example:* In China, resettlement in most sectors follows this model and is often implemented effectively. In rare cases, the entire resettlement planning and implementation process may be devolved to the local governments, but this devolution is more likely if resettlement takes place within one administrative jurisdiction, such as in rural development projects.

> *Project example:* In Vietnam, the First Highway Rehabilitation Project (Cr 2549) relied on a decentralized organizational scheme for carrying out resettlement activities. A project management unit of the Ministry of Transportation was responsible for supervising all actions and disbursing funds to provincial governments to cover costs. Provincial People's Committees in the 10 affected provinces were responsible for implementing the RP and overseeing the work of District People's Committees in 33 districts, which executed the required actions.

Checklist for Organizations Involved in Resettlement Implementation

A few general pointers for designing responsive and effective organizations are given below:

- Establish which organizations are responsible for delivering each entitlement and conducting each activity of the resettlement program.
- Involve the implementation organizations in resettlement preparation and planning. Their early involvement ensures that they know the contexts in which agreements were redefined during resettlement planning.
- Staff the implementation organizations promptly. Adequate organizational design will not, in itself, result in effective implementation unless the various positions are staffed at the right time.
- Review the jurisdiction, mandate, and financial authority of each organization involved in implementing resettlement. All too often, organizations assumed to be doing certain things are not actually authorized, competent, or adequately funded to do them. For example, NGOs can play an important role in resettlement, but they have no legal powers to

effect land acquisition and cannot be expected to replace the legally vested government officers who have this power.

- Build mechanisms into the project design for supervising and coordinating the work of key organizations. If none of the coordinating organizations have control over the agencies implementing key resettlement activities, any difficulties that arise may be difficult to resolve.
- Ensure that the project resettlement unit's reporting channels provide direct access to the key decisionmakers. Good monitoring is not effective unless project decisionmakers are adequately informed about issues and make timely decisions to resolve them. Without access to the decisionmakers in the project agency, a resettlement organization would be unable to promptly resolve resettlement issues.

Coordination with Local Governments

Displacement entails substantial socioeconomic disruption in the lives of the affected people. The aim of resettlement is to enable the DPs to reconstruct their livelihoods and lifestyles at the new sites. Some resettlement activities—such as physical relocation, payment of compensation, reconstruction of houses, and construction of basic infrastructure—can be undertaken by the project agency. Large parastatals may be able to do more by supporting development activities at resettlement sites and helping to bring about some amount of integration into the local economy.

However, many resettlement activities, especially those associated with economic rehabilitation of affected households and their integration into the local administrative settings, require support from local governments. Coordination with local government organizations is thus critical to successful resettlement. Resettlement programs that fail to coordinate closely with government agencies and do not involve them throughout the resettlement process can face substantial difficulties in implementation. Close involvement of local government organizations is required for the following:

- Census survey of affected people and properties;
- Land acquisition;
- Development and allocation of residential and agricultural resettlement sites;
- Integration of resettlement initiatives into local development plans;
- Support for income restoration programs—providing jobs, credit, information on local development packages, raw-material support, marketing support, and so forth;
- Consultations with affected people;
- Grievance redress mechanisms; and
- Integration of resettlement sites into local administrative systems.

11

Monitoring and Evaluation

Good institutional design makes implementation easier, but effective monitoring ensures it stays on track. Even projects with the best RPs and exceptionally supportive organizations are likely to run into problems and issues during implementation. Timely identification and resolution of these problems are critical to achieving desired resettlement outcomes. Effective monitoring is essential. To be most effective, monitoring needs to cover both internal monitoring, conducted by the project agency, and external monitoring, conducted by a qualified independent agency. While internal monitoring would primarily consist of a follow-up on the quantitative aspects of resettlement implementation and focus more on processes and delivery of inputs, external monitoring focuses more broadly on outputs, outcomes, and the qualitative aspects of implementation. Both internal monitoring and external monitoring cover the agreed benchmark indicators in the RP. This requirement prevents reporting against some local guidelines or other vague standards, a practice that sometimes reduces the validity and applicability of the findings of the monitoring program. A good-practice checklist of issues for internal and external monitoring would include the following:

Internal Monitoring

- An internal monitoring unit is explicitly designated within the project agency and may include representatives from the government agencies, NGOs, and other agencies. Good communication with field offices, as well as coordination with other implementation agencies, is factored into the design. Internal monitoring is carried out in accordance with detailed, specific terms of reference.
- The staff of the internal monitoring unit are familiar with the design of the resettlement program.
- Staff from the internal monitoring unit receive adequate training in the framework and methodology of internal monitoring.
- The internal monitoring unit regularly receives information and data updates from field offices.
- The unit staff participate in the project launch workshop, where the key monitoring benchmarks and the reporting process are discussed and agreed to.
- Resettlement data are collected under both household and impact categories and entered into a computer to make processing easier.
- Senior decisionmakers have explicitly agreed on a process for factoring monitoring reports into decisionmaking.

11

External Monitoring

- The external monitoring agency is identified by the appraisal stage, to facilitate discussions with the Bank appraisal mission on the scope and content of external monitoring. Having the same agency conduct socioeconomic surveys and external monitoring is acceptable. However, the consultants involved in resettlement planning are preferably not hired for external monitoring, as they have a vested interest in reporting smooth implementation.
- The external monitor—for example, a university, research institute, or NGO—verifies, in the field, some of the quantitative information submitted by the internal monitoring agency. This aspect is sometimes overlooked because of the qualitative focus of external monitoring.
- The project resettlement unit, the Bank resettlement specialist, and the monitoring agency discuss the proposed methodology for external monitoring. A good practice is to describe the methodology in the RP. An outline format for the external monitoring report is agreed to. Such agreement helps ensure that external monitoring reports cover all elements of resettlement implementation.
- The process of reviewing external monitoring reports and factoring them into resettlement decisionmaking is agreed to and described in the RP.

Training and Capacity Building

OP 4.12 provides for Bank assistance to borrowers for developing capacity to design and conduct resettlement operations. "In furtherance of the objectives of this policy, the Bank may at a borrower's request support the borrower and other concerned entities by providing

(a) assistance to assess and strengthen resettlement policies, strategies, legal frameworks, and specific plans at a country, regional, or sectoral level;
(b) financing of technical assistance to strengthen the capacities of agencies responsible for resettlement, or of affected people to participate more effectively in resettlement operations;
(c) financing of technical assistance for developing resettlement policies, strategies, and specific plans, and for implementation, monitoring, and evaluation of resettlement activities" (para. 32).

11

Resettlement organizations must deal with dynamic situations. The staff therefore need experience and knowledge to adapt to resettlement challenges. Furthermore, sensitivity and empathy are required to build cooperative relationships with DPs and cannot be assumed. Some staff may actually resent resettlement assignments, while many others continue to interpret their main objective as one of helping to implement the overall project. Effective implementation, as a consequence, hinges on both application of technical skills and an appropriate degree of commitment to resettlement principles and objectives.

For most projects, training and capacity building are essential to effective implementation. To this end, before a training program can be designed, the manager of the resettlement unit should usually conduct, or commission, a technical-skills assessment, comparing the existing skills and experience base of available staff with expected requirements. Although all staff likely understand the sequence of resettlement activities, a desirable approach may be to provide training in stages so that staff have more time to absorb and focus on actual phases of preparation or implementation (see CD Appendix 25, "Resettlement Training Program," for descriptions of multiweek training programs in two Bank projects).

Sensitivity to DPs and commitment to resettlement objectives are considerably more difficult to instill through formal training. Brief job reassignments or internships may be an effective way to build commitment. If those options are too expensive or impractical, some other method of giving staff exposure to DPs and their problems and uncertainties is needed.

Organizations with staff who require resettlement training may not have in-house sources of training. External sources of resettlement training include the following:

- *National-level training centers*—Some countries now have well-qualified training centers affiliated with major universities or colleges. These centers offer training programs for senior project staff, who can, in turn, train other project staff. Task teams wishing to suggest possible training venues to borrower agencies can consult the resettlement help desk at Bank headquarters for an up-to-date list of these institutions.
- *Project-level training*—Resettlement training is unlikely to be available in the vicinity of a given project, and sending all the people who need training to national centers may be impractical. Project-level training is more practical in such cases. Some or all of this training can be provided by personnel from national centers, by personnel from qualified NGOs, or by Bank resettlement specialists as part of project preparation. Similarly, local or regional specialists or NGOs involved in specific aspects of resettlement, such as microenterprise development or community irrigation management, can be called on to familiarize resettlement staff with key issues and methods. These topics can also be included in the project launch workshop. The project resettlement specialist or consultants can provide training for resettlement staff, including field personnel. Another possibility is a carefully structured study tour of projects in

11

neighboring provinces or countries. Study tours give agency staff an opportunity to not only see field conditions in another project, but also speak with colleagues elsewhere about implementation issues.

Training makes an important contribution to institutional capacity. Training activities should complement and support each other. The training should be appropriate for the intended audience. Senior managers are concerned with policy issues and have little interest in field problems, whereas resettlement staff are consumed by implementation issues but believe they have little influence on policy concerns. One recurring mistake is to provide policy training to field staff, but no operational training. Another is to provide policy orientation to senior managers, while giving no training to staff tasked with actual implementation. An effective training program emphasizes policy training for senior management and operational training for resettlement staff.

In many instances, project preparation grants or technical assistance funds can be used to pay for training abroad, in national centers, or in the project. Sending resettlement staff to similar projects in the country can be an inexpensive yet effective way of building resettlement capacity. Such interactions are particularly useful, because practitioners are involved in the exchanges, and the context, problems, and issues are likely to be similar.

Notes

1. Picciotto, R., Van Wicklin, W.A., III, and Rice, E.B. 2001. *Involuntary Resettlement: Comparative Perspectives*. New Brunswick, N.J.: Transaction Publishers, p. 20.

2. Bank experience suggests that subsidies can be paid for short periods without fostering DP dependency on project largesse. A similar proviso is appropriate for government provision of raw materials and marketing services, as well as other assistance. However, such support may be critical during the start-up period. Short-term support to help the DPs restore their income levels during the transition period must not, however, undermine long-term market sustainability. NGOs, community-based organizations, and DP groups can help in making this transition to long-term sustainability.

11

Chapter 12

Implementing Resettlement Plans

Resettlement outcomes depend on the quality of implementation. Even the best plans, prepared with tremendous attention to detail, do not by themselves improve the lives of resettlers—unless resettlement programs are also diligently implemented. Although resettlement planning in the projects of the World Bank and other multilateral development agencies has by and large improved in the last decade, resettlement implementation continues to be a challenge. This chapter outlines the key ingredients of successful implementation; it also discusses common problems and offers a number of practical tips to help those administering various aspects of a resettlement program.

Getting Ready for Implementation

The actions needed for successful resettlement implementation start during the final stages of project preparation. The first important step is to ensure that the implementing agencies are ready, and this should be done as follows:

- *Explain the key features of the resettlement plan to key project staff and all staff working in the resettlement implementation agency*—This step may sound obvious, but in many projects key staff of the project-implementing agency are often unaware of the actions proposed in the resettlement plan (RP). Also, if resettlement planning was carried out by a different agency, resettlement staff may not be fully aware of the details of the program. Therefore, the main features of the resettlement program should be explained to staff working on project implementation. The staff responsible for resettlement implementation should take part in a detailed discussion of the RP and of the issues and problems likely to arise during implementation. For projects with large-scale or complex resettlement, a good practice is to bring operational-level staff together for intensive training at a project launch workshop.
- *Relate the resettlement implementation schedule to adequate staffing levels at various stages*—Various staff and resources will be required at various

12

stages of resettlement implementation. As considerable time may be needed to recruit staff or mobilize the necessary resources, resettlement decisionmakers should be made aware of organizational and resource needs in advance.

- *Adequately staff and equip the resettlement implementation agency before implementation begins*—The resettlement agency should be adequately staffed and have the necessary resources and equipment (such as vehicles, computers, office space, and furniture) to implement the resettlement program. Again, this may sound obvious, but many resettlement programs suffer from inadequate staff, resources, and equipment. Because resettlement is often not the occupation preferred by government officials, finding enough adequately qualified staff for resettlement assignments may be difficult. Decisionmakers thus need to plan in advance for such activities.

- *Activate implementation coordination mechanisms*—Resettlement implementation usually requires close coordination of several government agencies. Having adequate coordination mechanisms is important, and they should be activated and functioning when resettlement implementation starts. Routine resettlement problems, especially likely to be encountered in the initial stages of implementation, become especially difficult to resolve without effective arrangements for coordination.

- *Continue consultations with displaced persons*—If a long gap between the resettlement planning and implementation stages occurs, the needs and priorities of displaced persons (DPs) may change, requiring some modifications in the resettlement program. Or the resettlement program may be substantially modified, requiring some form of consultation with DPs. In such cases, project officials should establish methods and venues for consultation.

- *Update census and socioeconomic surveys, if necessary*—In projects such as dams, with long gestation periods, a long time can elapse between the stage of census and socioeconomic surveys and the beginning of resettlement implementation. In such cases, key census and socioeconomic data should be updated before the start of implementation, because the data may have implications for resources and physical planning.

12

Initiating Implementation

This section provides tips that will be useful in implementing the typical resettlement program.

Payment of Compensation

Payment of compensation is an essential activity of almost all resettlement programs. The following measures help smooth the payment process:

- *Pay compensation into bank accounts and not directly to DPs*—Depositing compensation directly into accounts, rather than paying the DPs in person, helps reduce the incidence of graft and corruption in the compensation payment process. Compensation deposited in bank accounts is also less likely to be spent unproductively. Involving a bank in the compensation payment process exposes DPs to some savings and credit options that help them reconstruct their livelihoods. Often, these are joint bank accounts requiring the permission of both the DP and the resettlement agency.
- *Involve local nongovernmental organizations in the compensation process*—Where transparency may be an issue, involving local, operational nongovernmental organizations (NGOs) in the payment of compensation may be helpful. Where information is lacking, NGOs may help DPs decide on the optimum use of compensation for procuring productive assets.
- *Inform all household members about compensation payments*—Often, heads of households receive the compensation, although the compensation is for the benefit of all members of the household. Informing all members about the compensation can encourage more effective use of funds and prevent their being wasted on gambling or alcohol, for example.

Relocation

For resettlement programs that involve physical relocation of populations, the following measures would help in relocating people to resettlement sites:

- *Ensure that DPs are generally ready to accept specific resettlement sites*—Resettlement sites are selected during the resettlement planning phase, in consultation with the affected people. However, at the start of implementation, verifying that each affected household is willing to occupy its specific resettlement site is important. If the affected households find features of the specific sites highly disadvantageous or culturally inappropriate, site improvements or reallocation of sites may be advisable.
- *Prepare relocation sites before the date of the actual move*—The relocation sites (including community infrastructure and services) should be ready before people are relocated. Providing DPs access to the relocation site before the actual deadline for the move makes the transition smoother.

12

During the transition, the DPs can engage in productive activities in both the affected areas and the resettlement sites; these activities will provide them with a useful economic cushion during the resettlement process.

- *Assist DPs in the physical move*—Depending on the location of the affected area and the resettlement area, as well as on the DPs' preferences, DPs should be assisted in the actual physical move to relocation sites. If the permissible cash entitlement is insufficient to permit a move from a remote location, or if arranging suitable transportation is otherwise difficult, directly arranging transfer of people and assets (including salvage materials) is preferable.

Linkage of Resettlement Progress and Pace of Project Construction

Because land must be available for construction of new housing when required, key resettlement activities on a piece of land should be sufficiently completed before the land is likely to be required for construction. The activities to be completed before construction typically include the following:

- Detailed census and socioeconomic survey of affected households;
- Payment of compensation for affected assets;
- Identification of residential and agricultural resettlement sites (if required by the project) that are acceptable to DPs;
- Development of resettlement sites, including provision of civic amenities and the basic agricultural inputs required;
- Offer of resettlement sites for occupation by DPs;
- Offer of jobs, if provision of alternative employment is part of the resettlement package;
- Offer of training, seed capital, credit, and other agreed entitlements, if the resettlement package includes assistance for self-employment; and
- Payment of cash compensation for economic rehabilitation, if a cash option is selected by the DP.

Reconstruction and Relocation to New Housing

Where new housing is being constructed under the resettlement program, house layouts and designs, as well as the location of community infrastructure, should be determined with resettler participation and approval. DPs can help make the design meet their specific needs, such as space for livestock, gardens, and other activities not obvious to others. They should have a range of housing options, and these options should not be overly standardized. One option should allow

12

DPs to add their own resources so that they can obtain larger or better houses. Housing options should include a cash option, which would allow DPs to build their own houses or move elsewhere. This option can include a voucher applicable to a range of housing alternatives. Housing options should not exceed the financial means of DPs: mortgages, rent, utilities, and other costs should be manageable.

In many rural resettlement programs, an important question is whether the resettlers want to live in a nuclear community, on their respective farmlands, along roads, or according to some other alternative or combination of alternatives. Nuclear villages have the advantage of proximity to community infrastructure and other households, but they also increase the distance to agricultural lands for some community members. Living along roads makes transportation more convenient and may provide additional livelihood options. The resettling community should be allowed to choose the options best suited to their needs and their sociocultural preferences, and the implications of the options should be discussed with them.

- *Allocate housing*—New housing should be allocated on the basis of clearly defined criteria that the resettlers understand. If resettlement is in multistoried housing in urban areas, preference for the lower floors should be given to households with old people, households with physically disabled people, or households with commercially based livelihoods that require conversion of part of the house into a shop. After the households that require priority treatment are accommodated, others should be allocated housing on the basis of either a consensus within the community or a transparent, random process of allocation. Arbitrary allocation managed by the resettlement agency can be perceived by resettlers as an injustice and should be avoided.
- *Assist resettlers in managing construction of replacement housing*—Arrangements should be made to ensure that resettlers have enough time to dismantle old housing, transfer salvage materials or obtain new ones, and build new housing on an available and adequately prepared site. The pace and process of construction should be supervised by the implementing agencies so that any problems beyond the control of the resettlers can be addressed. Special arrangements may be necessary to provide the vulnerable (elderly people, female heads of households, or physically disabled people) with supplemental sources of labor for movement and reconstruction.
- *Arrange for transitional accommodation if needed*—Although housing should be ready before the physical relocation of resettlers from the affected area, short-duration transitional housing arrangements are sometimes necessary. During implementation, assistance with commuting

12

expenses or transportation may be required for the duration of the transition. Arrangements for moving assistance (or payment of moving expenses) for both the move into transitional housing and the move into long-term housing may also be required. Of course, if the transition extends beyond the originally intended period, all forms of transitional assistance must be extended as well.

Civic Infrastructure

- *Upgrade infrastructure in host communities*—If resettlers are moving into existing communities, the civic infrastructure of the host communities (for example, schools, health clinics, water supply and sewerage, and roads) should be expanded or upgraded. The level of community infrastructure and services in the new location should be the same as, if not better than, what the DPs had before. Improved civic infrastructure not only helps a host community cope with the increased demand, but also gives them a positive impression of the resettlement process. If the standard of civic infrastructure was higher in the affected area, the infrastructure in the host community should be strengthened to similar standards, to the extent feasible.

- *Construct new infrastructure*—Often resettlement programs construct new civic infrastructure and other facilities for resettlers, even if these DPs are moving into already populated areas. Use of such infrastructure and facilities should not be restricted to the resettling population, although for facilities such as schools, a preference can be given to resettling communities. If the new infrastructure created for resettlers is obviously superior to the existing facilities for the communities living in the vicinity, a good practice is to invest in improving the facilities of host communities. Absence of such measures could give rise to feelings of discontent in host communities.

- *Discuss maintenance arrangements*—Often, resettling communities and local governments do not fully appreciate the financial and organizational implications of operating and maintaining infrastructure after the resettlement phase, or they cannot afford these costs. Providing appropriate infrastructure—not necessarily the best infrastructure—at the resettlement sites is important. Discussing arrangements for handing over the operation and maintenance of local infrastructure to the local governments and resettling communities is also useful. Resettlement implementation should include provisions for training staff from local departments, as well as resettlers, in operation and maintenance of civic infrastructure, as appropriate.

12

Income Improvement Strategies

Before initiating planned income improvement strategies, the project team should reconfirm that these strategies are still feasible and generally acceptable to the DPs. For example, some DPs may have opted for jobs in state enterprises during the planning phase, when such jobs were presumed to be available. However, when implementation starts, the jobs may no longer be available if the economy has changed.

- *Initiate livelihood activities*—Some income improvement strategies, for example, development of horticulture, development of irrigation systems, or provision of jobs that require substantial upgrading of skills, require substantial lead times before income flows can start. In such cases, preparatory measures should begin well before the affected persons are deprived of present sources of income.
- *Provide inputs*—All inputs required for different types of income improvement strategies should be provided as early as possible so that DPs have enough time to implement the selected strategies. Providing various inputs, such as cash assistance, replacement land, pumping equipment, seeds, and fertilizers, can be complicated and time-consuming. Therefore, timetables in the RP (in the form of Gantt charts or critical path analysis) should be updated before the start of the implementation, and all the required actions should be completed on time. Activities on the critical path should be carefully followed up, because any delay can have adverse consequences for the entire income improvement program.
- *Provide information*—At the same time, arrangements should be made to implement other activities, such as provision of training, credit, and advice on markets, as well as marketing of goods and services produced by resettlers, as soon as possible. Many of these activities have long lead times and require coordination with many specialized agencies. The relative positions of these activities on the critical path for implementing income improvement strategies should be carefully determined, and the activities should begin at the appropriate times.
- *Provide transitional support*—If income recovery cannot be expected at the time of displacement, DPs should be provided with transitional support. Communities with subsistence livelihoods should normally receive food-based transition arrangements, but DPs practicing commercial agriculture or living in urban areas may prefer cash. Termination of assistance should be linked to monitorable benchmarks: either full development of the productive potential of income-generating assets; or attainment of agreed income levels. Providing gradually declining transition assistance

12

is advisable so that this assistance is not perceived as core income by DPs and they are not faced with abrupt termination of assistance at the end of the transition phase. If implementation problems hamper or delay income restoration measures, transitional support should continue until alternative approaches are formulated and adopted and start yielding incomes.

Monitoring and Evaluation

Monitoring of the resettlement program should begin at implementation and continue throughout the implementation phase. If an external, independent monitoring agency is to be engaged, the contractual arrangements should be finalized before the start of implementation. The agency can then monitor early resettlement, a time when many problems of timely provision of required inputs and services arise. Internal monitoring arrangements should also be promptly finalized. A process should be established for systematic tabling of the results of internal and external monitoring at the meetings of the group coordinating the resettlement program. Each coordination meeting should discuss the follow-up of the issues and problems identified through internal, and especially external, monitoring.

Grievance Redress

RPs in Bank projects include mechanisms for redress of grievances. Because of the inherent complexities in resettlement, some DPs will have complaints about some aspect of their circumstances. A complete absence of grievances should be carefully analyzed, as it may be an indicator of the inadequacy of the grievance mechanism. Before displacement is initiated, the officials responsible for handling grievances should have procedures ready for recording and processing grievances and recording official responses. The borrower (through a resettlement coordination group or resettlement leading group, if established) should regularly review progress in resolving grievances.

Adaptation When Things Do Not Go According to Plan

A recurring theme throughout these pages is that RPs should not be seen as blueprints to be followed rigidly during implementation. In the simplest of projects—where impacts are minor and can be mitigated quickly through payment of compensation—everything may well go according to plan. In most cases, however, resettlement is likely to be more complex and hence less predictable, and the RP should be considered more a document of estimation and guidance than a blueprint. Indeed, reviews of Bank resettlement experience indicate that the most successful implementation agencies are those that know when to adapt RPs to fit changing circumstances and can respond accordingly.

Many resettlement tasks are inherently complex. Economic rehabilitation is the obvious example, especially when DPs are required to shift to new and unfamiliar income-earning activities. These impacts can usually be anticipated in advance; indeed, providing feasible means for economic rehabilitation is a key element in resettlement planning. But effective implementation often requires close coordination of a number of agencies and often depends on the responsiveness of DPs to new opportunities and circumstances. Effective implementation is also influenced by the simple passage of time. Resettlement implementation does not occur in a vacuum—generally, the longer the implementation period is, the greater the likelihood that significant changes may occur in the project area. The complexities of agent coordination, DP responsiveness, and changes occurring in the project area cannot be wholly anticipated by even the most diligent resettlement planners.

The people responsible for resettlement implementation, monitoring, supervision, and evaluation have to use their judgment in difficult matters. Thorough resettlement planning is essential to successful implementation, but contingencies in the actual implementation environment can create significant gaps between the RP and reality. In most cases, though, the RP itself includes measures to improve responsiveness to such contingencies. Among them are the following:

- Contingency funds to meet increasing costs or unanticipated expenses;
- A formula (in some cases) for periodically updating compensation rates for various categories of affected assets;
- A resettlement coordination group or other key set of administrators designated as responsible for addressing unanticipated problems or issues;
- External monitoring, with terms of reference to identify issues of inadequate or obsolete planning;
- Grievance procedures by which DPs can seek redress for problems specifically affecting them but not anticipated by planners; and
- An early review of resettlement implementation (often in advance of the project mid-term review), which includes review of plan appropriateness or effectiveness.

Because, by definition, not all factors that may prove relevant during resettlement implementation can be identified in advance, only general guidance on being responsive and adaptive can be provided here. Although the need for

12

judgment may be inescapable, three general principles should influence all decisions to depart from agreed provisions in RPs:

- *Assistance of DPs is the fundamental objective*—Changes in the project environment may create unanticipated administrative burdens or greatly increase resettlement costs. Achieving efficiencies may be possible by changing classification schemes or service delivery mechanisms, but improving or restoring the incomes and living standards of DPs remains the fundamental objective.

- *Partnership with the borrower is essential to successful implementation*— Because RPs cannot reliably serve as blueprints, modifications are usually necessary for successful implementation. In complex resettlement operations unfolding over time, situations often arise that are beyond the direct control of both the Bank and the borrower, such as a general economic downturn in the area or an adverse shift in the terms of trade. In such circumstances, better results can be achieved through cooperative efforts to adjust the approach to resettlement or to devise an entirely new one. When this happens, the borrower should amend the project RP to describe the new approach to resettlement, and the amended RP should be reviewed and endorsed by the Bank.

- *Partnership with the DPs is also essential to successful implementation*—As a general rule, the Bank has no formal requirements to consult or inform DPs about changes occurring during implementation. As a practical matter, however, providing DPs with relevant information on changes is important. If planning changes are intended to allay the expressed concerns of DPs or cannot succeed without the active support of the DPs, the DPs should be consulted in some way while changes in planning are still at the proposal stage.

Circumstances Likely to Require Planning Changes

- *Changes occurring in the project area*—In urban or peri-urban areas, the Bank project area may be subject to changes initiated by many other sources. For example, other physical works undertaken by other agencies in the same area may cause deep confusion about who has been affected by what or who is responsible for what forms of resettlement assistance. Policy changes, too, may influence the effectiveness of resettlement programs. And other shifts in economic or political conditions may occur, without being directly caused by any agency. As a general principle, the borrower (and external monitoring agency) should track the receipt of all forms of agreed assistance by those affected by the Bank

12

project and ensure that the entitlements agreed in the RP are provided to all DPs.

- *Unanticipated adverse impacts*—In some cases, RPs make no provisions for certain adverse impacts that might arise during implementation. In such cases, the Bank and borrower should agree that eligibility criteria for resettlement will be extended to cover all the people affected and that appropriate remedies will be provided.

Project example: In China, the RP prepared for the Ertan Hydroelectric Project (Loan 3387) made no provision for land lost to subsidence along the reservoir banks. The borrower recognized those affected by subsidence as being project-affected and provided replacement land or cash compensation as remedial measures.

- *Changes in project siting*—Sometimes physical or financial considerations lead the borrower to make a change in the project design that results in a shift in siting. This may mean that some or all of the people previously identified through a census or surveys as eligible for assistance may not be affected after all, while people who may not have been surveyed or identified during resettlement planning will be affected. In China, for example, minor shifts in linear alignment are often made to lessen land acquisition and resettlement impacts. When shifts in siting would result in adverse impacts on a population that was not previously covered by the RP, however, works should not be initiated until the potentially affected people (and their assets) are surveyed and they are consulted about the planning measures and entitlements. If adverse impacts are categorically the same as those already established in the RP, planned entitlements or other forms of assistance may simply be extended to the new population (though compensation rates may vary from area to area). If adverse impacts are different from those already identified in the RP, project planners need to devise new entitlements or other forms of assistance.
- *Changes in compensation rates*—For various reasons, borrowers sometimes increase compensation rates during implementation from those agreed in RPs. This action may reflect changes in actual asset valuation since the plan was prepared or may be an inducement to encourage DPs to move at an earlier date (or to drop resistance to resettlement). Issues of possible collusion aside, increased compensation rates are not a matter of concern to the Bank. Sometimes, however, the borrower decreases compensation rates for land or other assets during implementation. In some cases, the borrower can demonstrate that the compensation rates agreed to in the RP were miscalculated or that the actual value of assets has declined. But any decrease in compensation rates deserves careful

12

scrutiny (and documentation) on the part of the Bank. Obviously, the Bank cannot accept a borrower's claim of insufficient financial resources as a satisfactory reason for decreasing or eliminating compensation. Under such circumstances, the Bank should work with the borrower to consider whether alternative assistance of equivalent value can be provided in lieu of compensation. Ultimately, however, the Bank should insist that the borrower pay compensation at replacement cost (or provide equivalent forms of assistance) as a matter of compliance with project legal documents.

- *Changes in remedial measures*—Instead of, or in addition to, payment of compensation, some RPs include remedial measures that may not be fully delivered during implementation. In many cases, some alternative or substitute may be readily available. Care must be taken, however, when measures intended to allow DPs to improve or restore their incomes are changed. The promise of employment for those losing agricultural land is perhaps the most important example. In some cases, the promised job never materializes. In other cases, the job may be lost in a short time through no fault of the DP. Where income restoration measures are to be changed during implementation, working with the DPs themselves to find feasible and acceptable alternatives is very important.

Documentation of Planning Changes

For the purposes of project supervision and evaluation, all significant changes to the RP during implementation should be recorded. For changes other than changes in the scale of impact, in the legal framework for resettlement, in the policy entitlements, in the resettlement sites, in the income restoration measures, or in the budget for resettlement, an aide-mémoire that notes the circumstances necessitating the change and the nature of the change agreed to with the borrower may be sufficient. Where the scale of resettlement is changing dramatically, significant impacts are being introduced, or reductions in compensation rates are proposed, the RP should be formally revised. Such changes would require an amendment of the project legal agreement.

12

Involuntary Resettlement in Selected Sectors

Chapter 13

Resettlement in Urban Areas

The Context of Urban Resettlement

In the Bank's current portfolio, most urban resettlement is associated with infrastructure projects (roads, transmission lines, pipelines, railways, and so forth) or projects to improve the urban environment (sewerage or sanitation management, for example). Successful urban resettlement requires attention to density and diversity, usually in a context of rapid change. High population density is an obvious hallmark of urban life. Although population density in the urban landscape creates opportunities (concentrated demand for goods and services, employment, and land and other natural resources), it also creates concentrated problems (pollution and waste disposal). Resettlement in urban areas is often expensive, because the public infrastructure must be built, rehabilitated, or upgraded in an area where people are living and working. As a consequence, even projects acquiring little land in urban areas can generate a fairly large displacement, and even temporary loss of land or other assets can cause severe and costly impacts.

The geography of cities reflects wide differences in land use. Residential areas vary in terms of income levels, standards of living, length of residence, and ethnic or regional affiliation. In terms of resettlement, three factors may affect urban diversity. First, political factors may be as important as economic or technical considerations in guiding project specification, site selection, or implementation. Second, the urban economy gives rise to specialization and diverse sources of income. Third, location may often be a key factor in the restoration of incomes and living standards. Because of urban diversity, social assessment is recommended as a routine step in resettlement planning (see chapter 7).

Another consideration is that urban growth is often recent, rapid, and uncontrolled. In many cities, resettlement plans (RPs) must take into account a dynamic process of urbanization in which density and diversity increase rapidly, often in uneven and unsanctioned ways. Land to be acquired is frequently inhabited by squatters, low-income families, or new migrants. These areas have thriving informal economic activities, unplanned growth, and mixed land use. Distinguishing between urban and peri-urban areas may be difficult, as improved communications and transportation bring previously remote areas

13

under the sway of the urban centers. As a consequence, borrowers can find themselves straddling competing social objectives. Land acquisition and displacement may be necessary to meet the rising demands for urban services. But designing socially sensitive projects often requires planners to meet high and costly compensation and rehabilitation standards and provide assistance to segments of the population lacking legally recognized rights. In addition, in a context of rapid change, merely restoring public infrastructure or service to preexisting levels may make little sense: preexisting levels are likely to be inadequate or obsolete, or soon may be. Such circumstances call for urban development planning, rather than for simple mitigation.

Urban displacement includes many of the issues of resettlement operations in other sectors, but four issues recur with particular frequency:

- Rapid increase in the size of the operation (which underscores the importance of planning);
- Coordination of government units, agencies, and service providers;
- Recognition of squatters and others lacking formal property rights; and
- Commingling of commercial and residential activities.

Recommended approaches for managing or resolving such issues are discussed in the following sections.

Importance of Initial Planning

Early resettlement planning is always advised, and the fact that resettlement costs can escalate quickly in urban areas underscores the importance of early planning. A good practice is to base initial project design on an assessment of social and demographic conditions and then revise it to incorporate information from public consultations. Timing is crucial, because resettlement mistakes can be especially costly in urban projects. Careful, early, and participatory planning avoids the major revision of investments (or opportunities) during implementation and helps ensure that resettlement provisions are accepted by displaced person (DPs). Similarly, early planning can help limit the duration of temporary disruption, which often weighs heavily on displaced residents or commercial enterprises.

Bank project experience demonstrates that reductions in the severity and scale of displacement and reductions in the opportunities for fraudulent claims can be significant dividends of effective early planning.

Minimizing Displacement

Technical considerations are fundamentally important in project design, but they are not the only factors to be taken into account. Environmental and social

13

factors are also important. In dense urban settings, minimizing displacement is likely to reduce overall project costs and make project implementation easier. Shifting project alignments or siting criteria, for example, can avoid concentrated pockets of people while having only a marginal impact on the project's technical performance. Similarly, changes in construction methods can reduce the extent or severity of impacts. Bank experience shows that it is advisable to minimize displacement, even at somewhat higher cost, as long as the project remains economically viable.

From the social perspective, resettlement costs may not be simply directly proportional to the number of DPs. Costs depend on the type and degree of impacts. Compensating a large number of people for minor or partial land acquisition may cost far less than physically relocating a few DPs and providing them with income-restoring alternatives. In urban projects, just as in others, minimizing both the number of people displaced and the severity of resettlement impacts—especially residential relocation and changes in employment—is necessary. Another good practice is to minimize the distance of any necessary relocation: families moving less than a kilometer in the city often find their lives and livelihoods are much less disrupted than those moving greater distances.

Project example: In Brazil, the Rio Flood Reconstruction and Prevention Project (Loan [Ln] 2975) changed the layout of ditches and adopted new construction techniques in order to reduce displacement by 8 percent, from 24,000 DPs to 22,200 DPs.

Project example: In China, planning revisions for the Shanghai Second Sewerage Project (Ln 3987) called for tunneling, wherever possible, to minimize surface disruption. One result was a large reduction in the amount of scarce housing that would have to be demolished, from the initial estimate of 106,480 square meters to 44,341 square meters.

Project example: Also in China, the Beijing Environment Project (Ln 3415; Credit [Cr] 2312) shifted the alignment of a sewer line to an opposite riverbank, thereby reducing population displacement by 83 percent, from an estimated 6,300 people to 1,049 people. The additional 34 million yuan in construction expense was more than offset by the estimated 270 million yuan saved in resettlement costs (in 2003, 8.2872 Chinese yuan renminbi [CMY] = US$1.00).

Project example: In West Bank and Gaza, the Solid Waste and Environmental Management Project sponsored a workshop with people residing near the site of the proposed new facility. The DPs recommended that the southern boundary be moved, to preserve 3.5 hectares of olive groves with significant historic, cultural, and economic value. The project

13

agency agreed. The DPs also suggested that a contiguous uncultivated area could be used instead, with much less disruption and social impact. The project agency implemented these recommendations, thus reducing the economic hardship caused by this investment in infrastructure.

Preventing Fraudulent Claims of Eligibility for Compensation

Bank policy recognizes the distinction between assisting urban residents living uncontested in the area before the project and assisting people who move into the area after the project is announced. People who come into the project area after a determined cutoff date, with the express purpose of qualifying for project assistance, are not eligible for any assistance. As Operational Policy (OP) 4.12 states, "Persons who encroach on the area after the cut-off date are not entitled to compensation or any other form of resettlement assistance" (para. 16).

Early resettlement planning is an important protection against opportunistic or fraudulent claims on resettlement assistance in urban areas. The key step is to establish an official cutoff date for eligibility. To prevent fraudulent claims from those arriving after the cutoff date, a census of the affected area to identify eligible residents and to establish the size and quality of structures, current land use, and other relevant facts is essential. The census is usually carried out in the initial stages of project identification and as soon as tentative location and physical boundaries of the project can be established. If final alignments are not known, surveying a wider area than may be acquired is advisable. If land acquisition is to affect commercial or industrial enterprises, establishing employment and ownership rosters, noting wages and incomes, is also important. Assembling a photographic record of potential sites at the time of the cutoff date may also be effective in discouraging fraudulent claims.

Normally, the cutoff date is when the census begins. An earlier cutoff date may be established, provided that the project area has been clearly delineated and information about that delineated area has been effectively and continuously disseminated, to prevent further population influx.

> *Project example:* In Bangladesh, the Jamuna Bridge Project (Cr 2569) suffered massive invasion on a riverbank that had been almost unpopulated. The establishment of a cutoff date and the availability of aerial photographs of the area taken about the time of the eligibility date enabled the project team to disqualify most of the opportunistic squatters.

Encouraging Public Participation and Responsiveness

Consultation and participation ensure a two-way flow of project information, providing the project team with opportunities to improve project design and

13

maintain a civic atmosphere more conducive to project performance. The effort invested in early planning to solicit the advice and cooperation of DPs—and build community support for project-related benefits—often yields significant dividends: improved project design, reduced displacement, diminished community resistance to the project, and greater community support in operating or maintaining project-related facilities or services. Furthermore, given the complexity of the income sources and location considerations involved in urban projects, consulting DPs and providing plans offering them a menu of options are especially important, because no single solution will likely fit all cases (see also chapter 7).

The following are some of the steps normally taken in the early stages of project design:

- Send out information on project objectives and potential impacts within the project area. Given the diversity of tenure arrangements, a good practice is to supplement legally required notification with other public announcements, to ensure that renters and others, as well as owners, are informed about the project.
- Conduct a census of project impacts, and then publicly display the results.
- Solicit information from potential DPs regarding valuation of losses and preferences for possible resettlement options.
- Send out information regarding compensation rates and other entitlements and the resettlement implementation schedule.
- Form a community-based committee to coordinate with the project resettlement agency.

Because urban areas are subject to rapid change, adjustments to plans are highly likely to be necessary throughout the implementation period. The need for consultations does not therefore end with initial planning. If changing conditions necessitate alterations in planning, the project team should solicit and consider the views and preferences of those potentially affected by such changes.

Project example: In China, the Guangzhou City Center Transport Project (Ln 4329) team organized a sophisticated consultation process. It sent out information about the investment through public meetings, brochures, newspaper articles, and television broadcasts. The project census and the pre- and post-move standard-of-living surveys provided other opportunities to answer DPs' questions. The project team also organized visits to resettlement sites before signing contracts with DPs. It also set up a computerized information system that DPs could use to review their housing options. It established grievance offices and a telephone hotline. The project team held a series of public meetings before

13

the move, to help people prepare for the relocation; and afterwards, to deal with unforeseen issues. It established people's committees in each new location. And the project team paid personal visits and provided small gifts to each DP family at the Chinese New Year, after relocation.

Project example: In Colombia, in the Bogotá Urban Transport Project (Ln 4021), the transport agency began a local information campaign when it discovered a great deal of misinformation among potential DPs. Almost everybody (96 percent) knew about the existence of the project—at least that it would widen the road—and some believed that the city administration would evict them and raze their houses. The vast majority of people, however, knew nothing about the formal procedures for negotiating property acquisition, and most renters had not been informed that they would have to move. To counteract rumors that could have caused unnecessary conflict, the transport agency began an information campaign using written and graphic materials, in combination with public meetings, to get out the facts about the urban road program. Meetings were held in residents' houses, after written invitations had been sent out 10 days in advance. Project authorities discussed the timetable for land acquisition, using a map depicting road rehabilitation, and distributed materials on land acquisition procedures. Project social workers followed up on these local meetings, answering any lingering questions and assessing the results of the meetings.

Project example: In West Bank and Gaza, the Solid Waste and Environmental Management Project team undertook a social analysis in delimiting a central waste site and closing unauthorized dumps contaminating the water aquifer. Public participation in project definition had numerous benefits. People initially understood neither the project objectives nor the deleterious consequences of their own actions in dumping and burning waste. Once they understood the project, they made valuable suggestions for improving waste management, including an increase in the number of waste containers. They also suggested collection fees and public education campaigns and made inputs into other aspects of project design.

Considering Gender Issues

13

Household composition is a major consideration in urban projects. Unlike in many rural areas, a significant percentage, even a majority, of the households in urban areas may be headed by women. Women heads-of-household are responsible for a gamut of domestic and productive activities and may as a consequence have little time or energy for dealing with additional issues related to displacement. A good practice is therefore to have resettlement planners assess both the extent of women-headed households and their particular concerns. For example, mothers who work may need childcare facilities, and elderly women may be unable to seek out replacement housing. Gender issues may also occur in the titling of property to women and their access to financial assistance, such as mortgages.

> *Project example:* In Brazil, the Rio Flood Reconstruction and Prevention Project (Ln 2975) team found that 66 percent of the households were headed by women, and this finding had implications for the design of resettlement programs. By contrast, the Parana Water Quality and Pollution Control Project (Ln 3503, 3504, 3505) team found that only 15 percent of the displaced households were headed by women, although this still translated into more than 1,000 people.

Coordination of Administrative and Financial Responsibilities

Successful design and implementation of urban projects usually require careful coordination of several layers of government and multiple line agencies. There is a tendency among Bank staff to deal with a single municipal agency as the project counterpart in planning and implementation, although one or more other agencies may be responsible for land acquisition and resettlement. In this situation, simple problems of coordination in timing and delivery quickly become far more complex, because agencies may not always communicate with each other and, indeed, may have conflicts in function, legal requirements, and strategic priorities. Clear administrative responsibility for implementing RPs and agreement on effective mechanisms to coordinate resettlement planning and implementation among various agencies involved are key to effective project implementation.

Administrative Coordination

Administrative coordination involves several related issues. Clearly defining the tasks involved, the concomitant administrative responsibilities, and the skills mix needed to carry out the tasks is necessary. Interagency coordination becomes necessary, because various agencies are involved and their administrative capacity to act effectively, especially at the municipal level, may need strengthening.

In addition, resettlement itself is invariably complex. The many tasks to be performed range from urban planning to the issuance of land acquisition

13

notices, to provision of resettlement-site infrastructure, to payment of compensation, to provision of employment or other forms of economic rehabilitation. A substantial number of governmental agencies scattered horizontally across several jurisdictional levels are therefore likely to be involved in any operation. In urban water supply projects, some of the adverse impacts may also involve rural residents.

Urban administrations usually have a dedicated agency for land acquisition. Even well-staffed and well-trained agencies, however, may have developed capacity only for land acquisition and compensation practices, which may be seen as sufficient in domestically funded projects. The skills mix is broader for effective resettlement planning and implementation. Expertise in real estate, spatial planning, microenterprise development, and microfinance may be necessary to meet the broader development objectives of resettlement. RPs need to identify the roles of, and assign specific responsibilities to, the various agencies that will be involved in planning and implementing resettlement. If an agency cannot assign qualified staff, the project authority may seek assistance elsewhere—for example, within the nongovernmental organization (NGO) community.

A central resettlement coordinating committee, consisting of representatives from all agencies involved, is usually necessary when urban resettlement requires coordination of multiple agencies or jurisdictions. The central committee may have subcommittees, each focused on a particular task. Thus, depending on the project, a subcommittee may be formed for land acquisition and negotiation, another for new housing land development, and another for economic assistance. Overall authority can be assigned to the senior officer in the project agency responsible for resettlement, and this person would coordinate the work of each subcommittee. In short, an appropriate skills mix, appropriate coordination of relevant agencies, and a clear delineation of responsibilities and authority are essential ingredients of success.

Project example: In China, the Shanghai Urban Environment Project (Ln 3711) suffered from a weak project-coordinating office, which undermined otherwise exemplary efforts. As a supervision mission noted, resettlement units had been established at the municipality and town levels, as planned in the RP. While the town land planning and management agencies played a major role in coordinating land acquisition and compensation payment, various government agencies had responsibility for other aspects of resettlement implementation. For example, county labor departments were responsible for employment and pension schemes. However, the project office failed to function effectively as a central resettlement management unit because there was no effective mechanism to coordinate the work of various units. This deficiency gave rise to a failure to report and monitor project activities and to great variation in performance.

13

Financial Planning and Coordination

To ensure that resettlement is adequately funded, the RP needs to assess existing or potential sources of funds for administrative agencies responsible for compensation, entitlements, or other aspects of the resettlement (see also chapter 9). Not uncommonly, local municipal bodies are assigned responsibility for payment of compensation or provision of housing and urban infrastructure to affected people in their jurisdiction, though they may receive no budgetary supplement or taxing authority to cover the additional expenses. As a consequence, they may prefer to dedicate available resources to other priorities, especially if they are excluded from the project design and negotiation processes.

In the early stages of project preparation, the Bank task team must ensure that the borrower agency agrees to bear financial responsibility for resettlement and that lack of funds will not be used as an excuse for nonpayment of agreed-on entitlements. By appraisal, the task team ensures that estimated resettlement costs are reflected in overall project costs and that all entities identified as financially obligated to support resettlement are aware of their obligations. The Bank team also verifies arrangements to direct funds to their intended destinations. As a general principle, fund-flow arrangements should involve the least number of intermediaries. Passing compensation funds, in particular, through several agencies or jurisdictions increases the likelihood of delay or inappropriate deductions.

To ensure availability of adequate funds during implementation, RPs include the following:

- Detailed cost estimates for all cost categories, including contingencies;
- Budgetary allocations linked to financial year and project phase;
- Financial responsibility and sources of funds for each activity;
- Funding commitments from all responsible agencies; and
- Mechanisms for monitoring and Bank supervision of financial flows.

Project example: In Brazil, the Water Quality and Pollution Control Project (Parana component; Ln 3503, Ln 3504, Ln 3505) authority estimated unit housing costs at $2,500, even though a finished low-income housing unit in the capital of Curitiba cost $7,500 (all dollar amounts are current U.S. dollars). As a consequence, urban relocation costs were seriously underestimated and had to be revised during implementation.

Project example: Also in Brazil, the Water Quality and Pollution Control Project (São Paulo component; Ln 3503, Ln 3504, Ln 3505) authority estimated land and housing prices at the time of project design, but without sufficient provision for inflation and price increases. Consequently, the cost estimates had to be increased almost 70 percent,

13

to match prevailing prices in the low-income housing market at the time of acquisition.

Limits of Bank Financing in Urban Projects

A good practice is for the Bank task team to explain, in the early stages of resettlement planning, that many resettlement costs can be paid through Bank loan proceeds. The Bank does not, as a general rule, disburse for simple transfer costs—for example, cash payment of compensation for land or existing structures. All expenses that generate added value, however, can be disbursed against. Areas of potential Bank financing are significant in urban resettlement. Bank financing can be applied to all forms of land improvement, including development of resettlement sites. Bank financing can also be included for replacement housing construction costs, provision of public infrastructure, enterprise development, microcredit schemes, and job creation programs. Bank financing, or other special financial arrangements, may also be available for pilot innovations in urban resettlement.

> *Project example:* In Brazil, the Rio Flood Reconstruction and Prevention Project (Ln 2975) financed 60 percent of resettlement costs (the state component) through Bank financing; the rest came from a federal contribution.

Resettlement of Urban Squatters

Property rights are not well developed in many urban areas, whether wealthy or poor. Resettlement, however, often affects the urban poor disproportionately, and the question of title is of particular importance for them. Furthermore, because poverty alleviation is the fundamental goal of Bank lending, the Bank places resettlement in a development framework. Displacement of low-income squatters or slum communities often provides opportunities for moving beyond narrow mitigation of adverse impacts to promoting community development, security of tenure, and rational land use. These are also the objectives of many urban improvement programs.

Entitlements for People without Security of Tenure

Bank resettlement policy provides for compensation for lost assets and restoration of incomes and living standards. Where property rights and administrative procedures for land acquisition are institutionalized and effectively applied, principle usually differs little from practice. People with customary rights but no formal legal standing are in a complicated category. For purposes of formulating

13

compensation policy, the census identifies residential and commercial tenure arrangements for people lacking formal rights, such as the following:

- Residents claiming ownership of private land but lacking legal title
- Tenants
- Squatters on public lands
- Squatters in public safety zones: drains, riverbeds, or rights-of-way
- Owners of enterprises lacking licenses or property titles
- Marketers
- Mobile and itinerant vendors.

RPs must include measures to assist each group of DPs lacking secure legal tenure and, if relevant, to improve (or at least restore) their incomes and living standards.

For each category of DPs, tenancy claims are documented, along with other available information, to determine duration of residency or other eligibility criteria. Payment of taxes, enrollment in schools, records of participation in community activities, registration to vote, and testimony of community members are examples of alternative forms of documentation that can be used to determine duration of residency. Payment of taxes or permit fees or testimony of suppliers or customers can similarly be used to establish the duration of an unlicensed enterprise.

Each category of DPs is entitled to distinct treatment. People designated as squatters because they lack title to private land they have purchased or inherited are treated as fully and legally entitled to land compensation and other benefits. Residents with such ownership claims usually receive assistance to gain title to their land and are treated in the same manner as those with legal title.

Tenants, who by definition are not property owners, receive assistance to find new housing and to move. In practice, tenants usually receive some multiple of their monthly rent or lease payments, to cover the cost of identifying and moving to alternative housing or commercial space.

Squatters and renters of informal housing on public lands and in public safety zones may constitute the most contentious category of DP. Altering the mix of resettlement assistance is one mechanism for bridging gaps between legal codes and Bank policy. For example, the Bank does not insist on the *legal entitlement* of squatters on public land to compensation for land. Instead, the Bank requires only compensation for structures or other fixed improvements on the land and provision of resettlement assistance for residential relocation (and economic rehabilitation, if applicable) needed to resettle displaced squatters. In short, these DPs receive compensation for their house and assistance to find new housing and to move, but they receive no compensation for the land they were occupying.

13

The owners of enterprises are treated in much the same manner as households. Similarly, marketers who pay license fees are recognized as legitimate renters and receive assistance to locate new venues and to move. Itinerant and mobile vendors with established work histories may also receive assistance through provision of alternative space for continuing their activities after relocation.

A good practice is to seek community endorsements of census results and identified categories of tenure rights. To offset some of the costs of displacement, encourage community support, and discourage future unplanned encroachment, planners can use the RP as a vehicle for improving DPs' security of tenure, along with improving titling systems more broadly. At the very least, the project is expected to provide secure tenure at any resettlement sites it establishes. In urban projects, a component to improve management and protection of public space may also be desirable.

Project example: In Brazil, the Bahia Water Resource Management Project (Ln 4232) required resettlement of DPs lacking legal title to the land they occupied. In phase I of this project, before resettlement, the state provided legal services, which secured, free of charge, the equivalent of property deeds for all untitled, bona fide landowners in the affected area. Those who opted for cash compensation were therefore qualified to receive the appraised full market value for their land. This approach was adopted in phase II also.

Project example: Also in Brazil, the Fortaleza Metropolitan Transport Project (Ln 7083) agency assisted families in regularizing their personal and property documents, without cost to them. The project agency also provided the DPs with documentation for newly acquired housing. Where providing formal legal title for new housing was not possible (for example, where the subdivision itself was not yet regularized), the project agency provided alternative documentation, such as a certificate of occupancy or a certificate of use concession.

Project example: In Colombia, the Santa Fe I Water Supply and Sewerage Rehabilitation Project (Ln 3952, Ln 3953) offered legal owners monetary compensation for 120 percent of the replacement value of their house and lot or replacement of the house at no cost, as well as monetary compensation for economic losses in domestic and commercial activities. Landholders without legal title received indemnification for 100 percent of the replacement value of their house and lot or replacement property at no cost, plus monetary compensation for impacts on economic activities. Renters received six months' rent, if they had been resident for less than two years; or one year's rent, if resident for more than two years.

13

Adverse Impacts on Mobile Enterprises

Urban residential and commercial areas in most developing countries often have informal (unauthorized or unlicensed) economic activity. Displacement of informal enterprises can be disastrous for people deriving their incomes from them and deprives communities of access to products or services. Potentially displaced formal and informal enterprises should be identified, and appropriate remedies should be devised. Those remedies will vary, however, depending on the nature of the enterprise and the impacts that will likely affect them.

Formal and informal enterprises with fixed premises are entitled to assistance, according to the degree of adverse impact. Vendors with recognized rights or formal licenses have established property rights and are *entitled* to resettlement and rehabilitation assistance. However, many informal enterprises are mobile, operating with carts or easily reassembled structures adjacent to well-traveled shopping areas, railways, bridge approaches, or road intersections. These displaced businesses lose no land or other fixed assets. Bank policy, therefore, does not mandate assistance for unlicensed mobile vendors who are not directly displaced by acquisition of land or other fixed assets. Nonetheless, Bank policy does recognize the need to pay particular attention "to the needs of vulnerable groups among those displaced, especially those below the poverty line . . . who may not be protected through national land compensation legislation" (OP 4.12, para. 8).

Clearly, displacement can adversely affect such enterprises if they lose proximity to other businesses or access to an established clientele. Effective remedial action for mobile vendors should, therefore, be seen in the broad context of urban development and land-use planning. Provisions can be made for development of alternative market areas. Where possible, new market areas should be close to the original site, to provide access to an existing clientele. Alternatively, new market areas may be promoted in high-growth areas or other areas with access to significant levels of customer traffic. Bank funds can be used for development of new market sites, including construction of shops, roads, and other improvements.

Project example: In Brazil, the Fortaleza Metropolitan Transport Project (Ln 7083) had to move a street fair that had been meeting weekends and Mondays at the site of one of the proposed viaducts. More than 100 itinerant merchants had temporary sidewalk stalls, where they sold a wide variety of merchandise, including fresh meat and vegetables, clothing, and household articles, to the neighborhood people. Some of the merchants were full-time sellers, rotating to various marketplaces; others were local residents who supplemented their income selling goods at the market. The market had been meeting for more than 10 years, and it was

13

growing. The project resettlement specialist therefore advised the project agency to register all merchants in place on two successive weekends within a year of construction start-up, to establish eligibility. Meanwhile, Metro Fortaleza, the project agency, created a new, improved market space to relocate eligible vendors, close to where they formerly had their stalls.

Project example: In India, the National Highways Project (Ln 4559) designated small commercial areas within local bus stations in order to accommodate vendors displaced by the widening of the roads in towns and villages.

Residential Relocation in Urban Projects

In many urban projects, identification of replacement land and provision of replacement housing are serious constraints. For land, calculation of replacement cost is made more complex by gross disparities in land prices or, in some cities, the absence of a functional land market. Meanwhile, high land costs and rapid population growth combine to produce a chronic housing shortage in many cities. Projects requiring demolition of housing—especially low-income housing—can easily exacerbate the problem of homelessness.

Resettlement of DPs is usefully seen in the broader context of an urbanization process. Urban areas in most developing countries are undergoing rapid changes in land use—both in urban centers and in urban fringes—as a result of intracity movement of people in various income groups.

Provision of replacement housing often is a crucial ingredient in urban resettlement planning. Remedies usually take some variant of two basic forms. In some cases, those losing housing are relocated to newly developed housing sites. In other cases, projects follow "fill-in" resettlement strategies, in which DPs obtain vacant existing housing, or new housing is constructed on vacant lots scattered throughout several areas.

Replacement Cost for Urban Land

Land replacement, whether in kind or in cash, recognizes not only the quantity of land acquired, but also its characteristics, such as location and productive capacity. For land in urban areas, location accounts for great differences in value. A parcel of land in the inner city, because of its centrality, may be worth many times the same sized plot in a peripheral area. Such an inner-city plot may also have advantages of location not compensated by, for example, a larger plot in a more distant area.

13

Urban volatility also complicates land valuation. In several countries (China, India, the Philippines, and others), the Bank has required special arrangements to adequately compensate landowners, because domestic legislation allows the government to acquire urban land at a discount. Given the explosive growth of many peri-urban areas, the real estate value of land can vastly exceed legal compensation levels. Replacement cost in such settings is often a product of negotiations. If adequate compensation arrangements cannot be agreed on, significant delays in acquisition timetables can occur.

Participatory processes are especially important in urban areas, because of the great diversity of needs and wishes. Some risk-averse individuals, such as the elderly and single parents, may prefer that project agencies find or provide replacement land. A good practice is therefore to include that possibility among the options. Other people may prefer cash compensation, pegged to the value of high-priced urban land. This approach satisfies Bank policy, but it may be exorbitantly expensive and may fail to contribute to orderly urban planning or even to satisfy DPs' preferences. In practice, a mix of compensation and other benefits that together constitute acceptable replacement or restoration of living standards is more appropriate. For example, larger land parcels, improved housing standards, and access to improved infrastructure and community services can partially offset the higher unit value of acquired land. Under some circumstances, the government may provide significant benefits to DPs or their communities through preferential policies, such as fee or zoning waivers.

Replacement Housing in Urban Areas

The high cost of urban land, combined with rapid population growth, produces chronic shortages of affordable housing in many cities. Providing replacement housing, when displacement is substantial, usually takes some combination of two basic forms: large-scale relocation to new housing, often provided at fairly distant sites; and fill-in resettlement, on vacant lots or in housing scattered throughout the project area.

Large-scale Relocation

Large-scale relocation has important advantages. It involves economies of scale in construction, increases the overall housing supply, and gives urban planners another tool for influencing the direction of urban growth. But it raises issues of affordability and public management; and when built at a distance from current housing, the new housing raises additional issues of increased transportation costs and employment.

When relocation sites are to be provided, RPs must address the adequacy and affordability of public housing or private housing financed or constructed

13

285

by the project. Low-income families and squatter households may lack the resources to pay mortgages or utility and other fees and may have to sell their allotted housing. Furthermore, relocated families may not appreciate the improved services and housing conditions at the relocation site, especially if the improvements entail additional expenses. Successful resettlement therefore screens DP families for some level of financial capacity and provides the assistance needed for these families to participate in the scheme.

In assessing replacement housing in new sites, it is important to look beyond physical attributes (for example, size, number of rooms, plumbing and electricity, quality of building materials). New sites need to be safe and accessible, and the new tenants must be screened for problems such as alcoholism and drugs. In multistory public housing, financial and managerial arrangements need to be in place for maintenance of buildings and grounds and for delivery of community services. Building cooperatives charged with maintenance are an important innovation for managing these issues.

Resettlement sites located away from the place of work may result in increased household expenditures for transportation. A good practice is to have RPs include strategies to mitigate increased transportation costs. A subsidy for commuting costs is a common strategy.

When jobs are lost as a consequence of the project, the resettlement site must be selected to ensure employment and income-generating opportunities. Loss of jobs is a difficult, short-term problem in new housing developments that, in the beginning, have few shops and services. Several community areas for informal economic activities may be provided at suitable locations within the resettlement site.

Project example: In El Salvador, the Earthquake Reconstruction Project (Ln 2873) relocated DPs in a new housing project, some 15 kilometers from the capital. Follow-up studies documented the dearth of jobs in the new area, especially of jobs such as tailoring and tortilla selling, which depended on proximity to government offices.

Fill-in Resettlement

Fill-in resettlement—locating DPs to available space within the affected area, rather than to another area—also has advantages. Many cities do not have public housing or space for constructing substantial additional housing. Other cities cannot afford large-scale construction of new relocation sites or the infrastructure for them. Small-scale construction, or programs to identify vacant housing, can increase occupancy while providing a much broader range of options to displaced families, at more economic cost. Several projects in Brazil have pioneered a novel approach to fill-in resettlement they call chess, after the popular

13

board game. In this approach, some better-off slum families move to new apartments, and their former homes are upgraded for occupation by poorer families living in precarious or unsafe areas in the slum.

The possibility of new squatters arises when the rehabilitated area has empty spaces. Dedicating these small spaces to public uses is one way to avoid such invasions. In Brazil, neighborhood residents have formed committees to design and oversee these small spaces, which give people a place to meet and socialize, something that had not been available to them before.

> *Project example:* In Brazil, the Water Quality and Pollution Control Project (São Paulo–Guarapiranga program; Ln 3503, Ln 3504, Ln 3505) provided the options of either new apartments or upgraded dwellings in the slum. Applicants for the available apartments were screened for financial and social acceptability. Those who moved to apartments were happy, as they saw this as a step up the social ladder. Meanwhile, the houses they left behind were upgraded for poorer families, who were living in precarious and environmentally unsafe areas in the newly cleared slum. This approach assisted many more families than would have been possible otherwise, reduced the overall cost of the resettlement program, and created far less social disruption than if the entire slum community had been moved to another area.

Location Issues in Urban Resettlement

Urban DPs have diverse preferences regarding resettlement sites, because for them, different locations have different advantages. DPs with lower incomes may be more interested in access to workplaces or markets. Others may be more interested in the quality of their living environment. Some may prefer to remain as close as possible to relatives or friends. Whatever a family's reasons, few will want to move far from their current residence.

The possibilities of meeting these expectations are limited by affordability of available housing and by urban zoning or other restrictions. Land for resettlement sites in the vicinity of workplaces is often either unavailable or prohibitively expensive. Therefore, providing multiple location options helps to meet the diverse preferences of displaced families.

Development of resettlement sites may also promote a variety of housing approaches (Box 13.1). These approaches include provision of "sites and services," where fully serviced plots with long-term security of tenure are offered to DPs; and "shell-housing" or "core-housing" arrangements, which provide for incremental construction. A good practice is to consult with the DPs and to have them participate in selecting sites and housing approaches. All costs associated

13

Box 13.1 Vertical Resettlement: A Tool for Urban Renewal

In the India Mumbai Urban Transport Project (Ln 4665; Cr 3662), about 100,000 residents of urban slums and shanties have been resettled in high-rise buildings, as part of an approach that holds promise. The displaced persons (DPs) were living along railway tracks and roads that needed to be upgraded as part of the project. Most of the DPs did not have any titles to the affected land. After consultations with the Bank, local nongovernmental organizations (NGOs), and the DPs, Maharashtra state and Indian Railways authorities designed a program to relocate DPs to apartment buildings, each with seven floors, as close as possible to their current locations. Because of the importance of social mobilization and the difficult task of getting DPs to adapt to new residential patterns, the tasks of designing and implementing the resettlement program were given to two reputable NGOs, SPARC and National Slum Dwellers Federation, which were already working actively among the DPs. Because time was needed to acquire and develop some of the urban sites, provision was made for temporary housing close to the permanent resettlement sites.

To reduce the total cost of the resettlement program, the government helped establish a market in tradable development rights, which enabled builders who constructed buildings for resettlement at subsidized rates to construct additional commercial space, beyond what would otherwise be allowed under development regulations in other commercial locations in Mumbai.

More than 50,000 people have already been resettled under the program and have expressed high levels of satisfaction with the resettlement program. The potential success of the resettlement program is evident from early indicators: (a) no defaults have occurred on the loan component of the housing assistance; (b) residents have formed cooperative societies for maintenance and other activities; (c) electricity and water tariffs and maintenance fees are paid regularly by all DPs; (d) women-led small-savings and loans groups have been established in every building; and (e) DPs have adapted quite well to living in high-rise buildings.

Because of the success of this experiment, the Government of Maharashtra has been encouraged to follow a similar approach when relocating people from other slum areas in Mumbai to high-rise buildings, thus freeing up for redevelopment some of the most expensive urban land in the world. If successful, this approach could offer valuable lessons on addressing the problem of unorganized urban development in many cities around the world.

---

with the development of resettlement sites, including construction of replacement housing, can be funded by the Bank. RPs typically contain information on final relocation sites and housing.

Project example: In Brazil, the Fortaleza Metropolitan Transport Project (Ln 7083) assisted scattered displaced families to find their own new housing. It could do this because the total number of displaced families was fairly small (319 families, along the entire 17-kilometer route) and because Fortaleza has a large, active housing market. Metro Fortaleza, the project agency, provided social, technical, and legal assistance to any

13

family, to ensure that the goals of resettlement policy were met. Also, the project expropriated properties gradually, to avoid provoking real-estate speculation and a spike in housing prices. And it made a single, lump-sum compensation payment for assets acquired from each family, to enable them to quickly purchase new housing.

Project example: In China, the Tianjin Urban Development Project (Cr. 2387) provided replacement housing for 4,600 families. Rather than being assigned to units, resettlers were given vouchers they could use for residence rights in any of the city's 18 new housing developments. The value of the vouchers reflected the size and quality of the original housing, as well as its location. By extending the range of choice for displaced families, the program offered many advantages. Those families obtaining vouchers could shop for preferred housing sizes and location (in effect mimicking voluntary real-estate transactions). They could surrender the voucher for 60 percent of its value in cash. If the displaced families selected housing worth less than the voucher amount, they received half of the difference in cash. If they selected housing worth more than the voucher amount, the government bore 20–50 percent of the additional cost. And those people who did not wish to relocate away from their small businesses could exchange their voucher for the housing of others willing to move out of the area. The voucher system was well received, and it reduced local opposition to resettlement.

Urban Improvement: Opportunities for Resettlement as Development

When resettlement is integrated into project planning from the earliest stages, the diversity and complexity of the urban landscape may present development opportunities, as well as constraints. An urban setting provides innovative possibilities to lessen displacement or the severity of its impacts. Conversely, where urban living conditions are substandard, resettlement can be designed to enable poor and vulnerable urban populations to benefit from their displacement. The following sections discuss broad categories of interventions offering opportunities to mainstream resettlement into the urban development process.

Improvement of Housing Standards

Instead of attempting to recreate the status quo, standard resettlement practice for the Bank is to use minimum standards for housing size and safety when resettling people from substandard dwellings. The Bank accepts local minimum standards

---

Box 13.2   Housing Affordability and Willingness to Pay

Replacement housing must be affordable to all categories of displaced families. In general terms, affordability can be calculated as a proportion of household income spent on housing. Bank policy is that as a general principle, because resettlement is involuntary, a household cannot be compelled to pay more for replacement housing than it would otherwise.

In practice, many displaced households may be *willing* to pay for improvements in the size or standard of their housing, or they may wish to use resettlement assistance to shift from renting to owning their own housing. When such cases are prevalent, some projects formulate housing strategies by calculating a housing affordability ratio (based on the proportion of monthly income that the household is *willing* to spend on housing and the available financing terms) expressed in terms of a multiple of annual household income.

Unrealistically high standards may put even reasonably good housing out of reach for low-income groups in urban areas. Moreover, getting even minimally acceptable housing that is affordable for such groups is often difficult. Two partial remedies can improve the picture:

- The affordability ratio is often proportional to the security of tenure. Long-term security of tenure makes many people more willing to spend a higher proportion of income on housing.
- Long-term financing on attractive terms encourages people to purchase homes. With attractive terms, many people are willing to spend a higher proportion of income on housing, as a form of savings.

However, some families are likely to attach a lower priority to spending on housing than to spending on education or something else. The choice of improved, but more costly, housing is made willingly only in the context of favorable options.

---

where they exist. Resettlement planning simply promotes reasonable size and safety standards where they do not already exist. Of course, providing housing of acceptable standards on terms the poor cannot afford makes no development sense (Box 13.2).

Slum Improvement Programs

Many planners now favor slum-upgrading programs over slum removal. Attempts to eradicate slums often generate unintended problems: slums are recreated elsewhere, the supply of low-cost housing is depleted, and the supply of unskilled or low-cost labor is separated from areas of existing demand. This approach is also extremely expensive, as new housing has to be built in peripheral areas, the slum dwellers have to be relocated, and the new projects have to be maintained.

Although physical improvement remains the primary objective, slum-upgrading schemes generally enable most of the existing slum dwellers to remain in place as the intended beneficiaries. This community-based approach is likely to maintain or improve the housing supply and leaves residents in the same proximity to neighbors, services, and sources of income. Resettlement may arise, however, if physical improvements require reduction in population density. If the potential for benefits (higher living standards, security of tenure, new economic opportunities) is high, the community itself may be able to identify ways to redistribute people and opportunities on a voluntary basis. In such cases, a good practice is for the project agency to ensure that the affected community, acting through participatory decisionmaking processes, supports the upgrading program; and that everyone in the community who would be adversely affected agrees to the arrangements the community accepts for their relocation or compensation. If land or structures are ceded involuntarily, however, relevant provisions of OP 4.12 necessarily apply. Virtually all costs of slum upgrading (except compensation for involuntarily ceded land) are eligible for Bank project financing.

Land Consolidation Programs

Given diversity in land use and the prospect of rapid economic change, a partial loss of land in an urban setting may lead to significant improvement in incomes or living standards. Land consolidation is one example. Urban land consolidation typically involves amalgamation and redistribution of land parcels so that facilities and services, such as paved roads, walkways, electricity, schools (or other community facilities), or water and sanitation lines, can be provided or improved. Each participant typically loses some portion of land and may even be relocated within the program area. In return, however, each participant typically benefits from improvements that make the value of the remaining parcel higher than that of the previous, larger one. Systematic and uniform improvement within the community reduces as well the helter-skelter additions to roads and water lines that create chronic problems in many cities.

Given compelling assurances that residual property values will increase significantly, most residents in an area designated for land consolidation may *voluntarily* accept the program. If so, contractual arrangements can place land consolidation on a "willing buyer, willing seller" basis, significantly reducing the need for land acquisition (see also "Voluntary Resettlement," in chapter 1). For land ceded involuntarily, however, the requirements of OP 4.12 fully apply. Virtually all land consolidation costs (except compensation for involuntarily ceded land) are eligible for project funding.

Land consolidation can be promoted by government agencies under urban renewal or redevelopment plans, or land consolidation may be undertaken by

13

residents themselves or by private sector developers. In such cases, the cost of providing improved community services can be met by selling some portion of the area for private commercial use. Salient features of successful land consolidation programs include the following:

- Extensive consultation and collaboration with the affected community during project design and implementation.
- Attractive potential benefits, minimizing the need for involuntary land acquisition (people who do not wish to participate have the option of accepting compensation for assets at replacement cost, as well as other resettlement benefits, as applicable, but would lose out on the significant benefits from improvements in infrastructure and provision of services resulting from area development).
- Transitional arrangements to provide adequate housing, transportation, or other services during the consolidation period.
- Long-term security of tenure for all displaced families, including squatters and those with weak titles.
- Equitable distribution of post-development benefits.

Economic Rehabilitation in Urban Projects

Income restoration is invariably one of the greatest resettlement challenges, even in urban areas (see chapter 4, "Compensation and Income Restoration," and Chapter 8, "Income Improvement," for elaboration). Urban areas generally have more favorable conditions for economic rehabilitation: they have large, dynamic economies, unlike those of distant, stagnant rural areas. Nonetheless a good practice is to limit the distance required for relocation, as it can be difficult for people to find new jobs, and commuting times and costs can become unacceptably large. Peri-urban areas are even more favorable, as they often have widespread economic growth.

> *Project example:* In China, the Hubei Environment Project (Ln 3966; Cr 2799) benefited from the dynamic economy of a peri-urban area. The villages affected by the proposed water treatment plants had experienced rapid development with the installation of village industries and the decline in farming. These industries provided a huge job market for the displaced villagers, and most affected laborers were able to find a job, usually in the same industries as in their village, and had medical, educational, and pension benefits.

One recurring issue is the difference between the emphasis in OP 4.12 on rehabilitation measures and the narrower emphasis in borrower legislation on compensation for expropriated assets. Compensation for lost physical assets may replace housing but does little to compensate for lost employment. Because

13

economic life in an urban setting is often highly diversified, and incomes for most people depend on formal or informal employment, the RP needs to address the issue of economic rehabilitation if any DPs lose income or livelihoods.

A second issue is the prevalence of informal economic activity. Residents in many cities rely on unlicensed enterprises, subsist in part on barter or reciprocity arrangements, or engage in other activities that may be overlooked or discounted by project officials. Furthermore, because unlicensed vendors and shopkeepers are in an insecure position, they make few or no investments in the kinds of fixed assets that are eligible for compensation. Again, a resettlement approach focusing primarily on compensation for lost assets is unlikely to provide these business people with adequate opportunities to restore their livelihoods.

In reviews of urban RPs, the need to provide feasible arrangements for economic rehabilitation arises repeatedly. Even where impacts on informal vendors and shopkeepers are recognized, for example, replicating opportunities for them in new and changed surroundings is often quite difficult. However, attention to physical and socioeconomic issues enhances the prospects for satisfactory planning, as follows.

Distance of Relocation

Because affordable, available replacement housing sites are more likely to be found along the more distant suburban perimeter, residential relocation may involve fairly large distances, even greater than 10–20 kilometers. A combination of large distances and poor transportation between the new town and old employment opportunities can create unemployment, or it can split families if employed workers stay behind in the city to earn an income.

Assistance for DPs Needing Employment

One alternative is to coordinate with public transportation services, to ensure that such services are available and affordable. Projects may also subsidize commuting costs. In some cities, finding or providing alternative employment for relocated DPs or providing them incentives to find their own income-generating opportunities may be just as sensible. In some projects, relocated DPs are given preference in hiring for public employment.

> **Project example:** In China, the Shanghai Metropolitan Transport Project (Cr 2296) provided subsidies for DPs forced to commute an additional 12–15 kilometers after relocation.

> **Project example:** Also in China, the Guangzhou Urban Project (Ln 4329) subsidized commuter costs for DPs for a year after their move.

In the informal economy, distant relocation may rupture interdependent relationships between rich and poor or between ethnic groups or castes previously

13

living close to one another. Even if satisfactory arrangements are made to restore formal employment to one or more members of a household after relocation, informal income or subsistence activities may be overlooked or discounted, contributing to further vulnerability and impoverishment.

A good practice is to minimize new employment requirements.

A good practice is to avoid relocation requiring loss of employment or change of occupation. If such impacts are unavoidable, the RP needs to detail significant effort and expenditure directed at mitigative measures. The RP needs to identify impacts that would cause any affected people to lose employment or to change occupations, and the RP should indicate what alternative employment or opportunities will be offered to restore livelihoods. In these instances, transitional assistance (a short-term job or outright subsidy) is, as good practice, to be provided until alternative employment is available. Any workers losing employment, moreover, should be given the option of alternative employment. They should under no circumstances be forced to bear the risks and costs of finding alternative employment. However, in many cities, some former workers may prefer cash settlements that allow them to start small businesses.

Assistance for Business

Distant relocation may force the owners of businesses to compete in a less favorable environment, because competitors may be more numerous or better established, consumers may be poorer or scarcer or have different tastes, or reputation and goodwill may be altogether extinguished. The simple provision of a place for conducting business may not be sufficient for income restoration. A good practice is therefore to have the RP assess the feasibility of income restoration in proposed new locations and state what transitional wage and profit assistance will be provided to employees and owners of businesses for an adequate interim period. (This assistance can take the form of short-term employment, as well as outright subsidies.) Good practice also suggests that business owners be provided with options allowing them to assess for themselves whether their existing business is restorable or new business opportunities would be preferable.

> **Project example:** In Brazil, the Minas Gerais Water Quality and Pollution Control Project (Ln 3554) team conducted an employment survey in a new settlement built 20 kilometers from an old residential area. Thirty-nine percent of the economically active DP population was still working in industries near the former community, and another 17 percent was self-employed in the old area. In total, 56 percent of the DP population depended on activities in their old, now distant area. As a result, almost two-thirds of the DPs complained of problems related to distance, and more than one-third claimed a loss of income because of higher

13

transportation and living costs. In addition, the DPs complained that lack of public services in the new area forced them to use schools, clinics, and hospitals in their old area.

Project example: In India, the Nathpa Jhakri Hydroelectric Project (Ln 3024) offered businesses the option of a new location or a cash payment. Sixty-five shopkeepers chose a new site and transfer assistance; 33 others chose payment for the loss of their business.

Obstacles to Income Restoration at the Relocation Site

The complexity and rich variety of urban living conditions make it practically impossible to provide a list of potential obstacles to income restoration. Urban projects have a remarkable ability to present new challenges—if they are identified. Thorough resettlement planning is the key to identifying and addressing the various problems sometimes impeding income restoration after people are relocated. Here are some examples:

- Compensation can be inadequate if it does not factor in all urban taxes, fees, or licensing costs. A good practice is to include all such official transaction costs in transition allowances or to have the RP ensure that such costs are waived.
- Alternative arrangements are to be provided if municipal zoning at the new site prohibits small-scale income-generating activities.
- Where DPs remain partially dependent on subsistence gardens, a good practice is to allocate private or community plots.
- In societies with an institutionalized division of labor between men (formal economic activity) and women (informal or subsistence activities), RPs must provide productive opportunities that will allow women to continue to contribute to household incomes. In some settings, another good practice is to identify opportunities through resettlement to improve the position of women (such as ensuring joint title to replacement assets or providing new educational opportunities).

Community and Public Infrastructure in Urban Projects

In urban settings, public infrastructure is both a major focus of project investment and a major cause of resettlement. Project planning must be carefully integrated so that new investments do not cause deterioration of existing water, sewerage, or other services in specific areas. Similarly, new or improved service can create shifts in population densities or property values that require more

13

295

investment in infrastructure and more displacement. The costs of repair or replacement of public infrastructure can also be exceedingly high. But because urban living standards depend heavily on such community-level services, such costs must be factored into project assessment and borne by the project. Finally, infrastructure planning needs to be forward-looking, as restoration of existing levels or qualities of infrastructure may make little practical sense in rapidly changing urban environments.

Restoring or Replacing Public Infrastructure

Survey and census instruments assess the kind, extent, and quality of existing public infrastructure in areas affected by the project. In projects without significant relocation of people, the RP discusses how existing services are to be restored, replaced, or improved. If the project involves significant relocation of people or development of resettlement sites, the RP includes arrangements for providing public infrastructure to meet minimum community standards or standards prevalent in the project-impact area, whichever is higher. A good practice is to plan for water, sewerage, and waste disposal arrangements that meet or exceed environmental standards and impose no environmental degradation on other areas.

The RP addresses financial requirements and responsibilities for infrastructure, as well as the capacity of agencies to effectively restore public services in a timely manner. If the project has disrupted the operation or maintenance of infrastructure, the RP also includes handover arrangements that will return responsibility for operating and maintaining infrastructure services to local service agencies. In a similar vein, the RP addresses any cost-recovery provisions or other arrangements that require DPs to bear additional expenses for access to infrastructure. Finally, it presents the provisions for restoration of educational and public health facilities and other community-level religious, cultural, and civic facilities, as appropriate. If new sites are to be built close to existing neighborhoods, arrangements to improve infrastructure include equitable treatment for host populations.

Creating Public Spaces

Many slums lack public areas for communal activities. Small unused areas created by urban upgrading will often be invaded by squatters if left unoccupied. Organizing neighborhood meetings to decide on the use of unused public spaces is a recommended practice, not only to eliminate the possibility of squatter invasions, but also to foster the social solidarity of the residents. Such spaces can be used productively for playgrounds and meeting areas, and such use of public space will also foster social solidarity and increase security.

13

Project example: In Brazil, the Water Quality and Pollution Control Project (São Paulo-Guarapiranga component; Ln 3503, Ln 3504, Ln 3505) developed playgrounds and parks from the small, irregular plots remaining after roads, sewers, and drains were built. These public areas provided a place for children to play and adults to visit. As a result, the community experienced more solidarity, and squatter invasions were less likely.

Urban Linear Projects

Linear projects (improving sewerage, widening roads, and so forth) in urban areas can affect a large number of people. Resettlement planning should be based on identified potential impacts, rather than on undifferentiated asset loss. Impacts may be temporary, such as loss of use or access during construction. Temporarily displaced people and businesses may be provided lump-sum compensation for inconvenience or loss of clientele. When marginal strips of land are acquired for road widening, the impact may be minor (defined as affecting less than one-fifth of the land area). People marginally affected by loss of assets may also be given compensation: replacement cost estimated on the basis of average land values or construction costs in the area.

Often, for DPs, the potential benefits of linear infrastructure improvements are likely to outweigh marginal adverse impacts. Road improvements, for example, typically result in assets that are worth much more than the assets lost. The Bank accepts that after delivery of all compensation or other entitlements, the borrower may impose new or higher property taxes on people whose property appreciated with the infrastructure improvements. The Bank does not accept potential increases in the value of assets in lieu of compensation for involuntary acquisition, for the simple reason that such benefits may be uncertain or take years to accrue, and without compensation, families may be forced to sell remaining assets in the interim.

If impacts on assets located along a linear urban corridor are marginal but many people are displaced, the administrative cost of asset valuation and other resettlement activities may become excessive. In fact, the cost of conducting a detailed valuation of replacement cost for every marginally affected asset can exceed the value of the compensation. If impacts are likely to be minor, alternative steps are recommended to determine appropriate compensation arrangements. These arrangements include the following:

- Preparation of the inventory of affected assets;
- Identification of marginal impacts;
- Categorization of marginal impacts; and

13

- Formulation of compensation measures for each category, based on average replacement cost for land and other assets in the area.

Cash compensation for expropriated assets in cases of marginal impact is acceptable.

Because cash is fungible, urban residents can use it to make their own tradeoffs in housing, employment, quality of life, or other considerations. Cash compensation may be appropriate when housing markets are viable, the cash compensation is sufficient to purchase replacement housing, and those receiving cash compensation have sufficient information about market conditions (see OP 4.12, para. 12). In other words, cash compensation is preferable if it provides alternatives for DPs; it is inappropriate, however, if it only transfers the problem of finding suitable and affordable alternatives from the project to the DPs.

13

Chapter 14

Resettlement in Linear Projects

The Context of Linear Resettlement

Linear projects—roads, railways, transmission lines, pipelines, and irrigation canals—have a long but fairly narrow corridor of impact. This defining characteristic creates both advantages and difficulties. Narrow strips of land generally displace few people. Indeed, linear projects may require only temporary dislocation while roads are rehabilitated or transmission lines are installed. But the long, narrow project corridor may make administrative coordination difficult if the project passes through many local areas. And coordinating and consulting with relatively small, dispersed groups of displaced persons (DPs) poses similar logistical considerations.

The resettlement impacts of linear projects are often less severe than those of large-area projects, such as dams, because narrow corridors tend to require acquisition of only parts of people's properties. Land acquired in linear projects frequently consists of a strip along property frontages. Acquiring these strips may not require relocation of occupants or users and typically may not negate the economic viability of landholdings. Linear projects can usually be rerouted to avoid heavy concentrations of population and to avoid large-scale resettlement. If relocation is needed, though, people can usually be resettled in the same area—sometimes, especially in rural zones, even on the same plot of land. Nonetheless, even small-scale land acquisition can result in significant hardships for some DPs. In rural areas, linear projects may bisect existing holdings or isolate communities from their productive resources and employment centers; in urban areas, they may dislodge many people without secure title.

Although linear projects usually have less severe impacts than other projects, they still pose considerable challenges in resettlement planning. Consultation and participation may be difficult if the project stretches across many areas. Projects involving roads or railways frequently necessitate resettlement of people without secure title, which can raise legally or political issues. Assessing and remedying partial (and often temporary) impacts can be complex and difficult. And the projects may be phased over several years, so issues of organizational coordination are likely to arise, underscoring the importance of

14

monitoring systems. This chapter offers technical guidance for dealing with these issues.

Linear Projects and Their Corridors of Impact

Linear projects all share the same defining characteristic—a long, narrow project zone—but each type of project has its own particularities. This section discusses the differences in road, pipeline, transmission line, and rail projects, in terms of width of the project corridor and extent of probable impacts.

Roads and Highways

Road and highway projects either build new roads or improve existing ones. This distinction is relevant in terms of land acquisition. Opening up a corridor for a new road requires substantially more land acquisition, and the negative impacts are usually more severe, than in road rehabilitation or upgrading. Although the extent and scale of resettlement may differ in the two situations, challenges related to resettlement have to be addressed in each.

Existing roads usually already have an established right-of-way (ROW). Although new land may need to be acquired for bypasses, curve straightening, or roadside improvements, the acquisition is likely to be more modest than in projects to build completely new roads. Even in projects involving little or no formal land acquisition, displacement may nevertheless take place—sometimes on a large scale—within an existing ROW.

Under Bank policy, the negative impacts on occupiers of public land should be mitigated.

Resettlement impacts are generally confined within a fairly narrow "corridor of impact," the area that is unsafe, where people are not permitted to occupy structures, carry out business activities, or cultivate land. The width of this corridor varies, depending on the type of road. The corridor may not be as wide as the legal ROW, but it is typically wider than the minimum required for pavement, shoulders, and roadside improvements (for example, parking zones, bus stops). For purposes of resettlement planning, the corridor of impact includes the immediate safety zone and any areas that impact directly on people's livelihoods. Whatever has to be removed or demolished, whether permanently or temporarily, is by definition inside a corridor of impact, and people suffering losses caused by the project should be assisted in improving or at least restoring their standards of living after resettlement.

No fixed or predetermined width can be established for the corridor of impact, because it will vary according to local conditions. For example, a safety zone for a good road with a high volume of fast-moving traffic may be considerably

14

wider than that of a less traveled rural road. In one state in India, the average width of the corridor of impact for a two-lane rural highway is 20 meters, within a ROW averaging 30 meters.

Project example: In India, the Andhra Pradesh State Highways Project (Loan [Ln] 4192) rehabilitated existing roads with an established ROW. Although road rehabilitation provided an opportunity to clear the ROW of all occupiers, the project undertook socioeconomic studies and engineering designs to determine which of the occupiers were within the ROW but outside the immediate corridor of impact. This led to changes in engineering design that eliminated some resettlement. Project authorities also agreed to allow those people technically within the ROW but outside the corridor of impact to continue residing, farming, or working as they previously were, thus further reducing the required resettlement.

Road and highway projects have different impacts in rural and urban areas, as population density and socioeconomic diversity tend to be higher in urban settings (see also chapter 13, "Resettlement in Urban Areas"). Substantial physical dislocation in rural settings can often be avoided by moving homes back a short distance, but this solution is more difficult in an urban area. And economic activities take place along the road in urban and rural areas, but the impact on street vendors and shopkeepers is generally higher in urban areas, where vendors are more closely packed. Finding alternative spots for shopkeepers and vendors is, therefore, often necessary.

Urban road improvements may generate significant indirect effects, both positive and negative. A bypass around a populated area, for example, may result in local merchants losing their customer base. A good practice, therefore, is to have socioeconomic analyses extend beyond impacts directly related to land acquired, to identify opportunities to mitigate adverse indirect impacts. However, road development in urban areas also generally results in appreciation of property values along the road. Because the extent of appreciation is variable and benefits all property owners along the road, not only those who may have lost some land for road construction, appreciation cannot be used as a proxy for compensation. If property values increase as a result of a Bank project, any "betterment taxes" levied on property owners can also be imposed on people who have lost some land.

Project example: In Nigeria, the Lagos Urban Transport Project (Credit [Cr] 3720) took as its definition of "corridor of impact" the sidewalks and walkway areas parallel to the arteries to be rehabilitated. This definition was based in the need to clear walkways of merchants and vendors so that pedestrians would not have to walk in the street. In most instances, sellers could be relocated either farther back within the ROW or along

14

nearby commercial streets. However, congested areas with thousands of vendors required participatory studies, both to determine the extent of relocation necessary and to identify possible solutions.

Another question in urban transport resettlement is whether compensation should be paid at the preproject replacement cost of land or at the anticipated postproject replacement cost. At issue here is the potential problem of finding replacement land in the same area if compensation is calculated on the basis of preproject land prices. Paying compensation at anticipated postproject land rates could make the entire project infeasible and might fail to account for the benefits accruing to those who continue to have residual lands after the acquisition. If land prices are expected to substantially increase after project development, paying compensation at preproject replacement cost, as early as possible during project implementation, is advisable so that people can purchase replacement land in the vicinity. The project team should monitor land prices so that it can find suitable land through special mechanisms if problems arise.

Gas and Oil Pipelines

Most pipelines do not require much land or resettlement, as they are built within an existing road ROW to facilitate access and maintenance. Others are underground, so impacts may be largely temporary. The corridor is generally narrow, typically 6–18 meters wide. And its alignment can be modified to avoid or minimize unnecessary displacement.

More significant land acquisition may be necessary for pumping stations, treatment plants, access roads, or storage facilities. A good practice is to assess the land and resettlement requirements of the pipeline, together with those of the ancillary structures, to arrive at a comprehensive resettlement plan.

Establishing a pipeline ROW does not generally require transfer of land ownership. Instead, restrictions are placed on the use of the land within the corridor. Pipelines might permanently constrain activities, such as forestry, or cultivation of crops that require plowing. They also impose restrictions on building structures. Because they can affect incomes and living standards, however, limitations on use warrant compensation or other forms of assistance. Easement fees and payment for any crop damage, for example, are appropriate compensation for people whose fields may be subject to periodic intrusion for maintenance.

Security and safety considerations frequently make some displacement unavoidable. Safety considerations may require, for example, displacement of people in the vicinity of the pipeline, where they face the dangers of oil leaks, gas escapes, or explosions. In many cases, the need to protect pipelines from vandalism or sabotage may lead project planners to design perimeters of exclusion. In such cases, proper safety measures must be observed, even where they entail displacement, and the necessary extent of resettlement must not be understated.

Like other linear projects, pipelines can cause unanticipated indirect displacement. Pipelines crossing through isolated forests, natural parks, or indigenous reserves, for example, can promote unintended colonization. This colonization can in turn have negative impacts on the cultures and livelihoods of people who depend on these resources. In these cases, careful consideration of long-term effects is recommended, before planners make irreversible decisions about alignments. Participatory assessment of environmental and social risks is highly recommended, to help prepare an appropriate mitigation action plan.

> *Project example:* In Bolivia, the Oleoducto Project to transport gas through the Amazon to consumption centers of Brazil implemented a strict policy to avoid uncontrolled colonization of the area and deleterious contact with local groups. Project authorities forbade any unnecessary contact between project employees and local populations and maintained a careful record of all necessary contacts.

Water and Sanitation Systems

In urban areas, construction or rehabilitation of water and sanitation systems tends to generate significant levels of displacement, both permanent and temporary, especially in areas with low incomes and informal housing. If large numbers of people have to be relocated, or entire communities are to be disrupted, RPs have to address the impacts on the entire community. To minimize the temporary adverse impacts, which can be substantial in urban areas, construction documents need to incorporate special provisions on the duration and timing of construction, as well as appropriate construction technologies to be adopted by the contractor. These provisions are also incorporated into the environmental management plan for the project and are monitored as part of the plan and as part of construction supervision.

Because the benefits of slum upgrading and avoidance of disasters in risk-prone areas directly target the poorest and more marginalized communities, minimization of displacement may not be desirable. In these projects, displacement may be a project objective if, for example, the communities request the project to be implemented in their neighborhood, knowing that some people will be able to stay while others have to move; water and sanitation works will significantly improve community living conditions; or people forced to move receive similar benefits and incentives in alternative locations.

> *Project example:* In Brazil, the Water Quality and Sewerage Project (São Paulo-Guarapiranga component; Ln 3503, Ln 3504, Ln 3505) sought to

14

protect the watershed for the reservoir of São Paulo. Because removing residents from the watershed area would be impossible for economic and historical reasons, the project aimed to improve the sewerage and drainage systems within the watershed area. Even this more limited development of infrastructure required major localized resettlement. The resettlement became an integral component of the project. The project offered a range of housing options, from new apartments to upgraded shanty dwellings, according to the resources of the DPs. This approach benefited many more people than otherwise and maintained the social fabric in the area, as well as upgrading social services, such as playgrounds, public security, and clinics.

Irrigation Systems

Irrigation canals are similar to pipelines in many respects, but they also have distinctive features. Usually, farmers losing land also receive benefits from the new irrigation infrastructure. Such projects present unique opportunities to optimize resettlement and establish an equitable distribution of costs and benefits. Also, land reform and land consolidation schemes may enable families facing water shortages to relocate to plots vacated by others, in exchange for irrigation benefits that make their remaining holdings far more productive.

Transmission Lines

Depending on technical specifications, transmission lines require a corridor of impact 12–25 meters wide, or even more in the case of high-voltage electric lines (500 kilovolts or more). Although the impact of a tower is likely to be slight, especially in rural areas, transmission lines extending hundreds of kilometers may produce a significant aggregate displacement, especially if the lines cannot avoid more heavily populated areas.

Transmission lines themselves do not require land acquisition, except for the towers. Instead, an ROW is established, imposing restrictions on land use. Local laws and regulations determine these constraints; for example, height restrictions might be imposed on crops grown under transmission lines. In most cases, existing structures are not permitted to remain underneath transmission lines. Some countries expressly prohibit digging or mining near towers, while permitting activities such as cattle ranching.

For reasons of safety or unresolved environmental issues, many countries specifically forbid residential or commercial use of land underneath or near transmission lines. Subject to various restrictions, some countries do allow people to live under transmission lines. (In China, for example, displacement may be

14

minimized by raising the height of the towers, rather than removing the people living under them.) In some cases, restrictions will extend to 50 meters from the line axis, depending on electromagnetic fields, interference with communications, or other factors.

Construction of the transmission line does not require purchase of much land, but construction of associated works, such as power substations, might entail displacement. Building or widening access roads to towers can also affect property use, and restrictions on land use can affect incomes. As with compensation for pipelines, an easement fee, combined with payment for any crop damage, may be an appropriate way to compensate for periodic access. Such easement fees range from 5 to 20 percent of the replacement cost of the affected land. In most cases, no compensation is paid for a decrease in property value as a result of construction of transmission lines.

> *Project example:* In Cambodia, the Phnom Penh Power Rehabilitation Project (Cr 2550) paid landowners an easement fee equivalent to 2 percent of the value of the land or free installation of an electricity connection. (Consumption costs would be the landowners' responsibility.) The owners could continue to use the land for purposes not interfering with the lines; crops, trees, and any structures built on the land had to be less than 3 meters high.

> *Project example:* In China, the Hunan Power Development Project (Ln 4350) raised the height of high-voltage transmission towers, wherever possible, to meet the technical standard of 6.5-meter clearance above any houses to comply with the national law and so to reduce the extent of relocation.

> *Project example:* In Senegal, the Regional Hydropower Development Project (Cr 2970, Cr 2971, Cr 2972) sited high-voltage power lines as much as possible within the ROW of the national highway, to avoid land acquisition.

Railways

Depending on the technology, a railway corridor is typically 16–24 meters wide. In many instances, squatters occupy existing railway corridors, which are among the most accessible urban spaces and have little other value. This feature is one of the main reasons why displacement of population is so high for the rehabilitation or privatization of railways.

Valid safety and security considerations entail the restriction of human habitation in railway corridors. Minimizing displacement may be inappropriate if human habitation poses risks to local residents or to people on passing trains.

14

305

However, the ROW of railway corridors is often wider than necessary. Under such conditions, project planners can move residents back a few meters and provide adequate safety measures, such as fences or pedestrian overpasses.

In all forms of linear resettlement, case-by-case analysis of impacts is recommended, even if impacts are predominantly partial. In many cases, even slight land loss might be critical to families living at or below the poverty line. Alternatively, linear projects may cut across areas where land has been fractionated into small, supplemental garden plots.

Participation and Minimization of Resettlement

By their nature, linear projects usually involve many stakeholders over considerable distances. The fact that roads, pipelines, transmission lines, and other types of linear projects typically run hundreds of kilometers means that they involve many areas. In some cases, they may even cross from one country into another. Because project authorities cannot be familiar with the particularities of each local area, public consultation and participation in project design are especially important for minimizing resettlement.

OP 4.12 requires the least possible displacement of people. To ensure the least displacement in linear projects, early screening of the entire corridor or corridors is essential. Such screening can be carried out in coordination with an environmental assessment, in close collaboration with those responsible for engineering designs and overall project management.

With early screening, it is often possible to shift the alignment of the proposed road, transmission line, or pipeline to reduce negative impacts. Good practice is to take into account a variety of concerns: how many structures may have to be demolished, areas where the population density is high, land or wells that are productive, producing trees that may have to be cut down for a power transmission line, and so forth. Detailed strip maps documenting existing land usage, economic activities, and environmental concerns are therefore usually prepared for the entire corridor, to inform the planning and final designs. Even a slight shift of a meter or two in the centerline of a road may avoid significant negative social or environmental impacts.

Effective screening usually entails consultation with potentially affected local people, as well as local officials. To be meaningful, the consultation process gives the stakeholders an opportunity to consider options and state their opinions. As good practice, the participation reports document how the views of the affected populations have been taken into account in project designs. As consultation and participation are important in both social and environmental assessments, the consultation process should integrate both dimensions, rather than considering them separately.

14

The consultative screening process can provide valuable information on

- Whether to shift the corridor, from marginal adjustments to a choice of alternative routes;
- Whether to construct a bypass around a populated area in a road project;
- Where to place underpasses or overpasses; and
- How safety measures can be introduced in specific areas.

In such diverse settings, consultation, public information, and local participation in the project need to be organized differently than in more localized projects. Typically, only a few of the people in any one area along the corridor may be involved or affected by the project. A community-based approach may therefore not be sufficient or appropriate for consultation and involvement of DPs. Because of the dispersed nature of the DPs, expecting a sense of common identity among them is unrealistic. Expecting different people to act as one collective body, represented by people with whom they may have nothing in common, is also unrealistic. A good practice is to set up consultative groups, grievance bodies, and participatory implementation units to adequately represent different categories of stakeholders.

Project example: In China, the Second Henan Highway Project (Ln 4027) informed and involved DPs throughout the activity. Local government regularly posted the amount of compensation received and its expenditure. The local township governments also proactively ensured the productive use of village compensation. The resettlement villages established village financial management groups, which proposed uses for compensation funds. These proposals were reviewed in the village councils and then cleared by the township government. Consultations were also conducted to determine the most appropriate locations for overpasses and underpasses, to help reduce disruption to communities living along both sides of the highways.

Project example: In India, the National Highways Authority of India (Ln 4559) instituted local consultations on the proposed routing of the major roads to be rehabilitated. In one town, residents preferred to route the highway around their community, rather than widen the existing road through town. To support their argument, they walked the Authority officials along the proposed new alignment of the road around the town and pointed out that 80 percent of the new alignment was on unoccupied land already owned by the government. The Authority's engineers recognized the cogency of the residents' argument and rerouted the highway.

Project example: In Senegal, the Regional Hydropower Development Project (Cr 2970, Cr 2971, Cr 2972) organized a series of meetings at

14

various administrative levels to inform officials and local residents of the nature of the project. First, official meetings were held in the prefecture office for district officers. These meetings explained the purpose of the project, sketched the route of the transmission line, and discussed the compensation program. Then district officers held local meetings to get that same information out and identify the individual landowners who would be affected by the project. At the same time, a grievance committee was established at the prefecture level, to hear and resolve complaints about project implementation.

With even the best coordinated approach from the various project authorities, civil works may be delayed by public protests. In some countries, local people may be supported, or even encouraged, to block construction. While these demonstrations often represent legitimate claims and grievances, they are sometimes the result of a lack of communication and proper consultation. Costly misunderstandings can be avoided by involving local stakeholders from the earliest stages. Experience also shows that careful consultation and coordination with local groups is essential to developing an appropriate framework for entitlements and to getting people's acceptance for this framework. The additional administrative and financial costs of undertaking detailed consultation and coordination are, in fact, investments, contributing to smoother implementation, greater ownership, and project sustainability.

Linear projects require consultation mechanisms.

OP 4.12 (para. 8) states that RPs will pay particular attention to vulnerable groups and insists that they be adequately represented in project consultations. Because they are geographically dispersed, DPs in linear projects may be disadvantaged in obtaining representation. But because whole communities are usually not directly affected, and few are physically displaced, detailed consultations may not be carried out. However, even though land acquisition may be slight, linear projects can produce adverse impacts on broader communities, such as severed access to resources. As these impacts might be identified only through consultations, Task Team Leaders need to ensure that DPs along the entire length of the project are consulted (Box 14.1).

Project example: In China, the Urumqi Urban Transport Project (Ln 4590) originally neglected a dozen households that would not be directly forced to relocate but would have been trapped in an almost inaccessible location between the ring road and an adjacent rail line. After consultation with these households, the project agency agreed to consider them project affected and provided them with the same benefits as other DPs. Other linear projects have constructed overpasses or underpasses to

14

Box 14.1   Consultation and Minimizing Displacement in Guatemala

The Guatemala Rural Roads Project (Ln 4260) had among its subcomponents the rehabilitation of an interstate road connecting the Sierra and Pacific lowlands. Rehabilitation of that road was expected to promote development of several municipalities, as well as tourism and commercial transport. The road was initially designed by engineers on the basis of standard technical and economic considerations. Poor rural families that were facing displacement from their land and houses asked the ministry of transport to realign parts of the road, to reduce displacement. A joint field inspection, with engineers, transport specialists, local authorities, and family households, subsequently took place.

Variations in the alignment were discussed in a fruitful exchange of technical, economic, and social considerations. As a result, it was suggested that instead of widening the road on both sides of a central axis, the project should widen only one side. This design would significantly reduce displacement and cut project costs. However, the variants adopted would have affected some big farms. The farm owners, who also participated in the consultations, agreed to the new alignments in exchange for small improvements, such as better farm entrances or a bypass for farm workers and equipment. Where displacement of farm workers living along the road was unavoidable, agreements were reached with farm owners to relocate families to other areas near the farms so that they could keep their jobs. The same scheme was adopted by local governments, which provided land for relocating DPs in exchange for small works to improve town entrances or intersections with highways.

In this case, early consultation led to incorporation of social concerns along with the economic and technical standards. This process led to alterations in design that minimized displacement; identified small benefits, to offset some of the unavoidable negative impacts; and yielded a more equitable distribution of resettlement costs and benefits. Safety standards were maintained, and the project stayed within budget.

---

provide good-quality access for people cut off by new transport or infrastructure corridors.

Impacts on Vulnerable Populations

Like any investment, linear projects can impact vulnerable populations. In towns and urban areas, road and sanitation projects typically displace both informal economic enterprises and residents without secure title. In rural areas, linear projects may run through areas of indigenous populations. This section takes up each of these situations.

Informal Economic Enterprises

Widening of roads and railways frequently displaces enterprises located along or within the ROW, as well as creating economic opportunities for others. During

14

project preparation and design, the project team considers such impacts and assesses whether benefits are equitably distributed. Displacement may affect poor people disproportionately, as the more resourceful people may have the means to take advantage of economic opportunities. Better access to distant markets, for example, will most benefit people with a surplus to sell and the means to transport it. Losses usually occur immediately, as a result of land acquisition and project construction, whereas economic opportunities are likely to arise much later. Under such uncertainty, a reasonable approach is to concentrate on mitigation and compensation of economic losses, giving special attention to those who rely entirely on subsistence economic activities.

Informal traders and mobile vendors are included in the RP.

Improving an existing road may require space previously occupied by informal traders, mobile vendors, and others whose living depends on access to passersby. A good practice is to ensure that these weaker groups have continued access to clients and suppliers. Disruption of their activities affects not only the people who lose their business opportunities, but also the users of their goods and services. The project team needs to address this through good project design and try to relocate these economic activities in planned shopping areas, on open shoulders, or in other commercial facilities along the transportation corridors, while ensuring safety and the flow of traffic.

Different solutions may be appropriate for different categories of DPs. In the case of truly mobile vendors, all that may be required is to ensure that space is available for them to carry on with business. People expected to lose permanent or semipermanent structures should be fully compensated or assisted with moving and rebuilding in a new place. Such relocation is at no cost to the displaced population. If necessary, the RP makes provisions for subsistence allowances during the transition until recovery of the previous level of economic activity. Street vendors with fixed structures and licenses are entitled to relocation and restitution of their activities and to similar access to clients and markets.

Residents without Secure Title

Because transport corridors are also economic corridors, and governments often fail to exclude private use of public ROWs, projects involving road or railway improvements frequently displace squatters and encroachers. Because in most countries squatters and encroachers have no claim to resettlement assistance under local law, providing them with assistance under Bank-supported projects can raise sensitive issues with borrowers (Box 14.2). Formalizing such assistance through publicly announced resettlement programs may meet with strong resistance. Local officials want to avoid encouraging or rewarding what they see as

---

Box 14.2   Inconsistent Treatment of Squatters and Encroachers

Official views on, and practices relating to, squatters and encroachers are not always unequivocal or consistent. Experience demonstrates the following:

- To get political support, local elites and politicians sometimes encourage occupation of public land by squatters and encroachers.
- Settlements regarded as illegal are often regularized, and the occupants are given legal land tenure.
- Courts have sometimes ruled in favor of squatters' occupancy rights and sometimes in favor of evicting them (as in the case of the India Haryana National Highways Project).
- In India, the Ministry of Environment and Forests has developed guidelines for resettlement issues in linear projects, such as roads and railways. These guidelines explicitly state that squatters may be given assistance for relocation, but these guidelines are not well known among state authorities.

---

illegal use or occupation of public property. They are understandably worried about setting precedents that will establish expensive new entitlements and may undermine legal property systems by encouraging a new influx of public land invaders, particularly urban migrants.

An early census covering the entire planned corridor of impact is essential in establishing a baseline for the existing population. The census also creates a documented inventory of existing assets, such as structures and trees, that may be affected.

Reaching an early understanding and agreement about an entitlement framework can safeguard the economic viability of households and avoid giving the same legal entitlements to encroachers as to legal titleholders. Many governments recognize de facto rights of squatters and encroachers, often based on length of occupation. Recognizing that squatters and encroachers are generally among the poorest people, resettlement programs should direct special attention and support to them, to prevent further impoverishment.

Indigenous People

Linear projects may traverse areas inhabited by indigenous populations. Such instances raise two major concerns. First, the project should take the views of the local population into account while making decisions relating to the location, design, and alignment of the infrastructure and agree on how to pay any compensation or royalties. Since the project may take community land, the project's financing of community services selected by the local population, such as clinics and schools, is appropriate.

14

Second, construction needs to be managed to limit workers' contact with the local populations in the short term. Similarly, in the longer run, steps need to be taken to avoid the spontaneous migration into the area that the project's access roads may encourage.

Projects crossing lands occupied by indigenous people are required to meet Bank policy on indigenous peoples and develop an Indigenous People's Development Plan.

Project Phasing, Censuses, and Studies

Resettlement impacts can be determined only after final designs specify the corridor of impact. Final designs are unlikely to be complete at project start-up; in linear projects, final designs often are completed in stages. Civil works may well start along some areas of the corridor a year or two before designs are complete for the entire alignment.

Different activities related to planning and implementation of physical works and resettlement need to take place sequentially for any given stretch of corridor. But across the project area, these activities can be happening in parallel during the lifetime of the project. Careful coordination is required to avoid delays in resettlement activities that will hold up civil works or to prevent civil works from taking place on a stretch of corridor before appropriate resettlement activities. The following is an example of the phasing and coordination of some of these activities.

Activity	Time line
• Initial social screening, coordinated with environmental assessment and other feasibility studies • Initial consultations with stakeholders • Decision on choices of corridor	
• Census and baseline survey • Policy framework: Agreement on categories of impacts and appropriate entitlements	
• Preparation of resettlement action plan: time-bound implementation plan for entitlements	

Activity	Time line
• Final designs, indicating corridor of impact	
• Detailed overview of DPs within corridor of impact	
• Consultations with DPs about the project; presentation on entitlements and options	
• Registration and preparation of identity cards	
• Revisit DPs to discuss and finalize options	
• Issuance of identity cards	
• Updating of resettlement action plan	
• Implementation of resettlement action plan within relevant corridor segments	
• Civil works, not to be started on any segment before relocation and assistance	

Linear projects with known corridors of impact at the time of project appraisal require an RP with full population census and an inventory of the assets to be acquired; linear projects with corridors that can only partly be known at appraisal require a resettlement policy framework for the entire project and an RP for those sections where the corridor is known (an RP must be presented later for sections where the corridor is unknown at the time of project appraisal).

When the entire route of a linear project is known, the project team conducts both a census of DPs and an asset inventory so that it can develop the RP in time for appraisal.

In linear projects with a preliminary design identifying only general corridors of impact by the time of project appraisal, precise identification and enumeration of DPs and their assets cannot be undertaken by appraisal. In such circumstances, the project should include the following:

- A policy framework establishing categories of entitlements to apply after precise identification and enumeration of DPs.

14

313

- For segments of the project for which engineering specifications are available (and for all land acquisition occurring in the first year of the project), a full census of all DPs and a detailed and complete inventory of land and assets to be acquired.

- For segments of the project for which engineering specifications are not fully known, a corridor of maximum impact to serve as the basis for a full census of all people possibly affected, including a *simple listing* of land and structures that may be acquired. This simple listing will serve to estimate resettlement costs. These procedures will protect the project against fraudulent claims, as all potential DPs and major assets will have been registered. When specific project requirements become known, the RP must be updated to include a socioeconomic survey and a valuation of assets to be acquired.

Similarly, projects with subprojects that may involve involuntary resettlement should present a resettlement policy framework (OP 4.12, para. 26) for the entire project, along with an RP for each subproject or component that involves resettlement and will be initiated in the first year of the project. The RP for subsequent subprojects involving resettlement must be presented before the respective subprojects are approved for Bank financing. The borrower is responsible for "preparing a resettlement plan in accordance with the framework, for each sub-project giving rise to displacement, and furnishing it to the Bank for approval prior to implementation of the sub-project" (BP 4.12, endnote 8). A good practice is to develop the RPs for subprojects that could not be completed by appraisal within the first year of the project.

> *Project example:* In Nigeria, the Lagos Urban Transport Project (Cr 3720) developed, for appraisal, a policy framework to guide any resettlement activities. Furthermore, road rehabilitation was scheduled to avoid any resettlement in the first year of the project so that a master RP could be developed to cover most, if not all, the subproject areas to be rehabilitated in subsequent years.

RP preparation can be done in stages.

Census and survey procedures for projects with linear resettlement differ from those in most other projects in one important respect: because final technical designs often cannot be known over hundreds of kilometers by appraisal, final alignments or the precise corridors of impact are impossible to determine. The remedy is either to deliberately extend the census and surveys to include the maximum envelope of impact or to estimate the resettlement impact in the areas where the route has yet to be finalized and conduct the census and socioeconomic survey at a later date.

14

If preliminary designs are poorly defined, the maximum envelope of impact may cut a fairly broad swath, making census and survey taking more expensive and time-consuming. Nonetheless, identifying and enumerating the total potentially affected population and their assets will provide information for the final design process and establish a basis for entitlements, protecting the project from fraudulent or opportunistic resettlement claims. Of course, only those actually affected following final design would be eligible for resettlement assistance.

Some linear projects involve subcomponents whose locations are simply unknown (for example, a choice will be made between various routes on the basis of screening and feasibility studies still to be carried out). In such circumstances, numbers from similar areas can be extrapolated to estimate likely resettlement impacts. This estimate may be useful for planning and budgeting, but it does not identify and enumerate people potentially entitled to assistance. As soon as a choice has been made about a corridor, a census of the potentially affected population must be undertaken.

The partial land acquisition characteristic of many linear projects also makes it difficult to carry out accurate surveys. Often, the feasibility of making a living in the remaining area is difficult to assess. Although categories of impact (such as more than 20 percent of a plot taken) can be useful in devising entitlements, case-by-case assessment is highly recommended to ensure that households with particular vulnerabilities are not overlooked.

The initial project resettlement estimates must be updated as soon as possible, and the planning documents must be revised accordingly.

The RP presented at appraisal will likely cover both the known and the unknown alignments. In these cases, the initial RP must be updated to incorporate revisions in the estimates of the initial plan. Failure to update the RP can lead to shortfalls in financial resources, as well as imprecise monitoring benchmarks.

Project example: In China, the population census and asset inventory are often carried out on the basis of preliminary planning studies. Although most project authorities update the asset inventory once government approves the final plan, few also revise the census of affected people. A May 2000 review of resettlement in transport projects in China found that only the Fujian Provincial Highway Project (Ln 3681) and the Inland Waterway Project (Ln 3910) updated both the DP census and the asset inventory to accord with the final transport plan. In the other projects, the asset inventory, but not the population census, was updated.

Project example: Similarly, also in China, the May 2000 sectoral review found that all seven projects experienced substantial increases of 20 percent or more in the land area to be taken. Three factors were behind the

14

315

increase in expected impacts. First, technical design changes were a factor. In the Second Henan Highway Project (Ln 4027), for example, redesign increased the land area to be acquired by 25 percent; the number of households requiring relocation, by 82 percent; and the overall resettlement costs, by 57 percent. Second, survey errors, which were due largely to the inexperience of the field staff, accounted for some of the discrepancy. Third, delays in resettlement planning caused significant discrepancies. Project agencies tended to withhold the final inventory survey until the central government cleared the engineering designs. Consequently, the RP would be based on preliminary routing and an early asset inventory so that timely financing could be obtained. Projects that consulted with the Bank, such as Fujian Provincial Highway (Ln 3681) and Inland Waterways (Ln 3910), redid both the census and the asset inventory and updated their RP. Other projects, by contrast, updated only the asset inventory and never revised their RP.

Compensation is normally paid just before the land is actually required.

If project implementation is to be phased, the actual compensation and resettlement should not take place several years ahead of the construction phase for a particular segment of the project. Several reasons weigh against premature resettlement:

- People are likely to resent being asked to move long before the land is actually required.
- The people displaced, or others, are likely to reoccupy the space required if too much time passes between relocation and construction.
- If compensation or assistance is paid several years before people actually move, their situation may have changed, and the assistance is likely to be regarded as insufficient. Children will have come of age; the money will have been spent; and the price of replacement land will have risen.

Administrative Coordination

Planning and implementation will generally involve coordination of several—and sometimes quite different—public and private agencies. When a project crosses from one administrative jurisdiction into another, those in charge of overall coordination and decisionmaking will have to take account of differences in constraints and capacities and establish suitable mechanisms for allocating responsibilities, especially financial responsibilities and those needed for timely delivery of compensation and other assistance.

Linear projects require coordination, not just off the various agencies or jurisdictions involved, as noted above, but also of the environmental, socioeconomic,

14

and technical aspects of project planning and implementation. A rapid initial assessment enables project authorities to make more informed decisions regarding alignments on the basis of a matrix of screening criteria, including social impacts.

A key principle is that no civil works can be undertaken on any stretch of the alignment before land acquisition for the respective stretch has been completed and compensation or assistance has been delivered according to an agreed RP. Unless the various components of the project are carefully coordinated and implemented according to plan, project authorities may come under strong pressure to give civil contractors access to stretches of the alignment before all required resettlement work for the respective stretch of the alignment has been completed. This pressure may include financial liability, such as in claims for demurrage payments, and may prove extremely costly.

Project example: In China, the Hunan section of the National Highways II Project (Ln 4124) early on established a project resettlement office to coordinate the population census and social surveys. Subsequently, resettlement offices were established at the city, county, and township levels. An experienced member of the project resettlement office was appointed in each newly established field office during implementation, and staff members resided permanently in the field. Moreover, the city and county offices were equipped with computers, and the staff were trained to use the technology. As a result of this preparation and organization, all line departments were able to coordinate easily in resettlement implementation.

Project example: Also in China, the Guangzhou City Center Transport Project (Ln 4329) established five district resettlement offices. Under each district office, resettlement units or stations were set up in convenient locations in various parts of the areas affected. Each station had from one to seven staff, depending on impacts in the area. In addition, new resettlement staff attended a series of training programs covering resettlement policy, entitlements, consultation and participation, and computer technology. The project also implemented a computerized resettlement and rehabilitation information system. The system held such key information as DP census data, compensation agreements, confirmation of agreements, confirmation of relocation and demolition work, and information on housing sources. With this system, project officials could determine in an instant the entitlement for each DP and the basis for this calculation. Finally, the central project office assigned one staff member to oversee the work of each district station, to ensure coordination of project units.

14

*A good practice is for task teams to address issues
of multijurisdictional coordination.*

If linear projects extend across more than one major administrative jurisdiction (for example, interprovincial highway or railway projects), RPs and appraisal reports need to address coordination of planning and implementation and provide evidence that plans are acceptable in each of these jurisdictions. If socioeconomic conditions or resettlement impacts vary between jurisdictions, separate RPs for each jurisdiction may be preferable; alternatively, one RP with different implementation plans for each jurisdiction might suffice. In any case, the organizational responsibilities and financial arrangements must be described.

Monitoring

Monitoring gives project management timely information on progress in implementation, including information on DP complaints. Project management is responsible for reviewing the findings of the monitoring program and determining whether any remedial actions are necessary. A monitoring system is particularly helpful in linear projects covering long distances. The project agency simply cannot track developments in all areas, even if it has the expertise to do so. A reporting system is therefore crucial if the central office is to keep abreast of local developments.

Project agencies need to monitor implementation at the local level.

In linear projects, the project agency typically contracts with local authorities to carry out any required land acquisition, compensation payment, and relocation and economic rehabilitation of DPs. The contracts specify the nature and extent of the work and the per-unit cost. Once the contract is signed, the project agency expects the local government or contractor to carry out the work within budget.

A good practice is for the project agency to monitor implementation and the delivery of compensation through local administrative units. In one instance, in China, administrative agencies at various levels each levied charges that together amounted to 40 percent of the total land compensation and in some counties fully half of the compensation. Although the funds were invested for other public purposes, they were intended as direct compensation for the DPs; any other use was inappropriate.

*Inflation puts pressure on local officials, so monitoring helps
verify payments.*

Exogenous factors, such as inflation, can upset the original calculations, and local agencies may find themselves expected to carry out the contracted tasks at the stipulated cost even though actual costs may have risen significantly. Central project management can learn of such unexpected variation in compensation and other assistance only through periodic and independent monitoring.

> *Project example*: In China, in the Shaanxi Provincial Highways Project (Ln 2952), the provincial government unilaterally reduced the agreed compensation for land. Payment for land acquired then ranged from one-third to three-quarters of the agreed rates, with no payment at all for uncultivated land. Similar underpayments would be made for affected structures, both through lowering of the rates and through depreciation. Provincial officials acknowledged that the decision to lower compensation rates was, in part, an attempt to keep costs within the budget, as the costs for land acquisition and structural demolition had risen beyond project estimates. These discrepancies were discovered only during project supervision, because project management had not implemented a program of systematic, periodic monitoring.

Mid-term reviews are useful for verifying performance in the field.

RPs prepared before appraisal are based on data that can become inaccurate by the time of implementation. In some linear projects, for example, submitting a full RP for appraisal may be possible, but the long duration of implementation may make survey data obsolete and planning assumptions erroneous. As OP 4.12 recognizes, resettlement monitoring needs to be routine, because social and technical uncertainties are inherent in project implementation. Early implementation review is useful for maintaining the validity of RPs and resettlement activities and for helping improve resettlement performance, based on lessons from early implementation.

Summary of Key Elements

Linear projects can be summarized as follows:

- Early and iterative assessment of alternative alignments and technical designs is the most useful tool for reducing displacement.
- When displacement is unavoidable, on-site relocation by moving structures back is often the simplest and most efficient way to diminish the severity of impact.
- The construction documents must include provisions for minimizing temporary dislocation. These provisions should include precise scheduling of construction and the use of appropriate construction technology to reduce disruption.

14

- When on-site relocation is impossible, relocation to the nearest feasible site is often desirable, as increasing distance is likely to increase socio-economic disruption.
- Understanding why people live within an ROW or along a corridor is usually the most important element in designing successful resettlement operations.
- Finding a compromise between DPs' needs (for example, access to resources or clients) and projects' needs (such as safe and efficient transport) is frequently the key to assessing project feasibility and costs.
- When a precise corridor cannot be specified, doing a census or survey over a larger envelope of possible impact is the best way to identify categories of impact, estimate resettlement costs, and prevent fraudulent claims.
- Relocating DPs to nonessential lands within or adjacent to the existing ROW lowers costs and improves resettlement outcomes.
- Establishing a cutoff date for eligibility as soon as project designs are ready is the most efficient way to prevent fraudulent claims for assistance.
- If a linear project will displace only a few people, turning to the market for replacement plots and houses will simplify the resettlement process and increase the satisfaction of the affected families.
- Because the populations displaced along a long linear corridor may be culturally heterogeneous, standardized resettlement solutions may not work. Case-by-case solutions may be required.
- If the affected population is dispersed, negotiation with each family or economic unit may be more effective than negotiating with community representatives.
- Communities should be consulted to determine the location of underpasses and overpasses for people, livestock, and vehicles.
- Whenever possible, people adversely affected are to be made project beneficiaries. For example, they should be provided with access to energy, in transmission line projects; with transportation, in rural road projects; with serviced plots, in irrigation projects; or with water and improved hygienic conditions, in water and sanitation projects.
- Permitting continued seasonal use of nonessential areas within the ROWs and in areas under transmission lines may be especially important for the poorest segments of society.
- Incorporation of project bays, parking spaces, and so forth within the main designs will greatly help in relocating street vendors and others in the informal economy, while ensuring safety for users of roads and railways.

14

Chapter 15

Dams and Resettlement: Building Good Practice

The Context of Dam Construction

At some stage of development, most countries with water resources to economically exploit have built dams for energy, irrigation, and drinking water. Hydropower is a nonpolluting source of energy, generated in increasing amounts for the expanding needs of growing populations. Dams provide an important means of storing water, critical for irrigation and agricultural production. Once built, dams entail lower costs and maintenance than other sources of energy and provide other benefits, such as flood control, inland transport, and income from fisheries and tourism.

Dams, however, are not built without significant cost. In addition to having substantial adverse impacts on the physical environment, they can disrupt the lives and lifestyles of people displaced from the reservoir area and those dependent on this area. People can also be displaced by the dam itself, access roads, construction camps, irrigation canals, transmission lines, and other infrastructure. Unless thorough surveys are conducted of people who will be adversely affected by dams, predicting all the expected adverse impacts of dam construction is especially difficult. Any impacts that are not fully identified are difficult to fully mitigate. Poorly planned and implemented dams can devastate local socioeconomic systems, leaving people without comparable and acceptable alternatives.

Large dam projects can require complex and difficult resettlement operations if a large reservoir is produced in a populated area. Reservoirs can inundate entire narrow river valleys, forcing people to move out of the area and completely reconstruct their lives. If nearby areas are already used, finding replacement land for resettlement becomes very difficult or expensive. Dams usually take several years to build. The time needed for planning, constructing, and filling large reservoirs can discourage investment in the area and cause losses to area residents. Losses can even occur before construction begins. Without proper and timely reconstruction of their livelihoods, affected people can be caught in a long and arduous transition phase.

Dams are often built in remote areas. These areas tend to lack dynamic economies able to readily absorb people displaced from their traditional means of

15

livelihood. Many people in these areas are farmers whose families have worked the same land for generations. Their skills tend to be location specific and difficult to apply to any other occupation. Often, they are risk-averse and not psychologically prepared to move and begin a new occupation in an unfamiliar location, especially if they are elderly or settled in their ways. Sometimes, these upland areas are inhabited by indigenous people or ethnic minorities that have a close relationship with their land, and the loss of this relationship adds to the adverse impacts of dam construction. The land likely to be submerged behind a dam could be supporting a distinct culture, with language, customs, and traditions that are unique to the area. Resettlement of people from such locations is a much more difficult process and may be successful only if the affected people agree that acceptable alternatives exist, and those alternatives are actually offered to them.

Dams have the potential to produce significant gains, but they can have major adverse impacts if they are not carefully selected and constructed. Therefore, improving the decisionmaking processes for dam building and internalizing current international good practice are both critical. Those who are trying to select the best dams and build them well need to focus on refining the answers to the following questions: Is the particular dam being proposed the best means to fulfill the identified current or future needs of the population? After a dam is selected for construction, what processes need to be followed to successfully plan, design, and implement the resettlement?

This chapter discusses involuntary resettlement issues related to dam construction. It reviews innovative decisionmaking processes recently used in selecting the right dams for construction and proposes the mainstreaming of these processes. It covers in detail the special processes that should be followed to resettle people affected by dams. Some of the findings and recommendations of the World Commission on Dams (WCD) are given as a useful point of departure for planning and implementing resettlement. The chapter proposes a developmental approach to resettlement that contributes as much to the well-being of those adversely affected by the construction as it does to the well-being of others who directly benefit from dams.

The social impacts of large dams can be broadly divided into two categories: impacts mitigatable through careful planning and implementation; and others that normally are difficult to mitigate and therefore need to be addressed through good project design. The debate about large dams will benefit if better approaches are developed to address both categories of impacts.

Attention in the debate needs to turn to the development of international, good practice standards for resettlement. Stakeholders in this debate should help establish practical guidelines for selecting the right dams for construction; systems and procedures to promote successful resettlement; and forums and mechanisms to mainstream useful lessons and experiences. Implementing resettlement programs on the basis of agreed norms and standards would answer a lot of the criticism of reservoir resettlement. It would also help crystallize the residual, difficult-to-mitigate resettlement issues, for a more focused discussion among researchers and practitioners. Unless this crystallization of issues occurs, the debate will do little to help the plight of the thousands of people annually affected by large dams.

An impressive body of knowledge has developed, based on the experience gained and lessons learned from the implementation of reservoir resettlement. Multilateral and bilateral development institutions, project review panels, government agencies, nongovernmental organizations (NGOs), local institutions, resettlement researchers and practitioners, and people affected by resettlement have contributed to this effort. It is now possible to suggest the key steps that should be followed and the important issues that need to be addressed to increase the likelihood of successful resettlement in dam projects. The following paragraphs elaborate issues to be addressed for successful resettlement planning and implementation.

Organizational Capacity and Commitment

Assessment of Institutional Capacity for Resettlement Planning and Implementation

A key issue in selecting a dam for construction and smoothly implementing resettlement is the institutional capacity of the agencies involved. Dam resettlement is highly complex and can pose a formidable challenge to institutions engaged in conventional development programs. Although participation of displaced persons (DPs) helps the project planners make the right decisions and choices, and adequate budgeting helps ensure they have the money to pay for these choices, the resettlement program still needs competent institutions to implement the complex set of activities involved in reservoir resettlement.

Large-scale resettlement programs can be extremely difficult from the institutional perspective, and institutional constraints may force planners to accept less than optimum solutions to resettlement problems. Factors that may contribute to this complexity are the following:

- The multiple administrative jurisdictions spanned by a typical reservoir resettlement program;
- A possible lack of commitment to resettlement issues among primarily construction-oriented project agencies;
- Weak institutional capacity of government agencies in the remote areas where dams are normally constructed;

15

Box 15.1   Criteria for Assessing Adequacy of Institutional Commitment and Capacity

The following are some of the criteria for assessing the commitment and capacity of agencies responsible for planning and implementing resettlement programs:

- Willingness to make the necessary policy and institutional changes to develop an adequate framework for the resettlement;
- Willingness and ability to design and implement an effective consultation campaign involving key stakeholders, especially the affected people;
- Willingness to allow independent, external monitoring and evaluation of the resettlement program;
- Past experience in implementing resettlement programs, including capacity and willingness to provide adequate resources and take necessary corrective actions to achieve satisfactory outcomes;
- Willingness to undertake an assessment of staffing, both of numbers and of skills, and the necessary recruitment or training, based on the results of the assessment;
- Capacity of allied agencies, and the adequacy of the mechanisms to coordinate the work of other agencies; and
- Ability to successfully implement pilot resettlement programs.

- The complex interface between the project implementing agency and the local governments in control of land and mandated to implement the development programs essential to resettlement;
- The large number of implementing agencies to be coordinated;
- A possible conflict between the project's resettlement entitlement policies and those of local jurisdictions;
- The difficulties in preserving staff continuity and institutional memory over the long duration of a reservoir resettlement program;
- The need for household-focused institutions capable of addressing the different circumstances of each household; and
- The institutional vacuum commonly encountered in the maintenance phase, when the project agency needs to hand responsibility for resettlement infrastructure over to local agencies.

Project decisionmakers need to assess the capacity and commitment of the key institutions responsible for resettlement, before they select a project for construction (Box 15.1). If suitable capacity does not exist, efforts to create it should precede dam construction.

Capacity Building in All Relevant Agencies

Sometimes the project agency, being a new corporate entity, manages to create adequate capacity within the project resettlement unit, but complementary capacity is lacking in other local agencies that play a key role in resettlement implementation. Efforts to strengthen capacity should target not only the project agency, but also all the key local agencies involved in resettlement planning, implementation, and postimplementation maintenance. This may not be easy, given the typically large number of institutional jurisdictions of these agencies. Even more difficult is to create durable institutional capacity in local agencies, because of rapid staff turnover, which the project may not have any control over.

Involvement of Local Institutions Likely to Be Engaged in Operation and Maintenance

Resettlement should be planned and implemented with the full involvement of local institutions responsible for delivery of resettlement-related development programs and maintenance of the resettlement program after project completion. Resettlement-site facilities, when constructed without the involvement of local institutions, are difficult to sustain beyond the stage of project completion, owing to problems in handing over resettlement infrastructure to local agencies.

> *Project example:* In Lesotho, the Highlands Water Project (Loan [Ln] 4339) never fully integrated investments in roads, schools, and other public facilities into the work programs of local agencies. As a result, these well-intended initiatives ended up becoming a liability for the resettlers and therefore unsustainable.

Resettlement Planning

A Panel of Experts for Preparing and Implementing the Resettlement Program

Given the scale and significance of resettlement issues in dam projects, the use of a panel of independent, reputed resettlement experts to design the resettlement program can help capture international best practice. The panel of experts can also help ensure that the actions described in the agreed RPs are appropriately implemented. Such expertise is routinely employed in projects with large-scale resettlement, usually as part of an environmental review panel. The use of such panels in the planning stage can help a resettlement program improve substantially, as demonstrated by the impressive preparation of the resettlement components of the Ghazi Barotha Hydropower Project in Pakistan and the proposed Nam Thuen II Project in Lao People's Democratic Republic. The reports from the panel of experts should be made public after the draft report is revised to take into account the initial comments of the project agency.

Systems for Preparing, Reviewing, and Approving Resettlement Plans

Although carefully prepared RPs are required for most projects assisted by multilateral and bilateral institutions, no mechanisms are usually established to prepare and review similar RPs for projects financed by national and regional governments. Experience shows that the quality and likelihood of successful resettlement planning are improved by involving the technical expertise of government or consultants; and by establishing a system of review and approval by capable state and national agencies. For example, in China, RPs for locally funded hydropower projects need to be approved by qualified state and national agencies. RPs for reservoir projects in China are, consequently, of a much higher standard than those in countries without the requirement for such approvals.

Developing resettlement planning capacity in the institutes responsible for designing the dam is effective. It promotes close and early collaboration between resettlement planners, design engineers, and the representatives of the people likely to be affected. This collaboration, in turn, often helps reduce the scale of resettlement and integrate the resettlement program into the main project. Such collaboration can be seen in China, where most dam design institutes have capable resettlement planning staff working with the design engineers from the earliest stages of project conception.

The RP, prepared with the participation of affected people and agreed to by the project agency and the regulator (government) or the financier (international or local), needs to be incorporated into the legal framework established for the project as a binding obligation on the project developer. The link between adequate implementation of the resettlement program and the construction of the dam should also be clearly reflected in the legal agreements.

Framework for Compliance with Agreements

The RP provides the framework for compliance with the agreed roles and responsibilities of the various stakeholders, especially the resettlement implementation agency. The plan needs to be readily available and understandable to the affected people. The RP describes the following:

- Details of the impacts of land acquisition and resettlement;
- Provisions for compensation;
- Arrangements for physical relocation and economic rehabilitation;
- Institutional arrangements for delivering entitlements and undertaking other development activities;
- Schedule of implementation and its linkage with dam construction;
- Provisions for the continuing participation of DPs in the resettlement process;

- Costs and budgets and provision of funding;
- Resettlement performance indicators;
- Arrangements for internal and external monitoring; and
- Mechanisms for grievance redress.

The RPs should clearly list the activities to be completed in an area before the people occupying that area are relocated to resettlement sites.

If the dam is constructed by a private sector developer, the developer and the government need to reach an agreement on the developer's responsibility for implementing satisfactory resettlement and the government's responsibilities regarding provision of support to acquire land and to provide staff for the schools and other facilities constructed under the resettlement program. Evolving good practice suggests that agreement between the developer and the government should also include a performance bond, supported by a financial guarantee to be triggered if the developer has not adequately fulfilled its resettlement responsibilities.

The provisions of Operational Policy (OP) 4.12 on compliance with agreed plans are similar to good international practice developed under dam projects. Mechanisms promoting compliance with the resettlement agreements and the use of an independent panel of experts are covered in the Bank's resettlement policy and are routinely resorted to in Bank-supported dam projects. However, governments are ultimately responsible for implementation, coordination, and oversight of resettlement programs. Good practice also suggests the use of trust funds to finance the ongoing obligations for monitoring and auditing, activities that must continue for the life of the project. Royalties from the dam itself could fund ongoing initiatives.

Minimization of Displacement

Selection of Dams for Construction

The process of selecting dams may not always be based on a thorough analysis of alternatives. Dams are generally identified for construction on the basis of local demand for energy, water, and flood control. Comparisons, if made, are sometimes restricted to a handful of alternative sites on the same river. Efforts are rarely made to identify alternative dams at the national or regional level or to compare dam building with other ways of fulfilling the same objectives. The pioneering efforts of a few national governments and NGOs, however, are gradually changing this ad hoc approach. A good practice emerging in the international dam-building community is to select a particular dam for construction only after careful analysis of all other feasible alternatives, which may not even involve the construction of a dam. Along these lines, several countries have followed a methodology for screening and ranking dam investments. This methodology uses the extent and severity of resettlement impacts as key criteria in selecting dams. Application of this methodology would help minimize resettlement impacts associated with dam building.

This methodology was adopted in Norway in 1985, where it was used to select 116 sites for dam projects (3,000 megawatts) out of 320 potential sites; 58 other sites (1,500 megawatts) that were considered feasible for hydropower projects were not selected for construction, as hydropower generation at those sites would have been in strong competition with other uses. The dam projects chosen for most sites in the Norwegian exercise had no direct adverse social impacts, because few people lived in the reservoir areas. Similar exercises have been conducted in Brazil, Colombia, Nepal, and Vietnam, with various degrees of scope and rigor. This methodology contributes to nationally agreed decisions, so it may help prevent the delays and costs that result from the conflicts and protests that sometimes arise when certain dam sites are chosen.

Use of Dam Design to Reduce Displacement and Resettlement Impacts

Beyond the analyses to determine whether a dam is the preferred option for providing energy, water supply, or flood control and to determine which dams have the highest priority for construction—based on technical, economic, environmental, and social criteria—a range of design options can be developed for any specific dam. First, more than one location can be chosen, upstream or downstream of the indicated location. Second, the dam can be raised to various heights. Third, the dam operation regime can range from year-round run of the river to year-round impoundment of river flows. Adjusting any of these three design characteristics can significantly change the displacement impact of a dam.

> *Project example:* In Thailand, the site of the Pak Mun dam (Ln 3423) was moved 1.5 kilometers downstream, and the dam height was reduced by 5 meters. The combined effect of these two design changes was to reduce the length and surface area of the reservoir by more than half. This, in turn, decreased the number of people to be relocated, from 20,000 to about 1,500. Power benefits were reduced by only one-third.

Use of Barriers to Minimize Displacement and Resettlement Impacts

Besides dam design, dikes or other barriers can be used to shape the reservoir and reduce the need for resettlement. Certain vulnerable areas, or even houses, can be given protective walls. Generally, such measures are a cost-effectiveness

issue, and they are used mainly when they are cheaper than relocating and rehabilitating affected people.

Project example: In China, the Shuikou Hydroelectric Project (Ln 2775)
built protective walls at the twin tails of the reservoir around Nanping,
a city of 200,000 people, thus greatly reducing the number of affected
people. One village along the edge of the reservoir avoided relocation by
opting for a protective wall. Finally, the number of people who would
have been relocated was reduced from 32,000 living within an area subject to a 1-in-20-year flood event to 16,100 people living within an area
subject to a 1-in-10-year flood event, because of strengthened evacuation plans for a greater flood event.

Project example: In Thailand, the Pak Mun Hydroelectric Dam (Ln 3423)
backfilled areas to raise them above the level of the future reservoir. This
measure avoided relocation of houses, schools, temples, and other community infrastructure.

Assessment of Resettlement Impacts

Early, Detailed Surveys of Who Is Affected, How, and When

In addition to identifying the precise scope and extent of impacts on all affected people, knowing when the various communities will be affected is also
important. Dams take several years to build, and the reservoir expands in annual
increments. The reservoir rises higher and spreads farther behind the wall of the
dam in successive years, resulting in a three-dimensional expansion of the zone
of impact. This pattern has implications for resettlement planning. Households
from many communities along the river are all affected at the same time.
However, they may not wish to resettle with households from other communities affected at the same time and are likely to prefer resettlement next to their
as-of-yet unaffected fellow community members. To ensure acceptable relocation options for the affected communities, therefore, resettlement sites for all
communities need to be made available well in advance of full displacement.
This requirement has implications for resources and land acquisition schedules.
Substantial institutional capacity is also needed to initiate resettlement activities simultaneously at a large number of sites.

Project example: In India, in the Sardar Sarovar (Narmada) Project
(Ln 2497; Credit [Cr] 1552), the Government of Gujarat, one of the
three state governments participating in the project, had to acquire land
far in excess of the annual requirement in order to accommodate people
from villages that were, until then, only marginally affected. This change

was due to the preference of affected people of the same village to be resettled together, even though a gap of a few years occurred between the relocation of people living at the lower reaches, close to the river, and that of people living higher up, along the slopes of the valley. Resettlement sites, therefore, had to be acquired and developed far in advance of their actual use by affected people.

Upstream and Downstream Impacts

The resettlement policy applies to direct impacts, but dams affect people both upstream and downstream of the area immediately surrounding the reservoir. For example, areas downstream of a dam may have previously benefited from seasonal water flows and silt, which contributed to agriculture, but a dam may regulate and change the pattern of those flows. Dams may also interrupt fish migration to areas upstream of the dam. Downstream farmers and upstream fishers are not considered displaced, as they are not directly affected by land acquisition or physical relocation, but they may suffer indirect effects. The Bank's environmental assessment policy or social assessment should be used to identify impacts that can be mitigated through either the environmental management plan or the resettlement plan.

> *Project example:* On the Mali—Senegal border, the Manantali Dam, a non-Bank project, has released water in managed floods to help restore floodplain agriculture downstream. Projects have installed fish ladders to help fish migrate past dams.

Temporary, Partial, and Other Impacts

Although most people affected by dam building require permanent relocation, some do not. Some structures and other assets can be saved through protective measures, such as dikes and backfilling of land. People suffering temporary impacts require assistance during the period when they have restricted use of their homes, land, and other assets.

In identifying adverse impacts, project planners need to emphasize temporary and partial impacts, because these are likely to be missed in resettlement planning. For example, households living on the periphery of the reservoir may lose land only for a few days once every few years, as a result of high floods. A survey of permanent impacts of the reservoir might ignore these completely. Consultations with this group of periodically affected people will help identify feasible compensation options. Lands likely to be submerged in a 1-in-100-year flood should ideally be acquired, but project planners can evaluate the tradeoffs between outright acquisition of land and compensation for losses during temporary submergence in high floods once every few years.

Reservoirs can leave behind islands or render areas less accessible, thus making it harder and more expensive to get to markets and services and imposing other difficulties. These need to be mitigated, or the affected people need to be compensated. For example, tributaries of the dammed river may need bridging to maintain previous levels of accessibility. Wells may have to be redug. Some people may have to be relocated, even though their land is not necessary to the project, because it becomes unviable after the reservoir is filled.

Consequences of Inadequate Surveys of Impacts and Affected People

The planning process for many dams is based on an inadequate assessment of adverse impacts (Box 15.2). In some instances, entire categories of impact are

---

Box 15.2   Typical Adverse Social Impacts of Reservoirs

Typical adverse impacts of reservoir construction are as follows:

- Land taking for the reservoir and the dam itself;
- Relocation of residences;
- Impacts on access to common-property resources, such as forests in the vicinity of the proposed reservoir, for grazing, fuel, or fodder collection;
- Temporary impacts on houses and agricultural land at the edge of the reservoir during flooding season, including riverbank gardens;
- Temporary impacts on houses from construction noise, flying debris, and other nuisances and dangers;
- Disruption of fishing in the downstream stretches of the river and impacts on downstream agriculture;
- Temporary annual flooding of houses at higher levels in the rainy season during dam construction;
- Impacts on communities left behind that had depended on relocated communities;
- Breakup of communities;
- Impacts on host communities, especially overcrowding and increased pressure on public infrastructure;
- Disruption in seasonal use of the river by people living outside the edge of the proposed reservoir;
- Impacts of construction of other dam infrastructure, such as access roads, transmission lines canals, power house, contractors' and workers' colonies, and borrow pits; and
- Health impacts, especially waterborne diseases, such as malaria, as a result of standing water.

---

missed at the planning stage. Although it is fairly easy to survey those people whose land, houses, and other assets will be taken for the dam, others who might be using the river and its catchment for collecting forest products, seasonal fishing, grazing, and similar activities are easy to miss. Because many of these uses are typical of common-property natural resources and are not privately owned, they are often overlooked. The remoteness of most dam sites also makes surveying more difficult.

Often, impacts of operating dams are not adequately identified or mitigated. Such impacts include temporary flooding during construction, floods at higher than normal levels, and emergency releases into the downstream channel. Adequate flood-warning systems should be established, in consultation with the affected people; all resettlement planning should take into account 1-in-100-year flood levels; and mechanisms to compensate for incremental impacts of the dam should be included in the RP. The WCD report discusses this issue.

> *Project example:* In Thailand, the pre- and midproject baseline socioeconomic surveys of the people affected by the Pak Mun Dam Project (Ln 3423) did not adequately cover adverse impacts along the river, because only those losing houses or land were surveyed, not other nearby residents who fished the river. Because of this deficiency, the otherwise highly successful resettlement became embroiled in controversy. The claims made by communities regarding loss of fishing habitats and incomes and the counterclaims made by government agencies have become almost impossible to verify.

In some cases, resettlement planning has focused mainly on people affected by the reservoir and did not identify others affected by the construction of irrigation canals, power houses, and auxiliary facilities. Also overlooked are those not directly affected by the reservoir but dependent on the DPs.

> *Project example:* In India, in the early stages of implementation of the Sardar Sarovar (Narmada) Project (Ln 2497; Cr 1552), people affected by construction of canals, access roads, and other project construction facilities were not included in the project-affected people. Subsequent discussion of these impacts resulted in the inclusion of people affected by such activities, and this wider consideration is now standard for all Bank dam-building projects.

Without thorough surveys during the earliest stages of project planning, determining the range and the extent of impacts is difficult. This lack of thoroughness also dilutes the effectiveness of consultations with affected groups, as many affected groups may not be identified at the time of consultations.

Consequently, it becomes difficult to assess feasibility of resettlement options, prepare accurate budgets, or deliver resettlement entitlements to people affected in all categories of impact.

> *Project example:* In India, in the Sardar Sarovar (Narmada) Project (Ln 2497; Cr 1552), the deficiencies in the initial survey of project impacts made subsequent implementation difficult, even when the policy and institutional environments were substantially strengthened. The exact number of households at various elevations or households in various categories of impact was not identified in the initial surveys, and the project agencies found it difficult to prepare credible annual plans to assist them.

Establishing a baseline socioeconomic survey is a requirement of OP 4.12.

Impacts of the Long Gestation Period for Dam Construction

The area likely to be submerged by a dam does not benefit from additional investment in infrastructure development from the time the project is announced until the area is finally submerged. This period can extend from 2 to 10 years or in certain circumstances even longer. The affected people are often unable to expand their houses or invest in other developments during this period, because project agencies are reluctant to compensate for investments made after the property census surveys have been completed. To promote shorter gestation periods, project agencies could be required to increase compensation by 10 percent for each year of delay from the time surveys are conducted until the time the community is actually displaced. This would provide a disincentive for project agencies to delay resettlement implementation and give affected people some level of compensation for benefits foregone as a result of the long gestation period for dam construction.

> *Project example:* In India, in the Upper Krishna II Irrigation Project (Ln 3050; Cr 2010), the national land acquisition law provided a framework for paying compensation in three parts: (a) the market value of the assets; (b) a solatium of 15 percent of the market value, because of the compulsory nature of the land acquisition; and (c) annual interest at 5 percent for any delayed compensation payments. In 1984, the project doubled the solatium to 30 percent. Interest was increased to 9 percent for the first year and to 15 percent for subsequent years. Combined with inflation in land prices, per acre compensation rates increased from $380 in 1978 to $1,500 for dryland and $2,300 for irrigated land in 1997 (all dollar amounts are current U.S. dollars). The long gestation period significantly increased resettlement costs.

15

Consultation and Participation

Most problems with the design and implementation of resettlement components of dam projects can be traced back to a failure to identify and involve key stakeholders in the decisionmaking process. This failure can be avoided through use of the methods described in the following sections.

Mechanisms for Consulting Affected People throughout Planning and Implementation

The process of consultation should ensure full disclosure of information on the project. Affected people should be involved in selecting resettlement sites and economic rehabilitation programs, and these consultations should continue throughout resettlement implementation and monitoring.

Direct consultations with DPs are important. Although consultations with representatives have some advantages, ensuring that the views being relayed by them are those of the affected people is important. Key issues such as location of resettlement sites, types of economic rehabilitation, and timing of resettlement need to be discussed directly with the DPs. Representation by outside agencies, whether governmental or nongovernmental, can sometimes be based on mistaken assumptions and can feed on stereotypical notions of what DPs "should" feel or want, ignoring their actual preferences.

> *Project example:* In Brazil, in the Itaparica Resettlement and Irrigation Project (Ln 2883), Polo Sindical, the main NGO representing the affected people, insisted that land-based resettlement next to the reservoir was the only acceptable option. But the costs of preparing substandard lands for irrigated agriculture proved to be exorbitant (almost $250,000 per household). Incomes from irrigated plots were still insufficient and had to be supplemented with additional income assistance and with subsidies for irrigation water. However, direct communication with the affected people might have identified feasible alternatives. Similarly, although the Narmada Bachao Andolan (Save the Narmada Campaign) in the Sardar Sarovar (Narmada) Project (Ln 2497; Cr 1552) claimed to represent all affected people, it offered no assistance to people who gradually gave up their opposition to the project and opted for resettlement.

In the process of determining representation, therefore, a distinction needs to be drawn between those who represent issues and standpoints and those who represent the affected people, although the two groups may not always be mutually exclusive. Good resettlement design relies on mechanisms to directly involve the affected people in decisionmaking.

Consultations should be viewed as inputs into a process with a clear time frame and expected outputs. To be effective, consultation and participation need to be structured and closed ended. Processes of consultation in which the stakeholders are unclear about what is expected of them, or what they can expect, do not lead to good decisionmaking. Without a clear framework, participatory exercises run the risk of becoming ends in themselves and of failing to improve the quality of the resettlement program. Well-structured participation, with a clear time frame—and all parties having a stake in the outcomes—helps significantly to improve resettlement planning and implementation.

Provision of Information to Affected People

Having information on the project, its impacts, and the proposed mitigation strategies is a basic right of affected populations. Providing such information is the necessary first step in the design of any credible resettlement program. Resettlement affects people in fundamental ways: all the major determinants of their life—occupations, housing conditions, lifestyles, social relationships, and support systems—change significantly. Unless the project agency informs them about the proposed resettlement program, they are unable to effectively participate in its design. Under such circumstances, the information vacuum is filled by other, perhaps unreliable sources.

> *Project example:* In Colombia, in the Guavio Hydropower Project (Ln 2008), the affected people lacked information on the procedures for directly negotiating compensation with the project authority. The affected people were exploited by unscrupulous mediators, who offered them cash payments of only about 50 percent of the project authority's compensation rates.

Lack of reliable project-related information and lack of involvement of affected people in resettlement aspects of the project lead to conflict. By polarizing the various stakeholders, conflicts make resettlement issues that are difficult to begin with even more difficult to resolve. Lack of information sharing also has adverse effects on the design of the resettlement program. In the absence of full disclosure and the resulting exchange of ideas, resettlement programs are not likely to achieve desired outcomes. Mechanisms for reaching out to potentially affected people in the earliest stages of resettlement planning include the following:

- Regular meetings in each potentially affected village;
- Distribution of brochures with images (knowledgeable people are needed to follow up and answer any questions);

- Posting of information on community information boards, as in China (for example, in the Shaanxi Roads Project, a non-Bank project);
- Standardized placement of brochures in local government offices, so that people always know where to find this information;
- Appointment of one or more resettlement contact persons in each potentially affected community, to be the conduit for relevant information;
- Involvement of local, operational NGOs working in the area; and
- Project information booths at local festivals.

Noninteractive media, such as radio or TV, should be avoided in the early stages of resettlement planning, as they may fail to address people's questions and concerns. Once the affected people have a clear understanding of the resettlement program and have built sufficient faith in the resettlement agency, electronic media can be used to provide updates. The detailed information—such as the criteria for eligibility, entitlements, and compensation rates—needs to be in brochures or some other readily accessible printed form. Literate neighbors may need to interpret for the illiterate, but the literature places physical proof of their rights in the hands of resettlers.

Consultations with affected people should continue throughout project planning and implementation. Projects should establish sources of regular information that are credible to the affected people. A number of effective mechanisms can be used to provide information and promote consultations:

- Operational NGOs working in the project area can be a particularly good source of information, as they can often provide timely and credible information to the affected people. They can also help assess impacts of a particular change from the people's perspective.
- A regular meeting (usually monthly) between project staff and affected people, preferably at the same location and the same date or day of every month, can be an effective mechanism for ongoing consultations. The regular scheduling of these meetings would help to avoid the difficult logistics sometimes required for planning such events.
- Appointment of village or hamlet contacts from among the affected people can help create durable two-way communication between project agencies and affected people. Project planners need to be assured, however, that the selected representatives have the confidence of all the affected people. As contact persons are always resident in the community, they can effectively identify the real views or concerns of affected people on an ongoing basis.

Depending on local context and constraints, the project team should use as many of these mechanisms as possible. Regular interaction with the affected people provides an important feedback mechanism for monitoring, and it ensures effective communication and participation.

Consequences of Inadequate Involvement of Affected People

Programs are rarely successful if designed and implemented by centralized project agencies without fully involving the affected people, the local governments, and other stakeholders. Specialist knowledge on resettlement can never replace people's own assessments of the appropriateness of resettlement options to their circumstances. Designing effective resettlement programs is difficult without the involvement of key stakeholders; implementing them is even more so. Systematic stakeholder involvement acts as a self-correcting mechanism, enabling project agencies to identify problems as soon as they arise and to find workable solutions.

Key stakeholders in a resettlement program are the following:

- The affected people;
- People's representatives;
- Host populations;
- The national or provincial government supporting the project;
- NGOs or organizations of civil society working in the area;
- Local governments of the affected area and the resettlement area;
- The project developer;
- Other private sector firms involved in the project;
- Funding agencies;
- Consultants conducting various studies; and
- Engineering and resettlement units in the project design and implementation agencies.

Project example: In Lao PDR, the Nam Thuen 2 Hydroelectric Project put in place a comprehensive process for consultations with all key stakeholders from the early stages of project planning. A number of multistakeholder consultations were held. Participants included the concerned national government representatives, interested private sector developers, international and local NGOs, the directly affected people, representatives of local governments in the project area, and local and international media. The consultations helped forge a consensus on the proposed development and mitigation plans for the project and addressed legitimate concerns of various stakeholders.

The WCD report recommends a negotiated decisionmaking process, in which all key stakeholders negotiate and sign off on the project and the proposed mitigation measures. Although this may be a desirable approach to decision-making, it makes certain assumptions about development processes that are not borne out by experience. It assumes that all DPs have common interests and concerns and that it is possible to agree on an optimum project configuration that fully satisfies all stakeholders. The notion of negotiated decisionmaking processes also challenges the concept of the state's right to use eminent domain for larger public interest. Even if formal negotiation is not possible, the resettlement planning process should involve all stakeholders, ensure that they have an opportunity to express their views and concerns, and verify that the decisionmaking process fully takes these views and concerns into account. The decisionmaking process should include mechanisms to transparently address claims and concerns of stakeholders with dissenting views, and the results of this process should be made public.

Consultation with the Host Communities

Good resettlement design includes host communities as beneficiaries of the resettlement program. At the very least, host communities should feel they can welcome the resettlers and should not perceive any conflict with the incoming population. Organizing site inspections for potential resettlers gives them an opportunity to directly interact with host communities and assess for themselves the suitability of living among specific host populations. The carrying capacity of each host site needs to be assessed to determine the number of resettlers it can accommodate without overloading existing infrastructure. The civic infrastructure of host communities should be upgraded to the same level as the newly built infrastructure for the resettlers. Any new infrastructure or services provided for the DPs should also be offered to the host community.

> *Project example:* In Togo, the Nangbeto Hydroelectric Project (Cr 1507, Cr 1508) provided host communities with boreholes and other services. This initiative made it easier for the host communities to accept the resettlers. As long as the host communities had the same level of facilities and services as the resettlers, they did not object to the resettlers moving into their midst. Only later, when land became scarce and the borehole pumps began to break down because of lack of maintenance, did tensions develop between resettlers and host communities.

Systems for Grievance Redress

Local mechanisms, if effective, should be relied on to air and resolve the grievances of the affected people. Proposed redress mechanisms should be discussed with, and be acceptable to, the affected people. They should provide clear information on who to approach and how, when to expect a response, and what to do if a response is inadequate. A provision for appeal through the legal system should be available, and the project should provide legal assistance to affected people who wish to lodge an appeal.

Project example: In Thailand, the Pak Mun Hydroelectric Project (Ln 3423) established an effective grievance redress system, after a host of unresolved grievances threatened the smooth implementation of the project. The grievance system had two main components: a mechanism to effectively collect all grievances of potential DPs and a mechanism to expeditiously resolve grievances. The project authorities opened public grievance booths in the project area, conveniently accessible from the affected villages, for timely collection of grievances. A high-powered grievance redress committee was established; it was chaired by the provincial governor, and its members consisted of heads of key government departments, the heads of local government in the project area and representatives of potential DPs. The committee promptly redressed grievances, contributing substantially to the success of the resettlement program.

Rehabilitation Strategies

Resettlement as Development

When planned and implemented diligently, reservoir resettlement programs can be effective vehicles for substantial social and economic development for the affected people. Resettlement programs help provide better economic resources, renewed civic infrastructure, and increased access to markets. Successful resettlement programs, building on the existing social capital of affected communities, have resulted in improved literacy and health indicators; increased incomes and standards of living, as defined by the affected people themselves; and enhanced access to economic opportunities—all of which may have been difficult to achieve without the resettlement program.

Successful rehabilitation strategies mitigate all impacts, offer a menu of options, tap into the development potential in the general project area, and build on the opportunities generated by the project. Economic rehabilitation activities based on careful analysis of resettlers' aptitudes and the patterns of demand and supply of commodities and services have helped affected people benefit from the economic growth in the area. Well-designed reservoir resettlement can thus open up substantial opportunities for the resettlers.

Project example: As another example, the Saguling and Cirata dam projects (Ln 3602), in Indonesia, built rehabilitation programs based on the fisheries potential created by the reservoir. By 1992, several years after the dams were completed, fishing in the reservoir was producing 10,000 tons of fish annually, or 25 percent of the fish coming into Bandung, a city of 3 million people. The value of the fish is seven times that of the rice produced from the same land before inundation. Annual fishing incomes of resettlers are eight times higher than they would have been had these people continued farming the rice paddies flooded by the dams.

Feasibility of Sharing Project Benefits with DPs

The resettlement planning process should explore the possibility of sharing project benefits with DPs. The Bank's policy on involuntary resettlement requires that DPs benefit from the project. The WCD report lists the following types of project benefits that could be offered to DPs:

- Project revenue benefits can include a percentage share of project revenues or royalties. The project can be viewed as a joint enterprise, with affected people having a share of equity.
- Project benefits can include provision of irrigated land and supply of electricity, access to irrigation water and reservoir fisheries, and preference in obtaining contracts to manage recreational or water transportation facilities.
- Project construction and operation benefits include preference for employment in construction and other project activities, as well as training and financial support for contracts to provide goods and services to the project.
- Resource benefits can include preferential access to, or custodianship of, catchment resources for defined exploitation or management, catchment development (planting fruit trees or reforestation), access to pumped irrigation from the reservoir, and benefits from managed flows and floods.
- Community services benefits include provision of better and higher levels of service in healthcare, education, transportation, and water supply; and income support for vulnerable households; agricultural support services, including preferential planting materials and other inputs; and community forests and grazing areas.
- Household-related services can include skills training; transition support; interest-free loans for economic activities; housing improvement; provision of start-up livestock; access to public works; free or subsidized labor-saving devices or productive machinery; and preferential electricity rates, tax rates, and water charges.

The eligibility for, and level of, benefits to be provided should be assessed on the basis of the needs, preferences, and capacities of affected people. The form and extent of benefits should be clearly described in the RP and agreed to by the affected people.

Affected People as Shareholders in the Dam Project

One of the innovative mechanisms for making DPs partners in development calls for making them shareholders in the dam project. They could receive a part of the compensation payable to them in the form of cash or other economic rehabilitation measures, and the rest would contribute to their equity in the dam project. This mechanism may help the resettlement program achieve sustainable long-term economic rehabilitation. The resettlers would not be required to make difficult investment decisions in an uncertain environment, and it might contribute to a more even benefits stream. However, this mechanism would need to be used with some caution. First, the project needs to have a sufficient guarantee of profitability—a loss-making project would expose the people to a high risk of losing their resettlement entitlements. Second, it assumes that this approach would bring incremental benefits for DPs, which may not be true. Although this is an innovative method to make DPs real partners in the development process, it should be offered as an option, not a blanket entitlement. Depending on the risk-taking profile of the DPs, they may want to use part of their compensation to subscribe to project equity.

Land-Based Resettlement Strategies

Reservoir projects, like other types of project, should give preference to land-based resettlement strategies for those displaced from land-based livelihoods, if that is the preference of the resettlers. These strategies will work if sufficiently good-quality land is available. If too many people have to be resettled for the quantity or quality of available land, however, then land-based strategies may be insufficient. In that case, additional strategies may be necessary, including moving people to more distant areas or shifting them, based on consultations with them, to less land-intensive or non-land-based resettlement strategies.

> *Project example:* In China, the planners of Yantan Hydroelectric Project (Ln 2707), situated in an isolated and hilly area, found that local resources were too limited to accommodate income restoration for all DPs. Therefore, 3,600 people were relocated to two sugar estates near the rapidly developing coastal zone. These resettlers' incomes more than tripled. Another 11,500 were relocated to another state farm near the provincial capital.

Project example: Also in China, in the Ertan Hydroelectric Project (Ln 3933), 62 percent of resettlers remained in rural areas. Most of the people relocated to urban areas earned incomes surpassing their predisplacement incomes by 2000. Some rural resettlers recovered their former incomes by 2000, but more of them had remained in their original villages than expected, simply moving up hillsides. This led to crowding and lower incomes. The project, therefore, is undertaking a second round of resettlement for 3,000 people suffering farmland shortage and another 600 whose incomes were affected by reservoir-induced land erosion. Policy and Human Resource Development grants and the reservoir area maintenance fund (about $1.5 million per year) are being used to develop the most promising income-generating activities, improve the productivity of land, and provide jobs for surplus laborers and postrelocation support for rural resettlers, until they have recovered their incomes, which is expected by 2005.

One of the most direct forms of the use of resettlement as a development strategy is to move affected people from the catchment area into the command area so that the increased economic potential of the irrigated area will provide them with greater economic opportunities.

Project example: Moving resettlers into the command area has worked well in several large dam projects, including the Andhra Pradesh II (Ln 2662; Cr 1665) and III (Ln 4166; Cr 2952) and the Gujarat Medium II (Cr 1496) irrigation projects, in India; the Daguangba Multipurpose (Ln 3412; Cr 2305) and the Lubuge Hydroelectric (Ln 2382) projects, in China; and the Ceará Water Resources Project (Ln 4190), in Brazil.

The Bank's resettlement policy requires that preference be given to land-based strategies for those displaced from land-based livelihoods. However, as land-based resettlement strategies are perceived as more secure than non-land-based investment strategies, the evaluation of the feasibility of land-based resettlement proposals tends to be less thorough. The assumptions about the ease of re-creating land-based livelihoods have not always proven valid in actual practice, especially those regarding the availability of adequate replacement land and the ability of the affected people to cultivate it. Being a marketable fixed asset, land does offer greater security than business- or employment-based resettlement, especially for communities practicing traditional forms of agriculture or otherwise unfamiliar with non-land-based economic activities. However, if the income restoration potential of agriculture depends on the transfer of new farming skills, the outcome could be just as difficult to predict as the sustainability of jobs. Many resettlers do not have the skills or experience needed to manage the transition to irrigated, market-oriented agricultural systems.

Project example: In India, the Upper Krishna II Irrigation Project (Ln 3050; Cr 2010) shifted some affected people from rainfed to irrigated agriculture. But without agricultural extension services, they lacked knowledge of irrigation practices. Faced with an abundance of irrigation water after lifetimes of enduring scarce water, they overwatered their fields, causing salination of the soil and leaching of nutrients. This outcome led to a small, second wave of displacement, this time because of waterlogged fields. Furthermore, even though unauthorized irrigation is prohibited, government authorities were not able to halt its spread along the shores of the reservoir.

Project example: Also in India, some people affected by the Maharashtra III Irrigation Project (Cr 1621) moved into the command area. But they did not receive irrigation, because they were relocated to plots too high to be reached by gravity-fed irrigation, or they were at the tail (dry) end of irrigation systems, or they had to wait many years for irrigation systems to be constructed to reach them. In the Upper Krishna II Irrigation Project (Ln 3050; Cr 2010), the command area was developed so many years after people were displaced from the catchment area that they had to be relocated elsewhere. Instead, migrants from other areas moved into the command area and received the benefits. Synchronization of command area development with resettlement is crucial.

Project example: In India, in the Maharashtra Composite III Irrigation Project (Cr 1621), and in Indonesia, in the Kedung Ombo Multipurpose Project (Ln 2543), many people displaced by dams simply moved up the hillsides surrounding the reservoir. This led to crowding in the host communities on those hillsides. Another problem was that the upland soils, water availability, and other conditions affected crop choices and yields. Again, the DPs' lack of knowledge indicated the need for agricultural advice on how to cope with conditions significantly different from those of the fertile river valley.

Such movement is sometimes detrimental to the social capital that exists in the affected communities and may not be preferred by the DPs.

Project example: In India, some resettlers in the Maharashtra Irrigation II Project (Credit 954) preferred to move into the unaffected part of the catchment area, as they had strong links with local political leaders and various user associations. The social capital generated through these relations was more important to them than the promised allocation of irrigated farmland. This example underscores the need to avoid making any assumptions about the adequacy of sites without consulting the affected people.

Project example: In Brazil, the economic rehabilitation of the people affected by the Itaparica Resettlement and Irrigation Project (Ln 2883) was based on the cultivation of poorly drained, poor-quality soils that were highly prone to salinization. Despite huge expenditure on improving the agricultural potential of the resettlement sites ($50,000 per hectare for irrigation, and total resettlement expenditures of nearly $250,000 per household), the amount of cultivable land available was insufficient to accommodate the resettlers. Further complicating efforts at income restoration were poorly developed markets, expensive fertilizers and other inputs, insufficient extension services, inadequate transportation systems, and inadequate credit and funds to complete the resettlement operation.

Non-Land-Based Resettlement Strategies

Given the difficulties of land-based resettlement strategies, especially where reservoirs inundate entire valleys, non-land-based strategies often play a significant role in creating new livelihoods for affected people. This requires creative use of limited land resources and the development of non-land-based income-generating strategies.

Project example: In China, the Shuikou Hydroelectric Project (Ln 2775) adopted a development approach. Because most of the resettlers could not re-create their former valley-bottom rice-farming livelihoods, they switched to mainly land-intensive or non-land-based livelihoods, deriving their income from township and village enterprises (TVEs), retail shops along the new highway, tree crops, livestock, higher value agriculture (for example, backyard mushroom farming), and so forth. Although traditional agricultural sectors were expected to provide 74 percent of the jobs, in actuality they provided only 26 percent. Several years were required to recover predisplacement incomes, but in the two years after reservoir filling, incomes of a sample of 524 households increased 44 percent and were set to bypass those of nonaffected neighboring villages.

Because only a few skilled people are required for the operation and maintenance of dams, dams do not tend to be a major source of jobs. Nonetheless, dam projects can offer temporary or permanent employment to some affected people, often unskilled labor for construction. Temporary jobs help DPs make the transition to new livelihoods. And permanent employment, if sustainable, can help solve the income restoration problem.

Project example: In India, the Upper Krishna II (Ln 3050; Cr 2010) and Maharashtra III (Cr 1621) irrigation projects employed DPs as laborers in the construction of the canals in the command area, where they were being resettled, thus directing project benefits toward resettlers in two ways and linking their temporary and permanent livelihoods. Several dam projects—in China, India, Pakistan, and Vietnam—gave affected people priority for permanent jobs. Several dam projects in China provided opportunities for affected people to set up water transportation services.

Technical, Legal, Financial, and Economic Feasibility of Strategies and Options

The objective of the resettlement program should be to improve or at least restore, in real terms, the incomes and standards of living of the affected people. Many multilateral and bilateral lending institutions and national governments have adopted this goal for their resettlement operations. RPs should aim to improve the standards of living of the affected people; restoration of living standards should be the minimum benchmark against which the performance of the resettlement program should be measured. Because a gap of several years can occur between initiation of the project and actual displacement of a community, restoration of incomes and standards of living should be to the same level as that before project initiation or that before displacement, whichever is higher. This approach helps address situations in which economic growth in the project area improves the incomes and standards of living until the time of actual displacement, as well as those in which investments in the project area dry up after the announcement of the project, resulting in declines in incomes and standards of living. To use the "with and without the project" analysis to guide the design of the resettlement program is also helpful. Using this type of analysis helps in reestablishing standards of living at levels comparable to, or higher than, those that would have been achieved without the displacement.[1]

Regardless of the type of economic activities the resettlement program is based on, thorough analyses of the feasibility of these activities need to be conducted before they are offered as real options to the affected people. The feasibility analyses need to focus on the following aspects:

- *Technical*—Is the technology available to the resettlers adequate to support the type of activity?
- *Legal*—Are any legal obstacles in the way of assisting the affected people? (For example, local land ceilings may not allow provision of replacement land at the same level.)
- *Economic*—Are the demand and supply patterns propitious for the goods or services the resettlers are supposed to market?
- *Financial*—Are start-up capital and credit available at affordable terms?

- *Social and cultural*—Do considerations of the capacity and preferences of the resettlers to undertake the proposed activity underpin the detailed feasibility analysis of the resettlement options?

The nearly complete economic displacement resulting from dam projects also offers opportunities for constructing new bases for livelihoods, if adequate precautions are taken to protect DPs who find it difficult to make a transition to different modes of production. Those among the affected people who have the required technical skills and the capacity to bear some risk may find the non-land-based rehabilitation programs attractive. A menu of economic rehabilitation options should be offered to the affected people, and they should make the final selection on the basis of their skills, aptitudes, preferences, and risk-taking abilities.

All the resettlement options offered to DPs must be real options; that is, they must be feasible options the people can implement. If DPs are offered a number of options but the DPs consider only one of these options feasible, then the resettlement program is not in fact offering resettlement options. Worse, when the people do not have much faith in the commitment and capacity of local institutions to implement detailed resettlement strategies, they may end up opting for the only alternative they are familiar with, which may be the cash option. Thus, to avoid situations in which the people opt for only one or two resettlement alternatives familiar to them because they consider the resettlement package flawed or impractical, project planners must fully establish the feasibility of any given resettlement option before it is included in the list of options offered to the DPs. Feasibility of various options needs to be assessed, not exclusively by resettlement specialists, but by specialists in the respective fields—the same range of technical specialists as used in other agricultural and rural development projects. Income improvement strategies need to be designed with the same rigor and due diligence as in a stand-alone income generation project.

> *Project example:* In China, the Xiaolangdi Resettlement Project (Cr 2605) undertook several forms of feasibility analysis of rehabilitation options. Economic rates of return were calculated for a variety of types of land (irrigated and dryland), crops (vegetables, fruits, and fish ponds), and industrial activities (large enterprises and TVEs). The first eight TVEs that were established paid wages one-third higher than county-owned enterprises and paid off their initial investment (averaging $100,000) in less than one year, thus confirming their feasibility. Individual and household pre- and postresettlement incomes, including other sources of income, were estimated for all counties and townships. Farm models were prepared for estimating incomes that could be expected from agricultural activities.

As important as a thorough feasibility analysis of various income improvement strategies is, the process of consulting DPs on the selection of options is even more crucial. Local operational NGOs, if present in the project area, can explain the strengths and weaknesses of various options to the DPs and help them select the options best suited to their situations.

Project example: Technical and economic feasibility is often insufficiently analyzed. In China, the Shuikou Hydroelectric Project (Ln 2775) planted orchards of orange trees, but they were unsuitable for that microclimate and had to be dug out and replaced with other fruit trees. Furthermore, too many orchards were planted, and local markets were saturated with certain varieties of fruit. In Indonesia, some people displaced by the Kedung Ombo Multipurpose Project (Ln 2543) joined the transmigration program. Some of those sent to Sumatra were directed to grow rice, but a thick layer of peat lay under half of the cleared area, making rice farming impractical. But the area could have supported other crops, such as oil palm or even maize.

Feasible Resettlement Alternatives and Mitigation of All Impacts

Feasible resettlement entitlements need to be designed for all categories of impact. Inadequate identification of adverse impacts and the failure to design mitigation measures for each of these are major factors in the failure of resettlement programs. To prevent such a failure, formal and extensive consultations need to be carried out with the affected people. The range of impacts, as well as acceptable compensation or resettlement alternatives, needs to be identified through broad consultations with the affected people. After feasible alternatives have been identified, the affected people need to be consulted again so that they can exercise their choice. Failure to design mitigation measures for one or more categories of impact, even when the impacts are minor, can trigger general discontent among large sections of the affected population. Quite often, seasonal, temporary, or marginal impacts, as well as impacts resulting from loss of access to common-property resources, are overlooked, even though they can significantly affect a section of the affected population. Underreporting of impacts on grazing, seasonal fishing, collection of minor forest produce, and so forth is not uncommon in resettlement planning.

Project example: Sometimes, too many resettlers choose the same options, even though many more are available. In India, too many affected people in the Upper Krishna Project (Ln 3050; Cr 2010) used their income-generating grants to purchase ox teams and carts, grain milling

15

machines, and herds of goats, reducing the economic return from each of those options, as supply exceeded demand.

Detailed Feasibility Assessment of Resettlement Sites

Resettlement site selection requires consultations with individual households—approval given by community representatives on behalf of various households is insufficient. Resettlement sites should (a) be acceptable to the resettlers; (b) have the capacity to support the incomes and living standards of the people to be resettled; (c) provide for population growth; (d) supply infrastructure and services better than, or at least similar to, those available to DPs before displacement; and (e) be incorporated into the jurisdiction of local government agencies before the completion of the resettlement program. Inadequate analysis of, or attention to, these issues can give rise to serious problems during implementation and beyond.

Project example: In China, the Xiaolangdi Resettlement Project (Cr 2605) undertook a detailed feasibility assessment of resettlement sites. The general strategy was to rehabilitate most people in farming activities. An area that was flood land, but would be better protected from floods by the dam, was identified as containing 12,333 hectares of land that could be brought into year-round cultivation and absorb 41,800 people. Three other downstream areas that were already scheduled for land warping (diverting sediment-laden flows onto waste land) to improve their productivity were also identified as areas that could absorb resettlers. Irrigation, land leveling, and the use of fertilizers were other means of improving land to absorb resettlers. For example, the Houhe Dam and Irrigation Scheme would improve the productivity of an estimated 5,000 hectares, sufficient to absorb 16,000 resettlers and still benefit the host area. The project authority developed detailed guidelines for identifying resettlement areas and deciding which resettlers should move to which areas. Incomes were to be increased by at least 10 percent. Below the county level, individual resettlement sites were selected from host areas that had per capita landholdings of more than half a hectare. The sites had to be large enough to support a village of several hundred people. The sites also had to have good geological conditions, access to water supply, adequate communications, and no environmental problems.

Project example: In the Sardar Sarovar (Narmada) Project (Ln 2497; Cr 1552) in India, affected people in Maharashtra state demanded resettlement to degraded forest land that, nevertheless, was technically classified as a forest conservation area. When the search for alternative areas acceptable to the affected people failed to yield any results, the Indian government "declassified" the forest area and made it available for agricultural and residential resettlement sites. The layout and design of the resettlement site were then prepared based on consultations with affected people.

Financial Arrangements

Resettlement Entitlements and Activities

All resettlement programs and activities should be costed realistically and included in the project budget. Accurate estimation of the costs for preferred resettlement alternatives requires broad consultations with the affected people. A resettlement cost table should include estimates of the costs associated with the following activities:

- Conducting the census and socioeconomic surveys of the affected people;
- Conducting resettlement studies and preparing resettlement planning documents;
- Hiring and training resettlement agency staff;
- Taking land, structures, and other assets;
- Procuring land for resettlement sites;
- Developing resettlement sites;
- Conducting feasibility analyses of the proposed income improvement strategies;
- Implementing income improvement strategies;
- Moving DPs and their household effects to the resettlement site;
- Providing transition allowances and arrangements;
- Reconstructing community infrastructure, transportation networks, and utilities;
- Undertaking consultation and participation activities during planning and implementation;
- Carrying out monitoring and evaluation; and
- Establishing and maintaining a grievance redress system.

Compensation and other resettlement costs should be linked to an acceptable local price index, and on this basis the costs should be revised semiannually. Provision should also be made for physical contingencies.

Compensation for Affected Assets

Compensation should be calculated at replacement cost for affected assets. Many national legal systems provide for compensation significantly lower than replacement cost (also see "Calculation and Application of Replacement Cost," in chapter 4). Compensation for affected structures is usually calculated by deducting depreciation from replacement cost. This practice constitutes a major constraint on achieving the objective of income restoration. Mechanisms need to be established to bridge the gap between locally permissible compensation and the replacement cost of affected assets. Clear responsibility for funding the resettlement program needs to be established, including mechanisms to ensure that resettlement funding will not suffer disproportionately as a result of any project financing problems. Realistic assessments of costs and prompt payment of compensation and other entitlements help prevent conflicts and consequential delays in the resettlement program.

Nonmonetary Costs of Resettlement

In addition to the above-mentioned costs, which can be calculated in monetary terms, resettlement also entails costs that are difficult to quantify. Most project cost analyses ignore the environmental and social costs of projects. Cost-benefit analyses do not typically take into account nonmarket incomes, costs of non-priced essential services, cultural assets, the psychological costs of dislocation, the value of the community social capital, or the value of market access.[2] Resettlement programs should be redesigned to minimize these nonmonetary costs, with the help of extensive consultations with DPs.

Internalized Resettlement Costs

Another imperative is to internalize the full costs of resettlement in the project budget. Where expressing such impacts in economic terms is undesirable or impossible, planners should consider them separately, as parameters in the multicriteria analysis discussed earlier. Internalizing costs helps planners assess the real cost of resettlement and factor it into assessments of the feasibility of specific subprojects. The artificial externalization of resettlement costs could make projects appear less expensive than they actually are and distort the rates of return, possibly leading planners to make the wrong choices.

The typical resettlement costs—those associated with land acquisition, physical relocation, and economic rehabilitation at resettlement sites—are easy to identify, but they are often underestimated because inadequate allowance is made for inflation and other contingencies. The generally late identification of detailed resettlement costs also contributes to underestimation. In addition, other costs are sometimes missed or ignored in computing resettlement budgets. During the design stage, such costs are not adequately determined by the census and survey of populations and impacts. In many dam projects, the number of people finally affected turns out to be substantially higher than the initial estimates.

Project example: In Turkey, the Bank appraisal of the Izmir Water Supply and Sewerage Project (Ln 2828) estimated that 3,700 people would be adversely affected, but the final number turned out to be about 13,000. Similar underestimates of affected people include 135, instead of 15,000, in the Ruzizi II Project (Cr 1419), in Zaire; 1,000, instead of 5,500, in the Guavio Hydropower Project (Ln 2008), in Colombia; and 8,000, instead of 19,000, in the Madhya Pradesh Medium Irrigation Project (Cr 954), in India.

The planning process of many dam projects also underestimates temporary or partial impacts, and consequently it underestimates the cost of mitigating them.

Project example: The Operations Evaluation Department (OED) study[3] of eight large dam projects found that resettlement costs escalated significantly above estimates in half the cases: in India, the costs of the Upper Krishna II Irrigation Project (Ln 3050; Cr 2010) at project closing had increased 39 percent, and the increases were expected to reach 65 percent before completion of resettlement. In Thailand, the Pak Mun Project (Ln 3423) resettlement costs increased 67 percent; in Indonesia, the Kedung Ombo Project (Ln 2543) resettlement costs increased 120 percent; and in Brazil, the Itaparica Resettlement and Irrigation Project (Ln 2883) resettlement costs more than quadrupled, to nearly $1.5 billion. None of these projects underestimated the number of people affected, but they did underestimate the difficulty and expense of income rehabilitation programs, as well as the need to significantly increase land compensation rates in the face of rapidly rising land prices. Only one of the projects that OED studied, the Nangbeto Hydropower project (Cr 1507; Cr 1508), in Togo, kept resettlement costs within 10 percent of estimates.

In addition to contributing to suboptimal decisionmaking in project selection, inaccurate estimation of costs inappropriately makes the form and scope of resettlement alternatives offered to people contingent on the funds available for resettlement. Once the resettlement costs are inadequately identified, the arbitrary costs are often frozen, and the funding for costs identified at a later stage is then difficult to find. In some instances, the entitlements offered to affected people have been determined on the basis of arbitrary funding limits imposed by project agencies and derived from early cost estimates, rather than detailed budget estimates from the cost of entitlements and activities of the resettlement program.

As well as estimating the total cost of resettlement, project planners need to focus on the distribution of costs and benefits. Dams have a disproportionate impact on resettlers, and benefits often go to the landed and urban residents. Although cost-benefit analysis assesses the "total" effect of the project, it often does not ask who is paying the costs, who is receiving benefits, or who is losing.[4]

In recent years, considerable research has been carried out in the Bank to improve the economic analysis of projects. This research shows that projects assisted by the Bank tend to overestimate net benefits if costs are borne by the public sector but benefits are enjoyed by the private sector.[5] The undesirable effects of overestimating benefits are exacerbated by inadequate attention to issues of distribution. Resettlement costs, therefore, need to be compared, not only with the benefits accruing to project beneficiaries, but also with the benefits that a well-designed resettlement program can bring to the affected people themselves. The results of such analysis should be shared with key stakeholders and the public.

Project Revenues Used to Finance Resettlement Costs

Dam projects, especially those producing hydropower, generate revenue streams that can be shared with the people they displace. These revenues can be used for any purpose that benefits affected people: to provide community infrastructure, support local development programs, or generate additional revenues (Box 15.3).

Box 15.3   Laws for Hydropower Revenue Sharing with Affected Communities

Brazil, Colombia, and China have all passed legislation that earmarks part of project revenues for area development and resettlement activities. Brazilian Law 7990/89 mandates that 6 percent of electricity-sales revenues of power plants generating more than 10 megawatts be paid as royalties: 10 percent to the federal government, 45 percent to the host state, and 45 percent to the affected municipalities. Colombia Law 56/91 requires that 4 percent of annual electricity revenues generated by a hydroelectric project be allocated to municipalities in that plant's area: 2 percent are for reforestation and other environmental mitigation activities; and 2 percent, for social infrastructure, such as schools, roads, and rural electrification. Chinese legal frameworks for revenue sharing began in 1981, and by 1991 the state council issued a regulation that allocates $0.00056/kilowatt-hour (approximately 1 percent of revenues) for the first 5–10 years after completion of resettlement to a reservoir maintenance fund. The fund is used to compensate or restore the means of livelihood for people affected by the reservoir and maintain reservoir structures, drinking water, irrigation, and transportation used by those relocated. This arrangement helps ease the pressure to raise funds before project implementation and finance, through project revenues, the recurring resettlement costs of economic rehabilitation and community development programs. However, it can be successful only in the cases of profitable projects that generate revenues.

Source: Van Wicklin, Warren A., III. 1999. "Sharing Project Benefits to Improve Resettlers' Livelihoods." In M. Cernea, ed., *The Economics of Involuntary Resettlement: Questions and Challenges*. Washington, D.C.: World Bank; and World Commission on Dams. 2000. *Dams and Development: A New Framework for Decision Making*. London: Earthscan.

A community development or resettlement fund can also be used to address outstanding issues after resettlement is complete. Such a fund could help meet operations and maintenance costs of infrastructure, help meet transition period needs of resettlers, and help deal with contingencies related to income restoration measures.

Assessment of Risks to the Resettlement Program

Before a resettlement program is accepted as feasible and implementable, a thorough risk analysis must be conducted. Resettlement planners and decisionmakers should remember the vital difference between taking and imposing risk and between voluntary risk takers (the financiers and government decisionmakers) and involuntary risk bearers (the DPs). As voluntary risk takers, private companies manage their increased exposure to risk by requiring higher financial rates of return. Their risk management procedures are well developed; they use contractual agreements and sophisticated third-party recourse and arbitration mechanisms. Similarly, government decisionmakers weigh risks of undertaking dam projects against risks of not undertaking them. Unlike the above risk takers, however, the DPs are those on whom risks are imposed. The risks to displaced communities are compounded if they have no say in the decisions related to their future but have to bear the consequences. They often depend on the capacity of the government or the developer to manage the resettlement program on their behalf.

Involuntary resettlement is a complex process that affects every aspect of the life of the DPs. Reestablishment of livelihoods and acceptable lifestyles is difficult enough under the most favorable circumstances, without the tight implementation schedules and threats of cost escalation in development projects. The resettlement process can be viewed as a megaproject that includes subprojects dealing with issues of health, education, infrastructure, agriculture, microcredit, the environment, and business and social development. Successful resettlement requires not only that all these subprojects be satisfactorily implemented, but also that they be well coordinated with each other and implemented in tandem. Most resettlement programs make overoptimistic assumptions about the ability of implementing agencies and DPs to successfully implement a complex set of activities. Such overoptimism in the planning process should be balanced with a thorough analysis of the risks that could affect implementation.

A number of frameworks for risk analysis have been propagated by resettlement practitioners and researchers. The risks and reconstruction model is one such framework. This model lists the key risks faced by DPs: landlessness; joblessness; homelessness; social, economic, and political marginalization; food

15

insecurity; increased morbidity and mortality; loss of access to common-property resources; and loss of sociocultural resilience in a community. (For a discussion of the risks and reconstruction model, see "Risk Analysis" in chapter 8.) In addition, the following types of risk need to be assessed in the design of a resettlement program:

- Institutional risk associated with the capacity of agencies responsible for the resettlement, including the capacity to coordinate the many activities involved in a resettlement program;
- Financial risk associated with the timely availability of adequate funding for all resettlement activities, including risks of major cost escalation resulting from project delays;
- Technical risk associated with changes in any of the underlying factors and assumptions of the proposed mitigation strategies (such as an assumption that irrigated agriculture will be feasible, which the soil or drainage features discovered during implementation may prove wrong).
- Macroeconomic risk associated with changes in demand for the goods and services supplied by DPs or in supply of inputs needed for production.
- Risk of changes in people's needs and preferences during resettlement implementation (sometimes, after elaborate planning has been carried out, people change their minds about the location that is acceptable to them).
- Risk of nonimplementation of the project after completion of detailed planning and initiation of implementation.

A detailed analysis of these risks should accompany the resettlement planning process, to avoid unintended or unforeseen adverse consequences. Mechanisms to address some of these risks can be incorporated into the resettlement plan (RP) (for example, contingency financing arrangements in case of cost escalation; a more thorough feasibility analysis of proposed mitigation measures). Others may be difficult to plan for. Innovative mechanisms, such as trust funds or sharing of project revenues with displaced communities, may be needed to help mitigate such risks during implementation.

Institutional Arrangements

Adequate Arrangements During the Resettlement Transition Period

Reservoir resettlement, with its inherent disruption and reestablishment of livelihoods and community life, often entails a long transition period, during which the various productive resources offered to DPs reach their full potential for income generation. Community structures, which can provide an in-built mechanism for support, also take time to reestablish. To ensure improvement in incomes soon after displacement, the resettlement program needs to provide support during the transition period until the productive resources provided to the DPs achieve their full potential. Transition support can take the form of cash allowances, provision of food grains, employment, or maintenance of access to productive land before submergence. DPs can continue to cultivate their lands until these lands are submerged, and they can practice drawdown agriculture along the edges of the reservoir during the transition period. The RP needs to include a careful estimate of the time required for various economic activities to attain their full potential, and it needs to include provisions for support of DPs during this period. The plan should also include a process for making decisions to terminate transition support after an agreed duration.

> *Project example:* In China, the Shuikou Hydroelectric Project (Ln 2775) planted trees several years before resettlers were to move, and the trees were near maturity by the time of the resettlement. In Indonesia, the Kedung Ombo Multipurpose Project (Ln 2543) did not plant oil palm trees until six years after resettlers moved, and the trees did not reach maturity and full yield until six years later. Even then, 12 years after moving, some resettlers had still not received their oil palm trees. These delays were caused by the private company that was supplying the oil palm trees—it wanted to gradually increase oil palm production as the market expanded. But this policy did not meet the income needs of the resettlers.

Strong Institutional Design to Deliver What the Project Has Promised

Resettlement institutions need to be multisectoral, given that a resettlement program involves a diverse range of activities, such as land acquisition, impact measurement, physical relocation, job and credit provision, land development, and training. A mix of institutions—government agencies, the project implementation unit, specialized technical agencies, and experienced NGOs and other civil society organizations—is necessary for successful resettlement implementation. In addition to institutions involved in implementation and those providing community services, successful resettlement requires a capable project design agency and sector, state, and national regulatory agencies.

The design of resettlement institutions needs to take into account the fact that the specific circumstances of each household undergoing resettlement are likely to differ. Unlike administration of other development functions involving delivery of a few services that lend themselves to an aggregated approach to implementation, resettlement, with impacts that affect all aspects of the resettlers' lives, requires an approach customized for households. The project implementation unit needs the assistance of grassroots organizations to help each affected household benefit from the entitlements and other services provided by the project agencies.

Project example: In India, the Sardar Sarovar (Narmada) Project (Ln 2497; Cr 1552) agency in Gujarat (the state responsible for the resettlement of almost 70 percent of the displaced households) developed an effective institutional setup in consultation with the Bank. The setup consisted of the following:

- A strong resettlement agency (Narmada Resettlement Agency), with a corporate structure designed to expedite decisionmaking and implementation and with the capacity to perform most line functions (such as technical surveys, purchase of land in the open market, development of infrastructure at resettlement sites);
- Strong local government agencies, strengthened with the help of special assistance provided by the project and tasked to perform only the functions outside the mandate of the Narmada Resettlement Agency; and
- Local NGOs with substantial experience in implementing development programs in the area, who could help customize the resettlement entitlements to the specific needs of each displaced household.

Linkage of Dam Construction to the Implementation of Resettlement

The pace of dam construction needs to be linked to completion of resettlement activities. The reservoir level should be raised to successively higher levels only after specified resettlement activities are completed for households at those levels. This linkage of the resettlement and construction schedules has been established as regular practice in all Bank projects involving involuntary resettlement. The RP needs to clearly list the specific activities to be completed before the "green light" can be given to proceed with the physical displacement of a household. Green-light activities are generally the following:

- Payment of compensation at replacement cost for all affected assets;
- Allocation of productive resources to the households;
- Start of income generation activities;
- Supply of a serviced resettlement site and housing;
- Payment of moving allowances or moving support; and
- Start of transition period arrangements.

Project example: The Upper Krishna II Irrigation Project (Ln 3050; Cr 2010), in India, has the largest resettlement operation of any Bank-assisted project. The project faced many problems and delays. Most of the affected people were supposed to move to the command area, but the command area was not developed in tandem with dam construction. The Narayanpur Dam was completed in 1982, and the reservoir began filling. Although filling was delayed and not completed until 1999, in 1996 unusually heavy rains led to a 1-in-10-year flood. About 20,000 people had to be relocated under emergency conditions. Resettlement still did not catch up with construction, and in 1997 another 8,000 people had to be similarly relocated because of flood waters. They were housed in temporary sheds, awaiting construction of their permanent houses. Many affected people had to spend their compensation money and did not have enough left to build new houses until additional housing grants enabled them to rebuild their houses.

Monitoring and Supervision

All resettlement operations need monitoring, but the need is especially acute in large dam projects. Large dam projects are complex and difficult; often cause affected people to change occupations; sometimes move affected people significant distances, in phases, over a long period and require them to adjust to different environments; often do not go according to plan; span multiple administrative jurisdictions; and require handover to local agencies long after the dam itself is complete. None of the dam projects in the 1998 OED evaluation of involuntary resettlement went according to plan, but the best indicator of ultimately successful resettlement was how competently resettlement agencies monitored the effectiveness of implementation, identified problems, and took corrective action.

Clear Benchmarks and Indicators for Monitoring Implementation

Bank policy on involuntary resettlement requires a review of resettlement implementation in the early stages to assess the adequacy of the resettlement program and make necessary modifications to improve subsequent implementation. Wherever possible, monitoring by the project agency should be complemented by monitoring and evaluation by a qualified, independent agency. Implementers and monitors should have a clear, common understanding of the goals of the resettlement program and how they will be measured. Monitoring reports need to be regularly reviewed by decisionmakers and should form the basis of decisions to improve implementation. It is not uncommon to find monitoring and implementation proceeding on two different tracks, with little learning taking place through the monitoring exercise. In the case of dams with

15

major resettlement impacts, regular internal and external monitoring should be supplemented by the work of international panels for overseeing resettlement implementation. The results of internal, as well as external, monitoring should be available to the DPs.

> *Project example:* In India, the Upper Indravati Hydroelectric Project (Ln 2278; Cr 1356) established an independent panel of experts to review its progress on various environmental and social issues, including resettlement. The panel visited the project twice a year to review the implementation of agreements reached in earlier visits. The panel also assessed, on a continuing basis, the adequacy of institutional, financial, and other arrangements.

Resettlement Supervision beyond the Resettlement Program

On the basis of a study of eight large dam projects partly financed by the Bank in the mid-1980s, OED (1998) recommended that regular supervision of the resettlement program continue until the objectives of the program are achieved. Completion of the main dam and the exit of the main funding agency from the project have often resulted in a decline in emphasis on resettlement issues, even though the objectives of the resettlement program may not have been achieved. Based on OED's recommendation and Bank experience in resettlement, the revised resettlement policy of the Bank, OP/BP 4.12 states that a project is not to be considered complete until the RP is fully implemented by the borrower. On completion of the activities included in the resettlement program, an assessment is needed to determine the extent to which the DPs' incomes and standards of living have been restored. This assessment is generally accomplished through a follow-up socioeconomic survey. The survey results help in determining the need, if any, for follow-up efforts; it also serves as a useful basis for designing them. The Bank will continue to supervise the resettlement program, if necessary, beyond project completion.

Good practice in resettlement is continuously incorporating the learning that takes place in programs using a variety of implementation strategies and institutional models. Resettlement practice has evolved significantly in the Bank through the experience and suggestions of its resettlement staff and the knowledge gained from other lending, resettlement, practitioner, academic, and research organizations. This experience and this knowledge have become an effective mechanism of learning, which is best demonstrated by the incorporation of the key lessons into the revised resettlement policy of the World Bank.

Notes

1. Cernea, M. 1988. Involuntary Resettlement in Development Projects: Policy and Guidelines in World Bank Financed Projects. Vol. 1. Washington, D.C.: World Bank. Technical Paper 80.

2. Pearce, D.W. 1999. "Methodological Issues in the Economic Analysis of Involuntary Resettlement Operations." In M. Cernea, ed., *The Economics of Involuntary Resettlement: Questions and Challenges*. Washington, D.C.: World Bank.

3. Operations Evaluation Department. 1998. *Recent Experience with Involuntary Resettlement*. Washington, D.C.: World Bank.

4. Cernea, M. 1999. "Why Economic Analysis Is Essential to Resettlement: A Sociologist's View." In M. Cernea, ed., *The Economics of Involuntary Resettlement: Questions and Challenges*.

5. Devarajan, S., Squire, L., and Suthiwart-Narueput, S. 1995. *Reviving Project Appraisal at the World Bank*. Washington, D.C.: World Bank.

15

Chapter 16

Resettlement in Natural Resources Management and Biodiversity Projects

Operational Policy (OP) 4.12 provides several important clarifications of earlier policy statements concerning the nexus of involuntary resettlement, natural resources management, and biodiversity protection. These clarifications—related to applicability of the policy, objectives of the policy, and instruments to be used to implement the policy—are necessary for several reasons. First, the involuntary resettlement policy is not meant to substitute for a broader social policy. Instead, it covers only project-related social and economic impacts of the direct taking of land or of the restriction of access to legally protected areas. Although Bank projects may have a wide range of social and economic impacts not directly related to the taking of land or the restriction of access, the involuntary resettlement policy, with good justification, does not cover such impacts.

Second, a balance is needed between the objectives of the Bank's involuntary resettlement policy and those of its policy on management of natural resources and biodiversity, particularly critical natural habitats. If applied in isolation from one another, environmental and social policies can be mutually defeating and can undermine efforts to reduce poverty. But if they are applied thoughtfully and contextually, the policies can be mutually supportive, and the possible tradeoffs between them can be managed.

Third, a special resettlement instrument is needed to address adverse impacts that restricted access to protected areas might have on livelihoods. This instrument should also take into account the dynamic interplay of protected area management, community participation, and poverty reduction.

Policy Applicability

With regard to the applicability of the policy, two important clarifications are introduced. The first is that, with respect to natural resources management projects, the Bank's policy covers only direct economic and social impacts. Specifically, it covers adverse impacts on livelihoods that result from Bank-assisted investment projects and are caused by "(a) the involuntary taking of land resulting in (i) relocation or loss of shelter; (ii) [loss] of assets or access to assets; or (iii) loss of income sources or means of livelihood . . . ; or (b) the involuntary restriction of access to legally designated parks or protected areas" (OP 4.12, para. 3 [b]).

The policy underscores a distinction between impacts of the outright taking of land and those of measures restricting access to or use of resources in parks or protected areas, without physical dislocation of the affected people. Two important types of impact related to natural resources can be distinguished:

- *Involuntary taking of land*—In this case, the project results in the loss of land, other assets, or means of livelihood, regardless of whether the affected person is physically displaced. Examples are (a) the creation of a legally protected area (or more precise demarcation of boundaries of an existing park) that results in physical displacement of people, loss of shelter, or other nonresource assets; (b) the construction of a dam that affects the incomes of those who previously fished in the area now occupied by the dam's reservoir, even if those fishers did not lose land or housing.
- *Involuntary restriction of access to parks or protected areas*—In this case, access to natural resources is restricted to meet the objectives of resource management or biodiversity protection in legally protected areas, as a result of the project.

These two types of impact are covered by the policy. But, although the policy applies *equally* to each of these two types of impact, it is applied *differently* in each case. Both the policy objective and the resettlement instrument vary slightly for each case. These two aspects are discussed in more detail below.

The second clarification (OP 4.12, endnotes 6, 8) on policy application provides for two specific natural-resource exclusions: the policy does not apply to projects involving national or regional regulation of natural resources to promote their sustainability; or to community-based projects that restrict access to natural resources outside of parks or protected areas where the scope and extent of restrictions are decided by the involved communities themselves (even though some individuals in the community might disagree).

In the first case, restrictions on use are imposed through national or regional environmental management programs, and the restrictions apply broadly and are not site specific. In such cases OP 4.12 does not apply. Rather, good practice suggests that social analysis (since it is not site or project specific) should be done, and policy measures should be put in place to address social impacts, including, as appropriate, social safety nets for vulnerable groups.

In the second case, restrictions on use are devised under community-based projects (as when governmental agencies are not imposing the restrictions and when the area under consideration is not part of a legally designated park, reserve, or other form of demarcated protection zone). In such cases the community is considered the legitimate decisionmaking entity, and any restrictions the community decides to impose on its members are viewed as voluntary. Thus, OP 4.12 does not apply, although the Bank must still satisfy itself that the community-based decisionmaking processes are genuinely participatory and voluntary.

Policy Objectives

OP 4.12 also clarifies the policy objectives as applied to involuntary restriction of access to parks or protected areas (OP 4.12, endnote 4). An overall objective of the involuntary resettlement policy is to mitigate the adverse impacts of resettlement by assisting displaced persons (DPs) in their efforts to improve or at least restore their livelihoods to predisplacement levels. In the case of involuntary restriction of access to parks or protected areas, however, the policy clarifies that resettlement assistance is more constrained than in the more general case. In projects involving restriction of access to parks or protected areas, the objective is generally to maintain the sustainability of natural resources or biodiversity protection, in line with the Bank's policy on natural habitats. There is thus a need to balance the objectives of OP 4.12 and those of OP 4.04 (Natural Habitats), which prohibits any measures resulting in significant conversion or degradation of critical natural habitats, including parks and protected areas. In such projects the objective of the involuntary resettlement policy is to improve or restore the livelihoods of DPs *while maintaining the sustainability of parks or protected areas, which could present particularly difficult challenges in some contexts.*

Throughout the world, governments and citizens are becoming more aware of the need for sustainable management of natural resources and protection of critical natural habitats. As population levels continue to climb in virtually all developing countries, sustainability of resources use has emerged as a key challenge in poverty reduction. Governments and local residents recognize that they need to cooperate in managing natural resources and biodiversity, to ensure sustainability of the benefits derived from them. But government regulations for resource management tend to fail unless supported or accepted by local populations, and natural resources, if degraded by overuse, are unable to meet communities' needs. This complex interplay of natural resources and the communities who depend on them needs to be taken into account in resettlement planning.

Policy Instruments

OP 4.12 also provides important clarifications of the resettlement instrument (paras. 7, 31) to be used in cases involving involuntary restriction of access to parks or protected areas. Because both the taking of assets and restrictions on

16

Table 16.1   Choice of Resettlement Instruments

	Physical relocation or dispossession of assets	Restriction on use of or access to natural resources without physical relocation or dispossession of assets
Outside parks or protected areas	Resettlement policy framework or resettlement action plan	None[a]
Inside parks or protected areas	Resettlement policy framework or resettlement action plan[b]	Process framework or plan of action[c]

[a]Operational policy (OP) 4.12, endnotes 6 and 8.
[b]OP 4.12, endnote 9.
[c]A protected area management plan can serve as the plan of action, provided it adequately covers the appropriate topics.

resource use can adversely affect incomes or living standards, OP 4.12 requires appropriate measures to avoid, minimize, or otherwise mitigate adverse impacts that arise in either case. But in cases involving restrictions on resource use in parks or protected areas, the approaches taken in assessing impacts and planning for their mitigation differ significantly. Table 16.1 shows the range of available resettlement instruments and situations in which they are appropriate.

The traditional resettlement instruments—resettlement action plan and resettlement policy framework—are prepared for projects where land acquisition directly results in dispossession of assets, loss of income, or physical relocation, whether inside or outside protected areas (as shown in the first two columns of Table 16.1). In those cases in which there is no physical relocation these traditional resettlement instruments are unsuitable for project impacts resulting from the involuntary restriction of access to legally designated parks or protected areas. In such cases, application of these instruments poses operational difficulties, because it is not practical to presume that all livelihood impacts of proposed restrictions can be predefined. The nature of the restrictions and the specific interventions needed to restore people's livelihoods typically cannot be known in advance. Therefore, application of the traditional instruments would be difficult to operationalize, undermine the objectives of the project, and compromise the process orientation.

Bank requirements shift the focus away from a priori plans, with detailed implementation arrangements, toward review of participatory processes to be used in formulating and implementing restrictions on resource use. To fulfill policy requirements, the borrower is required to prepare, before appraisal, a new instrument that is more appropriate for addressing issues of restricted access to protected areas. This new instrument—the process framework—describes the participatory process by which communities and the project's authorities or other relevant implementing agencies will jointly recommend land- or resource-use restrictions and decide on measures to mitigate any significant adverse impacts of these restrictions. A plan of action, which describes specific measures to assist people adversely affected by the proposed restrictions, would be submitted for approval by the Bank during project implementation and before the enforcement of the restrictions. As shown by the final entry in the third column of Table 16.1, the process framework and plan of action approach may be used when the Bank supports newly designated parks, reserves, or protected areas or efforts to improve existing ones by strengthening or extending restrictions, provided no physical relocation or dispossession of assets occurs.

Elements of a Resettlement Process Framework

Key elements of a process framework (OP 4.12, paras. 7, 31) describe the "participatory process by which". . .

"(a) Specific components of the project will be prepared and implemented."

This section of the process framework should describe how, and to what extent, potentially affected groups or communities are to participate in defining and determining restrictions. It should also describe how measures to assist potential DPs will be identified and selected. This section should mention which methods of participation and decisionmaking (for example, open meetings, selection of leaders or councils) will be used.

Essentially, the process framework is meant to codify a participatory approach, which is considered best practice for conservation activities in officially designated parks and protected areas. Experience has consistently shown that externally imposed regulations or restrictions tend to fail for a variety of reasons. In some cases, local resource users simply do not know about or understand the regulations. In others, local resource users (or users coming from more distant locations) choose to ignore or circumvent them. In yet other cases, the regulators may impose restrictions on resource use without fully realizing the important role such resources play in the subsistence or livelihoods of the affected people. Because parks and protected areas are usually situated in remote areas and their boundaries are porous, governments acting without community support find it costly, if not impossible, to regulate resource use through legal instruments.

16

Community participation in the design and enforcement of conservation activities helps to ensure active support. The community identifies acceptable alternatives to current patterns of resource use and identifies distribution patterns it deems to be equitable. In other words, if conservation activities are to succeed, the people affected must be convinced that the arrangements are reasonable. If sustainability requires local residents to stop or reduce hunting or the felling of trees, for example, then those residents must be confident that they can obtain alternative sources of food or building materials. Mitigation, however, need not be one for one. For instance, local communities are often those who register decline in availability of resources (or decline in resource base), and they are often concerned for the future sustainability of those resources. Therefore, experience shows that local, especial indigenous communities are often willing to reduce resource use, if they are supported by protected area management and they perceive that they can sustain their livelihood in the future.

The key to the process framework approach is establishing an appropriate degree and quality of community participation in conservation activities. The process framework must thus address the quality of the process of consultation and participation (for example, issues of leadership and representation, distributional equity, and special treatment for people vulnerable to specific hardship), with participatory arrangements that can adequately be monitored to ensure that the agreements reached are executed. The process framework approach offers an alternative to traditional resettlement planning. And it is more appropriate where the active support of communities is vital to achieving more sustainable patterns of resource use. Under this approach, communities have a right to participate in deciding on the nature of the resource restrictions and the measures necessary to mitigate adverse impacts arising as a consequence.

"(b) The criteria for eligibility of displaced persons [for any form of assistance] will be determined."

A clarification of OP 4.12 is that eligibility criteria for resettlement assistance related to impacts of involuntary restriction of access to parks or protected areas (endnote 18) are handled differently. This difference in treatment allows the flexibility to exclude from resettlement assistance anyone involved in clearly illegal, unsustainable, and destructive activities (such as wildlife poachers or dynamite fishers), if including these people would undermine the objective of the project or the sustainability of the park or protected area.

Just as the framework should describe how potentially affected groups or communities will be involved in identifying and assessing the significance of adverse impacts, it should also describe how the local population will be involved in establishing criteria for eligibility for assistance. Although the process framework approach allows the local population to participate in decisionmaking on eligibility criteria, ensuring the framework will enjoy the support of government agencies involved in the program is also important.

The framework should identify groups that may be particularly vulnerable to hardship as a result of new or strengthened restrictions on access to natural resources, such as those segments of the community who are more heavily dependent on protected area resources for their livelihood (for example, grass-cutters, collectors of non-timber forest produce). Two other issues warrant careful consideration in some cases. First, the framework should consider how the interests of nonresidents, who also may use the resources, are to be accounted for. Second, the framework may need to justify the exclusion of people engaging in some forms of resource use (for example, poaching of protected wildlife or opportunistic encroaching into areas already subject to customary resource management) as illicit or inappropriate for sustainable resource management. The challenge faced by communities and other stakeholders is how to establish appropriate criteria to determine what is poaching and opportunistic, as opposed to genuine livelihood activities.

"(c) Measures to assist the displaced persons in their efforts to improve their livelihoods, or at least to restore them, in real terms, while maintaining the sustainability of the park or protected area, will be identified."

The framework should describe how groups or communities will be involved in determining the most equitable and just sharing of access to resources under restricted use and for identifying possible alternative resources available for use and opportunities to offset losses. This section should describe the method for adversely affected community members to make collective decisions and decide on options available to them as eligible individuals or households. The framework should also describe enforcement provisions, clearly delineating the responsibilities of the community and those of government agencies in enforcing restrictions on the use of these resources. In general, affected communities are likely to use one or more of four strategies:

- *Devising transparent, equitable, and fair ways of more sustainably sharing the resources*—Recognition of rights to resources and more transparent resource management practices may significantly reduce pressure on forest products, for example.
- *Obtaining access to alternative resources or functional substitutes*—Access to electricity or biomass energy may eliminate overuse of timber for firewood, for example.

- *Obtaining public or private employment (or financial subsidies)*—Local residents may need alternative livelihoods or the means to purchase resource substitutes.
- *Providing access to resources outside the park or protected area*—Of course, a framework promoting this strategy must also consider impacts on the people and the sustainability of the resources in these other areas.

Once identified in the process framework, measures to assist DPs are articulated in the plan of action and implemented in accordance with this plan, as part of the project (OP 4.12, paras. 10, 31).

"(d) Potential conflicts or grievances involving DPs will be resolved."

The framework should describe community processes for addressing the disputes or complaints of affected groups or communities. A key aspect may be the role of government in mediation and in the enforcement of agreements. The framework should also describe processes for addressing the grievances of the individuals or households in the affected communities that are dissatisfied with eligibility criteria, the design of mitigation measures, or patterns of actual implementation. The framework should describe the distribution of responsibilities between government agencies and the communities themselves in the event of unanticipated problems or impacts or the failure of mitigation measures.

Implementation and monitoring arrangements will be made.

In addition, the framework should define in the action plan how measures to assist the DPs following the imposition of restrictions and to improve and restore their livelihoods will be monitored and how impacts will be carefully recorded while the project is in progress.

Plan of Action

A plan of action describes the nature and scope of any restrictions, their anticipated social and economic impacts, the people eligible for assistance, and the specific measures to assist these people. The plan of action is to be submitted for Bank approval during project implementation and before any enforcement of restrictions. The plan specifies the timing of the imposition of restrictions and describes the scope of and methods for monitoring the extent and the significance of adverse impacts and the effectiveness of measures designed to assist DPs and maintain the sustainability of the park or protected area. As a general principle, these arrangements should include opportunities for the affected population to participate in monitoring activities. A protected area management plan can serve as the plan of action, provided it adequately covers the appropriate topics.

Bank Procedures for the Resettlement Process Framework and Plan of Action

In many respects, Bank procedures for developing the resettlement process framework are similar to those of other resettlement planning instruments. As with resettlement action plans and policy frameworks, a draft process framework must be prepared by the borrower, and the Bank must satisfy itself that the framework conforms to OP 4.12, as a condition for project appraisal. However, as the process framework must itself be based, in part, on results of previous consultations, preparatory work should begin well before the appraisal stage.

As is the case in all projects involving resettlement in any form, the project task team should explore with the borrower the nature of impacts and planning alternatives early in the project identification stage. Because of differences in planning requirements and processes, deciding on the appropriate planning instrument at an early stage is likely to save time and money in project preparation.

Whenever the process framework approach is to be used, receipt of an acceptable framework is a condition of appraisal. If remaining deficiencies are minor, appraisal may be allowed to proceed. During project appraisal, the task team assesses the adequacy and feasibility of the proposed participatory process and ensures that any remaining deficiencies in the draft process framework are remedied. As in all projects involving resettlement, the appraisal process should establish that the borrower, as well as the affected communities, possesses adequate commitment and capacity (including identified financial resources) to implement the resettlement. Because mitigation measures and other alternatives are to be identified only during the implementation stage, however, assessing the feasibility of resettlement measures at appraisal is impossible.

Before appraisal can be said to be complete, a final process framework, reviewed and accepted by the Legal Department and the regional safeguards unit, must be formally submitted by the borrower. The Project Appraisal Document summarizes the agreed resettlement arrangements. The project legal documents include a reference to resettlement arrangements, including the need for the borrower to prepare a subsequent plan of action for Bank review and acceptance, before enforcement of any new or strengthened restrictions on resource use begins.

Because the process framework approach defers preparation and review of resettlement alternatives until the implementation stage, the development of a specific plan of action is a crucial step in the entire process. The plan of action (which can take the form of a natural resources management plan, if appropriate) is an outcome of a process of information, consultation, participation, and joint decisionmaking between the official agencies and the communities regarding the mutually acceptable level of resource use. It describes the specific measures to be taken to assist adversely affected people, and it describes the arrangements

16

for implementing these measures. The borrower discloses the plan of action in the project area in a form and language understandable to the affected communities; the task team places the plan of action in the InfoShop to ensure public access to it.

Through regular project supervision, the task team

- Ensures that potential DPs have opportunities to participate in developing the specific plan of action, described in the process framework;
- Reviews and approves the plan of action before the borrower begins to enforce access restrictions; and
- Assesses, through field inspection and review of monitoring reports, whether agreed measures have been effectively implemented, as planned, or alternative measures are necessary.

As with all projects involving involuntary resettlement, responsibility for supervision continues until all agreed measures have been implemented. The project is not considered complete until the borrower has implemented all of the measures described in the plan of action. If, at project completion, resettlement measures have not led to satisfactory results (in both livelihoods and resource sustainability), the task team should work with the borrower to decide on appropriate follow-up measures.

World Bank Involuntary Resettlement Policy, OP/BP 4.12

Involuntary Resettlement OP 4.12

1. Bank[1] experience indicates that involuntary resettlement under development projects, if unmitigated, often gives rise to severe economic, social, and environmental risks: production systems are dismantled; people face impoverishment when their productive assets or income sources are lost; people are relocated to environments where their productive skills may be less applicable and the competition for resources greater; community institutions and social networks are weakened; kin groups are dispersed; and cultural identity, traditional authority, and the potential for mutual help are diminished or lost. This policy includes safeguards to address and mitigate these impoverishment risks.

Policy Objectives

2. Involuntary resettlement may cause severe long-term hardship, impoverishment, and environmental damage unless appropriate measures are carefully planned and carried out. For these reasons, the overall objectives of the Bank's policy on involuntary resettlement are the following:

   (a) Involuntary resettlement should be avoided where feasible, or minimized, exploring all viable alternative project designs.[2]

   (b) Where it is not feasible to avoid resettlement, resettlement activities should be conceived and executed as sustainable development programs, providing sufficient investment resources to enable the persons displaced by the project to share in project benefits. Displaced persons[3] should be meaningfully consulted and should have opportunities to participate in planning and implementing resettlement programs.

   (c) Displaced persons should be assisted in their efforts to improve their livelihoods and standards of living or at least to restore them, in real terms, to pre-displacement levels or to levels prevailing prior to the beginning of project implementation, whichever is higher.[4]

Note: OP and BP 4.12 together replace OD 4.30, *Involuntary Resettlement.* This OP and BP apply to all projects for which a Project Concept Review takes place on or after January 1, 2002. Questions may be addressed to the Director, Social Development Department (SDV).

1

Impacts Covered

3. This policy covers direct economic and social impacts[5] that both result from Bank-assisted investment projects,[6] and are caused by
   (a) the involuntary[7] taking of land[8] resulting in
       (i) relocation or loss of shelter;
       (ii) lost of assets or access to assets; or
       (iii) loss of income sources or means of livelihood, whether or not the affected persons must move to another location; or
   (b) the involuntary restriction of access[9] to legally designated parks and protected areas resulting in adverse impacts on the livelihoods of the displaced persons.
4. This policy applies to all components of the project that result in involuntary resettlement, regardless of the source of financing. It also applies to other activities resulting in involuntary resettlement, that in the judgment of the Bank, are (a) directly and significantly related to the Bank-assisted project, (b) necessary to achieve its objectives as set forth in the project documents; and (c) carried out, or planned to be carried out, contemporaneously with the project.
5. Requests for guidance on the application and scope of this policy should be addressed to the Resettlement Committee (see BP 4.12, para. 7).[10]

Required Measures

6. To address the impacts covered under para. 3(a) of this policy, the borrower prepares a resettlement plan or a resettlement policy framework (see paras. 25–30) that covers the following:
   (a) The resettlement plan or resettlement policy framework includes measures to ensure that the displaced persons are
       (i) informed about their options and rights pertaining to resettlement;
       (ii) consulted on, offered choices among, and provided with technically and economically feasible resettlement alternatives; and
       (iii) provided prompt and effective compensation at full replacement cost[11] for losses of assets[12] attributable directly to the project.
   (b) If the impacts include physical relocation, the resettlement plan or resettlement policy framework includes measures to ensure that the displaced persons are
       (i) provided assistance (such as moving allowances) during relocation; and
       (ii) provided with residential housing, or housing sites, or, as required, agricultural sites for which a combination of productive

potential, locational advantages, and other factors is at least equivalent to the advantages of the old site.[13]

(c) Where necessary to achieve the objectives of the policy, the resettlement plan or resettlement policy framework also includes measures to ensure that displaced persons are

(i) offered support after displacement, for a transition period, based on a reasonable estimate of the time likely to be needed to restore their livelihood and standards of living;[14] and

(ii) provided with development assistance in addition to compensation measures described in paragraph 6(a) (iii), such as land preparation, credit facilities, training, or job opportunities.

7. In projects involving involuntary restriction of access to legally designated parks and protected areas (see para. 3(b)), the nature of restrictions, as well as the type of measures necessary to mitigate adverse impacts, is determined with the participation of the displaced persons during the design and implementation of the project. In such cases, the borrower prepares a process framework acceptable to the Bank, describing the participatory process by which

(a) specific components of the project will be prepared and implemented;

(b) the criteria for eligibility of displaced persons will be determined;

(c) measures to assist the displaced persons in their efforts to improve their livelihoods, or at least to restore them, in real terms, while maintaining the sustainability of the park or protected area, will be identified; and

(d) potential conflicts involving displaced persons will be resolved.

The process framework also includes a description of the arrangements for implementing and monitoring the process.

8. To achieve the objectives of this policy, particular attention is paid to the needs of vulnerable groups among those displaced, especially those below the poverty line, the landless, the elderly, women and children, indigenous peoples,[15] ethnic minorities, or other displaced persons who may not be protected through national land compensation legislation.

9. Bank experience has shown that resettlement of indigenous peoples with traditional land-based modes of production is particularly complex and may have significant adverse impacts on their identity and cultural survival. For this reason, the Bank satisfies itself that the borrower has explored all viable alternative project designs to avoid physical displacement of these groups. When it is not feasible to avoid such displacement, preference is given to land-based resettlement strategies for these groups (see para. 11) that are compatible with their cultural

1

preferences and are prepared in consultation with them (see Annex A, para. 11).

10. The implementation of resettlement activities is linked to the implementation of the investment component of the project to ensure that displacement or restriction of access does not occur before necessary measures for resettlement are in place. For impacts covered in para. 3(a) of this policy, these measures include provision of compensation and of other assistance required for relocation, prior to displacement, and preparation and provision of resettlement sites with adequate facilities, where required. In particular, taking of land and related assets may take place only after compensation has been paid and, where applicable, resettlement sites and moving allowances have been provided to the displaced persons. For impacts covered in para. 3(b) of this policy, the measures to assist the displaced persons are implemented in accordance with the plan of action as part of the project (see para. 30).

11. Preference should be given to land-based resettlement strategies for displaced persons whose livelihoods are land-based. These strategies may include resettlement on public land (see footnote 1 above), or on private land acquired or purchased for resettlement. Whenever replacement land is offered, resettlers are provided with land for which a combination of productive potential, locational advantages, and other factors is at least equivalent to the advantages of the land taken. If land is not the preferred option of the displaced persons, the provision of land would adversely affect the sustainability of a park or protected area,[16] or sufficient land is not available at a reasonable price, non-land-based options built around opportunities for employment or self-employment should be provided in addition to cash compensation for land and other assets lost. The lack of adequate land must be demonstrated and documented to the satisfaction of the Bank.

12. Payment of cash compensation for lost assets may be appropriate where (a) livelihoods are land-based but the land taken for the project is a small fraction[17] of the affected asset and the residual is economically viable; (b) active markets for land, housing, and labor exist, displaced persons use such markets, and there is sufficient supply of land and housing; or (c) livelihoods are not land-based. Cash compensation levels should be sufficient to replace the lost land and other assets at full replacement cost in local markets.

13. For impacts covered under para. 3(a) of this policy, the Bank also requires the following:

    (a) Displaced persons and their communities, and any host communities receiving them, are provided timely and relevant information,

1

consulted on resettlement options, and offered opportunities to participate in planning, implementing, and monitoring resettlement. Appropriate and accessible grievance mechanisms are established for these groups.

(b) In new resettlement sites or host communities, infrastructure and public services are provided as necessary to improve, restore, or maintain accessibility and levels of service for the displaced persons and host communities. Alternative or similar resources are provided to compensate for the loss of access to community resources (such as fishing areas, grazing areas, fuel, or fodder).

(c) Patterns of community organization appropriate to the new circumstances are based on choices made by the displaced persons. To the extent possible, the existing social and cultural institutions of resettlers and any host communities are preserved and resettlers' preferences with respect to relocating in preexisting communities and groups are honored.

Eligibility for Benefits[18]

14. Upon identification of the need for involuntary resettlement in a project, the borrower carries out a census to identify the persons who will be affected by the project (see the Annex A, para. 6(a)), to determine who will be eligible for assistance, and to discourage inflow of people ineligible for assistance. The borrower also develops a procedure, satisfactory to the Bank, for establishing the criteria by which displaced persons will be deemed eligible for compensation and other resettlement assistance. The procedure includes provisions for meaningful consultations with affected persons and communities, local authorities, and, as appropriate, nongovernmental organizations (NGOs), and it specifies grievance mechanisms.

15. *Criteria for Eligibility.* Displaced persons may be classified in one of the following three groups:
   (a) those who have formal legal rights to land (including customary and traditional rights recognized under the laws of the country);
   (b) those who do not have formal legal rights to land at the time the census begins but have a claim to such land or assets—provided that such claims are recognized under the laws of the country or become recognized through a process identified in the resettlement plan (see Annex A, para. 7(f)); and[19]
   (c) those who have no recognizable legal right or claim to the land they are occupying.

16. Persons covered under para. 15(a) and (b) are provided compensation for the land they lose, and other assistance in accordance with para. 6. Persons covered under para. 15(c) are provided resettlement assistance[20] in lieu of compensation for the land they occupy, and other assistance, as necessary, to achieve the objectives set out in this policy, if they occupy the project area prior to a cutoff date established by the borrower and acceptable to the Bank.[21] Persons who encroach on the area after the cutoff date are not entitled to compensation or any other form of resettlement assistance. All persons included in para. 15(a), (b), or (c) are provided compensation for loss of assets other than land.

Resettlement Planning, Implementation, and Monitoring

17. To achieve the objectives of this policy, different planning instruments are used, depending on the type of project:
    (a) a resettlement plan or abbreviated resettlement plan is required for all operations that entail involuntary resettlement unless otherwise specified (see para. 25 and Annex A);
    (b) a resettlement policy framework is required for operations referred to in paras. 26–30 that may entail involuntary resettlement, unless otherwise specified (see Annex A); and
    (c) a process framework is prepared for projects involving restriction of access in accordance with para. 3(b) (see para. 31).
18. The borrower is responsible for preparing, implementing, and monitoring a resettlement plan, a resettlement policy framework, or a process framework (the "resettlement instruments"), as appropriate, that conform to this policy. The resettlement instrument presents a strategy for achieving the objectives of the policy and covers all aspects of the proposed resettlement. Borrower commitment to, and capacity for, undertaking successful resettlement is a key determinant of Bank involvement in a project.
19. Resettlement planning includes early screening, scoping of key issues, the choice of resettlement instrument, and the information required to prepare the resettlement component or subcomponent. The scope and level of detail of the resettlement instruments vary with the magnitude and complexity of resettlement. In preparing the resettlement component, the borrower draws on appropriate social, technical, and legal expertise and on relevant community-based organizations and NGOs.[22] The borrower informs potentially displaced persons at an early stage about the resettlement aspects of the project and takes their views into account in project design.

20. The full costs of resettlement activities necessary to achieve the objectives of the project are included in the total costs of the project. The costs of resettlement, like the costs of other project activities, are treated as a charge against the economic benefits of the project; and any net benefits to resettlers (as compared to the "without-project" circumstances) are added to the benefits stream of the project. Resettlement components or free-standing resettlement projects need not be economically viable on their own, but they should be cost-effective.

21. The borrower ensures that the Project Implementation Plan is fully consistent with the resettlement instrument.

22. As a condition of appraisal of projects involving resettlement, the borrower provides the Bank with the relevant draft resettlement instrument that conforms to this policy, and makes it available at a place accessible to displaced persons and local NGOs, in a form, manner, and language that are understandable to them. Once the Bank accepts this instrument as providing an adequate basis for project appraisal, the Bank makes it available to the public through its InfoShop. After the Bank has approved the final resettlement instrument, the Bank and the borrower disclose it again in the same manner.[23]

23. The borrower's obligations to carry out the resettlement instrument and to keep the Bank informed of implementation progress are provided for in the legal agreements for the project.

24. The borrower is responsible for adequate monitoring and evaluation of the activities set forth in the resettlement instrument. The Bank regularly supervises resettlement implementation to determine compliance with the resettlement instrument. Upon completion of the project, the borrower undertakes an assessment to determine whether the objectives of the resettlement instrument have been achieved. The assessment takes into account the baseline conditions and the results of resettlement monitoring. If the assessment reveals that these objectives may not be realized, the borrower should propose follow-up measures that may serve as the basis for continued Bank supervision, as the Bank deems appropriate (see also BP 4.12, para. 16).

Resettlement Instruments

Resettlement Plan

25. A draft resettlement plan that conforms to this policy is a condition of appraisal (see Annex A, paras. 2–21) for projects referred to in para. 17(a) above.[24] However, where impacts on the entire displaced population are

minor,[25] or fewer than 200 people are displaced, an abbreviated resettlement plan may be agreed with the borrower (see Annex A, para. 22). The information disclosure procedures set forth in para. 22 apply.

Resettlement Policy Framework

26. For sector investment operations that may involve involuntary resettlement, the Bank requires that the project implementing agency screen subprojects to be financed by the Bank to ensure their consistency with this OP. For these operations, the borrower submits, prior to appraisal, a resettlement policy framework that conforms to this policy (see Annex A, paras. 23–25). The framework also estimates, to the extent feasible, the total population to be displaced and the overall resettlement costs.

27. For financial intermediary operations that may involve involuntary resettlement, the Bank requires that the financial intermediary (FI) screen subprojects to be financed by the Bank to ensure their consistency with this OP. For these operations, the Bank requires that before appraisal the borrower or the FI submit to the Bank a resettlement policy framework conforming to this policy (see Annex A, paras. 23–25). In addition, the framework includes an assessment of the institutional capacity and procedures of each of the FIs that will be responsible for subproject financing. When, in the assessment of the Bank, no resettlement is envisaged in the subprojects to be financed by the FI, a resettlement policy framework is not required. Instead, the legal agreements specify the obligation of the FIs to obtain from the potential subborrowers a resettlement plan consistent with this policy if a subproject gives rise to resettlement. For all subprojects involving resettlement, the resettlement plan is provided to the Bank for approval before the subproject is accepted for Bank financing.

28. For other Bank-assisted project with multiple subprojects[26] that may involve involuntary resettlement, the Bank requires that a draft resettlement plan conforming to this policy be submitted to the Bank before appraisal of the project unless, because of the nature and design of the project or of a specific subproject or subprojects, (a) the zone of impact of subprojects cannot be determined, or (b) the zone of impact is known but precise sitting alignments cannot be determined. In such cases, the borrower submits a resettlement policy framework consistent with this policy prior to appraisal (see Annex A, paras. 23–25). For other subprojects that do not fall within the above criteria, a resettlement plan conforming to this policy is required prior to appraisal.

29. For each subproject included in a project described in para. 26, 27, or 28 that may involve resettlement, the Bank requires that a satisfactory resettlement plan or an abbreviated resettlement plan that is consistent with the provisions of the policy framework be submitted to the Bank for approval before the subproject is accepted for Bank financing.

30. For projects described in paras. 26–28 above, the Bank may agree, in writing, that subproject resettlement plans may be approved by the project implementing agency or a responsible government agency or financial intermediary without prior Bank review, if that agency has demonstrated adequate institutional capacity to review resettlement plans and ensure their consistency with this policy. Any such delegation, and appropriate remedies for the entity's approval of resettlement plans found not to be in compliance with Bank policy, are provided for in the legal agreements for the project. In all such cases, implementation of the resettlement plans is subject to ex post review by the Bank.

Process Framework

31. For projects involving restriction of access in accordance with para. 3(b) above, the borrower provides the Bank with a draft process framework that conforms to the relevant provisions of this policy as a condition of appraisal. In addition, during project implementation and prior to enforcing of the restriction, the borrower prepares a plan of action, acceptable to the Bank, describing the specific measures to be undertaken to assist the displaced persons and the arrangements for their implementation. The plan of action could take the form of a natural resources management plan prepared for the project.

Assistance to the Borrower

32. In furtherance of the objectives of this policy, the Bank may at a borrower's request support the borrower and other concerned entities by providing
   (a) assistance to assess and strengthen resettlement policies, strategies, legal frameworks, and specific plans at a country, regional, or sectoral level;
   (b) financing of technical assistance to strengthen the capacities of agencies responsible for resettlement, or of affected people to participate more effectively in resettlement operations;
   (c) financing of technical assistance for developing resettlement policies, strategies, and specific plans, and for implementation, monitoring, and evaluation of resettlement activities; and
   (d) financing of the investment costs of resettlement.

1

33. The Bank may finance either a component of the main investment causing displacement and requiring resettlement, or a free-standing resettlement project with appropriate cross-conditionalities, processed and implemented in parallel with the investment that causes the displacement. The Bank may finance resettlement even though it is not financing the main investment that makes resettlement necessary.

34. The Bank does not disburse against cash compensation and other resettlement assistance paid in cash, or against the cost of land (including compensation for land acquisition). However, it may finance the cost of land improvement associated with resettlement activities.

Notes

1. "Bank" includes IDA; "loans" includes credits, guarantees, Project Preparation Facility (PPF) advances and grants; and "projects" includes projects under (a) adaptable program lending; (b) learning and innovation loans; (c) PPFs and Institutional Development Funds (IDFs), if they include investment activities; (d) grants under the Global Environment Facility and Montreal Protocol, for which the Bank is the implementing/executing agency; and (e) grants or loans provided by other donors that are administered by the Bank. The term "project" does not include programs under adjustment operations. "Borrower" also includes, wherever the context requires, the guarantor or the project implementing agency.

2. In devising approaches to resettlement in Bank-assisted projects, other Bank policies should be taken into account, as relevant. These policies include OP 4.01 *Environmental Assessment*, OP 4.04 *Natural Habitats*, OP 4.11 *Safeguarding Cultural Property in Bank-Assisted Projects*, and OD 4.20 *Indigenous Peoples*.

3. The term "displaced persons" refers to persons who are affected in any of the ways described in para. 3 of this OP.

4. Displaced persons under para. 3(b) should be assisted in their efforts to improve or restore their livelihoods in a manner that maintains the sustainability of the parks and protected areas.

5. Where there are adverse indirect social or economic impacts, it is good practice for the borrower to undertake a social assessment and implement measures to minimize and mitigate adverse economic and social impacts, particularly upon poor and vulnerable groups. Other environmental, social, and economic impacts that do not result from land taking may be identified

1

and addressed through environmental assessments and other project reports and instruments.

6. This policy does not apply to restrictions of access to natural resources under community-based projects, i.e., where the community using the resources decides to restrict access to these resources, provided that an assessment satisfactory to the Bank establishes that the community decisionmaking process is adequate, and that it provides for identification of appropriate measures to mitigate adverse impacts, if any, on the vulnerable members of the community. This policy also does not cover refugees from natural disasters, war, or civil strife (see OP/BP 8.50, *Emergency Recovery Assistance*).

7. For purposes of this policy, "involuntary" means actions that may be taken without the displaced person's informed consent or power of choice.

8. "Land" includes anything growing on or permanently affixed to land, such as buildings and crops. This policy does not apply to regulations of natural resources on a national or regional level to promote their sustainability, such as watershed management, groundwater management, fisheries management, etc. The policy also does not apply to disputes between private parties in land titling projects, although it is good practice for the borrower to undertake a social assessment and implement measures to minimize and mitigate adverse social impacts, especially those affecting poor and vulnerable groups.

9. For the purposes of this policy, involuntary restriction of access covers restrictions on the use of resources imposed on people living outside the park or protected area, or on those who continue living inside the park or protected area during and after project implementation. In cases where new parks and protected areas are created as part of the project, persons who lose shelter, land, or other assets are covered under para. 3(a). Persons who lose shelter in existing parks and protected areas are also covered under para. 3(a).

10. The *Resettlement Sourcebook* (forthcoming) provides good practice guidance to staff on the policy.

11. "Replacement cost" is the method of valuation of assets that helps determine the amount sufficient to replace lost assets and cover transaction costs. In applying this method of valuation, depreciation of structures and assets should not be taken into account (for a detailed definition of replacement cost, see Annex A, footnote 1). For losses that cannot easily be valued or compensated for in monetary terms (e.g., access to public services, customers, and suppliers; or to fishing, grazing, or forest areas), attempts are made to establish access to equivalent and culturally acceptable resources and earning opportunities. Where domestic law does not meet the standard

1

of compensation at full replacement cost, compensation under domestic law is supplemented by additional measures necessary to meet the replacement cost standard. Such additional assistance is distinct from resettlement assistance to be provided under other clauses of para. 6.

12. If the residual of the asset being taken is not economically viable, compensation and other resettlement assistance are provided as if the entire asset had been taken.

13. The alternative assets are provided with adequate tenure arrangements. The cost of alternative residential housing, housing sites, business premises, and agricultural sites to be provided can be set off against all or part of the compensation payable for the corresponding asset lost.

14. Such support could take the form of short-term jobs, subsistence support, salary maintenance, or similar arrangements.

15. See OD 4.20, *Indigenous Peoples*.

16. See OP 4.04, *Natural Habitats*.

17. As a general principle, this applies if the land taken constitutes less than 20% of the total productive area.

18. Paras. 13–15 do not apply to impacts covered under para. 3(b) of this policy. The eligibility criteria for displaced persons under 3(b) are covered under the process framework (see paras. 7 and 30).

19. Such claims could be derived from adverse possession, from continued possession of public lands without government action for eviction (that is, with the implicit leave of the government), or from customary and traditional law and usage, and so on.

20. Resettlement assistance may consist of land, other assets, cash, employment, and so on, as appropriate.

21. Normally, this cutoff date is the date the census begins. The cutoff date could also be the date the project area was delineated, prior to the census, provided that there has been an effective public dissemination of information on the area delineated, and systematic and continuous dissemination subsequent to the delineation to prevent further population influx.

22. For projects that are highly risky or contentious, or that involve significant and complex resettlement activities, the borrower should normally engage an advisory panel of independent, internationally recognized resettlement specialists to advise on all aspects of the project relevant to the resettlement activities. The size, role, and frequency of meeting depend on the complexity of the resettlement. If independent technical advisory panels are established under OP 4.01, *Environmental Assessment*, the resettlement panel may form part of the environmental panel of experts.

23. See BP 17.50, *Disclosure of Operational Information* (forthcoming) for detailed disclosure procedures.

24. An exception to this requirement may be made in highly unusual circumstances (such as emergency recovery operations) with the approval of Bank Management (see BP 4.12, para. 8). In such cases, the Management's approval stipulates a timetable and budget for developing the resettlement plan.

25. Impacts are considered "minor" if the affected people are not physically displaced and less than 10% of their productive assets are lost.

26. For purpose of this paragraph, the term "subprojects" includes components and subcomponents.

1

OP 4.12—Annex A

1. This annex describes the elements of a resettlement plan, an abbreviated resettlement plan, a resettlement policy framework, and a resettlement process framework, as discussed in OP 4.12, paras. 17–31.

Resettlement Plan

2. The scope and level of detail of the resettlement plan vary with the magnitude and complexity of resettlement. The plan is based on up-to-date and reliable information about (a) the proposed resettlement and its impacts on the displaced persons and other adversely affected groups, and (b) the legal issues involved in resettlement. The resettlement plan covers the elements below, as relevant. When any element is not relevant to project circumstances, it should be noted in the resettlement plan.

3. *Description of the project.* General description of the project and identification of the project area.

4. *Potential impacts.* Identification of
   (a) the project component or activities that give rise to resettlement;
   (b) the zone of impact of such component or activities;
   (c) the alternatives considered to avoid or minimize resettlement; and
   (d) the mechanisms established to minimize resettlement, to the extent possible, during project implementation.

5. *Objectives.* The main objectives of the resettlement program.

6. *Socioeconomic studies.* The findings of socioeconomic studies to be conducted in the early stages of project preparation and with the involvement of potentially displaced people, including
   (a) the results of a census survey covering
      (i) current occupants of the affected area to establish a basis for the design of the resettlement program and to exclude subsequent inflows of people from eligibility for compensation and resettlement assistance;
      (ii) standard characteristics of displaced households, including a description of production systems, labor, and household organization; and baseline information on livelihoods (including, as relevant, production levels and income derived from both formal and informal economic activities) and standards of living (including health status) of the displaced population;
      (iii) the magnitude of the expected loss—total or partial—of assets, and the extent of displacement, physical or economic;

    (iv) information on vulnerable groups or persons as provided for in OP 4.12, para. 8, for whom special provisions may have to be made; and

    (v) provisions to update information on the displaced people's livelihoods and standards of living at regular intervals so that the latest information is available at the time of their displacement.

(b) Other studies describing the following

    (i) land tenure and transfer systems, including an inventory of common property natural resources from which people derive their livelihoods and sustenance, non-title-based usufruct systems (including fishing, grazing, or use of forest areas) governed by local recognized land allocation mechanisms, and any issues raised by different tenure systems in the project area;

    (ii) the patterns of social interaction in the affected communities, including social networks and social support systems, and how they will be affected by the project;

    (iii) public infrastructure and social services that will be affected; and

    (iv) social and cultural characteristics of displaced communities, including a description of formal and informal institutions (e.g., community organizations, ritual groups, nongovernmental organizations [NGOs]) that may be relevant to the consultation strategy and to designing and implementing the resettlement activities.

7. *Legal framework.* The findings of an analysis of the legal framework, covering

(a) the scope of the power of eminent domain and the nature of compensation associated with it, in terms of both the valuation methodology and the timing of payment;

(b) the applicable legal and administrative procedures, including a description of the remedies available to displaced persons in the judicial process and the normal timeframe for such procedures, and any available alternative dispute resolution mechanisms that may be relevant to resettlement under the project;

(c) relevant law (including customary and traditional law) governing land tenure, valuation of assets and losses, compensation, and natural resource usage rights; customary personal law related to displacement; and environmental laws and social welfare legislation;

(d) laws and regulations relating to the agencies responsible for implementing resettlement activities;

(e) gaps, if any, between local laws covering eminent domain and resettlement and the Bank's resettlement policy, and the mechanisms to bridge such gaps; and

(f) any legal steps necessary to ensure the effective implementation of resettlement activities under the project, including, as appropriate, a process for recognizing claims to legal rights to land—including claims that derive from customary law and traditional usage (see OP 4.12, para. 15b).

8. *Institutional framework.* The findings of an analysis of the institutional framework covering

(a) the identification of agencies responsible for resettlement activities and NGOs that may have a role in project implementation;

(b) an assessment of the institutional capacity of such agencies and NGOs; and

(c) any steps that are proposed to enhance the institutional capacity of agencies and NGOs responsible for resettlement implementation.

9. *Eligibility.* Definition of displaced persons and criteria for determining their eligibility for compensation and other resettlement assistance, including relevant cutoff dates.

10. *Valuation of and compensation for losses.* The methodology to be used in valuing losses to determine their replacement cost; and a description of the proposed types and levels of compensation under local law and such supplementary measures as are necessary to achieve replacement cost for lost assets.[1]

11. *Resettlement measures.* A description of the packages of compensation and other resettlement measures that will assist each category of eligible displaced persons to achieve the objectives of the policy (see OP 4.12, para. 6). In addition to being technically and economically feasible, the resettlement packages should be compatible with the cultural preferences of the displaced persons, and prepared in consultation with them.

12. *Site selection, site preparation, and relocation.* Alternative relocation sites considered and explanation of those selected, covering

(a) institutional and technical arrangements for identifying and preparing relocation sites, whether rural or urban, for which a combination of productive potential, locational advantages, and other factors is at least comparable to the advantages of the old sites, with an estimate of the time needed to acquire and transfer land and ancillary resources;

(b) any measures necessary to prevent land speculation or influx of ineligible persons at the selected sites;

(c) procedures for physical relocation under the project, including timetables for site preparation and transfer; and

(d) legal arrangements for regularizing tenure and transferring titles to resettlers.

13. *Housing, infrastructure, and social services.* Plans to provide (or to finance resettlers' provision of) housing, infrastructure (e.g., water supply, feeder roads), and social services (e.g., schools, health services);[2] plans to ensure comparable services to host populations; any necessary site development, engineering, and architectural designs for these facilities.

14. *Environmental protection and management.* A description of the boundaries of the relocation area; and an assessment of the environmental impacts of the proposed resettlement[3] and measures to mitigate and manage these impacts (coordinated as appropriate with the environmental assessment of the main investment requiring the resettlement).

15. *Community participation.* Involvement of resettlers and host communities,[4] including

(a) a description of the strategy for consultation with and participation of resettlers and hosts in the design and implementation of the resettlement activities;

(b) a summary of the views expressed and how these views were taken into account in preparing the resettlement plan;

(c) a review of the resettlement alternatives presented and the choices made by displaced persons regarding options available to them, including choices related to forms of compensation and resettlement assistance, to relocating as individual families or as parts of preexisting communities or kinship groups, to sustaining existing patterns of group organization, and to retaining access to cultural property (e.g. places of worship, pilgrimage centers, cemeteries);[5] and

(d) institutionalized arrangements by which displaced people can communicate their concerns to project authorities throughout planning and implementation, and measures to ensure that such vulnerable groups as indigenous people, ethnic minorities, the landless, and women are adequately represented.

16. *Integration with host populations.* Measures to mitigate the impact of resettlement on any host communities, including

(a) consultations with host communities and local governments;

(b) arrangements for prompt tendering of any payment due the hosts for land or other assets provided to resettlers;

(c) arrangements for addressing any conflict that may arise between resettlers and host communities; and

1

(d) any measures necessary to augment services (e.g., education, water, health, and production services) in host communities to make them at least comparable to services available to resettlers.

17. *Grievance procedures*. Affordable and accessible procedures for third-party settlement of disputes arising from resettlement; such grievance mechanisms should take into account the availability of judicial recourse and community and traditional dispute settlement mechanisms.

18. *Organizational responsibilities*. The organizational framework for implementing resettlement, including identification of agencies responsible for delivery of resettlement measures and provision of services; arrangements to ensure appropriate coordination between agencies and jurisdictions involved in implementation; and any measures (including technical assistance) needed to strengthen the implementing agencies' capacity to design and carry out resettlement activities; provisions for the transfer to local authorities or resettlers themselves of responsibility for managing facilities and services provided under the project and for transferring other such responsibilities from the resettlement implementing agencies, when appropriate.

19. *Implementation schedule*. An implementation schedule covering all resettlement activities from preparation through implementation, including target dates for the achievement of expected benefits to resettlers and hosts and terminating the various forms of assistance. The schedule should indicate how the resettlement activities are linked to the implementation of the overall project.

20. *Costs and budget*. Tables showing itemized cost estimates for all resettlement activities, including allowances for inflation, population growth, and other contingencies; timetables for expenditures; sources of funds; and arrangements for timely flow of funds, and funding for resettlement, if any, in areas outside the jurisdiction of the implementing agencies.

21. *Monitoring and evaluation*. Arrangements for monitoring of resettlement activities by the implementing agency, supplemented by independent monitors as considered appropriate by the Bank, to ensure complete and objective information; performance monitoring indicators to measure inputs, outputs, and outcomes for resettlement activities; involvement of the displaced persons in the monitoring process; evaluation of the impact of resettlement for a reasonable period after all resettlement and related development activities have been completed; using the results of resettlement monitoring to guide subsequent implementation.

Abbreviated Resettlement Plan

22. An abbreviated plan covers the following minimum elements:[6]
    (a) a census survey of displaced persons and valuation of assets;
    (b) description of compensation and other resettlement assistance to be provided;
    (c) consultations with displaced people about acceptable alternatives;
    (d) institutional responsibility for implementation and procedures for grievance redress;
    (e) arrangements for monitoring and implementation; and
    (f) a timetable and budget.

Resettlement Policy Framework

23. The purpose of the policy framework is to clarify resettlement principles, organizational arrangements, and design criteria to be applied to subprojects to be prepared during project implementation (see OP 4.12, paras. 26–28). Subproject resettlement plans consistent with the policy framework subsequently are submitted to the Bank for approval after specific planning information becomes available (see OP 4.12, para. 29).

24. The resettlement policy framework covers the following elements, consistent with the provisions described in OP 4.12, paras. 2 and 4:
    (a) a brief description of the project and components for which land acquisition and resettlement are required, and an explanation of why a resettlement plan as described in paras. 2–21 or an abbreviated plan as described in para. 22 cannot be prepared by project appraisal;
    (b) principles and objectives governing resettlement preparation and implementation;
    (c) a description of the process for preparing and approving resettlement plans;
    (d) estimated population displacement and likely categories of displaced persons, to the extent feasible;
    (e) eligibility criteria for defining various categories of displaced persons;
    (f) a legal framework reviewing the fit between borrower laws and regulations and Bank policy requirements and measures proposed to bridge any gaps between them;
    (g) methods of valuing affected assets;
    (h) organizational procedures for delivery of entitlements, including, for projects involving private sector intermediaries, the responsibilities of the financial intermediary, the government, and the private developer;

1

(i) a description of the implementation process, linking resettlement implementation to civil works;

(j) a description of grievance redress mechanisms;

(k) a description of the arrangements for funding resettlement, including the preparation and review of cost estimates, the flow of funds, and contingency arrangements;

(l) a description of mechanisms for consultations with, and participation of, displaced persons in planning, implementation, and monitoring; and

(m) arrangements for monitoring by the implementing agency and, if required, by independent monitors.

25. When a resettlement policy framework is the only document that needs to be submitted as a condition of the loan, the resettlement plan to be submitted as a condition of subproject financing need not include the policy principles, entitlements, and eligibility criteria, organizational arrangements, arrangements for monitoring and evaluation, the framework for participation, and mechanisms for grievance redress set forth in the resettlement policy framework. The subproject-specific resettlement plan needs to include baseline census and socioeconomic survey information; specific compensation rates and standards; policy entitlements related to any additional impacts identified through the census or survey; description of resettlement sites and programs for improvement or restoration of livelihoods and standards of living; implementation schedule for resettlement activities; and detailed cost estimate.

Process Framework

26. A process framework is prepared when Bank-supported projects may cause restrictions in access to natural resources in legally designated parks and protected areas. The purpose of the process framework is to establish a process by which members of potentially affected communities participate in design of project components, determination of measures necessary to achieve resettlement policy objectives, and implementation and monitoring of relevant project activities (see OP 4.12, paras. 7 and 31).

27. Specifically, the process framework describes participatory processes by which the following activities will be accomplished

(a) *Project components will be prepared and implemented.* The document should briefly describe the project and components or activities that may involve new or more stringent restrictions on natural resource use. It should also describe the process by which potentially displaced persons participate in project design.

(b) *Criteria for eligibility of affected persons will be determined.* The document should establish that potentially affected communities will be involved in identifying any adverse impacts, assessing of the significance of impacts, and establishing of the criteria for eligibility for any mitigating or compensating measures necessary.

(c) *Measures to assist affected persons in their efforts to improve their livelihoods or restore them, in real terms, to pre-displacement levels, while maintaining the sustainability of the park or protected area will be identified.* The document should describe methods and procedures by which communities will identify and choose potential mitigating or compensating measures to be provided to those adversely affected, and procedures by which adversely affected community members will decide among the options available to them.

(d) *Potential conflicts or grievances within or between affected communities will be resolved.* The document should describe the process for resolving disputes relating to resource use restrictions that may arise between or among affected communities, and grievances that may arise from members of communities who are dissatisfied with the eligibility criteria, community planning measures, or actual implementation.

Additionally, the process framework should describe arrangements relating to the following

(e) *Administrative and legal procedures.* The document should review agreements reached regarding the process approach with relevant administrative jurisdictions and line ministries (including clear delineation for administrative and financial responsibilities under the project).

(f) *Monitoring arrangements.* The document should review arrangements for participatory monitoring of project activities as they relate to (beneficial and adverse) impacts on persons within the project impact area, and for monitoring the effectiveness of measures taken to improve (or at minimum restore) incomes and living standards.

Notes

1. With regard to land and structures, "replacement cost" is defined as follows: For agricultural land, it is the pre-project or pre-displacement, whichever is higher, market value of land of equal productive potential or use located in the vicinity of the affected land, plus the cost of preparing the land to levels similar to those of the affected land, plus the cost of any registration and transfer taxes. For land in urban areas, it is the pre-displacement market

1

value of land of equal size and use, with similar or improved public infrastructure facilities and services and located in the vicinity of the affected land, plus the cost of any registration and transfer taxes. For houses and other structures, it is the market cost of the materials to build a replacement structure with an area and quality similar to or better than those of the affected structure, or to repair a partially affected structure, plus the cost of transporting building materials to the construction site, plus the cost of any labor and contractors' fees, plus the cost of any registration and transfer taxes. In determining the replacement cost, depreciation of the asset and the value of salvage materials are not taken into account, nor is the value of benefits to be derived from the project deducted from the valuation of an affected asset. Where domestic law does not meet the standard of compensation at full replacement cost, compensation under domestic law is supplemented by additional measures so as to meet the replacement cost standard. Such additional assistance is distinct from resettlement measures to be provided under other clauses in OP 4.12, para. 6.

2. Provision of health care services, particularly for pregnant women, infants, and the elderly, may be important during and after relocation to prevent increases in morbidity and mortality due to malnutrition, the psychological stress of being uprooted, and the increased risk of disease.

3. Negative impacts that should be anticipated and mitigated include, for rural resettlement, deforestation, overgrazing, soil erosion, sanitation, and pollution; for urban resettlement, projects should address such density-related issues as transportation capacity and access to potable water, sanitation systems, and health facilities.

4. Experience has shown that local NGOs often provide valuable assistance and ensure viable community participation.

5. OPN 11.03, *Management of Cultural Property in Bank-Financed Projects.*

6. In case some of the displaced persons lose more than 10% of their productive assets or require physical relocation, the plan also covers a socioeconomic survey and income restoration measures.

Involuntary Resettlement BP 4.12

Note: OP and BP 4.12 together replace OD 4.30, *Involuntary Resettlement*. This OP and BP apply to all projects for which a Project Concept Review takes place on or after January 1, 2002. Questions may be addressed to the Director, Social Development Department (SDV).

1. The planning of resettlement activities is an integral part of preparation for Bank-assisted projects.[1] During project identification, the task team (TT) identifies any potential involuntary resettlement[2] under the project. Throughout project processing, the TT consults the regional social development unit,[3] Legal Vice Presidency (LEG), and, as necessary, the Resettlement Committee (see para. 7 of this BP).

2. When a proposed project is likely to involve involuntary resettlement, the TT informs the borrower of the provisions of OP/BP 4.12. The TT and borrower staff
   (a) assess the nature and magnitude of the likely displacement;
   (b) explore all viable alternative project designs to avoid, where feasible, or minimize displacement;[4]
   (c) assess the legal framework covering resettlement and the policies of the government and implementing agencies (identifying any inconsistencies between such policies and the Bank's policy);
   (d) review past borrower and likely implementing agencies' experience with similar operations;
   (e) discuss with the agencies responsible for resettlement the policies and institutional, legal, and consultative arrangements for resettlement, including measures to address any inconsistencies between government or implementing agency policies and Bank policy; and
   (f) discuss any technical assistance to be provided to the borrower (see OP 4.12, para. 32).

3. Based on the review of relevant resettlement issues, the TT agrees with the Regional social development unit and LEG on the type of resettlement instrument (resettlement plan, abbreviated resettlement plan, resettlement policy framework, or process framework) and the scope and the level of detail required. The TT conveys these decisions to the borrower and also discusses with the borrower the actions necessary to prepare the resettlement instrument,[5] agrees on the timing for preparing the resettlement instrument, and monitors progress.

4. The TT summarizes in the Project Concept Document (PCD) and the Project Information Document (PID) available information on the nature and magnitude of displacement and the resettlement instrument to be used, and the TT periodically updates the PID as project planning proceeds.

5. For projects with impacts under para. 3(a) of OP 4.12, the TT assesses the following during project preparation:
   (a) the extent to which project design alternatives and options to minimize and mitigate involuntary resettlement have been considered;

1

(b) progress in preparing the resettlement plan or resettlement policy framework and its adequacy with respect to OP 4.12, including the involvement of affected groups and the extent to which the views of such groups are being considered;

(c) proposed criteria for eligibility of displaced persons for compensation and other resettlement assistance;

(d) the feasibility of the proposed resettlement measures, including provisions for sites if needed; funding for all resettlement activities, including provision of counterpart funding on an annual basis; the legal framework; and implementation and monitoring arrangements; and

(e) if sufficient land is not available in projects involving displaced persons whose livelihoods are land-based and for whom a land-based resettlement strategy is the preferred option, the evidence of lack of adequate land (OP 4.12, para. 11).

6. For projects with impacts under para. 3(b) of OP 4.12, the TT assesses the following during project preparation:

(a) the extent to which project design alternatives and options to minimize and mitigate involuntary resettlement have been considered; and

(b) progress in preparing the process framework and its adequacy in respect to OP 4.12, including the adequacy of the proposed participatory approach; criteria for eligibility of displaced persons; funding for resettlement; the legal framework; and implementation and monitoring arrangements.

7. The TT may request a meeting with the Resettlement Committee to obtain endorsement of, or guidance on, (a) the manner in which it proposes to address resettlement issues in a project, or (b) clarifications on the application and scope of this policy. The Committee, chaired by the vice president responsible for resettlement, includes the Director, Social Development Department, a representative from LEG, and two representatives from Operations, one of whom is from the sector of the project being discussed. The Committee is guided by the policy and, among other sources, the *Resettlement Sourcebook* (forthcoming), which will be regularly updated to reflect good practice.

Appraisal

8. The borrower submits to the Bank a resettlement plan, a resettlement policy framework, or a process framework that conforms with the requirements of OP 4.12, as a condition of appraisal for projects involving

1

involuntary resettlement (see OP 4.12, paras. 17–31). Appraisal may be authorized before the plan is completed in highly unusual circumstances (such as emergency recovery operations) with the approval of the Managing Director in consultation with the Resettlement Committee. In such cases, the TT agrees with the borrower on a timetable for preparing and furnishing to the Bank the relevant resettlement instrument that conforms with the requirements of OP 4.12.

9. Once the borrower officially transmits the draft resettlement instrument to the Bank, Bank staff—including the Regional resettlement specialists and the lawyer—review it, determine whether it provides an adequate basis for project appraisal, and advise the Regional sector management accordingly. Once approval for appraisal has been granted by the Country Director, the TT sends the draft resettlement instrument to the Bank's InfoShop.[6] The TT also prepares and sends the English language executive summary of the draft resettlement instrument to the Corporate Secretariat, under cover of a transmittal memorandum confirming that the executive summary and the draft resettlement instrument are subject to change during appraisal.

10. During project appraisal, the TT assesses (a) the borrower's commitment to and capacity for implementing the resettlement instrument; (b) the feasibility of the proposed measures for improvement or restoration of livelihoods and standards of living; (c) availability of adequate counterpart funds for resettlement activities; (d) significant risks, including risk of impoverishment, from inadequate implementation of the resettlement instrument; (e) consistency of the proposed resettlement instrument with the Project Implementation Plan; and (f) the adequacy of arrangements for internal, and if considered appropriate by the TT, independent monitoring and evaluation of the implementation of the resettlement instrument.[7] The TT obtains the concurrence of the Regional social development unit and LEG to any changes to the draft resettlement instrument during project appraisal. Appraisal is complete only when the borrower officially transmits to the Bank the final draft resettlement instrument conforming to Bank policy (OP 4.12).

11. In the Project Appraisal Document (PAD), the TT describes the resettlement issues, proposed resettlement instrument and measures, and the borrower's commitment to and institutional and financial capacity for implementing the resettlement instrument. The TT also discusses in the PAD the feasibility of the proposed resettlement measures and the risks associated with resettlement implementation. In the annex to the PAD, the TT summarizes the resettlement provisions, covering, inter alia, basic information on affected populations, resettlement measures, institutional

1

arrangements, timetable, budget, including adequate and timely provision of counterpart funds, and performance monitoring indicators. The PAD annex shows the overall cost of resettlement as a distinct part of project costs.

12. The project description in the Loan Agreement describes the resettlement component or subcomponent. The legal agreements provide for the borrower's obligation to carry out the relevant resettlement instrument and keep the Bank informed of project implementation progress.[8] At negotiations, the borrower and the Bank agree on the resettlement plan or resettlement policy framework or process framework. Before presenting the project to the Board, the TT confirms that the responsible authority of the borrower and any implementation agency have provided final approval of the relevant resettlement instrument.

Supervision

13. Recognizing the importance of close and frequent supervision[9] to good resettlement outcomes, the Regional vice president, in coordination with the relevant country director, ensures that appropriate measures are established for the effective supervision of projects with involuntary resettlement. For this purpose, the country director allocates dedicated funds to adequately supervise resettlement, taking into account the magnitude and complexity of the resettlement component or subcomponent and the need to involve the requisite social, financial, legal, and technical experts. Supervision should be carried out with due regard to the Regional Action Plan for Resettlement Supervision.[10]

14. Throughout project implementation the TL supervises the implementation of the resettlement instrument ensuring that the requisite social, financial, legal, and technical experts are included in supervision missions. Supervision focuses on compliance with the legal instruments, including the Project Implementation Plan and the resettlement instrument, and the TT discusses any deviation from the agreed instruments with the borrower and reports it to Regional Management for prompt corrective action. The TT regularly reviews the internal, and, where applicable, independent monitoring reports to ensure that the findings and recommendations of the monitoring exercise are being incorporated in project implementation. To facilitate a timely response to problems or opportunities that may arise with respect to resettlement, the TT reviews project resettlement planning and implementation during the early stages of project implementation. On the basis of the findings of this review, the TT engages the borrower in discussing and, if necessary,

amending the relevant resettlement instrument to achieve the objectives of this policy.

15. For projects with impacts covered under para. 3(b) of OP 4.12, the TT assesses the plan of action to determine the feasibility of the measures to assist the displaced persons to improve (or at least restore in real terms to pre-project or pre-displacement levels, whichever is higher) their livelihoods with due regard to the sustainability of the natural resource, and accordingly informs the Regional Management, the Regional social development unit, and LEG. The TL makes the plan of action available to the public through the InfoShop.

16. A project is not considered complete—and Bank supervision continues—until the resettlement measures set out in the relevant resettlement instrument have been implemented. Upon completion of the project, the Implementation Completion Report (ICR)[11] valuates the achievement of the objectives of the resettlement instrument and lessons for future operations and summarizes the findings of the borrower's assessment referred to in OP 4.12, para. 24.[12] If the evaluation suggests that the objectives of the resettlement instrument may not be realized, the ICR assesses the appropriateness of the resettlement measures and may propose a future course of action, including, as appropriate, continued supervision by the Bank.

Country Assistance Strategy

17. In countries with a series of operations requiring resettlement, the ongoing country and sector dialogue with the government should include any issues pertaining to the country's policy, institutional, and legal framework for resettlement. Bank staff should reflect these issues in country economic and sector work and in the Country Assistance Strategy.

Notes

1. "Bank" includes IDA; "loans" includes credits, guarantees, Project Preparation Facility (PPF) advances, and grants; and "projects" includes projects under (a) adaptable program lending; (b) learning and innovation loans; (c) PPFs and Institutional Development Funds (IDFs), if they include investment activities; (d) grants under the Global Environment Facility and Montreal Protocol for which the Bank is the implementing/executing agency; and (e) grants or loans provided by other donors that are administered by the Bank. The term "project" does not include programs under adjustment operations. "Borrower" also includes, wherever the context requires, the guarantor or the project implementing agency.

1

2. See OP 4.12, *Involuntary Resettlement.*

3. Unit or department in the Region responsible for resettlement issues.

4. The Bank satisfies itself that the borrower has explored all viable alternative project designs to avoid involuntary resettlement and, when it is not feasible to avoid such resettlement, to minimize the scale and impacts of resettlement (for example, realignment of roads or reduction in dam height may reduce resettlement needs). Such alternative designs should be consistent with other Bank policies.

5. Such actions may include, for example, developing procedures for establishing eligibility for resettlement assistance; conducting socioeconomic surveys and legal analyses; carrying out public consultation; identifying resettlement sites; evaluating options for improvement or restoration of livelihoods and standards of living; or, in the case of highly risky or contentious projects, engaging a panel of independent, internationally recognized resettlement specialists.

6. See BP 17.50, *Disclosure of Operational Information* (forthcoming) for detailed disclosure procedures.

7. For projects with impacts covered under para. 3(b) of OP 4.12, the analysis referred to in (b) and (d) above is carried out when the plan of action is furnished to the Bank (see para. 15 of this BP).

8. In the case of the resettlement policy framework, the borrower's obligation also includes preparing a resettlement plan in accordance with the framework, for each subproject giving rise to displacement, and furnishing it to the Bank for approval prior to implementation of the subproject.

9. See OP/BP 13.05, *Project Supervision.*

10. The Plan is prepared by the regional social development unit in consultation with the TTs and Legal.

11. See OP/BP 13.05, *Implementation Completion Report.*

12. The ICR's assessment of the extent to which resettlement objectives were realized is normally based on a socioeconomic survey of affected people conducted at the time of project completion, and takes into account the extent of displacement, and the impact of the project on the livelihoods of displaced persons and any host communities.

Checklist for Census Information

Persons:

- Aggregate number of individuals and households in each affected category
- Age, gender, occupation of every individual (see list of PAP categories vulnerable to census exclusion)

Property:
Personal property including details of ownership of

- structures: houses, farm buildings, shops, industrial structures, grain drying area, latrines
- land and type: irrigated or nonirrigated, woodlots, grassland, wasteland, etc. A description and estimate of the value of standing crops on land
- other: livestock, wells, trees

Public and common property:

- land: village common lands, gathering and foraging areas, fishing areas, etc.
- structures and facilities: schools, health facilities, burial grounds, panchayats, temples, community centers, public transport, banks, co-ops
- infrastructure: drinking and other water systems, access and internal roads, electricity and other power sources

PAP incomes from other sources, including:

- farm-based income
- off-farm labor
- informal sector activities

Source: India Resettlement Handbook, World Bank, 1995, p. 39

Appendix 3

Census Forms

Table 1 Data to Be Collected on All Affected Households in Census or Combined Census/Socioeconomic Survey

Serial #	ID #	Name of head of household	Names of Other Eligible Household members (*)	Total # of Household members	District Location	Block & Plot no.	Impact	
1	345	Sunil Patel	Dipak Patel Sandya Patel	6	Malgudi district	Block*: Plot # 3456, Ram Marg	Irrigated 3 ha	Unirrigated 4 ha F/H

Source: India Resettlement Handbook, World Bank, 1995, Annex 3.

(*) = where applicable
(**) = Legend for tenure categories:
F/H = freehold title
L/H = lease holder
TEN/SC = sharecropping or other tenancy arrangement
CUST/USU = usufruct rights and customary occupancy
S/E = squatters/encroachers, without legal title

Land acquired		House area		Primary source of income	Secondary source of income	Estimated PAF total income	Estimated cash compensation (*)				Other cash entitlements	
Irrigated	Unirrigated	Acquired	Not acquired				Irrigated	Unirrigated	House	Improvements	Relocation grant	Subsistence (Y or N)
2 ha.	3 ha.	60 m²	0 m²	Farm: sharecropping	• Weaving • Bicycle repairs	R. 1700 per month (or per year where incomes have seasonal variation)	R.****	R.****	R.****	R.****	R. 2000	N

(*) Surveys should set out the per unit costs on compensation (e.g., per sq.m. of irrigated/unirrigated land; per sq.m of different quality dwellings)

Other non-cash entitlements		House type and quality (*)	Impact category under C.I. R&R policy (**)
# eligible for job	# eligible for training		
1	4	Type 2: good quality	A (i) + A (ii)

(*) House quality legend:
Type 1: permanent dwelling (e.g., pukka: brick walls, concrete roof)
Type 2: semi-permanent (e.g., brick walls, titled or thatched roof)
Type 3: temporary dwelling (e.g., kuccha: wooden frame, thatched roof)

3

Table 2 Subproject Level Data Summary Table (by Village)

Name of village	No. of PAFs under Coal India Compensation and Rehabilitation policy categories (*) and (**)					No. of PAPs eligible for jobs	Total no. of PAFs (***)	Total land and amount acquired			
	A (i)	A (ii)	B (i)	B (ii)	B (iii)			Private—total and acquired	Revenue—total and acquired	Common—total and acquired	Forest—total and acquired
Malgudi	800 (4000)	1200 (5200)	2000 (8000)	800 (3800)	400 (1600)	750	4200 (19,060)	– 2000 ha. Total – 1600 ha. acquired	– 250 ha. Total – 200 ha. acquired	– 100 ha. Total – 90 ha. acquired	– 250 ha. Total – 100 ha. acquired

(*) Legend for PAP categories: (These categories are only indicative and would vary by project)

A (i) = person from whom land acquired, including tribals cultivating under traditional rights

A (ii) = person whose homestead is acquired

B (i) = sharecroppers, land lessees, tenants, and day laborers

B (ii) = landless tribals

B (iii) = persons without title whose homestead is lost

(**) = Numbers in brackets are total PAPs in households in each category

(***) = Total PAF and PAP numbers less than A (i) – B (iii) totaled due to overlapping impact categories

Age categories (no. of PAPs)			
0–15	15–32	33–59	60+
3,500	5,030	7,075	3,455

Occupational categories (no. of PAFs)				
Ag. Self employed	Ag. wage labor	Non-land self-employed	Non-land wage labor	Others
4,326	7,547	887	377	23

Income categories (no. of PAFs)			
Below poverty line	Poor	Middle	Well off
1032	2398	602	167

Table 3 Subproject Level Public Facilities/Services and Common Resources Acquired for Projects

Village no.	Village name	Schools	Health clinics	Public buildings	Religious buildings	Common grazing areas	Rivers and/or river access	Forests with foraging access	Roads—tarred and unsealed
3–15	Malgudi	1 (10 rooms for 500 primary and secondary students)	2 with basic primary care facilities (3 rooms each)	– 1 panchayat of 60 sq. m. – 1 community center of 30 sq. m	– 1 mosque – 1 temple	50 ha.	River 2 kms. away with fishing access	25 ha.	– 1 tarred access road; – 2 dirt roads

Table 4: Detailed Household Level Data from Sampled Survey or Combined Census and Socioeconomic Survey (i.e., Less Than c. 500 PAFs)

ID #	PAPs in household	Economically active		Age	Level of Education (*)	Income generating skills	Type of employment	Estimated total PAP income
		Full time	Part time					
345-1	Sunil Patel	Y	Y	48	N-I	Farming	Sharecrop	R. 600
345-2	Ratna Patel	Y	N	40	N-I	Weaving	Weaver coop	R. 400
345-3	Dipak Patel	Y	Y	22	M-L	Farming	Vege. Plot	R. 450
345-4	Sandya Patel	N	Y	18	M-L	Weaving	At home	R. 150
345-5	Ritu Patel	N	N	8	P-L	None		
345-6	Dilip Patel	N	Y	14	M-L	Bicycle repairs	At home	R. 100

Level of education legend:

L = literate
I = illiterate
N = no or less than 2 years formal schooling
P = primary school

M = middle school
H = high school
G = graduate

Distance to Drinking water	Distance to school	Distance to health facility	Distance to transport	Distance to work
0.6 km	0.85 km	1.3 km	3 km	0 km

Appendix 4

Terms of Reference for a Socioeconomic Study

Introduction

1. The Upper Indravati Hydro Project is located in the Koraput and Kalahandi districts of Orissa. In addition to generating 600 MW of electricity, it is also expected to irrigate 1.09 lakh ha of land. The foundation of the dam was laid in April 1978, though the environmental clearance was provided by the Environmental Appraisal Committee of the Department of Science and Technology, Government of India, only in 1979.

2. The catchment area of the project is about 2,630 sq km and the reservoir is expected to cover 12,865 ha. About 25,000 people living in 95 villages (44 in Koraput district and 51 in Kalahandi) were expected to be affected. Of these, 65 villages (31 in Koraput and 34 in Kalahandi) were to come under total submergence necessitating displacement of people, while in the other 30 villages only some agricultural land was to come under submergence.

3. The evacuation of project-affected persons—2,793 from Koraput and 2,528 from Kalahandi—has taken place in four phases in 1989, 1990, 1991, and 1992. The cutoff date for inclusion as PAPs has been fixed as January 1 of these years when evacuation took place.

4. The resettlement of the PAPs who were evacuated was an unorganized process and the PAPs had, on their *own*, settled *down* over a widespread area in four districts—Koraput, Kalahandi, Malkangiri, and Navrangpura—in 560 dusters. Of these 560 dusters, only 163 have more than 10 PAPs each with a total of 4,191. These dusters are eligible to receive the provision of social infrastructure.

5. The other clusters that have less than 10 PAPs are not eligible for social infrastructure. They are to depend on the facilities that are available within the "host villages," and this may affect not only the relations between the resettlers and the hosts, but also the effectiveness of the social infrastructure.

6. It is also not possible for the project authorities to correctly assess the actual number of PAPs as the process of including "major sons" is still

going on. Since the resettlement was an unorganized process, it is also not possible to assess the impact of the package of entitlements provided by the Government of Orissa on the socioeconomic conditions of the PAPs and the social infrastructure of the clusters in which they live, as they are too widespread.

7. Since the Government of Orissa's aim is to "improve or at least restore" the living standards, earning capacity, and production levels of the PAPs, a socioeconomic study is planned. Since a majority of the PAPs are *Adivasis*, the government has also concluded that they do not suffer from the project and that they are resettled and rehabilitated with emphasis on their social and cultural identity.

8. A socioeconomic study is expected not only to provide the actual number of affected persons, the impact of the government's efforts on their living standards and access to social infrastructure, but also the social, economic, and cultural factors that influence the process of their development through resettlement and rehabilitation.

Objectives of the Study

9. The objectives of the study are:

(i)   to develop a clear definition of "project-affected persons";
(ii)   to see whether all such persons have been included as project-affected persons;
(iii)   to see whether all PAPs who have been identified so far have received all benefits of the package;
(iv)   to assess the impact of the package on their living standards;
(v)   to see whether all clusters with more than 10 PAPs have adequate social infrastructure;
(vi)   to suggest ways to provide access to social infrastructure not only to these PAPs, but also to others in the clusters and "host" villages; and
(vii)   suggest appropriate policies that would help the PAPs not only to improve or regain their former living standards, but also to participate in this process.

The Study

10. The study will cover all the 5,321 PAPs and others who can be classified as PAPs and who live in the project-affected areas, and the 560 clusters. The study will administer individual family profile for all the PAPs and cluster profile for all the 560 clusters (Annexes 1 and 2).

Scope of the Study

11. On the basis of the interpretation and analysis of data, details, and information collected, the study is expected to provide inputs for policy formulation so that appropriate decisions could be made for the resettlement and rehabilitation of the project-affected persons. The study, in particular, should provide the following:

    (i)   demarcation of project-affected areas that are directly and indirectly affected by the project;
    (ii)   definition of project-affected persons and their actual number;
    (iii)   assessment of actual number of PAPs who have received all benefits of the package and have purchased the land;
    (iv)   assessment of actual number of PAPs who have received only a part of the package and the reasons for not receiving the entire package;
    (v)   assessment of the socioeconomic impact of the package on those who have received it fully and those who have received it partly;
    (vi)   assessment of the socioeconomic conditions of those who have purchased land and what could be done to improve their standards of living;
    (vii)   assessment of the impact of displacement of community's access to minor forest produce including fodder and firewood;
    (viii) assessment of impact of displacement on women's role and status;
    (ix)   assessment of the socioeconomic impact of the acquisition of different types of land, including forest land, on the PAPs in general and the Adivasi PAPs in particular;
    (x)   suggestions for improving the socioeconomic conditions of the PAPs, including women;
    (xi)   assessment of availability of social infrastructure within the clusters where PAPs have resettled or their access in the "host villages" and their impacts on use by the "host" community;
    (xii)   assessment of the possibility of regrouping the clusters so that PAPs have increased opportunities for improving their living standards and access to social infrastructure;
    (xiii) assessment of availability of adequate land from "willing sellers" for resettlement and rehabilitation;
    (xiv)   assessment of choices expressed by the PAPs for their resettlement and rehabilitation; and
    (xv)   suggestions for policy so that the socioeconomic and cultural conditions of the PAPs could be improved with their own participation.

Methodology of the Study

12. The study would use secondary data (census, land records, etc.) in addition to generating its own data through the *administration* of PAP Family Profiles and Resettlement Cluster Profiles in the field with emphasis on observation and discussion with the community, government officials, non-government officials, etc.

13. A Participatory Rural Appraisal, with the involvement of the community of the Village/Resettlement Clusters including its common resources and social infrastructure, would be an important aspect of the methodology if the community is organized, able and willing to participate. This is particularly so, as it will enable them to fully understand the process of their resettlement and rehabilitation.

14. While analyzing and interpreting data, it is necessary to give equal weight to quantitative and qualitative aspects so that it reflects a balanced reality of the situation.

15. At the end of the study, before the report is formally submitted, the findings are to be presented in a seminar. It is also necessary to provide all data, tables, etc., in dBase.

Source: India Upper Indravati Hydropower Project (n.d.), World Bank.

4

Matrix of Resettlement Impacts

Item	Unit	Hubei	Hunan	Jiangxi	Total
General					
Affected Counties	Units	16	7	6	29
Affected Township	Units	31	13	19	63
Affected Village	Units	84	52	36	172
A. Resettlement					
A1. Households to be resettled	Households	5,400	4,464	2,735	12,599
Urban Households	Households	3,216		1,556	4,772
A2. Population to be resettled	People	22,100	19,213	11,546	52,859
Urban Resettlers	People	12,871		6,037	18,908
A3. Houses needed to be replaced	sq. meters	802,216	1,028,956.76	472,074.18	2,303,247
A3.1 Enterprise Structures	sq. meters	400,331	249,215.44	235,014.73	884,561.20
Frame-structure	sq. meters	41,555		22,601.10	64,156.10
Brick-concrete-structure	sq. meters	201,509	125,724.25	174,010.50	501,243.80
Brick-wood structure	sq. meters	152,814	111,571.20	37,240.80	301,626
Wood (earth) structure	sq. meters		530.40		530.40
Miscellaneous	sq. meters	4,453	11,389.59	1,162.33	17,004.92
A3.2 Private house	sq. meters	401,885	779,741.32	237,059.45	1,418,686
Brick-concrete structure	sq. meters	160,454	210,157.43	132,198.75	502,810.20
Brick-wood structure	sq. meters	201,534	373,483.28	90,510.10	665,527.40
Wood (earth) structure	sq. meters		9,485.00		9,485.00
Miscellaneous	sq. meters	39,897	186,615.61	14,350.60	240,863.20
A4. Other fixed assets					
Fence wall	sq. meters	60,254	87,386.00	43,137.90	190,777.90
Ground	sq. meters	97,881	160,030.70	77,926.50	335,838.20
Water pool	sq. meters		4,927.90		4,927.864
Tower	sq. meters	66		35.30	101.30
Water well	pieces	122	1240	25	1386.937
Pressed-water well	pieces	227		444	671.40
Tomb	pieces	250	4408	1381	6039
Simple building	pieces	500		1364	1864.20

Item	Unit	Hubei	Hunan	Jiangxi	Total
A5 Trees (including fruits, timber)	mu	56783	143903	8812	209497.80
B. *Land*	mu	11334	18577.68	7786.60	37698.28
B1. Irrigation land	mu	2649	3054.16	5162.40	10865.56
B2. Dry soil	mu	3876	7085.53		10961.53
B3. Vegetable land	mu		2738.48		2738.48
B4. Water pond	mu	2246	1213.44	362.60	3822.04
B5. Frost	mu	844	2442.63	293	3579.63
B6. Hacienda	mu		466.25		466.25
B7. Land for house	mu		1577.19		1577.19
B8. Miscellaneous	mu	1719		1968.60	3687.60
C. *Infrastructure*					
C1. Traffic facilities					
a. concrete road surface	km	12.67			12.67
b. simple road	km	11.15	69.24		80.39
c. machine-plough road	km		43.62		43.62
C2. Electrical facilities					
a. low voltage transmission lines	km	118.03	124.72	7.98	250.73
b. 10 kV electrical transmission line	km	30.09	49.60	6.19	85.88
c. 35 kV electrical transmission line	km	3.60			3.60
d. transformation device	pc		9.70		9.70
C3. Telephone lines		379.50	109.59	28.78	517.87
C4. Broadcasting lines	km	99	23.68		122.68
C5. Water mains	km	5.63	3.90		9.530

Source: China Yangtze Basin Flood Control Project, Draft Final RAP, Executive Summary.

Appendix 6

Resettlement Entitlement Matrix

Project Impact	Affected Population/Entity	Compensation Policy	Other Measures
Loss of arable land resulting from permanent land acquisition	Arable land, vegetable garden, trees and orchard areas, reservoirs/ponds, located in the path of dyke strengthening and the farmer and worker population working these land areas	• Provision of equivalent land nearby (if available) • Cash compensation to village for arable land for both more and less than 1 mu per family categories (compensation unit prices based on output value of cultivated land, land compensation times, and relative land management regulations) • Detailed compensation rates in Table 3-2	• Readjustment of village land within affected villages and host villages where applicable • Use of cash compensation for farm intensification, crop diversification and other land development and agricultural extension techniques for more efficient use of land
Loss of land from temporary land acquisition	Arable and cultivable land located in the path of dyke strengthening	• Compensation for temporary land acquisition based on the annual output of the leased land plus the costs associated with land preparation and re-cultivation • Detailed compensation rates in Table 3-2	• Return of temporary land to the land user after use
Loss of settlements (including housing, auxiliary scattered trees and transfer subsidy)	Housing and auxiliary buildings in the path of dyke strengthening and the residential population living in the houses	• Compensation for housing including private housing (rural and urban) • Replacement land for households to be provided within the original village (internal settlement), if available • If replacement land not available provide alternative household enterprise location as close to the original location as possible (collective resettlement) • House-for house replacement in urban areas • Cash compensation based on original house	• Building materials may be salvaged from old housing or enterprise building to be utilized in new structures • Assistance to be provided to the resettlers in procurement of labor and material for construction of new housing • Provisions to be made for temporary housing and financial assistance accorded where rental support needed for temporary accommodation • Transportation/relocation allowance to be provided to the resettlers on household basis

Project Impact	Affected Population/Entity	Compensation Policy	Other Measures
Loss of crops	Crops located in the path of dyke strengthening	• Cash compensation to affected farmers based on the average of the previous three years production value	• Crop loss to be minimized to the extent possible by avoiding acquisition during harvesting
Loss of enterprises	Enterprise and workers employed with the enterprises	• Compensation for land and reconstruction of enterprises' structure/buildings and facilities • Compensation for loss in production and relocation of enterprises • Detailed compensation rates in Table 3-2	• Provision for continuance of employment of workers affected from enterprise relocation during the transition period through provision of temporary premises, or compensation for lost wages
Loss of settlement utilities	Water supply, power, and sanitation in resettled houses and enterprises	• Compensation for reconstruction or reconnection to water supply/sanitation and electricity (previous infrastructure) • Detailed compensation rates in Table 3-2	
Loss of public infrastructure	Roads, power supply, water supply, telecommunication, and media broadcast facilities in the affected areas	• Compensation to owners/operators for infrastructure replacement • Detailed compensation rates in Table 3-2	• Prompt allocation of land for reconstruction of public infrastructure including labor and material
Impact to vulnerable groups	Elderly, orphans, widows, and female headed households being resettled	• Additional cash allowances provided to vulnerable and economically disadvantaged groups • Detailed compensation rates in Table 3-2	• Prompt payment to vulnerable and economically disadvantaged groups early in the resettlement process
Loss of cultural property	No significant impacts arising from the project	• Not applicable	• Not applicable

Source: China Yangtze Basin Flood Control Project, Draft Final RAP, Executive Summary

Based on:
(a) *Land Management Act of the People's Republic of China, 1998*
(b) *Water Act of the People's Republic of China, 1988*
(c) *Land Compensation and Resettlement Regulation for Large and Medium-Sized Water Conservancy & Hydropower Projects, State Council promulgated Order No. 74, February 15, 1991*
(d) *Design Regulation for Flooded Reservoir Area Treatment at Water Conservancy and Hydropower Projects, 1985, the Ministry of Hydropower*
(e) *Investigation Details for the Reservoir-Flooded Physical Substances at Water Conservancy and Hydropower Project, the Ministry of Hydropower, 1986*
(f) *Standards for Village/Town Planning, the Ministry of Construction, September 27, 1993; Classification of Villages and Towns; Standards for Construction-Occupied Land*
(g) *Hunan Province Land Management Implementation Method, Hunan Province, April 28, 1992, Chapter 4, Land for National Construction*
(h) *Hubei Province Land Management Implementation Method, Hubei Province, September 3, 1987*
(i) *Jiangxi Province Implementation of Land Management Act, July 15, 1989, Chapter 4—Land for Use in State Construction*

6

Appendix 7

Resettlement Budget

Summary of Cost Estimates for Elevation 275m Relocatees
(in thousands yuan)

Descriptions	Total	Henan	Shanxi	Other
I. Rural Area	329,253.51	242,334.82	86,918.69	
1. Allowance for land compensation	145,749.98	103,315.12	42,434.86	
2. Rural residential sites relocation	169,987.81	129,322.06	40,665.75	
(a) Houses	104,500.85	78,155.25	26,345.60	
(b) Others	65,486.96	51,166.81	14,320.15	
3. Compensation for agricultural sidelines	3,494.38	1,973.76	1,520.62	
4. Compensation for small-sized hydraulic facilities	10,021.34	7,723.88	2,297.46	
II. Town Relocation	16,817.63	9,899.73	69,179	
1. Houses	10,450.91	5,764.95	4,685.96	
2. Others	6,366.72	4,134.78	2,231.94	
III. Cost of Industrial and Mineral Enterprises and Road Relocation	124,128.52	97,067.92	27,060.60	
1. Institutes outside towns	1,450.91	776.55	674.36	
2. Compensation for industrial and mineral enterprises	85,360.00	70,136.00	15,224.00	
3. Cost of the special items such as roads	37,317.61	26,155.37	11,162.24	
(a) Road	27,449.85	19,267.69	8,182.16	
(b) Power	5,928.82	3,985.52	1,943.30	
(c) Communication	988.71	732.38	256.33	
(d) Broadcasting	1,185.79	886.78	299.01	
(e) Compensation for pumping station in the reservoir	130.00	130		
(f) Compensation for ferries and ferryboats	73.00	73.00		
(g) Restoring the transportation in the reservoir	1,561.44	1,080.00	481.44	
IV. Reservoir Clearance and Public Health	1,251.00	909.35	341.65	
V. Compensation for Special Items	2,484.82	1,925.34	559.48	
VI. Relocation and Construction Cost for the Large Special Items above County Level	16,897.48			16,897.48
VII. Overhead Cost	7,469.05			74,609.05
(a) Implementation management	12,724.99			14,724.99
(b) Reconnaissance and design	7,362.49			7,362.49
(c) Reconnaissance and design of design institute	6,184.50			6,184.50
(d) Scientific studying	2,454.16			2,454.16
(e) Supervision and monitoring	4,908.33			4,908.33
(f) Technical training	1,646.27			1,646.27
(g) Contingency	34,358.31			34,358.31
(h) Counterpart funds with the World Bank	1,050.00			1,050.00
(i) Startup cost for resettlement agencies	1,920.00			1,920.00
VIII. Taxes for Farmland Occupation	16,425.03	12,340.86	4,084.17	
Total	581,867.04	364,478.02	125,882.49	91,506.53

Note: (8.2872 Chinese yuan renminbi = US$1.00).
Source: China Xiaolangdi Resettlement Project RAP, pp. 81–2.

Resettlement Timetable

Actions	1994	1995				1996				1997				1998			
	4Q	1Q	2Q	3Q	4Q	1Q	2Q	3Q	4Q	1Q	2Q	3Q	4Q	1Q	2Q	3Q	4Q
1 Inform local governments and affected persons																	
2 Conduct census survey																	
3 Conduct socio-economic survey																	
4 Obtain permissions																	
5 Approve land acquisition and borrowing																	
6 Sign contracts with local governments for LA&R																	
7 Finalize compensation and resettlement strategies																	
8 Finalize relocation sites (residential and industrial)																	
9 Fix compensation levels																	
10 Pay compensation																	
11 Complete construction of resettlement sites																	
12 Transfer people to new sites; relocate enterprises																	
13 Provide jobs to eligible persons																	
14 Demolition of buildings																	
15 Start construction																	

Source: China Second Shanghai Sewerage Project, Appraisal Report, Vol. 5, RAP, p. 70, July 1995.

8

Appendix 9

Resettlement Supervision Guidelines

1. This note provides generic TORs for what should be supervised about the resettlement component during upcoming missions and reported back as an attachment to Form 590s. Field visits to departure and receiving sites are a critical part of resettlement supervision, and adequate field time should be allocated to the resettlement component. Taking a resettlement specialist may be most useful for projects that involve significant displacement or particularly complex resettlement components.

2. The Bank's overall policy objective is to help people displaced by project activities restore or improve their income and productivity capacity. Thus, supervision should focus on whether executing agencies have developed a resettlement action plan able to achieve this goal, and on its implementation status. The main points to be addressed are:
   (i)   restoration of pre-displacement income levels;
   (ii)   organizational capacity for resettlement and follow-up;
   (iii) physical progress of relocation work;
   (iv)   consultation with affected people;
   (v)   compensation;
   (vi)   project-specific issues.
   To assist with the supervision work, a few, more detailed items are suggested for supervision for each of the above points, to be used as appropriate.

3. *Income Restoration*—Given the Bank's policy objectives of restoring lost incomes, supervision mission should concentrate on the following key items:
   (i)   Is there accurate baseline information of what pre-move income levels are?
   (ii)   Do the proposals amount to an appropriate set of measures to restore incomes?
   (iii) Are people's living standards and income levels being adequately monitored by the project authorities? and
   (iv)   In the mission's judgment, how long will it take for resettlers to recover their test living standards, and what measures will sustain them until then?

Where resettlement is land-based, missions should assess the quality of the studies done, the amount and pace of land identification, and how the acceptability of replacement land is evaluated. Proposals for using non-land-based income generating schemes either alone or in combination with land should be reviewed for the success of their performance.

4. *Baseline Numbers*—Missions should obtain the most up-to-date estimates of the numbers of people to be affected by loss of land, loss of house, or both. Where the basis for the resettlement estimate is not clear, they should ask the borrower to explain how the number was obtained, and the criteria used to determine when people only partially affected by the project are eligible for resettlement.

5. *Resettlement Organization*—Mission should (a) identify the position of the resettlement organization or unit within the overall project management structure; (b) assess the adequacy, numbers, and skills of resettlement staff; (c) review the efficiency of mechanisms that coordinate the different agencies involved in resettlement; (d) assess the usefulness of the role played by NGOs and local organizations and, where appropriate, indicate how it can be improved.

6. *Resettlement Budget*—Missions should review and evaluate detailed resettlement budgets. Resettlement budgets should at a minimum be divided into public and private compensation, and redevelopment costs for the resettled families. Missions should assess (a) the adequacy of overall resettlement budget; (b) actual expenditures; (c) per capita budgeted expenditure for resettlement; (d) provisions for adjusting budgets; (e) the availability of resources for field staff; (f) the causes of cost overruns or budgetary shortfalls. You may also wish to consult the technical annexes to World Bank Technical Paper No. 80 Involuntary Resettlement in Development Projects for more detailed financial and economic guidelines; it is available in Spanish, French, and English.

7. *Timetables*—The first, critical element to review is whether progress on the resettlement action program is proceeding in tandem with the main investment that is causing the displacement. Supervision should evaluate actual versus planned resettlement performance, and match deviations from the resettlement schedule against the overall project timetable. A second timetable concern refers to the adequacy of preparation of resettlement sites when resettlers are moved there, and supervision should assess both the mechanism to signal that preparation is ready as well as its effectiveness.

8. *Monitoring*—Supervision should review the work done by the project's monitoring systems. What is the methodology used to obtain data, who receives it, how is it processed through the executing agency, and how could it be improved?

9

9. *Consultation*—Resettlement plans normally include mechanisms for grievance/dispute resolution. Areas of particular concern include asset compensation, integration of resettlers with their host villagers, and timely delivery of promised benefits. Missions should check to see that such mechanisms do in fact exist, and are working.

10. *Compensation*—Common compensation issues include (a) whether compensation is at replacement cost; (b) compensation eligibility; (c) the efficiency of its delivery to the affected people; (d) hidden charges against compensation; (e) compensation for public property and private businesses.

11. Handover Concerns—Successful resettlement involves transferring all administrative responsibilities to the resettled people and their representatives. How will this be accomplished? Is there an adequate, phased program to devolve responsibilities, including budgetary resources?

12. *Proposals*—Progress to date, as well as difficulties and problems with the resettlement component that are identified by the supervision mission, should be discussed with the borrower in order to agree on actions for the next 6–8 months that will bring the resettlement into line with project agreements and policy guidelines.

13. *Reporting*—Detailed back-to-office reports should review the above points, and include proposals for what the Bank could do to provide technical or other assistance.

9

Glossary

Eminent Domain. The right of the state to acquire land, using its sovereign power, for public purpose. National law establishes which public agencies have the prerogative to exercise eminent domain.

Land Acquisition. The process of acquiring land under the legally mandated procedures of eminent domain.

Grievance Procedures. The processes established under law, local regulations, or administrative decision to enable property owners and other displaced persons to redress issues related to acquisition, compensation, or other aspects of resettlement.

Resettlement Strategy (Rehabilitation Strategy). The approaches used to assist people in their efforts to improve (or at least to restore) their incomes, livelihoods, and standards of living in real terms after resettlement. The resettlement strategy typically consists of payment of compensation at replacement cost, transition support arrangements, relocation to new sites (if applicable), provision of alternative income-generating assets (if applicable), and assistance to help convert income-generating assets into income streams.

Resettlement (Action) Plan. A resettlement action plan [RAP] is the planning document that describes what will be done to address the direct social and economic impacts associated with involuntary taking of land.

Stakeholders. A broad term that covers all parties affected by or interested in a project or a specific issue—in other words, all parties who have a stake in a particular issue or initiative. **Primary stakeholders** are those most directly affected—in resettlement situations, the population that loses property or income because of the project and host communities. Other people who have an interest in the project—such as the project authority itself, the beneficiaries of the project (e.g., urban consumers for a hydro-power project), and interested NGOs are termed **secondary stakeholders.**

Displaced Persons. The people or entities directly affected by a project through the loss of land and the resulting loss of residences, other structures, businesses, or other assets.

Relocatees, Relocated Communities, or *Resettlers.* Those groups of people who have to physically move to new locations as a result of a project.

Host Community (Hosts). The population in the areas receiving resettlers is called the host community or the **hosts.**

Project-Affected Family. Any family (household) that loses a home, land, or business interests because of land acquisition.

Eligibility. The criteria for qualification to receive benefits under a resettlement program.

Resettlement Entitlements. Resettlement entitlements with respect to a particular eligibility category are the sum total of compensation and other forms of assistance provided to displaced persons in the respective eligibility category.

Population Census. A complete and accurate count of the population that will be affected by land acquisition and related impacts. When properly conducted, the population census provides the basic information necessary for determining eligibility for compensation.

Asset Inventory. A complete count and description of all property that will be acquired.

Socioeconomic Survey (SES). A complete and accurate survey of the project-affected population. The survey focuses on income-earning activities and other socioeconomic indicators.

Initial Baseline Survey. The population census, asset inventory, and socioeconomic survey together constitute the baseline survey of the affected population.

Economic Rehabilitation. Economic Rehabilitation implies the measures taken for **income restoration** or economic recovery so that the affected population can improve or at least restore its previous standard of living.

Task Manager or *Task Team Leader.* In Bank parlance, the officer in charge of a Bank-supported project or activity.

Project Cycle. The process of identifying, planning, approving, and implementing a Bank-supported development activity. In the World Bank, the project cycle is divided into the following stages: **Identification, Preparation, Appraisal, Negotiations, Approval, Loan Effectiveness,** and **Implementation.**

Index

A

abbreviated RPs, 99, 389
acquisition of land, *see* land acquisition
action plan, *see* resettlement plan (RP)
administrative and legal procedures
    financing and costs, 189, 195–96
    linear projects, 316–18
    process framework, 32
    replacement costs, 53
    staffing, DP census and inventory of
        assets, 211–12
    urban resettlement, 277–78
adult offspring of eligible household, 49
agencies, *see* organizations and agencies
annuities as cash compensation, 68
appraisal, *see* project appraisal
asset inventory, *see* census of DPs and
        inventory of assets
Azerbaijan Republic Pilot Reconstruction
        Project, 16, 18

B

Bangladesh, Jamuna Bridge Multipurpose
        Project, 19, 55, 66, 196, 240, 274
Bank Procedure (BP) 4.12, 95, 393–98,
    see also more specific topics
    monitoring and supervision, 396–97
    project appraisal requirements,
        394–96
baseline survey, *see* surveys, socio-economic
        analysis, census of DPs and
        inventory of assets
benefits from projects for DPs, *see* benefit
        sharing
benefit sharing
    compensation calculations not
        including, 53

dam projects, 340–41, 352
income restoration/improvement, 171–76
biodiversity projects, *see* restrictions of
        access to protected areas
Bolivia, Oleoducto Project, 303
BP 4.12, *see* Bank Procedure (BP) 4.12
Brazil
    Bahia Water Resource Management
        Project, 282
    Ceará Integrated Water Resources
        Management Project, 172, 342
    Fortaleza Metropolitan Transport Project,
        282, 283–84, 288–89
    Itaparica Resettlement and Irrigation
        Project, 127, 170, 194, 334,
        344, 351
    legislation earmarking project revenue for
        resettlement costs, 352
    Machadinho Hydropower Project, 160
    Minas Gerais Water Quality and
        Pollution Control Project, 294–95
    Nova Jaguaribara Project, 74–75, 140, 142
    Rio Flood Reconstruction and
        Prevention Project, 273, 277, 280
    Salto Caxias Hydropower Project, 141
    Urban Development and Water
        Resource Management Project, 141,
        172–73
    Water Quality and Pollution Control
        Project, 6–7, 279–80, 287,
        294–95, 297
    Water Quality and Sewerage Project,
        303–4
budget, *see* financing and costs
buildings, *see also* residences
    movable structures, 60
    replacement costs, 57–60
Burkina Faso, Ouagadougou Water Supply
        Project, 12

businesses
    eligibility criteria, 38, 43–45
    severity of impact, 43–45
    urban resettlement, 294–95

C

Cambodia, Phnom Penh Power
        Rehabilitation Project, 140,
        231, 305
capacity building and training, 253–55,
        324–25
cash compensation, 66–69
    annuities, dividends, or shares, 68
    marginal impacts, 63, 298
    pensions, 68–69
    severity of impact, 40–41
CDD (community-driven development),
        101–2
census of DPs and inventory of assets,
        209–13
    checklist, 399
    defined, 418
    forms, 401–3
    linear projects, 312–16
    organizations and agencies responsible
        for, 233
change, allowing for, see flexibility and
        change
children as vulnerable population, 77,
        81–83
China
    Asian Development Bank Shaanxi Roads
        Project, 175
    Beijing Environment Project, 273
    Daguangba Multipurpose Project, 172, 342
    Ertan Hydropower Project, 171, 173, 179,
        267, 342
    Fujian Provincial Highway Project,
        315, 316
    Gansu Hexi Corridor Project, 22
    Guangzhou City Center Transport
        Project, 84, 131, 137, 275–76, 317
    Guangzhou Urban Project, 293
    Henan Highway Projects, 91, 198,
        307, 316
    Hubei Environment Project, 292
    Hunan Power Development Project,
        7, 305

Inland Waterway Projects, 58, 171, 221,
        315, 316
Inner Mongolian Highway Project, 58
Jiangxi Highway II Project, 58
legislation earmarking project revenue for
        resettlement costs, 352
Liaoning Environment Project, 68
lotteries used to fund elderly housing, 84
Lubuge Hydroelectric Project, 171, 172,
        174, 342
National Highways Projects, 220–21, 317
non-Bank highway project, 168
organizations and agencies responsible for
        resettlement implementation, 237,
        239, 250
regional design institutes, 192
replacement costs for land, 56
Second Red Soils Area Development
        Project, 69, 174
Shaanxi Provincial Highways Project, 319
Shanghai Metropolitan Transport
        Project, 293
Shanghai Sewerage Projects, 7, 19, 60,
        68, 69, 75, 131, 188, 237–38, 273
Shanghai Urban Environment Project,
        174, 188, 278
Shijiazhuang Urban Transport Project, 12
Shuikou Hydroelectric Project, 63–64,
        160, 170–71, 172, 175, 194–95, 329,
        344, 347, 355
Sichuan Agricultural Development
        Project, 23
Sichuan Power Transmission Project, 174
Southern Jiangsu Environmental
        Protection Project, 174
Taihu Basin Flood Control Project, 17
Tianjin Urban Development Project, 289
Tuoketuo Thermal Power Project, 12
Urumqi Urban Transport Project, 308–9
Wanjiazhai Water Transfer Project, 12, 175
Xiaolangdi Resettlement Project, 65, 69,
        201–2, 346
Yangtze Basin Flood Control Project,
        410–11
Yangtze Basin Water Resources Project,
        139–40, 195
Yantan Hydroelectric Project, 171, 172,
        175, 341
Yunnan Environment Project, 137

civic infrastructure, *see* community and
  public infrastructure
civil strife, 16–18
closing of project, *see* project closing or
  completion
collective ownership, 42–43, 48
Colombia
  Bogotá Urban Transport Project,
    14, 276
  Calle 80 Urban Transport Project, 73
  Guavio Hydropower Project, 335
  legislation earmarking project revenue for
    resettlement costs, 352
  Rio Grande Hydroelectric
    Project, 171
  Santa Fe I Water Supply and Sewerage
    Rehabilitation Project, 282
common property, 42–43, 48
community and public infrastructure
  financing and costs, 187, 192–93
  host communities, 89, 262
  household requirements, 77
  organization of, 122
  original area, community members
    remaining in, 91
  public spaces, creation of, 296–97
  replacement costs for community-owned
    facilities, 60
  resettlement implementation, 262
  urban resettlement, 295–97
community initiatives for income
  restoration/improvement, 181
community life organization, 122
community members remaining in original
  area after resettlement, 90–91
community-based natural resource
  projects, 24
community-driven development
  (CDD), 101–2
compensation, 51, *see also* cash
    compensation; land replacement;
    replacement costs
  children's economic contributions,
    allowing for, 83
  dam projects, 349–50
  entitlement matrix, 410–11
  financing and costs, 186–87, 192
  income restoration/improvement
    compared, 51, 158

payment of, 259
severity of impact, table of entitlement
  options, 40
supplementary payments, 53–54
tangible vs. intangible assets, 52–53
temporary acquisitions, 45–47
units of entitlement, 47–49, 78, 234
women's economic contributions,
  allowing for, 76
complaints, *see* grievance procedures
completion of project, *see* project closing or
  completion
consolidation of land, 291–92
consultant services, need for, 104
consultation and participation, 123–24
  changes in resettlement implementation
    process, 266
  dam projects, 333–39
  defined, 124–25
  importance of, 125–26
  linear projects, 306–9
  organizations and agencies responsible
    for, 234, 235–36
  practical issues and problems, 126–28
  project appraisal, 138–40, 149
  project closing or completion, 142, 151
  project cycle, 128–29, 130, 144–51
  project identification, 129, 144
  project implementation, 140–42,
    150–51
  project preappraisal, 138, 148
  project preparation, 130–37, 145–47
  urban resettlement, 274–76
  World Bank's role in, 142–43
contingency funds, 196–98, 200
contractors, *see also* organizations and
    agencies
  construction replacement costs based on
    quotes of, 57–58
  DPs as project contractors, 174–75
costs, *see* financing and costs
Côte d'Ivoire
  Azito Thermal Power Project, 12–13
  Rural Land Management and
    Community Infrastructure
    Project, 78
crops, replacement costs for, 61
cultural preferences of indigenous
  peoples, 80

D

dam projects, 321–23
  alternative resettlement strategies,
    347–48
  barriers, use of, 328–29
  benefit sharing, 340–41
  compensation, 349–50
  consultation and participation, 334–39
  design of dam, 328
  entitlements, 349
  environmental impacts, 329–33
  feasibility studies, 345–49
  financing and costs, 349–53
  grievance procedures, 338–39
  host communities, 338
  implementation of project linked to
    resettlement implementation, 260,
    356–57
  income restoration/improvement, 339–49
  land-based resettlement strategies,
    341–44
  local institutions' involvement in, 325
  minimization of displacement, 327–29
  mitigation of impacts, 347–48
  monitoring and supervision, 357–58
  non-land-based resettlement strategies,
    344–45
  organizations and agencies, 323–25,
    354–56
  resettlement preparation and planning,
    325–27
  resettlement sites, 348–49
  risk analysis, 353–54
  RPs, 325–27
  shareholders in project, DPs as, 341
  site selection, 327–28
  socioeconomic analysis, 329–33
  surveys, 329–33
  temporary/partial impacts, 330–31
  upstream and downstream impacts, 330
definitions, 417–18, *see also* under
    specific topics
depreciation of structures and replacement,
    58–59
development, resettlement as
  dam projects, 339–40
  urban resettlement, 289–92
disabled as vulnerable population, 84

disaggregation of the poor into socially
    meaningful groups, 73
disclosure requirements, 33–34, 54, 143
displaced persons (DPs), *see also*
    consultation and participation;
    employees; vulnerable populations
  benefit sharing, 340–41
  census and inventory of assets,
    see census of DPs and inventory
    of assets
  defined, 5, 417
  relocation of, 122, 259–60, 260–61
  temporary displacement, 45
dissemination of information, *see*
    consultation and participation
distance of relocation, 293–95
dividends as cash compensation, 68
documentation
  changes in resettlement
    implementation, 268
  DP census and inventory of assets,
    212–13
DPs, *see* displaced persons (DPs)

E

economic conditions, *see also*
    socioeconomic analysis
  impacts not attributable to involuntary
    land acquisition, 18–20
  income restoration/improvement,
    156–57, 160–61, 166–67
economic enterprises, informal or
    unlicensed, 86, 280–84, 309–10
economics of projects, *see* financing
    and costs
Ecuador, El Nino Emergency
    Project, 17
educational needs, 82–83
El Salvador, Earthquake Reconstruction
    Project, 286
elderly as vulnerable population, 83–84
eligibility criteria, 35, *see also* land tenure;
    severity of impact
  adult offspring of eligible household, 49
  businesses, 38, 43–45
  common property, 42–43
  defined, 418
  fraudulent claims, 87, 274

landowners, 36–37
nonlandowners, 37–38
OP 4.12, 8–10, 15–25, 375–76
organizations and agencies responsible
    for, 234
process framework, 30–31
residences, 43
restrictions of access to protected areas,
    366–67
severity of impact, 38–41
temporary involuntary acquisition,
    45–47
temporary permits for use or
    occupancy, 45
units of entitlement, 47–49, 78, 234
eminent domain, xxiv, 4, 17, 22, 24, 98
defined, 417
resettlement preparation and
    planning, 98
RP, 385–86
employees (DPs)
duration of unemployment and severity
    of impact, 44–45
eligibility criteria, 38, 44–45
projects as sources of employment,
    172–74
reemployment options for landless
    laborers, 41
rehabilitation, employment as, 69
temporary employment, 69
urban resettlement, 293–94
employees (resettlement implementation),
    see staffing
encroachers, 38, 85–87, 280–84, 311
entitlement see also eligibility criteria
defined, 418
matrix for, 410–11
severity of impact, table of options, 40
units of, 47–49, 78, 234
environmental impacts, see also natural
    resources
consultation and participation, 133–34
dam projects, 329–33
host communities, 88, 90
non-attributable to involuntary land
    acquisition, 19–20
survey or assessment, 208–9
evaluation, see monitoring and supervision
external monitoring, 219–21, 253

F

family or household as unit of entitlement,
    47–49, 78, 234
feasibility studies, see also surveys
dam projects, 345–49
income restoration/improvement, 161,
    170, 176, 177, 235–36
resettlement site selection, 121, 235
feasibility studies, resettlement site
    selection, 121, 235
field operations, DP census and inventory
    of assets, 212
fill-in urban resettlement, 286–87
financing and costs, 185–86
administration, 189, 195–96
annualization and itemization, 196
community infrastructure and services,
    187, 192–93
compensation, 186–87, 192
contingency funds, 196–98, 200
dam projects, 349–53
earmarking, 196
estimation of costs, 189–96
flexibility, importance of, 196
identification of costs, 186–89
income restoration/improvement,
    188–89, 194–95, 200
internalizing costs to project,
    350–52
monitoring and supervision, 202
nonmonetary costs of projects, 350
planning costs, 191–92
policy framework, 198–200
project
    internalizing costs to, 350–52
    revenue from project used to cover
    resettlement costs, 352–53
relocation costs, 187, 193–94
replacement, see replacement costs
reporting of costs, 186–89
resettlement site preparation, 188,
    193–94
responsibility, assignment of, 198
RP, 198, 199
sample budget, 412
urban resettlement, 279–80
World Bank disbursements for
    resettlement, 200–203, 280

flexibility and change
    financing and costs, 196
    linear projects, 312–16
    resettlement implementation, 264–68
    timetable for resettlement, 413
flow of funds, 196–98
focus groups, 135
fraudulent claims, 87, 274
funding, *see* financing and costs

G

gas and oil pipelines, 302–3
Gaza and West Bank, Solid Waste and
    Environmental Management
    Project, 273–74, 276
gender issues, 75–78, 276–77
glossary, 417–18, *see also* definitions under
    specific topics
grievance procedures
    committee, 243–44
    dam projects, 338–39
    defined, 417
    process framework, 31–32
    replacement cost calculations, 54
    restrictions of access to protected
        areas, 368
Guatemala
    Chixoy Hydroelectric Project, 126
    Rural Roads Project, 309

H

health status, monitoring, 77, 82–83
highways and roads, 300–302
host communities, 87–90, 262
    dam projects, 338
    defined, 418
household or family as unit of entitlement,
    47–49, 78, 234
housing, *see* residences

I

identification, *see* project identification
impacts, assessing, *see also* environmental
        impacts; socioeconomic analysis;
        surveys
    matrix of resettlement impacts, 408–9

implementation, *see also* project
        implementation; resettlement
        implementation
    relocation process, 259–60, 260–61
impoverishment risks and reconstruction
        (IRR), 163–64
income
    loss of income
        involuntary land acquisition, not
            directly attributable to, 18–19
        policy or program lending, attributable
            to, 15–16
    severity of impact affected by total
        income, 39–40
income restoration/improvement, 61–64,
        153–54, *see also* cash compensation;
        land replacement
    benefit sharing, 171–76, 240–41,
        340–41, 352
    community initiatives, 181
    compensation
        compared, 51, 158
        completion of process, 179–80
    consolidation of land, 291–92
    dam projects, 339–49
    defined, 155–57
    design strategies, 164–69
    distance of relocation, 293–95
    economic conditions, effect of, 156–57,
        160–61
    employment as rehabilitation, 69
    existing sources of income, analyzing,
        165–66
    feasibility studies, 161, 170, 176, 177,
        235–36, 345–47
    financing and costs, 188–89, 194–95, 200
    goal of resettlement policy, xxiv–xxv
    implementation of, 263–64
    land-based options, 64–66, 341–44
    land replacement, 169–71
    limits of responsibility, 161–62
    microfinance as tool for, 181–84
    monitoring and supervision, 177–81
    new opportunities, identifying, 166–69
    non-land-based options, 63–64, 171–75,
        344–45
    organizations and agencies responsible for
        feasibility studies, 235–36
        resettlement implementation, 247–48

poverty alleviation, 74–75
practical issues and problems, 157–62
process framework, 31
project closing or completion,
    verification prior to, 179
remedial actions, 180–81
reporting and review requirements,
    176–77
residences and other structures, use
    of replacement costs to improve,
    59–60
restrictions of access to protected areas,
    367–68
risk analysis, 161–64
urban resettlement
    development, resettlement as, 289–92
    economic rehabilitation, 292–95
vulnerable populations, 159
India
    Andhra Pradesh Highways Project, 85,
        301
    Andhra Pradesh Irrigation Projects, 172,
        181, 191, 343
    Bombay Sewage Disposal Project, 23
    Coal India Environmental and Social
        Mitigation Project, 15–16, 68, 81,
        174–75, 181, 237, 242
    Eco-Development Project, 13, 24–25
    employment of DPs on projects, 174
    Gujarat Medium II Project, 172, 342
    Hyderabad Water Supply and Sanitation
        Project, 13, 75
    Karnataka Power Project, 173
    Maharashtra Irrigation Projects, 172,
        173, 342
    Mumbai Urban Transport Project, 131
    Nathpa Jhakri Hydroelectric Project, 295
    National Highways Authority of India
        projects, 60, 131–32, 140, 238, 240,
        241, 242, 284, 307
    National Thermal Power Corporation,
        14, 174, 233, 249
    Orissa Water Resources Consolidation
        Project, 42, 55, 64, 66, 91, 172
    Sardar Sarovar Project, 66, 90–91,
        329–30, 332, 333, 348–49, 356
    Tamil Nadu Newsprint Project, 20
    Tamil Nadu Urban Development
        Project, 20

Tamil Nadu Water Resources
    Consolidation Project, 202
Upper Indravati Hydroelectric Project,
    65, 66, 358, 404–7
Upper Krishna Irrigation Projects, 10, 66,
    76, 125, 160, 168, 173, 192, 225,
    241, 333, 343, 344–45, 347–48, 351,
    356–57
indigenous peoples, 78–81, 311–12, 322
indirect economic impacts, 18–19
Indonesia
    Cirata Hydroelectric Project, 172, 339–40
    Jabotabek Urban Development
        Project, 86
    Kedung Ombo Multipurpose Project, 65,
        160, 167, 347, 351, 355
    Saguling Hydroelectric Project, 172,
        339–40
    Second Sulawesi Urban Development
        Project, 56
    Village Infrastructure Project, 23–24
inflation, 53, 196, 197, 318–19
informal economic enterprises, 86, 280–84,
    309–10
information requirements, 205–8, see also
    monitoring and supervision;
    reporting requirements; surveys
infrastructure, see community and public
    infrastructure
Integrated Safeguards Data Sheet (ISDS),
    105–7, 114 , 116
internal monitoring, 219, 252
internalizing costs to project, 350–52
interviews, 135, 214, see also surveys
inventory of DP assets, see census of DPs
    and inventory of assets
involuntary land acquisition, 4, 8, see also
    land acquisition, and more specific
    topics
involuntary resettlement, xvii–xix, see also
    more specific topics
    defined, 5
    domestic policies, encouragement of,
        13–14
    history of policy on, 3
    lessons derived from Bank experience in,
        xxvii–xxix
    need for sourcebook on, xxiv–xxvi
    OD 4.30, 3

involvement of DPs, *see* consultation and participation
IRR (impoverishment risks and reconstruction), 163–64
irrigation systems, 304
ISDS (Integrated Safeguards Data Sheet), 105–7, 114, 116

K

Kenya, Tana River Conservation Project, 7
key informant interviews, 135
Korea, Republic of
    Ports Development and Environmental Improvement Project, 42
    Pusan Urban Transport Management Project, 13

L

land acquisition, *see also* eminent domain
    applicability of OP 4.12, 8
    defined, 417
    involuntary, 4, 8
    open access or common property, 42–43
    organizations and agencies responsible for
        assessment process, 231–33
        resettlement implementation, 244–45
    survey or assessment, 208–9
    temporary, 45–47
    voluntary, 20
    voluntary land donation, 22–24
land consolidation, 291–92
land purchase, resettlement site, 121–22
land replacement, 62–63
    allowing alternatives to, 63–64
    dam projects, 341–44
    direct replacement, 64, 80
    income restoration/improvement via, 169–71
    indigenous peoples, 80
    indirect replacement, 65
    open access or common property, 42
    open-market purchase, 20–21
    peri-urban areas, 63
    policy requirements, 51
    severity of impact, 41
    unacceptability of replacement land to DPs, 65
land, replacement costs for, 54–57
land tenure, 35–38
    collective, 42–43, 48
    indigenous peoples, 79
    persons without, *see* nonlandowners
    registered title to land, 36–37
    secure title or use rights, people lacking, 85–87, 310–11
    severity of impact affected by, 39
    temporary permits, 45
landlords, *see* renters
language of project area, translation of key documents into, 243
Lao People's Democratic Republic
    IFC Sepon Gold Mine Project, 136–37
    Nam Thuen 2 Hydroelectric Project, 337
legal procedures, *see* administrative and legal procedures
Lesotho, Highland Water Project, 68, 133–34, 325
linear projects, 299–300, 319–20
    administrative coordination, 316–18
    census of DPs and inventory of assets, 312–16
    consultation and participation, 305–9
    defined, 299
    flexibility and change, 312–16
    gas and oil pipelines, 302–3
    irrigation systems, 303
    minimization of displacement as policy objective, 305–9
    monitoring and supervision, 318–19
    policy framework, 313–14
    project phasing and stages, 312–16
    railways, 305–6
    roads and highways, 300–302
    RP, 313–15
    surveys, 312–16
    transmission lines, 304–5
    urban resettlement, 297–98
    vulnerable populations, 309–12
    water and sanitation systems, 302–3
linked activities, applicability of OP 4.12 to, 10–14

living standards, *see* income
    restoration/improvement
local governments as organizations
    responsible for resettlement
    implementation, 249–51
local institutions' involvement in dam
    projects, 325
loss of income
    involuntary land acquisition, not directly
        attributable to, 18–19
    policy or program lending, attributable
        to, 15–16

M

Malawi, land reform program, 20, 41
Mali
    Manantali Dam, 330
    Regional Hydropower Development
        Project, 13
marginal impacts, cash compensation for,
    63, 298
market failure and microfinance, 182
market value, replacement costs for
    land at, 54–57
Mauritania, Regional Hydropower
    Development Project, 13
Mexico, Aguamilpa Hydroelectric
    Project, 172
microfinance as tool for
    restoration/improvement of
    income, 181–84
minimization of displacement as policy
    objective, 5–7
    dam projects, 327–29
    linear projects, 305–9
    urban resettlement, 272–74
mobile enterprises, 86, 280–84, 309–10
monitoring and supervision, 205–8,
    215–18
    BP 4.12 requirements, 396–97
    consultation and participation, 142
    dam projects, 357–58
    early review of resettlement
        implementation, 225–27
    elements of, 216
    external monitoring, 219–21, 253
    financing and costs, 202
    guidelines, 414–16
    income restoration/improvement, 177–81
    income restoration plans, review of,
        176–77
    indicators of performance, 218
    internal monitoring, 219, 252
    linear projects, 318–19
    OP 4.12, 377
    organizations and agencies responsible
        for, 252–53
    performance indicators, 218
    process framework, 32–33
    process model, 217
    resettlement implementation, 264
    resettlement preparation and planning,
        116–19
    restrictions of access to protected
        areas, 368
    World Bank involvement, 221–27
movable structures, 60
moving, *see* relocation
multiple subprojects, 27, 101

N

national resource management
    programs, 20
natural disasters, 16–18
natural resources, *see also* restrictions of
    access to protected areas
    community members remaining in
        original area after resettlement, 91
    community-based projects, 24
    host communities, 90
    income restoration/improvement by
        providing access to, 172
    national or regional management
        plans, 20
    national resource management
        programs, 20
    sustainability of, 367–68
negotiations, *see* project negotiations
new borrowers, special needs of, 106
new housing, reconstruction of and
    relocation to, 260–62
NGOs (nongovernmental organizations),
    132–33, 140–42, 167–68,
    176, 249
Nigeria, Lagos Urban Transport Project,
    301–2, 314

nongovernmental organizations (NGOs),
132–33, 140–42, 167–68, 176, 249
non-land-based resettlement strategies
dam projects, 344–45
income restoration/improvement, 63–64,
171–75
nonlandowners
eligibility criteria, 37–38
linear projects, 310–11
reemployment options for landless
laborers, 41
urban resettlement, 280–84
vulnerable populations, 85–87, 310–11
nonmonetary costs of projects,
compensation for, 350

O

OD (Operational Directive) 4.30, 3
oil and gas pipelines, 302–3
OP 4.12, *see* Operational Policy (OP) 4.12
open access or common property,
42–43, 48
open market purchase of land, 20–21
Operational Directive (OD) 4.30, 3
Operational Policy (OP) 4.12, xxiii, 3, 371
applicability, 8–10, 98–99, 372
Bank-financed projects triggering, 8
eligibility criteria, 375–76
interpretive issues, xxix
linked activities, 10–14
monitoring and supervision, 377
non-applicability, 15–25
objectives, 371
policy framework, 378–79, 389–90
process framework, 379, 390–91
required measures, 372–75
resettlement instrument,
determining, 376
resettlement preparation and planning,
376–77
restrictions of access to protected areas,
361–63
RP, 377–78, 384–89
scope of, 3–7
text and notes, 371–83
World Bank assistance to borrower,
379–80
organizations and agencies, 229–30

consultation and participation, 234,
235–36
dam projects, 323–25, 354–56
eligibility criteria, 234
income restoration/improvement
feasibility studies, 235–36
resettlement implementation,
247–48
land acquisition
assessment process, 231–33
resettlement implementation,
244–45
monitoring and supervision, 252–53
performance evaluation, 252–53
resettlement implementation, 237–38
central project management unit,
239–40
checklist for organizations involved in,
250–51
grievance committee, 243–44
land acquisition, 244–45
local field offices, 240–42
local governments, 249–51
NGOs, 249
organizational models for, 248–50
project agency, 249–50
project launch workshop, 238–39
relocation, 245–46
special service agencies, 244–48
steering committee, 242–43
resettlement preparation and planning,
230–36
resettlement site selection feasibility
studies, 235
RP elements, 388
surveys, 233
training and capacity building, 253–55
ownership of or claim to land, *see* land
tenure

P

PAD (Project Appraisal Document), 113,
176
Pakistan
Ghazi-Barotha Hydropower Project, 174,
180–81, 243
Left Bank Drainage Outfall Project, 42,
191, 193, 202

Palestine, West Bank and Gaza Solid Waste
and Environmental Management
Project, 273–74, 276
partial/temporary impacts of dam projects,
330–31
participation, *see* consultation and
participation
pavement dwellers, 86
performance evaluation, *see* monitoring and
supervision
peri-urban areas, land replacement in, 63
personnel, *see* staffing
Philippines
Leyte-Cebu Thermal Project, 171
Leyte-Luzon Thermal Project,
55–56, 172
Transmission Grid Reinforcement
Project, 56
physical relocation process, *see* relocation
pipelines, 302–3
plan of action, *see* resettlement
plan (RP)
planning requirements, *see* resettlement
plan (RP); resettlement preparation
and planning
Poland, coal sector restructuring
projects, 16
policy framework, 27–29
elements of, 389–90
financing and costs, 198–200
linear projects, 313–14
OP 4.12, 378–79, 389–90
restrictions of access to protected areas,
364–65
poverty, 72–75, 159
power transmission lines, 303–4
preparation, *see* project preparation;
resettlement preparation and
planning
private sector financial intermediation
projects, 100
process framework, 27, 28, 29–33
elements of, 390–91
OP 4.12, 379, 390–91
restrictions of access to protected areas,
364–70
surveys and monitoring, 207
processing requirements, *see* resettlement
preparation and planning

project agencies as organizations responsible
for resettlement implementation,
249–50
project appraisal, 114–15
BP 4.12 requirements, 100, 394–96
consultation and participation,
138–40, 149
Project Appraisal Document (PAD),
113, 176
project closing or completion
applicability of OP 4.12, 9–10
consultation and participation,
142, 151
income restoration/improvement verified
prior to, 179
information requirements, 208
RP implementation, completion of
project dependent on, 118–19,
224–25
project cycle, *see also* specific stages
consultation and participation,
128–29, 130
definition and stages, 418
project decision meeting, 111–14
project financing and costs
internalizing resettlement costs to
project, 350–52
revenue from project used to cover
resettlement costs, 352–53
project identification, 102–5
consultation and participation,
129, 144
information requirements, 207, 208
land acquisition assessment, 208–9
late identification, 119–20
preidentification, 97–102
project implementation
participation of DPs during, 140–42,
150–51
resettlement implementation linked to,
260, 356–57
project launch workshop, 238–39
project negotiations, 115–16
project preappraisal, 110–11, 138,
148, 208
project preparation
consultation and participation, 130–37,
145–47
stage of project cycle, 107–10

project quality enhancement review (QER), 105–7
public infrastructure, *see* community and public infrastructure
public safety zones, 86
public spaces in urban environments, creation of, 296–97

Q

quality enhancement review (QER), 105–7

R

railways, 305–6
RAP (resettlement action plan), *see* resettlement plan (RP)
recordkeeping
    changes in resettlement implementation, documentation of, 268
    DP census and inventory of assets, 212–13
regional resource management programs, 20
rehabilitative measures, *see* income restoration/improvement
relocation
    distance of, 293–95
    financing and costs, 187, 193–94
    implementation of, 259–60, 260–61
    new housing, 260–62
    organizations and agencies responsible for, 245–46
    process of, 122
remedial actions, income restoration/improvement, 180–81
renters
    eligibility criteria, 38
    public safety zones, 86
    urban resettlement, 280–84
replacement costs, 51, 52–54
    agricultural crops and trees, 61
    construction, 57–58
    dam projects, 349–53
    land, 54–57
    miscellaneous assets, 61
    nonlandowners, 86

public infrastructure and community-owned assets, 60
    residences and other structures, 57–60
    urban land, 284–85
replacement of housing in urban areas, 285–87
replacement of land, *see* land replacement
reporting requirements, 206
    income restoration plans, 176–77
    resettlement costs, 186–89
    supervision reports, 223–24
representativeness of participants, 127, 132–33
Republic of Korea
    Ports Development and Environmental Improvement Project, 42
    Pusan Urban Transport Management Project, 13
reservoirs, *see* dam projects
resettlement
    action plan, *see* resettlement plan (RP)
    costs, *see* financing and costs
    defined, 5
    impacts matrix, 408–9
    involuntary, *see* involuntary resettlement
    voluntary, 21–25
resettlement implementation, 257–58, *see also* organizations and agencies
    change, dealing with, 264–68
    completion of project dependent on RP implementation, 118–19, 224–25
    documentation of changes in, 268
    early review of, 225–27
    flexibility, importance of, 264–68
    income restoration/improvement, 263–64
    monitoring and supervision, 215, 264
    new housing, reconstruction of and relocation to, 260–62
    payment of compensation, 259
    performance evaluation, 264
    project implementation linked to, 260, 356–57
    public infrastructure, 262
    relocation, 259–60, 260–61
    restrictions of access to protected areas, 365–66, 368

resettlement instrument, determining, 27, 28, 99–102
  abbreviated RPs, 99, 389
  OP 4.12, 376
  policy framework, 27–29
  process framework, 27, 28, 29–33
  restrictions of access to protected areas, 363–65
resettlement plan (RP), 27, 28, 99
  abbreviated RPs, 99, 389
  completion of project dependent on implementation of, 118–19, 224–25
  dam projects, 325–27
  defined, 417
  disclosure requirements, 33–34, 54, 143
  elements of, 384–88
  financing and costs, 198, 199
  implementation, see resettlement implementation
  information requirements, 207, 208
  linear projects, 313–15
  OP 4.12, 377–78, 384–88
  restrictions of access to protected areas, 364–65, 368–70
  socioeconomic analysis for RP preparation, 213–15, 233, 384–85
  survey of existing uses of land, 42–43
resettlement preparation and planning, 95–96
  applicability of OP 4.12, 98–99
  appropriate resettlement instrument, determining, 27, 28, 99–102
  community life organization, 122
  consultant services, need for, 104
  dam projects, 325–27
  effectiveness of project dependent on, 116
  financing and costs of planning, 191–92
  irregular processing/late identification, 119–20
  monitoring and supervision, 116–19
  negotiations, 115–16
  OP 4.12, 376–77
  organizations and agencies, 230–36
  project appraisal, 114–15
  project decision meeting, 111–14
  project identification, 102–5
  project preappraisal, 110–11

project preidentification, 97–102
project preparation, 107–10
project quality enhancement review (QER), 105–7
relocation of DPs, 122
site selection, 120–22
support services organization, 122
time requirements, 109
resettlement site
  cost of preparing, 188, 193–94
  dam projects, 348–49
  design of, 121–122
  feasibility studies, 121, 235
  land purchased for, 121–22
  selection, 120–22
residences, see also urban resettlement
  eligibility criteria, 43
  new housing, reconstruction of and relocation to, 260–62
  replacement costs, 57–60
  severity of impact, 43
residual landholdings and severity of impact, 41
resources, see natural resources
responsible organizations, see organizations and agencies
restrictions of access to protected areas, 4–5,
  applicability of OP 4.12, 361–63
  eligibility criteria, 366–67
  grievance procedures, 368
  income restoration/improvement, 367–68
  monitoring and supervision, 368
  objectives of OP 4.12, 363
  process framework, 364–70
  resettlement implementation, 365–66, 368
  resettlement instrument, determining, 363–65
  RP, 364–70
  scrutiny of, 24–25
  sustainability of resources, 367–68
  voluntary restrictions, 24–25
  World Bank procedures, 368–70
review of performance, see monitoring and supervision
rights-of-way (ROW), projects involving, see linear projects

risk analysis
  dam projects, 353–54
  income restoration/improvement, 161–64
roads and highways, 300–302
Romania, coal sector restructuring
    projects, 16
ROW (rights-of-way), projects involving,
    see linear projects
RP, see resettlement plan (RP)
rural residences and eligibility criteria, 43
Russian Federation
  coal sector restructuring projects, 16
  Northern Restructuring Project, 22
Rwanda, National Highway Project, 14

S

salvage materials and replacement costs, 59
sanitation systems, 303–4
sector investment loans, 100
Senegal
  Manantali Dam, 330
  Regional Hydropower Development
    Project, 13, 134, 305, 307–8
severity of impact, 35, 38–41
  businesses, 43–45
  employees' duration of unemployment,
    44–45
  residences, 43
sewage systems, 303–4
shareholders in projects, DPs as, 341
shares as cash compensation, 68
sharing project benefits with DPs, see
    benefit sharing
site of resettlement, see resettlement site
socioeconomic analysis, see also census of
    DPs and inventory of assets
  dam projects, 329–33
  elements of, 215
  financing and cost issues, 190–91
  host communities, 88–89
  indigenous peoples, assessment of, 80
  land acquisition assessment, 208–9
  methodology, 407
  non-attributable to involuntary land
    acquisition, 19
  objectives, 405
  poor, social disaggregation of, 73
  RP preparation, 213–15, 233, 384–85

scope, 406
terms of reference for, 404–7
South Africa, national park enlargement
    project, 21
specific investment loans, 100
squatters, 38, 85–87, 280–84, 311
Sri Lanka, Northeast Irrigated Agriculture
    Project, 18
staffing
  census of DPs and inventory of assets,
    211–12
  sources of employment for DPs, projects
    as, 172–74
  training and capacity building, see
    training and capacity building
standards of living, see income
    restoration/improvement
street vendors, 86, 280–84, 309–10
structural adjustment loans, 15–16
structures, see buildings; residences
supervision requirements, see monitoring
    and supervision
support services, see community and public
    infrastructure
surveys, 205–8, see also census of DPs and
    inventory of assets; feasibility studies
  consultation and participation, 134–35
  dam projects, 329–33
  existing uses of land, 42–43
  interviews, 135, 214
  land acquisition and environmental
    impact assessment, 208–9
  linear projects, 312–16
  matrix of resettlement impacts, 408–9
  organizations and agencies responsible
    for, 233
  socioeconomic analysis for RP
    preparation, 213–15, 233
sustainability of resources, 367–68

T

Tajikistan, Pamir Energy Project, 191
Tanzania, Boundary Hills Lodge Project, 21
temporary employment as rehabilitation, 69
temporary permits and eligibility
    criteria, 45
temporary/partial impacts of dam projects,
    330–31

tenants, *see* renters
Thailand
    Pak Mun Hydroelectric Project, 126,
        159, 160, 172, 175, 190–91, 192,
        194, 328, 329, 339, 351
    Third Power System Development
        Project, 20, 65
timetable for resettlement, 413
title to land, *see* land tenure
Togo, Nangbeto Hydroelectric Project, 161,
    338, 351
traditional access to resources, restriction
    of, *see* restriction of access to
    conservation areas
training and capacity building, 253–55,
    324–25
translation of key documents into language
    of project area, 243
transmission lines, 304–5
trees, replacement costs for, 61
Turkey
    hiring preferences, 173
    Marmosa Earthquake Recovery Project,
        17–18

U

Uganda, Bujagali Power Project, 7
Ukraine, coal sector restructuring
    projects, 16
units of entitlement, 47–49, 78, 234
unresettled or undisplaced persons, 90–91
urban resettlement, 271–72
    administration, 277–78
    businesses, 294–95
    community and public infrastructure,
        295–97
    consolidation of land, 291–92
    consultation and participation, 274–76
    coordination of administrative and
        financial responsibilities, 277–80
    distance of relocation, 293–95
    employees (DPs), 293–94
    financing and costs, 279–80
    fraudulent claims, 274
    income restoration/improvement
        development, resettlement as, 289–92
        economic rehabilitation, 292–95
    land tenure, persons without, 280–84

linear projects, 297–98
location issues, 287–89
minimization of displacement as policy
    objective, 272–74
replacement costs for urban land, 284–85
replacement housing, 285–87
residences, 284
    affordability and willingness to
        pay, 290
    eligibility criteria, 43
    fill-in resettlement, 286–87
    improvement of housing standards,
        289–90
    large-scale relocations, 285–86
    location issues, 287–89
    replacement costs for urban land,
        284–85
    replacement housing, 285–87
    slum improvement programs, 290–91
    vertical resettlement, 288
vertical resettlement, 288
women, 276–77

V

vertical resettlement, 288
Vietnam
    Highway Rehabilitation Projects, 8, 14,
        237, 250
    Mekong Delta Water Resources
        Development Project, 58
    replacement costs for land, 56–57
voluntary land acquisition, 20–21
voluntary land donation, 22–24
voluntary migration projects, 21–22
voluntary resettlement, 21–25
voluntary restrictions of access to protected
    areas, 24–25
vulnerable populations, 71–72
    children, 77, 81–83
    community members remaining in
        original area after resettlement,
        90–91
    disabled persons, 84
    elderly persons, 83–84
    host communities, 87–90
    indigenous peoples, 78–81, 311–12
    informal economic enterprises, 86,
        280–84, 309–10

vulnerable populations (*continued*)
    linear projects, 309–12
    income restoration/improvement, 159
    nonlandowners, 85–87, 310–11
    poor persons, 72–75, 159
    secure title or use rights, people lacking,
        85–87, 310–11
    women, 75–78, 276–77

W

wars, 16–18
water and sanitation systems, 302–3
West Bank and Gaza, Solid Waste and
    Environmental Management
    Project, 273–74, 276
women as vulnerable population, 75–78,
    276–77

World Bank
    borrower assistance, 379–80
    BP 4.12, *see* Bank Procedure (BP) 4.12
    consultation and participation, role in,
        142–43
    disbursement of resettlement funds,
        200–202
    lessons derived from experience of,
        xxvii–xxix
    monitoring and supervision by, 221–27
    OP 4.12, *see* Operational Policy (OP) 4.12
    restrictions of access to protected areas,
        procedures for, 368–70

Z

Zambia, Power Rehabilitation Project,
    7, 234